CEREMONIES OF
CHARLES I

CEREMONIES OF CHARLES I

THE NOTE BOOKS OF JOHN FINET
1628 - 1641

Edited by

ALBERT J. LOOMIE, S.J.

NEW YORK
FORDHAM UNIVERSITY PRESS
1987

Printed in the United States of America

CONTENTS

The Note Books

Book III: October 1, 1628 to April 23, 1632

Book IV: May 11, 1632 to November 23, 1637

Book V: November 27, 1637 to ca. May 15, 1641

APPENDICES

ACKNOWLEDGMENTS

I am deeply grateful to Mr. C. Cottrell-Dormer for his generous permission to edit the original journals of Sir John Finet at Rousham House, near Steeple Aston, Oxfordshire. I am also indebted very much to the American Philosophical Society for a grant to begin research in the Finet papers and to Fordham University for a faculty fellowship to continue the editorial work on them. I am especially mindful of the help provided by Dr. David Rogers and the staff of the Bodleian Library at Oxford University, as well as the librarians at the Institute of Historical Research of the University of London, where many of the annotations and the information for the introduction were prepared. A photocopy of the rare original printing of *Finneti Philoxenis* (1656) was generously made available by the Folger Shakespeare Library in Washington, D.C. Crown Copyright documents from the Public Record Office in London have been transcribed with permission of the Controller of H. M. Stationery Office. Mr. Vincent Pascal, as my graduate assistant, helped me to compare the transcriptions from the Finet papers. Finally, a particular debt of gratitude must be recorded to the late Mr. Hugh Murray Baillie, formerly of the Historical Manuscripts Commission in London, for his unfailingly prompt responses to numerous inquiries. The mistakes that survive are my own.

Fordham University   A. J. L.

ILLUSTRATIONS

between pages 34 and 35

between pages 254 and 255

ABBREVIATIONS

III	The Third Book of Notes
IV	The Fourth Book of Notes
V	The Fifth Book of Notes
	Each is followed by Finet's original folio number, with ^{v} (verso) indicated as needed.
AGS E	Archivo General de Simancas, Sección de Estado (Spain)
AMAE	Archives, Ministère des Affaires Etrangères (Paris)
Bentley	Gerald E. Bentley, *The Jacobean and Caroline Stage* (Oxford, 1941 —; 7 volumes currently)
CSP	*Calendar of State Papers*
D	*Domestic*
S	*Spanish*
V	*Venetian*
	Volumes are cited by the years.
HMC	*Historical Manuscripts Commission*
PRO	Public Record Office (London)

INTRODUCTION

CHARLES I
AND THE CULTURE OF HIS COURT

VISITORS TO Inigo Jones's Banqueting House at Whitehall today can enjoy Peter Paul Rubens' striking ceiling panels portraying the apotheosis of James I. Here the celebrated defender of the divine right of kings is borne aloft on the back of an eagle accompanied by the allegorical figures of Justice and Religion, as symbols of his royal responsibilities to his subjects, to receive the laurel crown offered by Peace and Minerva, whose wise counsel had always guided him. By this splendid survival of a lost court culture,[1] dominant three centuries ago, the visitor is reminded that the hall was once alive, not only with now legendary theatrical presentations, but with the pageantry of public receptions for diplomats with their colorfully liveried attendants. Although the Banqueting House was completed during his father's regime, these paintings were an additional commission through which Charles I planned to enhance the prestige of his royal house in the eyes of foreigners, as well as of his own courtiers. As a narrator of royal diplomatic ceremonies, John Finet retains his special place in any study of this early Stuart court's politics and culture. During his thirteen years as Master of Ceremonies immediately before the civil war, he compiled the three small journals which are here published for the first time. In his pages Finet preserved attitudes and values typical of Charles's aristocratic circle, as well as of the foreign nobility who came to Whitehall, while he wrote a fairly continuous narrative about the diplomatic scenes in which he had a role. Accordingly his pages provide a mirror of the pageantry and conventions that were typical of the English diplomacy of that decade and are possibly the fullest extant chronicle of the regular procedures of any palace north of the Alps for these years.

Since, recently, historians have given increasing attention to the different court ceremonial traditions within the western European diplomacy of this era,[2] Finet's pages are a welcome clarification of the customs preferred by

---

[1] Graham Parry, *The Golden Age Restor'd: The Culture of the Stuart Court, 1603–42* (Manchester: Manchester University Press, 1981) is an admirable survey of the civilized environment of the early Stuart palace.

[2] A full review is in William Roosen, "Early Modern Diplomatic Ceremonial: A Systems Approach," *Journal of Modern History* 52 No. 3 (September 1980) 452–76.

Charles I. From 1628 to 1641 — the years covered in these note books — nearly a hundred accredited ministers, either resident or extraordinary, as well as over fifty other distinguished foreigners, entered Whitehall for the first time with Finet at their side.[3] The diplomatic ceremonial of Charles I was, of course, largely traditional to the English court before his accession to the throne, but since "the public pageantry of kingship" outside the royal palaces occurred far less frequently under him than under Elizabeth I,[4] Finet's narrative accurately established the king's special role in the elaborate official events that were infrequently recorded, or left to the eyes of only the privileged few in attendance. It has long been known that Charles's theatrical presentations held certain political overtones. Whenever foreign diplomats with their attendants returned to the Banqueting House to see a court masque, they were offered allegorical scenes that were "direct political assertions," where just as Neptune could tame the seas, or Pan could bring order to the wilderness' savage beasts, so would the king's wisdom create peace at home and in the commonwealth of nations.[5] Charles was not unique. A recent study of the spectacular public processions that were organized at times in Venice by the doges has shown that pageantry was used as "political pedagogy of a high order."[6] Foreign observers were also aware that Charles's official receptions revealed various grades of warmth and hospitality. A king's public behavior was carefully watched by both courtier and diplomat as a sort of weather gauge of Charles's friendship, or coolness, toward another state. Finet was equally alert to record the ways that visiting diplomats appeared to wage their own cold war by various calculated gestures meant to humilate or intimidate their rivals. Ultimately, by 1640, Charles's own foreign policy had proved to be without the resources and skill needed to achieve most of his ambitious goals, yet this need not detract from his proper instinct to create the suitable setting for his diplomatic activities.

[3] Gerald E. Aylmer, *The King's Servants* (New York: Columbia University Press, 1961) pp. 13–21 explains the pattern of authority in the palace household; Phyllis Lachs, *The Diplomatic Corps under Charles II and James II* (New Brunswick: Rutgers University Press, 1965) has a detailed picture of English diplomatic practices in the late-17th century; Maurice Keens-Soper, "François de Callières and Diplomatic Theory," *Historical Journal* 16 No. 3 (1973) 485–508 describes contemporary notions of a diplomat's duties.

[4] Malcolm Smuts, "The Political Failure of Stuart Cultural Patronage," in *Patronage in the Renaissance*, edd. Guy Fitch Lytle and Stephen Orgel (Princeton: Princeton University Press, 1982) pp. 165–87, esp. 172–74.

[5] Stephen Orgel, *The Illusion of Power: Political Theater in the English Renaissance* (Berkeley: University of California Press, 1975) pp. 51–57.

[6] Edward Muir, "Images of Power: Art and Pageantry in Renaissance Venice," *American Historical Review* 84 No. 1 (February 1979) 16–52.

A few misleading qualities in Charles's personality[7] are adroitly invented in John Finet's pages. Here he does not stammer, for in each public appearance the king, as the central figure, speaks unhesitatingly and concisely in English, or French. When needed, one of the king's council will later translate into Spanish, Italian, or Latin, but there is no sign of his speech impediment. Finet at times tried to show a regal warmth toward most diplomats by Charles's frequent invitation to mount the dais to be closer. The king is always placed in a harmonious setting, as he gravely listens to an address in the midst of his elegantly attired court. In the Banqueting House that was hung with his finest tapestries, for a first public audience of an ambassador extraordinary, the king stands patiently attentive to all the laudatory speeches. This was so even if the oration went on for over a half-hour in Latin. Since the king considered the ceremonies at Whitehall to be part of the decorum and splendor of his monarchy, he was sensitive to even the smallest details. Finet was instructed to be vigilant that a hat should not be worn by a diplomat in the king's presence without a previous invitation from Charles to do so. Further examples abound. Even though he had already received news by courier of the death of the archduchess Isabella in Brussels late in 1633, he demanded that Henry Taylor, her agent, appear before him with an official narrative of her passing, before he issued orders for an official period of mourning at court, during which he wore purple. Charles went out of his way to tell an ambassador, who mourned the death of his ruler but brought also news of the birth of an heir, that he fully approved his court dress of both black and white. If, on one occasion, a Venetian ambassador did not wear his dark red official robe to meet the king, Finet was careful to note that the diplomat also gave a reason for this change which satisfied Charles. The foreign diplomat might well consider it worth his while to postpone his first official audience, if the costly costumes of his retinue were not yet completed by their London tailors. Both Coloma from Spain and Oxenstierna from Sweden did this before beginning their diplomatic business, since they knew that their final elegance would delight Charles. From Finet's pages there is little doubt that Charles took pride in being the leading figure in a ceremony and, in fact, could, when the occasion offered, plan in considerable

---

[7] Two major biographies — Pauline Gregg, *King Charles I* (London: Dent, 1981 & Berkeley: University of California Press, 1984) and Charles Carlton, *Charles I: The Personal Monarch* (London: Routledge, Kegan Paul, 1983) — are available. Martin Havran, "The Character and Principles of an English King: The Case of Charles I," *Catholic Historical Review* 69 No. 2 (April 1983) 169–208 has a concise appraisal of his childhood years.

detail a ritual, such as that for the return of the insignia of the Garter of the deceased Gustavus Adolphus, or the ancient oath of fealty of a courtier.

Outside of a ceremony the king could be firm, even stubborn, in insisting on his own views of order and status, even when there were diplomatic risks in so doing. As will be seen later, he humiliated the Spaniard Necolalde, by treating him as if he had been only an agent. Similarly, since his sister Elizabeth, the widow of the Count Palatine, felt offended by the Polish king's recent marriage, Charles refused in 1637 to admit the Polish ambassador to his presence. The one person capable of securing an exemption from his regulations was his wife, Henrietta, for he gladly accepted her plea for special rights of access to the palace for French and Savoyard diplomats. Ultimately, Finet's image of Charles is that of a king who is confident and at ease in the midst of ceremony, yet highly sensitive to all the minutiae of proper decorum which he insisted had to be observed. Ceremonies here clearly had become one more example of the refined taste of the court of Charles I, where intellectuals, poets, dramatists, and artists were already encouraged to portray the king in an idealized fashion. A theologian such as William Laud was already hard at work by liturgical services and sermons urging obedience to divine-right kingship. Poets and playwrights contrived to produce polished and flattering celebrations in language of the virtues of the king and queen, who lead their subjects along a path of righteousness. The ambitions of this court have been particularly well reflected in portrait painting. Charles was without a doubt the premier art collector of his generation in England, a refined connoisseur and patron of painters, paticularly of Sir Anthony Van Dyke, his Principal Painter in Ordinary, whose lasting influence on English portraiture has been established, in addition to his role in introducing to London the finest contemporary styles of the Continent.[8] All the diplomats of this decade had an opportunity to view the king's superb art collection as well as the significant holdings of such wealthy courtiers as Arundel, Buckingham, or Pembroke, who outstripped others in the same fashionable trend.

While the failures of the king's diplomacy will be appraised elsewhere, it is important to note that Charles earnestly hoped that his ideals would produce a new moral and political order in England. In this he was not hypocritical but rather the victim of self-deception. It has been recently observed that by "collecting pictures and patronizing the arts Charles could indulge his personal fantasies, for unlike the world of parliament and politics he could control that of poets, playwrights and painters where every artistic piper soon realized

---

[8] Oliver Millar, *Van Dyke in England* (London: National Portrait Gallery, 1983) provides a thorough review of his influence.

the exact tune the king called and paid for — sometimes even better than the king himself."[9] Nothing typifies the court culture of the last year in which Finet served as master of ceremonies more than the presentation in 1640 of a final sumptuous masque, *Salmacida spolia*. Salmacis was the mythological site of a fountain, whose waters not only delighted the barbarians but inspired their leaders to seek peace with their foes. As will be seen, even in his own place there were exaggerated rumors of the king's preference for Spanish clients and Catholic courtiers, as well as resentment of his high-handed taxes and thorough support for Laud's religious innovations. Within this masque, however, the audience saw envious creatures and furies — Charles's critics — fall back in dismay before the appearance of a "Good Genius of Great Britain" who spoke in the midst of figures depicting Concord, Heroic Virtue, and Heavenly Wisdom of the right path for all to follow. Once again the all-too-familiar lesson was being taught, for the treasure of Salmacis was in fact the wisdom of the king. Outside that court theater, nevertheless, the real history of England was about to be written with a tragic role and very different lines for Charles I.[10]

[9] Charles Carlton, "The Personality of Kingship," in *Three British Revolutions*, ed. J. G. A Pocock (Princeton: Princeton University Press, 1980) pp. 188–89.

[10] A perceptive analysis of the growth of the Cavalier image of Charles's reign is found in R. Malcolm Smuts, *Court Culture and the Origins of a Royalist Tradition in Early Stuart England* (Philadelphia: University of Pennsylvania Press, 1987), pp. 245–91.

THE CAREER OF SIR JOHN FINET
AT COURT

THE ELDEST SON of a Kentish gentry family, John Finet was born in 1571 at Soulton near Dover.[10] Little is known of the earliest years of his life prior to his service overseas, as a "gentleman" in the company of the Governor of Flushing, Sir Robert Sydney, in the 1590s. After further travel on the Continent, by the opening of the reign of James I Finet had entered the employ of Thomas Wilson, secretary to Robert Cecil, earl of Salisbury, the principal adviser of the king. At this time he was selected for useful minor duties. For example, he was sent to carry the earl's instructions to Spanish commanders of troop convoys that had sought shelter in Dover harbor from the Dutch in July 1605. In the spring of the following year he journeyed through the Spanish Netherlands and France to send back reports on the English Catholic exiles and the situation at the court of Henry IV.[11] At the same time Finet also gained the friendship of John Whitgift, archbishop of Canterbury, for in his dedication of a translation that he published in 1606 he recalled that Whitgift had accepted his letters "sent him in my travailles," and sent "signes of his love" in return.[12] In the autumn of 1608 Salisbury selected Finet, and the physician Matthew Lister, to conduct his son and heir, William Cecil, on an elaborate grand tour of the Continent during 1609 and 1610.[13] This post, as experienced guide, was hardly a sinecure since the young peer was·thought "not easy to educate or amuse"; consequently, regular reports were prepared for the concerned earl during their leisurely journey through France and Italy.[14] Upon his return to England, Finet replaced Wilson as Salisbury's

[10] *Dictionary of National Biography* VIII 24–25.

[11] *Calendar of Marquess of Salisbury Manuscripts*, Historical Manuscripts Commission (London: H. M. Stationery Office) XVIII 321; XIX 249–50.

[12] His translation of the Savoyard diplomat René de Lucinge, *The Beginning, Continuance and Decay of Estates* (London, 1606; STC 16987).

[13] John Chamberlain, who disliked Finet, commented that he was "a travayler of no note or account but only preferred by Wilson." *The Letters of John Chamberlain*, ed. Norman McClure (*Memoirs*, American Philosophical Society; Philadelphia, 1939) Part One, 268.

[14] John W. Stoye, *English Travelers Abroad, 1604–67* (London: Jonathan Cape, 1952) 126–28; HMC *Salisbury Mss.* XXI 32, 45, 157, 212.

personal secretary, so that in 1611 Finet had an opportunity to learn more of the court and diplomatic matters through his patron's correspondence. He accompanied the earl to Bath where he fruitlessly sought relief from his fatal disease of dropsy.[15] The death of Salisbury in May 1612 left Finet without any official appointment, but his earlier friendship as tutor to the new earl of Salisbury, whose father-in-law, Suffolk, was lord chamberlain, probably explains his appointment as a second "officer of assistance" to Lewis Lewkenor, the official Master of Ceremonies. His stipend was small and his duties so infrequent that he could easily be spared for other minor offices such as membership in the suite of the young prince Charles on an official visit to Cambridge in 1613.[16] In the following summer of 1614 Finet brought to Madrid a small party of young courtiers on an official mission to present personal gifts from James I to Philip III.[17] After this, he returned to London to await the occasional call to assist Lewkenor. Two years later there was another diplomatic mission overseas to the court of Heidelberg, with letters for James's daughter Elizabeth, the wife of the Count Palatine. In March 1616, some months before his departure, he received knighthood. Possibly because he had little personal wealth, Finet delayed his marriage until relatively late in life. By the standards of the day it was advantageous for him to marry, in December 1617, Jane Wentworth, daughter of lord Henry Wentworth of Nettlestead in Suffolk, the sister of Thomas Wentworth, later first earl of Cleveland.[18] Secure at last through his friendship with the Cecil, Howard, and Wentworth families, Finet kept in step with the politics of the day by steering closer to the clique of Buckingham. Anthony Weldon, who wrote over thirty years later with contempt for the levity and decay of James I's regime, identified Finet as one of a trio in that new favorite's faction, who improvised raucous evening "pastimes" for the king's entertainment. Finet was the composer of "bawdy songs," which Edward Zouche sang and George Goring arranged for "fiddlers" to accompany.[19] His lyrics could be scandalous

---

[15] *The Letters of John Chamberlain*, Part One, 306–11; HMC *Calendar of Marquess of Downshire Manuscripts*, III 238–39, 285.

[16] William Berry, *Pedigrees of the Families of Kent* (London: Sherwood, Gilbert, Piper, 1830) p. 449.

[17] Chamberlain described James's gifts as a "rabblement" of "pied bulls and kine, greyhounds, spaniells, water dogges, cormorants, hunting horses, nagges, stone bowes, cross bowes, curious peeces, truncks and many things els that I remember not. . . ." *The Letters*, Part One, 563.

[18] Ibid., Part One, 516; Part Two, 42, 126.

[19] Zouch was privy councilor and Lord Warden of the Cinque Ports; Goring was later to be vice chamberlain for Henrietta. Arthur Weldon, *The Court and Character of King James* (London, 1651) pp. 84–85.

to some, for John Chamberlain reported a theatrical diversion at the palace of Theobalds in January 1618, where Finet sang a song "of such scurilous and base stuffe that it put the king out of his goode humor."[20] The privilege of survival at court came at a high price indeed for Finet, but in September 1618 his patience was rewarded by the valuable reversion, or right to the next appointment, of the office of Master of Ceremonies. His continuous presence at Whitehall was now assured, while his friendship with Buckingham outweighed the disastrous fall of the lord chamberlain, Suffolk. Finet attended each session of the trial of the earl and his countess for bribery and corruption so as to prepare reports of considerable detail for their son-in-law, Salisbury.[21] In the following years he appeared more frequently at Lewkenor's side while he became more familiar with the problems that various embassies could present. Later, in the spring of 1623, he sailed to the northern coast of Spain as a member of the suite of the earl of Rutland to receive Charles, Buckingham, and, as it was then expected, the Infanta Maria.[22] Four years later, with the death of Lewkenor in March 1627, Finet became Master of Ceremonies.

What credentials did he bring to the office? It is clear that he knew French, Spanish, Italian, German, and Latin, and from his travels had personal experience of the customs at several courts in western Europe. Furthermore, he had earned the confidence of several English diplomats who had served on the Continent. He was a regular correspondent of Dudley Carleton, who was at The Hague, about court events in London. Viscount Scudamore wrote to him from Paris and William Trumbull from Brussels. Thomas Philips gave him the keys to his London house during Philips' mission to Constantinople. Thomas Roe confided in him about his negotiations in Poland and would finally be named one of the executors of Finet's will.[23] He was asked by viscount Conway, when absent from Whitehall, to send his opinion about the mission of marquis Pompeo Strozzi, during the crisis of the duchy of Mantua's succession. The Lord Chancellor, the Secretary of State, the Comptroller of the royal Household — all mention Finet's friendly and advisory assistance.[24]

20 *The Letters of John Chamberlain*, Part Two, 131.

21 Lawrence Stone, *Family and Fortune: Studies in Aristocratic Finance in the 16th and 17th Centuries* (Oxford: Clarendon Press, 1973), pp. 276–81; HMC *Salisbury Mss.* XXIII, 95–102, 104–105, 131–33.

22 HMC *Third Report Appendix*, Devonshire Mss. p. 39.

23 PRO SP 14/177/12, Finet to Carleton, 24 Dec. 1624; CSP D 1625–26, p. 271; CSP D 1633–34, p. 161; CSP D 1637–38, p. 599; CSP D 1640–41, p. 80.

24 PRO SP 16/74/101, Finet to Conway, 24 Aug. 1627; CSP D 1635, p. 323; CSP D 1635–36, pp. 531–32.

What sort of a fortune did Finet acquire during his service at Whitehall? In his last will he mentioned that his London home, which consisted of "two houses with the garden houses to them and the inclosed peece of ground ad-joyning" on St. Martin's Lane, had been a grant from the earl of Salisbury. The site was convenient for his duties at Whitehall palace, near which he leased a stable for his own coach and horses.[25] His note books mention another house in Chiswick, which seems to have been leased for use when on duty nearby at Hampton Court. He also owned the parsonage at Kingston-iuxta-Lewes and several leases on properties in Kent from archbishop Laud. The day before he drew up his will he sold "certain lands, tenements and heredita-ments in Lincolnshire and elsewhere" to form a trust for his son, William. For his five daughters marriage portions varying from £1000 to £700 were prepared, as well as a bequest to his wife, relatives, and the poor of the parish of St. Martin's, where he was to be buried. He continued his services as Master of Ceremonies until six weeks before his death on July 12, 1641.

[25] PRO Probate 11, vol. 187/143, dated 22 May 1641. The estimated payments from his office are described in Appendix III, Table I.

THE NOTE BOOKS:
THEIR SOURCE AND CHARACTER

AT ROUSHAM HOUSE, Oxfordshire, are three hitherto unpublished manuscripts:

a. "My Thyrd book of notes and observations concerning ambassadors, etc. beginning at Michelmas 1628." 144 leaves numbered consecutively on the recto only, hand-drawn margins, original parchment binding, 6″ wide, 8″ long.

b. "My 4th booke of notes and observations concerning ambassadors, etc. beginning in May 1632." 156 leaves numbered consecutively as above, with margins, binding, and page size similar to the above.

c. "My fift book of notes and observations concerning ambassadors, etc. beginning in October 1637." 112 leaves numbered consecutively as above (with 67 blank pages), with margins, binding, and page size as before.

The first two original note books have not survived, but, as will be seen, their contents were put in print through the work of James Howell in 1656. There is also in the manuscripts of Rousham House a late-seventeenth-century volume stamped with the words "FINET'S NOTES" on the spine.[26] Here the original divisions of five note books are not retained, but many of Finet's corrections are included. However, this copyist occasionally rewrote sentences and incorporated, without notice, into this text some other incidents which he had read in other sources. It is highly likely that this copy was prepared for the convenient consultation of the later Masters of Ceremonies in the Cotterel family, once Finet's original notes came into their possession after the Restoration. Earlier, only fifteen years after Finet's death, James Howell published *Finetti Philoxenis: Som choice observations of Sir John Finet, knight, and Master of the Ceremonies to the two last Kings, touching the Reception, and Precedence, the treatment and Audience, the Puntillios and Contests of Forren Ambassadors in England.* This book covered diplomatic events which Finet had observed,

---

[26] 590 folios, numbered recto and verso, with additional unpaginated 20 folios of index, 8 3/4″ wide, 15″ long, hand-ruled margins with different cross-references and subject captions.

largely as Lewkenor's assistant, from October 1612 to February 1628. A comparison of it with the later manuscript known as "Finet's Notes" showed that only a short narrative of events from March to September 1628 — fifteen folios in length — had been omitted in Howell's edition.[27] His information was soon appreciated by more famous continental writers on diplomatic procedures, such as Abraham de Wicquefort and Gregorio Leti, who relied upon Howell for several examples of James I's court.[28] This book was fittingly dedicated to Philip Sydney, third viscount L'Isle, the grandson of the Robert Sydney with whom Finet had served at Flushing.[29] In his preface Howell pointed out the exceptional credentials of Finet, as "a knowing knight and well accomplished courtier" who wrote "being still upon the place himself and an actor in everything."[30] Curiosity exists as to why only an excerpt of Finet was published, and at the unlikely date of 1656. It can be suggested that as a royalist, living during the pseudo-monarchical Protectorate of Oliver Cromwell, Howell may have wished that Finet's authentic picture of the court of James I be an oblique reminder of the public dignity the English ruler should bring to his regime. Recently, Dr. Sharpe has noted: "During the 1640s and 1650s Howell, a royalist, published works in which historical parallels were vehicles for his political ideas. He thought the threat of disorder, which would loom with the curtailment of royal authority, was more serious than the question of the rights of the people."[31] Consequently, a truncated version of Finet was meant as a timely hint to the Lord Protector, who had been living in Whitehall palace since April 1654. The early note books discreetly concentrated on events under James I yet provided little on the regime of the executed Charles. Since it has been recently established that the Crom-

---

[27] London 1656, Wing STC, F 947. The book was first entered for publication on 27 November 1654 but printed in May 1656 (*Registers of . . . Company of Stationers, 1640–1708*, ed. E. Arber [London, 1913] I 460, II 56). By the terms of his will Finet ordered that his papers and "paperbookes" be entrusted to his son William.

[28] Abraham de Wicquefort, *L'Ambassadeur et ses fonctions*, 2 vols. (The Hague, 1680–1681); Gregorio Leti, *Il Ceremoniale historico e politico*, 6 vols. (Amsterdam, 1685).

[29] Howell knew the Sydney family from his own services, as Latin orator, with Philip Sydney's father on an embassy to Denmark in 1632, of which he wrote a short history (Oxford, Bodleian Library, Rawlinson Mss. Series C. Vol. 354).

[30] *Finetti Philoxenis* sig. A 5.

[31] Kevin Sharpe, *Sir Robert Cotton, 1586–1631: History and Politics in Early Modern England* (Oxford: Oxford University Press, 1979) p. 246. Later, Howell declared his credentials to write on diplomatic affairs to be his own service "by royal commission," for three years in Madrid, and several visits to France and "sundry courts in Italy" (Howell, *Proedria Basilike: A Discourse Concerning the Precedency of Kings* [1664] sig. B 1ᵛ).

wellian palace regime was carefully imitating earlier Stuart customs, but on a very reduced scale of expense,[32] Howell was safely preaching to the converted. By the end of the century his book fell into disuse until it would be rescued from oblivion by John Nichols in the early nineteenth century, who reprinted large selections from it in his widely quoted collection of descriptive memoirs of the Jacobean court.[33]

These three note books were not meant to be a simple register of visits to the courts by foreign notables, nor a commonplace book of examples of early Stuart court customs. They appear to be a conscientious record of each notable ceremony in which Finet, and the king usually, had a role. This resulted in an episodic narrative, for he focused on one diplomat, or a noteworthy public event, during which he excluded other happenings until he had finished. There are some scattered clues which indicate that weeks might pass before he returned to his book of notes. For example, in 1634 he described the attendance of the king and queen at one of the Inns of Court for the masque *The Triumph of Peace* only after its text was already printed. Some pages later he twice misdated, as of October, his picturesque journey in company with the Savoyard ambassador, San Germano, when it occurred, in fact, in August (IV 39ᵛ and 61). On other occasions he left blank the day of the month for a public audience, when he had forgotten it at the time of his writing the entry. The amount of space that Finet allotted to any particular diplomat seemed to reflect that person's prominence in the court's attention at that moment. There was also at times a personal enthusiasm at work in his satisfaction at a well-staged ceremony. For instance, the king's oaths of ratification for the peace treaty with France, in the presence of Chateauneuf at Windsor in 1629 and, again, for a peace with Spain, with Coloma as witness at Whitehall in 1630, are given in extensive detail. These were the occasions when he enjoyed playing the role of chronicler, for there was some satisfaction that a colorful spectacle would enhance Charles's reputation abroad.

---

[32] Roy Sherwood, *The Court of Oliver Cromwell* (London: Croome Helm, 1977) pp. 149–57.
[33] John Nichols, *The Progresses, Processions and Magnificent Festivities during the Reign of King James*, 4 vols. (London, 1828).

THE FOREIGN POLICY OF
CHARLES I

IT IS STRIKING how alert Finet remained to the rivalries and alignments of the western European states during the period covered in his note books. The aloof reserve between French and Spanish diplomats at Whitehall after 1630 was indeed an omen of the open warfare that would be declared across the channel in May 1635. He was fully aware that the cordial gestures between the French, Dutch, and Swedish representatives in London were a reflection of their common anti-Habsburg alliances already in place on the Continent. In contrast, the Spanish diplomats appeared in his pages to be isolated, if not ostracized, at many public events at Whitehall palace since, aside from their predictable close links to the agent from Brussels from 1629 to 1636, they could count upon the friendship only of occasional visiting envoys from Vienna or Lorraine. Until the summer of 1636 Finet always took for granted a close friendship between Venice and France, after which time he was careful to note that that republic's ministers were openly friendly with the Spanish embassy. The roots of these tensions between rival embassies were found in their private instructions from home, but they compounded the difficulties that Finet faced in making arrangements for Charles's many receptions and theatrical events.

Recalling the great power-struggles of the western European leaders can be of value in understanding the diplomatic context in which Finet labored.[34] In 1621 the Spanish court had decided to reopen its long and costly war to recover the northern provinces of the Low Countries, although these had, even by 1609, won their de facto independence as the Dutch Republic. The changing fortunes in this great contest suggested to King Charles the particular benefits he might pursue at either The Hague or Madrid. For this period before

---

[34] The domestic political pressures necessitating peace after 1628 are ably described in Conrad Russell, *Parliaments and English Politics, 1621–29* (Oxford: Clarendon Press, 1979) pp. 70–84; Charles's relations with the major foreign powers are described in G. M. D. Howat, *Stuart and Cromwellian Foreign Policy* (London: Black, 1974) pp. 40–68, and J. R. Jones, *Britain and Europe in the Seventeenth Century* (London: Arnold, 1966) pp. 1–25. The continuing wars on the Continent are explained in Geoffrey Parker, *Europe in Crisis, 1598–1648* (London: Harvester Press, 1979) pp. 182–267.

the English civil war one of his dominant preoccupations was the recovery of the patrimony of the Elector Palatine, his sister Elizabeth's husband, whose rash attempt to gain the title of king of Bohemia had been lost to the Habsburg claimant's forces on the battlefield near Prague in 1621. The Count Palatine had not merely lost the Bohemian crown; the Habsburg emperor had obtained support in the Diet to place his enemy under the ban of the empire and transfer the electoral title to Bavaria. During the period covered by these journals, Finet is sympathetic to the king's efforts to restore his sister's family's rights. The recovery of the Palatinate had been one of Charles's ambitions, even as prince of Wales, when he visited Madrid to seek the hand of the Infanta, Philip IV's sister, in the spring of 1623. The same dream was the cause of his disastrous naval campaign against Cádiz in the autumn of 1625, by which, in the first year of his reign, he planned to force Spain not merely to withdraw from the Palatinate but to coerce the emperor and the duke of Bavaria along similar lines. King Charles's failure led to his acceptance by 1630 of the treaty of Madrid,[35] in which Philip promised to intercede with the emperor Ferdinand on behalf of the Count Palatine. To no one's surprise, the Habsburg courts at Madrid and Vienna dragged their feet over any further concessions in this vexed question prior to 1640.

Notwithstanding this tension between the house of Stuart and that of Austria, France, the other great monarchy, did not develop an enduring friendship with England. Despite Charles's marriage in 1625 to Henrietta Maria, the sister of Louis XIII, he began in little over a year a second costly naval war against his brother-in-law. For this reckless adventure, there was at first a degree of popular support. First, sympathy had grown among English Protestants for the Huguenots, whose military and political power faced extinction by the superior forces of the French crown. Secondly, acute discontent had surfaced among English shipping and fishing interests against their French rivals, while, lastly, Charles's sudden decision to expel his wife's less-than-popular French entourage from Whitehall had offended the pride of King Louis. After Buckingham, as lord admiral, failed to achieve an expected success at La Rochelle in 1627, and later died at the hands of an assassin, a peace treaty between the two crowns was negotiated at Suze in 1629. Even then suspicions between Whitehall and the Louvre remained alive. Henrietta, no longer a competitor with Buckingham for influence over her husband, disapproved deeply of her brother's unwavering support for Richelieu, whom she held responsible not merely for the exile from France of her mother, Marie

[35] Albert J. Loomie, "Olivares, The English Catholics and the Peace of 1630," *Revue Belge de Philologie et d'Histoire* 47 No. 4 (1969) 1154–66.

de Médicis, but for the exclusion of the Queen Mother's faction from any influence at the French court. Accordingly, by 1635 Richelieu's overtures for a close Anglo-French alliance were treated with reserve once war had broken out between Spain and France. After many private conversations with Charles, the papal representative, George Conn, decided that the king did not have good relations with either Madrid or Paris, but the latter "was much worse and the activity of Richelieu underhanded and outrageous."[36]

What, then, of the court itself in which Finet had to arrange the visits of diplomats? Here two factions, which fluctuated in leadership, membership, and strength, competed for influence upon foreign affairs. Opposing the queen, who, despite her distaste for Richelieu, was considered a partisan of French interests, stood Richard Weston, later earl of Portland, who from 1629 to early 1635 urged the king toward a more Hispanophile view. Sharing his convictions were Thomas Wentworth, whose duties kept him for long periods in Ireland, Francis Cottington, and Francis Windebank, one of the Secretaries of State. Inevitably the chances that a Hispanophile outlook would prevail at court were further diminished by the death of Portland early in 1635. At this time Charles stressed his neutrality when Louis XIII declared war on Philip IV, for his recent costly offensive against both monarchs demonstrated the need for prudence. When Archbishop Laud began to assume more influence over Charles, his attention at first turned to questions of doctrine, ritual, and the selection of bishops for the Established Church. Charles encouraged Laud to make similar plans, based on these Arminian principles, for the church in Scotland and Ireland. To other courtiers, however, Charles's neutrality was seen to be a lost opportunity, for once again the Palatinate's future seemed to be vulnerable to English pressures. Some were confident that even talk of an alliance with France would quickly render Spain more accommodating, while others, such as Arundel, felt that English hostility would close the door at Madrid forever. At the same time a different quarrel raged over Charles's policy toward France's ally — and Spain's other adversary — the Dutch Republic. While many in Protestant England openly sympathized with Dutch resistance to the Catholic Habsburgs, certain commercial interests in London counseled restraint. To them Dutch success in the fishing and carrying trades was too great a threat to the declining English share in North Sea commerce. Furthermore the Spanish wars had begun to create a new prosperous role for Dover as an entrepôt for Spanish wool, silver, and

---

[36] PRO 31/9/124, Conn to Cardinal Barberini, 24 Sept. 1636: "Sua Maiesta non sta bene con Francia ne con Spagna, ma più biasima Francia et il proceder di Richelieu torbido et insolente."

fruit from the Biscayan ports to Flanders.[37] Finally, Charles and Henrietta, who were more sympathetic to the interests of the house of Orange, disliked the dominant commercial leadership of the province of Holland within the Dutch Republic itself. Charles's neutrality toward France and the Dutch Republic, however, remained a disappointment to many. Henrietta after 1637 found that many of her Protestant circle, such as Holland, Pembroke, and Northampton, who were more overtly anti-Spanish at that time, were complaining at her husband's indecision.[38] The queen in the final years of this decade was reduced to leading a smaller "popish" faction featuring such lesser courtiers as Walter Montague, Henry Percy, and Henry Jermyn, with whom the Protestant majority at court were far from comfortable. Finet's cautious references to Conn, the papal representative to Henrietta in London, was typical of the distance that most court officials were careful to preserve. The arrival of Marie de Médicis, the queen mother still in exile from France, in 1638 to remain in St. James's palace until 1641, as another unwanted symbol of court Catholicism,[39] only compounded the stress that Charles endured from courtiers who clamored for a change in his foreign policy.

The severe crisis in Scotland late in 1638 not only reduced Charles's freedom to choose sides in the continental power-struggles; it exposed for the first time his financial and military penury in the absence of a parliament which he was still reluctant to summon. A bold attack by the Dutch against a Spanish naval squadron sheltering within Dover harbor in the autumn of 1639 revealed in effect his inability to guarantee the protection of his own ports to Spain,[40] while he remained estranged from a Richelieu who did not hesitate to order the arrest of his nephew, the young Count Palatine, during a French offensive into the Empire. By 1640, when Finet wrote in his note books about the opening of the "Short" Parliament, the three major western powers — Spain, France, and the Dutch Republic — considered the English king an unreliable partner. Not one of them had compelling reasons to send

---

[37] Harland Taylor, "Trade, Neutrality and the 'English Road,' 1630–1648," *Economic History Review* Series 2, 25 No. 2 (1972) 236–60. S. L. Adams, "Foreign Policy and the Parliaments of 1621 and 1624," in *Faction and Parliament: Essays in Early Stuart History*, ed. Kevin Sharpe (Oxford: Clarendon Press, 1978) pp. 139–71, identifies the earlier Stuart Hispanophile grouping at court.

[38] Malcolm Smuts, "The Puritan Followers of Henrietta Maria in the 1630s," *English Historical Review* 93 No. 366 (January 1978) 43–45.

[39] Caroline Hibbard, *Charles I and the Popish Plot* (Chapel Hill: University of North Carolina Press, 1983) explains thoroughly the position of the court Catholics, pp. 72–109.

[40] Albert J. Loomie, "Alonso de Cárdenas and the Long Parliament, 1640–48," *English Historical Review* 97 No. 383 (April 1982) 289–91.

aid to him during his confrontation with parliament in 1641. In any case, by that time Spain was enduring the loss of Portugal, plus a major rebellion in Catalonia, in addition to continuing its interminable struggle against the Dutch Republic and France. Richelieu, for his part, still encountered dangerous aristocratic conspiracies at home as well as popular resentment over the heavy taxes needed for his large subsidies to the Dutch and the Swedes.[41] Even the Dutch Republic was facing an economic decline, accompanied by strident quarrels over the heavy taxes needed to support hostilities against Spain.[42] When Finet ended his journals in the spring of 1641, he must have been well aware, as many at court already sensed, that the king, whose image as a royal diplomat he had sought to protect, was entering into a struggle against a critical parliament without a chance of any substantial foreign support.[43]

[41] Victor–L. Tapié, *France in the Age of Louis XIII and Richelieu*, trans. David McN. Lockie (London: Macmillan, 1975) pp. 407–17.

[42] Jonathan Israel, *The Dutch Republic and the Hispanic World, 1606–1661* (Oxford: Clarendon Press, 1983) pp. 282–314.

[43] J. H. Elliott, "The Year of the Three Ambassadors," in *History and Imagination: Essays in Honour of H. R. Trevor Roper*, edd. Hugh Lloyd-Jones, Valerie Pearl, Blair Worden (London: Duckworth, 1981) pp. 165–81, explains the failure of the last negotiations for an alliance with Spain in 1640. A review of the reasons for the decline of the French and Spanish influences upon Charles is found in Albert J. Loomie, "The Spanish Faction at the Court of Charles I, 1630–8," *Bulletin of the Institute of Historical Research* 59 No. 139 (May 1986) 37–49.

THE OFFICE OF
MASTER OF CEREMONIES,
1603–1641

WHEN JAMES I inaugurated the office of Master of Ceremonies in the first year of his reign, he brought to Whitehall a title borrowed from diplomatic practices long established below the Alps. Since the mid-fifteenth century, clerks (*Magistri ceremoniarum*) had assumed a monopoly of ceremonial tasks for the papal chapel that included all the special liturgical activities of the presiding officials, as well as of the persons attending the services.[44] Inevitably, the duty of receiving, instructing, and guiding diplomatic visitors in a consistent manner began to be added to the normal work of the Roman master of ceremonies.[45] By 1483, John Burchard began his *Liber notarum* to record details as a guide for his successors, who were expected to continue his practice.[46] It was this public and secular portion of the Roman diplomatic customs which became in effect the charge of the new officer to be appointed by King James. He too was to be prepared to provide a dignified welcome, suitable lodgings, the proper schedule of visits to the king and his councilors, and to be tactful about precedence among diplomats and courtiers. On the Continent, the court of France had already seen the need. Earlier, by 1578, Henry III of France had appointed Jérôme de Gondy, a courtier of Franco-Italian background, to have sole charge of diplomats at the Louvre.[47] Henry

[44] Richard C. Trexler, "*Il Libro Ceremoniale*" *of the Florentine Republic by Francesco Filarete and Angelo Manfidi* (Travaux d'Humanisme et Renaissance 165; Geneva: Droz, 1978) pp. 18–20.

[45] Donald E. Queller, *The Office of Ambassador in the Middle Ages* (Princeton: Princeton University Press, 1967) pp. 191–96; Garrett Mattingly, *Renaissance Diplomacy* (Boston: Houghton Mifflin, 1955) pp. 55–82.

[46] Arnold H. Mathew, *The Diary of John Burchard of Strasburg* (London: Griffiths, 1910). Finet also called his journal a "Book of Notes." G. Constant, "Les Maîtres de Cérémonies du XVIe siècle: Leur diaires," *Mélanges d'Archéologie et d'Histoire* (Ecole Française de Rome) XXIIIe année, fascicules I–III (janvier–juin 1903) 161–229, fascicules IV–V (juillet–décembre 1903) 319–43, explains the origins and method of the diaries of the Masters in Rome.

[47] Albert J. Loomie, "The *Conducteur des Ambassadeurs* in Seventeenth Century France and Spain," *Revue Belge de Philologie et d'Histoire* 53 No. 2 (1975) 333–34. In 1585 Henry III of France created the office of Maître des Cérémonies at his court to direct the precedence within

had appointed a *conducteur des ambassadeurs* because of expanded diplomatic business, a fear of incidents resulting in friction, and his desire of adding dignity to his court. While foreign ambassadors were apparently grateful for the services of the *conducteur,* the character of the surviving sources does not permit a very detailed description of his relationship to the king, or his particular benefits to individuals in Paris.[48] In Spain, neither Philip II nor Philip III appointed this new officer, but the character of their international negotiations was less centralized in practice, since authorities in Brussels, Naples, Milan, and Lisbon handled regional matters and, because of war, there were fewer resident embassies in Madrid.[49] Later, in March 1626, after obtaining information from Spanish diplomats who served in Rome, Paris, and London, a committee of palace officers recommended to Philip IV that a *conductor de los embajadores* be attendant on the king.[50]

In planning his new office what improvements did James have in mind? Apparently, Elizabethan practices were erratic and wasteful, as the queen had simply continued her father's custom of picking any one of the twenty-five Gentlemen Pensioners on duty to speak an official welcome, at a short distance from London, or to escort the diplomat to his audience at the palace.[51] Otherwise, incidental problems were passed on to the lord chamberlain or added to

the palace of all courtiers: see Lucien Moreri, *Le Grand Dictionnaire historique* (Paris, 1740) 183.

[48] Theodore Godefroy's collection of notes on court ceremonies *Le Cérémonial de France* (Paris, 1619) had little material on diplomacy. After 1623 he and his son compiled twenty volumes of transcriptions, largely from the registers of the Hôtel de Ville of Paris, concerning court ceremonies for coronations, baptisms, etc., which served as the basis for their *Le Cérémonial François,* 2 vols. (Paris, 1649).

[49] Loomie (n. 47) 346–56. The reception of diplomats in Spain had been regulated by the palace ordinances compiled by order of Charles V in 1545. See *Etiquetas de la casa de Austria,* ed. Alonso Rodriguez Villa (Madrid, 1913) pp. 33–34.

[50] For a description of the duties of the *conductor* at a public audience in Madrid see Leti, *Il Ceremoniale* VI 769–74. For a private audience, H. J. Chaytor, "*Embajada Española*: An Anonymous Contemporary Guide to Diplomatic Procedure in the Last Quarter of the Seventeenth Century," *Camden Miscellany* (London: Royal Historical Society, 1926) XIV 23–25.

[51] For example, Giustiniani of Venice in 1515 was met twelve miles from London by a "Knight and a Doctor of Laws . . . with fifty horse" (*Four Years at the Court of Henry VIII,* ed. Rawdon Brown, 2 vols. [London, 1854] I 77–80). In July 1546 a French ambassador was met twenty-five miles from London by a "Gentleman of the Chamber" and five other courtiers (Germain Lefevre-Pontalis, *Correspondence politique de Odet de Selve* [Paris, 1888] p. 3). In 1564 the new Spanish ambassador had already been in residence before Elizabeth sent a Gentleman Pensioner to greet him, but in 1578 another ambassador was met at Gravesend by a Pensioner followed by a second with another greeting (CSP S 1558–67, p. 364; CSP S 1568–79, p. 564).

the agenda of the Privy Council. If there happened already to be in London another representative from the same state, it was not unusual for him to make arrangements for his compatriot's first interviews. Admittedly the last decade of Elizabeth's reign was not an active diplomatic period because of her estrangements from Madrid, Brussels, and Venice, and because of the unsettled conditions in France. Yet contemporary sources hint at other problems. André Hurault's narrative of December 1597 has a trace of bewilderment at meeting different Pensioners, "never one being sent twice," to announce his interviews with the queen. The embassy of the Maréchal de Biron in the summer of 1601 required nearly thirty letters from the privy council's secretariate directing officials on the route from Dover to London.[52] Whether it was the unsettled time of war, or the queen's known conservatism and frugality, that allowed this haphazard reception of diplomats to continue, James planned immediate reform for the era of peace which he sought. Typically, he did so with a lack of restraint, which Charles would be forced later to regret. The opulence of this Jacobean hospitality provoked nostalgia, over a half-century later, in the secretariate of Louis XIV. In its standing instructions to diplomats destined for England in the 1660s it noted: "Formerly there was rendered in England far more honor to our ambassadors than at present," for after landing at Dover the crown's hospitality began at once on the road to London. Within his palace, James would allow "an audience on the same dais as himself. . . . they would dine together at table and wash their hands in the same basin so that they almost seemed to be equals." Yet it was acknowledged that other courts had been less generous and that Charles I had to end "excessive honors."[53] For this new office James granted a stipend of £200 a year, a level of payment rarely permitted by Elizabeth.[54] Concurrently, a fashionable, but spurious, cachet of antiquity of the title was circulated, as appears in the pages of John Stowe's contemporary history.[55]

The Mastership was inaugurated at the palace in Greenwich by a warrant under the privy seal on May 21, 1603 to Sir Lewis Lewkenor, entrusting him with the care of "straungers of qualitie" so that they should be "with all

[52] *A Journal of All that was Accomplished by M. De Maisse*, edd. G. B. Harrison & R. A. Jones (London, 1931) pp. 18, 22–23; *Acts of the Privy Council*, J. R. Dasent, XXXII (1601–1604) (London: H. M. Stationery Office, 1907) 189–90, 205, 209.

[53] AMAE *Fonds divers: Angleterre*, 62 fol. 157.

[54] Anon., *A Collection of Ordinances . . . for the Government of the Royal Household* (London, 1790): "Queen Elizabeth's Annual Expense, Civil and Military," 241–57.

[55] John Stowe & Edmund Howes, *Annals of England* (London, 1631) 1037: "The auncient office of the ceremonies, having a long tyme voyd and almost forgotten, the king made Sir Lewes Lewkenor Master of The Ceremonies allowing thereunto all auncient fees."

respectes due them receaved, used and entertained both during their abode with us and their journeys also. . . ." Within three years the duties were further formalized by a patent of November 7, 1605 to Lewkenor as a "gentleman well languaged of good education and discretion."[56] At this time Lewkenor prepared a more specific description of his office, wherein he was expected to be "alwaies attendant about the courte with his servants and horses, himself and them fitly furnished . . . to entertayne and receave sutch foreyn ambassadors as shal repayre into this realme to do his majesty honor and service." In addition he was to "take care that they bee convenyently and fitly lodged and to have coaches to carry them "where the court shall then remayne." He was to arrange "theyr times of access and audience" and be fully informed about the "severall ranks, qualityes and degrees" of the diplomats. His purpose was to procure "by all possible means all favor, assistance and address for their negotiations."[57] At the same time, following the experience of Italy and France, an efficient subordinate — an *ayde* at the Louvre, or *sottomaestro* below the Alps — was to be appointed. James then established by another warrant the office of Marshall of the Ceremonies with a stipend of £100 a year. Decades later, Leti compared the smooth collaboration of a marshal with the master to that of a bellows to an organ's music. "He is to go about and leave instructions according to his orders, . . . he must possess courtesy, judgement and understanding of the world."[58] Even then, James had not finished. In a typical proliferation of court offices by another patent he ordered that two others, Sir James Murray and William Button, "in cases wher the said Lewkenor can not personally be by order of our chamberlain, to give attendance for the receipt and entertainment of all ambassadors."[59] Doubts about the need of two additional substitutes clouded from the start this tenuous and untitled office of "attendance." Every assignment depended on the good will of the lord chamberlain, or the Master; there was no other responsible authority. Regretting at the end of his reign this excessive number of officers surrounding the care of foreign diplomats, James ordered that, when Finet became Master, the office of "attendance" was "to cease and be discontinued."[60] Despite these expensive and wasteful beginnings, a convenient procedure for English diplomatic business had been created.

[56] PRO SP 14/16/26; Thomas Rymer, *Foedera Conventiones, Literae . . . Reges Angliae,* 20 vols. (London, 1704–35) VII.2, 144.

[57] PRO SP 14/16/26A, undated holograph.

[58] PRO SP 14/153/87, Lewkenor to Conway; Leti, *Il Ceremoniale* VI 700–701.

[59] PRO SP 15/135/126, undated copy.

[60] PRO SP 39/17, original patent 8 March 1625. Reviving the office for Woodward in 1630 was unnecessary since little need existed (Aylmer, 83–84, 103).

The episodic character of Finet's note books does not shed enough light on how much time was actually involved in his duties. Some clues to solve this problem are to be found in the surviving bills for disbursements submitted by Finet, for the period of 1628 to 1634. Since, as Master, he received a supplementary fee of £1 a day "in town," with diplomats at Whitehall or the City, and £2 for each day "outside," he used to identify each occasion with the number of days required. These bills, when approved by the chamberlain and vice chamberlain, provided a supplementary pay on top of his official salary.[61] From this, it is clear that extraordinary ambassadors occupied a major portion of the master's time and were equivalently important to the king and his councillors. The fees for his daily attendance during a long stay could mount up, so that Finet at times agreed to request but "the half of my ordinary allowance" on some bills, when his total became exorbitant.[62]

Behind this request for payment was a complex round of shuttling to and from various embassies as a messenger, or escort, to make sure the diplomat came to each arranged interview. Taking the year 1634, with a total of 136 days, as a sample, his notes record that he arranged, and was present in, the first audiences of two ambassadors extraordinary, Oxenstierne of Sweden and San Germano of Savoy, and the less elaborate welcomes for Correr of Venice and Pougny of France. There were public departures also for those two extraordinaries and official dismissals for Gussoni of Venice and Brassert of the Dutch Republic. A special audience was arranged for the agent from Brussels, Henry Taylor, to relate officially the news of the death of the Archduchess Isabella. There were twenty-three other private audiences of various diplomats to be arranged with the king. In addition, announcements, at Charles's request, of the Garter ceremonies had to be offered to each embassy and also places secured, for those who asked, to watch the elaborate public entry of the new lord mayor of London. There were troublesome debates over invitations to two major theatrical events: two performances of the spectacular *Triumph of Peace* at the Inns of Court, as well as Charles's own lavish masque *Coelum Britannicum*, at Shrovetide at Whitehall. Considerable efforts were spent upon arranging that the invited diplomats attended the christening of prince James. There were also other audiences of courtesy for Henrietta and the royal children that had to be planned. He noted also thirty-

---

[61] These fees are listed in Appendix III, Table I under "Allowances Paid."

[62] In 1630, with the right to 210 days of attendance on the French and Spanish ambassadors, he accepted the fee for 105 (PRO SP 16/164/48).

seven days "out of town," which were largely occupied in his assisting the Savoyard ambassador to be with the court then in progress.[63]

By placing the recorded disbursements of his court office beside the careful entries in his note books of the amount of gratuities that each diplomat or visitor gave him, a fairly reliable composite annual income can be estimated. The resulting table does not indicate a lucrative fortune but it is an accurate picture of substantial rewards for a lesser courtier in service at Whitehall. His average of more than £600 each year in direct payments, for a period of over thirteen years, was hardly negligible.[64]

---

[63] PRO SP 16/279/171 covering Nov. 1633 to Nov. 1634.

[64] Traditionally the salaries of English diplomats were not as high: see Gary M. Bell, "Elizabethan Diplomatic Compensation: Its Nature and Variety," *Journal of British Studies* 20 No. 2 (Spring 1981) 1–25.

CHARLES I AND
THE FOREIGN DIPLOMATIC CORPS

THE CITY OF LONDON

TO FOLLOW THE NOTEBOOKS more easily a brief review of Charles's special directives about the treatment of diplomats during their visit in London is in order. As a beginning, Finet's evidence about the less-than-smooth relations between the king and the City deserves attention. He was clearly aware that several wealthy householders were irritated at the clumsy procedure of Pembroke, the lord chamberlain, who might suddenly resort to Charles's "prerogative power to take up houses" in the City, when pressed to provide a residence for an important visitor. For example, when Carlos Coloma arrived, late in 1629, as ambassador extraordinary of Spain, Finet knew that the French ambassador still occupied the one official temporary residence for diplomats in London, which was the house of Sir Abraham Williams. Without naming the owners he seemed embarrassed to note the adroit excuses from each one who was asked to offer a residence and the last-minute discovery by the lord mayor of a suitable house, which the chamberlain had not named (III 55ᵛ–56). The offering of meager gifts of money by the City to the king always received a hostile comment. Early in 1634, for instance, he saw Charles decline the city's present of £2000 in gold "with some distaste and disgrace to the citizens" while the king announced his preference for a jewel worth twice that amount (IV 41). Later, there was more overt resentment toward the City when in 1639 he loyally approved Charles's decision not to make a public entry into London in the late summer, after his return from Berwick. At this time the City had shown "such poorness" (V 41ᵛ) in another grudging gift of money to defray his recent expedition to the north. Feelings at Whitehall continued to run high since he recorded that, shortly afterward, all privy councillors canceled their appearance at the inaugural banquet of the new lord mayor "upon a notice given them of some displeasure conceived by his majesty agaynst the city" (V 47).

There were, however, happier occasions recorded, since Finet had to deal with members of London's trading companies when they brought to Whitehall special representatives from countries where they did business. The Barbary

Company was helped by Charles's recognition of commissioners from the rebel city of Saley in Morocco in 1628 (III 2), but nine years later at its request he ignored the rebel cause by receiving publicly ambassadors from the new sultan. There were also expensive royal gifts in their honor (IV 152^v–153^v). In contrast, the poverty of the Muscovy Company's resources was noted after their shabby treatment of the czar's official agents in 1628 (III 8) and more clearly in 1634 (IV 71–71^v). The hard times that had also come upon a normally prosperous Levant Company were described in their skimpy hospitality to a courier, or chiaus, of the Turkish sultan in 1640 (V 88^v–91). On this occasion Charles agreed to pay part of their costs. A Persian merchant, whom Charles was prevailed upon to receive as an ambassador in 1637, was reported by Finet to say that he was pleased at the honors that Charles gave him, but that he was angry enough to threaten revenge upon the London merchants with whom he had done business. This did not augur well for the East India Company when they soughts benefits on the Persian coast (IV 136). A notable exception to Finet's dismal picture of the merchants trading in the Baltic seemed to be the representatives from the Hansa who expressed satisfaction with their success in London on different occasions in 1630, 1632, and 1635. Unfortunately, the merchants of the Eastland Company appear to have received little understanding from Charles when they pleaded for an official welcome to the ambassador of the king of Poland in 1637 out of consideration of "the danger of theyr and the states loss." Since Charles believed that the Polish king's recent marriage to a Habsburg princess had been a slight to his niece, the daughter of the late Elector Palatine, he told Finet to reply that "his honour was more dear to him than the merchants interest" (IV 149^v).

The Audiences at Whitehall

In 1627, after Finet assumed office, Charles reminded him that there must be a sequence of three "welcomes" to new ambassadors on first arrival at specified locations. This practice, while not new to the English court, had been reserved for special occasions in the past and designated sites at Greenwich, or the wharf at the Tower, had not been used invariably. At the beginning the Master of Ceremonies was to present a first welcome, in Charles's name, at Gravesend, at which time he was to establish the foreigner's official rank and credentials. While the ambassador still waited there, Finet had to return to London to discuss with the chamberlain the appropriate peer to offer a second welcome, in the king's name, and to arrange for barges or coaches for the entire retinue's journey. For an extraordinary ambassador, the second greeting must occur at Greenwich before the diplomat entered the king's barge, but for a resident ambassador this formal speech was to be made upon arrival at Tower wharf. In both cases, an earl was designated to welcome those from monarchies, a baron for those from a republic or duchy. Here the anxiety of Venice that it be treated in England on a par with the "crowned heads" stimulated fruitless appeals, each time, that a new Venetian ambassador be welcomed by an earl. At Tower wharf, city dignitaries and courtiers with a parade of coaches, including one or more from each friendly ambassador already in London, were to be ready to escort the new diplomat to his official residence. That night a "third" welcome was presented, usually by the younger son of a peer. By contrast to this expensive and time-consuming procedure, agents were to receive but one official greeting by the Master of Ceremonies, who escorted each one directly to his residence on arrival.

After this, the first public audience with Charles had to be planned. On the assigned day, an earl or baron, depending on the country of origin, was appointed to accompany the ambassador in the king's coach at the head of a procession of coaches to the gate of Whitehall. There the party dismounted to enter the courtyard amid trumpet fanfares and a line of the guard, to walk up the stone stairs next to the great hall, to proceed across the terrace into the palace. There the group entered a room, such as the empty council chamber which Finet usually called a "chamber of repose," to await word that Charles had entered the hall assigned by custom for a public audience. A resident ambassador was always first received in the Presence Chamber, but the extraordinary in the Banqueting House, in either of which Charles was seated beneath "the state," a canopy with the royal coat of arms behind his chair on a raised platform, while complimentary speeches from the ambassador and the king were heard and everyone studied the liveries of the foreigner's entourage and his proper bearing. After the ambassador returned to the "chamber of repose," Finet led him to the Withdrawing Chamber for the private interview with Charles where other letters were presented and diplomatic matters were discussed. Even if Henrietta were present at that first public audience, the occasion was considered to be officially with the king alone. A custom of having a separate interview with her, to present letters, was also observed on that same day. Then, moving for the last time to the "chamber of repose" to meet the rest of his escort, the ambassador was led back with similar ceremony to his residence. The first public audience of an agent, or "envoy," continued to remain a simpler affair involving only the Master as escort to the palace, to a "chamber of repose," and then to the Presence Chamber for the royal welcome.

It is evident in Finet's notes that, for all ranks, a ceremonial procession through certain interior rooms of Whitehall took place so as to show their great art collection[65] in as striking a fashion as possible. On the upper floor of Whitehall palace two adjacent areas of the state appartments which Finet called "the king's side" and "the queen's side" had a sequence of special rooms that Charles reserved for his diplomatic conferences. In order of importance for ceremony they were: Presence Chamber, Privy Chamber, Withdrawing Chamber.[66] The Presence, with its throne and cloth of State, was used only for the first and last public audiences of ambassadors and agents, or "envoys." Separated by a lobby was the Privy Chamber (not to be confused with the room where the council met), which was used by court officials in attendance but was rarely seen by diplomats. Close to this was the Withdrawing Chamber, which was preferred by Charles for his many interviews with diplomats since it was conveniently near other waiting rooms.[67] Here Charles arranged special meetings such as the knighting of Peter Paul Rubens (III 67ᵛ) in 1630. For public audiences of extraordinary ambassadors and other great occasions Charles directed that the Banqueting House be used, even if, at times prior to 1637, the scenery for a masque might be only partially dismantled. For other reasons Charles would freely include other parts of the palace. For the ratification of the treaty with Spain Finet recorded that Coloma was brought through the Great Hall, the Withdrawing Chamber, and the Presence Chamber into the king's chapel for the ceremony of the oaths. On this occasion the Banqueting House, true to its name, was the scene of a state dinner (III 94–96). Two days before there had been a proclamation of the treaty by a herald standing in the Inner — or Preaching — Courtyard, while the king and Coloma watched from above, at a window of the Council Chamber.[68] By personal preference Henrietta

[65] M. H. Cox & P. Norman, *London County Council Survey of London* XIII (St. Margaret Westminster) Part two (London, 1930) has a full history of the site of the palace; contemporary drawings of the palace are reviewed in E. Croft-Murray & P. Hulton, *A Catalogue of British Drawings* I (London: British Museum, 1960). The design of the Banqueting House and its purpose is explained in *The King's Arcadia: Inigo Jones and the Stuart Court*, edd. John Harris, Stephen Orgel, and Roy Strong (London: Arts Council of Great Britain, 1973).

[66] Hugh Murray Baillie, "Etiquette and the Planning of the State Apartments in Baroque Palaces," *Archaeologia* 101 (1967) 169–99, compares the designs of contemporary palaces.

[67] Peter Paul Rubens noted the "incredible quantity of excellent pictures, statues, and ancient inscriptions which are to be found in this court" in a letter to Pierre Dupuy of 8 August 1629. *The Lettrers of Peter Paul Rubens*, trans. and ed. Ruth S. Magurn (Cambridge: Harvard University Press, 1955) p. 320.

[68] Sketch plans of the upper and lower floors of Whitehall palace are available in *The Diary of John Evelyn*, ed. E. S. Beer, 6 vols. (London: Oxford University Press, 1955) III 247, and G. P. V. Akrigg, *Jacobean Pageant* (New York: Atheneum, 1962) pp. 398–400.

used her official rooms in a simpler fashion. Finet noted that her Privy Chamber was used for public visits of courtesy from diplomats. Otherwise, the queen received them in her Withdrawing Chamber, where it was not uncommon for the French and Savoyard diplomats also to stand about as they appeared in their own "domestic" fashion there. In their case Henrietta gave to the representatives of her brother, Louis, and her sister, Christine, her personal leave to come as a member of her own household, or family. This was not granted, however, to English representatives, in return, at Paris or Turin.[69]

The ceremonies apart, what did Charles expect Finet to do for subsequent diplomatic meetings? According to the note books, the Master was considered responsible for subsequent meetings with the king, and at times with the privy council. For this Charles decided upon a special route by which Finet avoided the crowded main gate, by leading the ambassador through a small door in the palace wall on King Street, across the privy garden to a private stair, named "Adam and Eve," to the upper floor of the palace. Normally a diplomatic visitor could not see any important officer without notice to Finet. The merchants of the Muscovy Company found this to be true in 1634, when they brought the czar's official courier to Whitehall and then left him for a whole day to wander "up and downe the lodgings of state" carrying his dispatches and "followed by some of his nation in theyr country habit" (IV 71) without seeing the king.

ROYAL HOSPITALITY

In a codicil to his last will, Finet recorded his special service "as the only meanes of saveing to his majestie above ten thousand pounds by keeping off, regulating and abating the excessive charge his majestie was at before, beyond other kings example, in defraying of ambassadors dyet and coaches without limitacion of tyme or number."[70] The "diet," or "defraying" of the extraordinary ambassador's retinue for a limited number of days after his arrival, had to be explained to each extraordinary ambassador. For example, in a note to the steward of the count of Oñate in 1636 Finet promised that the Spaniard would be given sumptuous daily provisions — including sixteen

---

[69] In 1637 Finet prepared a report for the earl of Leicester about the customs of the Louvre after receiving advice from Henri de Vic at Paris, in which he noted: "Your lordship is to expect no audiences, private or publick, ordinary or extraordinary, to be given you but by the introduction of the conductor of ambassadors" (IV 111, with original French letter in III 85–86ᵛ).

[70] PRO Probate 11/87/143 codicil of 6 June 1641.

dishes of meat — for six days for the eighty members listed in his entourage. The cost was paid from the accounts of the Cofferer of the king's household. These provisions, which he usually called "specie," were to be "disposed of and dressed by the ambassadors owne cookes. . . . Coales, lights and torches to be provided by the kinges officers as was also beer and wyne. . . . bread to be brought them every morning by talle. . . . theyr lodgings with hangings, bedding, sheets, stooles, tables to be furnished out also of the Kyngs standing wardrobe" (IV 124). These generous supplies were, by this date, a compromise. Earlier, in 1627, because of his financial straits from his wars, Charles had announced that he was terminating completely the offer of provisions, or "defraying" of extraordinary ambassadors. Accordingly Finet had to tell Pompeo Strozzi, at his arrival from Mantua, that there was to be "no more defraying" at court. This unexpected news inevitably provoked unintentional suspicions of hostility to that duke. After a period of reflection, Charles decided that it would be more fitting to match the courtesy shown by other states to English diplomats overseas. By this measure Chateauneuf was "entertained" the exact number of days in 1629 that Louis XIII had honored Thomas Edmondes, the English ambassador in Paris, for the ratification of the peace treaty. Because the king of Poland had been generous to Thomas Roe, two other Polish extraordinaries were "dieted" in 1631 and 1632. Probably the remarks in Finet's will refer to the final orders from Charles about "diet" in 1634 and 1635. In the summer of 1634, after three weeks of expensive fare for the marquis of San Germano, Charles ordered "the defraying of no ambassador shall continue longer than tyll the day of his fyrst audience be past" (IV 72). In practice this meant that, from the evening of his entry into his temporary official residence until the day of his public audience in the Banqueting House, he was "dieted" by Charles. From the note book it appears that firm efforts were made to keep the entertainment to about four days.[71] In March 1635, the Master of the Horse was told that an extraordinary ambassador was to have use of the king's coach no "farther or oftener then to and from theyr audiences" (IV 73-73ᵛ) at the palace. These two limitations, for which Finet apparently took credit later in his will, were a true economy in the expenses of the royal household. However, there still remained other outlays of money, particularly for official departure gifts, as will be seen.

It remained customary to arrange annually two special warrants exclusively for the use of resident diplomats. Each year the lord treasurer asked for a royal commission to pay to the customs farmers on behalf of these diplomats

[71] The extraordinary embassies recorded in the State Papers from 1 April 1629 to May 1641 came to a total crown expenditure of £5535.

only the tax they would have had to pay on purchasing wine. This tax exemption was limited to thirty tuns for ambassadors and fifteen for agents.[72] Finet noted that the origin of this privilege was "the frute of a consideration of King James that such ordinary ambassadors as should keep house and spend (as they must needs, having great familyes) much wine, might of the kyngs favor have it wyth less charge to them by as much as the impost came to . . ." (IV 135). Furthermore, gifts of venison from the royal forests were carried each summer to the houses of the residents. In 1635, this required that Finet request the earl of Holland, as Chief Justice in Eyre, to sign twenty-one separate warrants for each buck slain in the designated royal forest (IV 88ᵛ–89). He then arranged that they be distributed to the diplomat named in the warrant according to Charles's prescribed quota of three for an ambassador and two for an agent. If the diplomat was absent from London at the time of delivery, his warrant was declared void and torn up. At times, Finet received, as a gift, one of the bucks from an embassy, which he took pains to note in the margin of his journals.

HENRIETTA'S COURT AND HER "DOMESTICK" VISITORS

Although his official duties were obviously confined to the king's service, Finet's note books make it clear that he regularly consulted with Henrietta's lord chamberlain, the earl of Dorset, when diplomats desired an audience with her and also when their greetings to the royal children were to be presented. Although Finet did not mention her Catholic chapel, he was on good terms with the Queen's Almoner, the Bishop of Angoulême. With the arrival of the exiled Queen Mother Marie de Médicis in 1638, another royal household came into existence to which Finet occasionally arranged diplomatic visits. In many respects Henrietta's patronage of artists and selections of authors for her masques were similar to her husband's, so that the cultural atmosphere of her court was the same. Her lavish theatrical presentations were always considered to be her personal affair to which she offered her own invitations, so that Finet was spared a repetition of the troubles he recorded over diplomats attending the masques of Charles. The queen, as has been seen above, retained a leading political role at Whitehall, so her insistence that the representatives of her brother, Louis XIII, and of her sister, Christine of Savoy, should come to Whitehall as if "domesticks" of her household, ran

---

[72] 7560 gallons duty-free (with a tun rated at 252 gallons).

counter to the protocol on visits demanded by her husband. It will be seen in Finet's note books that he was uneasy that French and Savoyard diplomats had opportunities for private discussions with Charles whenever he visited his wife, or even to observe other diplomats when they were visiting her.

Chateauneuf, for instance, was able to be present to hear everything Coloma of Spain said to the queen in his private audience (III 66). Soon their privilege was judged by the two embassies to be a matter of right. To preserve it, Chateauneuf, to the irritation of Charles and his privy council, announced that he wished to cancel the ceremony of his public departure so as to have only a private, or "domestick," departure. Apparently, close advisers of Charles were uneasy at this freedom assumed by the two embassies, for Finet was ordered in 1634 to inform Pougny, the French ambassador, that he should not "surprise" the king by conversing with him "without the presence of his lords to assist . . . with their counsell" (III 77; IV 68). However, it is best to evaluate the perils of this strange exemption on an individual basis. In the spring of 1632, for example, the steward of Fontenay-Mareuil was arrested under charges that he had stolen the personal papers of the baron of Roche-chuart, a friend of Henrietta. As an embassy servant the steward received immunity from punishment, but Finet noted that during the remainder of Fontenay's stay the queen never gave him a "gracious look." Similarly, Oxenstierna of Sweden was invited by Charles "to hunt with him and to repayre domestically to court at his pleasure" (III 109^v, 111^v), yet he failed utterly to secure the purpose of his visit which was Charles's support for a command of troops in Germany. Despite his well "dieted" visit to the court in progress, San Germano never gained English approval for the duke of Savoy's claim to the title of king of Cyprus. At times, the French found the privilege so informal that some of their diplomatic messages seemed cheapened. Aware of this, Saint Nectaire and Pougny asked for an audience with Finet's "conduction" in April 1635 (IV 78^v), so as to give suitable gravity to their announcement that France had entered into a war against Spain. There was, undoubtedly, an element of satisfaction to Finet, in the directive he received in the spring of 1639, when the crisis in Scotland required that Charles travel to Newcastle. Then the French ambassador was told not "to wayte on his majesty in the expedition": as Finet explained, certain ambassadors were "so little subject to question or controul" that it was not proper to have them near, "particularly the French of so domestick accesse, to hearken after and to observe his majestyes motions and actions in a business of such weight and consequence" (V 40–41).

Quarrels over Rank

Throughout his entire period in office Finet was allowed by Charles to accept only two grades among foreign representatives: ambassador and agent, which could be, as has been seen, resident or extraordinary. The agent extraordinary would sometimes be called in these notes "envoy," if he represented a hereditary prince, or a "deputy" if he came from the Hansa or the Dutch Republic. Because of the English wars against France and Spain until 1629/30, only the Dutch and Venetian republics maintained ambassadors continuously from the accession of Charles in 1625 until the crisis of 1642. However, while Joachimi, the Dutch representative, remained the official appointee, he took leaves of absence and a deputy would be in charge. Venice regularly moved its ambassador out of London every three years. In one case, Charles expressed displeasure because he considered a new Venetian ambassador's previous post to be inferior to an appointment in England. In the second rank, and of minor importance, were the continuous presence of the agents of Florence and the exiled court of Bohemia. The archduchess in Brussels accredited her own agent, Henry Taylor, for a five-year period, but, from elsewhere in Europe, the number of resident diplomats for this decade before the civil war in London is meager. Denmark recalled its agent in 1632; Savoy kept a resident agent for but one three-year term. Sweden's Michael de Bloom appeared as agent in London for short periods as he served, at times, in other courts as well.

There was a surprising amount of trouble over the status of the Spaniards. In December 1634, the count of Umanes, the former ambassador to France, was nominated by Philip IV to England, and again, in January 1638, Gaspar de Bracamante, another veteran, was designated ambassador for London. Both appointees delayed interminably their arrival with excuses to the Spanish council that they were currently involved in litigation which demanded their attention. Olivares, *privado* of Philip, hesitated to appoint another ambassador because of two Castilian traditions: an official designate retained for a period the prescriptive right to his position; further, Olivares was hesitant to elevate anyone new to the higher rank since this personal status was retained.[73] Within the framework of this interim status Charles had to deal with Juan de Necolalde and later with Alonso de Cárdenas, who insisted that their rank was that of "resident," not agent. In Savoy, Venice, and Spain this title was recognized as higher than agent. Not so for Charles, who advised Finet that he would accept "no minister imployed here to be other than either am-

[73] *"Embajada Española"* (n. 50) 3.

Sir John Finet

Early nineteenth-century watercolor by George Perfect Harding, who copied a portrait since lost. The original was probably painted when Finet visited Venice in 1609; since he was Master of Ceremonies from 1627 to 1641, the inaccurate inscription must date from a later period.

WHITEHALL PALACE, EASTERN FRONT

Undated engraving by Wenceslaus Hollar, from a series done in Antwerp in 1647 ($6'' \times 13''$). His perspective from across the Thames shows, on the left, the Privy Stairs, where Finet noted that ambassadors sometimes entered the palace from a barge. Along the river were the queen's apartments when she stayed at Whitehall. The roofs of the Guard Chamber, Great Hall, and Chapel can be seen in front of the east façade of the Banqueting House.

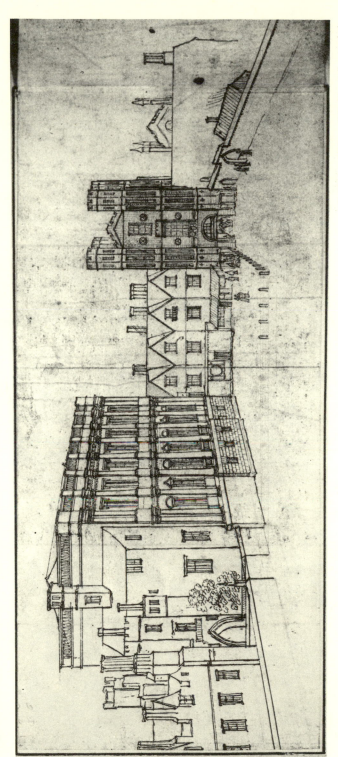

Whitehall Palace, Western Front

Unfinished folio-size drawing done by Wenceslaus Hollar in 1640. His perspective looks south on the public road, King Street. On the left is the Main Gate, through which ambassadors were brought for public audiences; in the center, Inigo Jones's Banqueting House, the site of many masques and audiences described by Finet; on the right, the Holbein Gate, through which the street continues past the wall of the Privy Garden toward the buildings of Parliament and the Abbey at Westminster, whose roofs are partly sketched. Between the Banqueting House and the Holbein Gate were apartments for courtiers, in one of which, Finet noted, the duchess of Chevreuse lived after 1638.

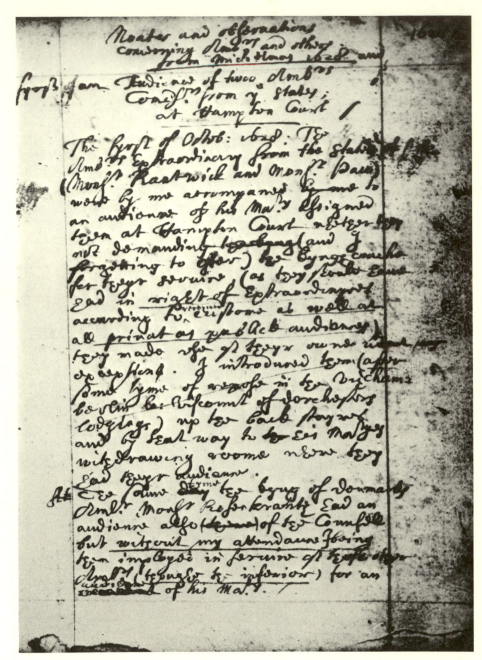

JOHN FINET'S HOLOGRAPH

His entry for October 1, 1628, on page 1 of the original third Note Book at Rousham House (6″×8″).

bassador or agent." To add to the controversy Necolalde replied that to him an agent was "but half a resident in quality and entertainment" (IV 146), and it was known that Gerbier in Brussels and Hopton in Madrid carried credentials from Windebank as "agent resident."[74]

The majority of diplomats received at Whitehall were temporary appointments. Extraordinary ambassadors stayed for visits that varied from the three weeks of the marquis de St. Chaumont to the twenty months of the count of Oñate. Although their secret negotiations were frequently of utmost consequence, Charles's reaction to all these special diplomats was unpredictable in his number of interviews, invitations to masques, ceremonies, and final departure gifts. Later, after the Restoration, Charles Cotterell, the Master of Ceremonies, recalled Charles's policy as operating "according to the quality of the persons sending or sent" balanced by a "consideration of them for kindness, interest or obligation."[75] There was always economy as well. Extraordinary agents, or "envoys," were restricted to a minimum of ceremony.[76] On one occasion Charles summoned the French ambassador to protest that "too much honor" was being given to English extraordinary agents, after their arrival at Saint-Germain, to offer Charles's congratulations at the birth of the dauphin in 1638. He warned that if Louis persisted in providing carriages and special honor to persons of this lower rank, he intended to decide the matter by a treaty article.[77]

THE THEATER AND THE GARTER CEREMONIES

Comedies and court masques at Whitehall, as well as ceremonies for the Order of the Garter, are mentioned in Finet's notes, since the attendance of diplomats at them could create problems for him. For many years there had been quarrels over the placing of seats near the royal chair at the Banqueting House.[78]

[74] By the end of the century an agent was considered by de Wicquefort not a true diplomatic minister but a member of an embassy responsible for commerce (*L'Ambassadeur* I 56, 60). By then Charles II was following continental practice by also nominating residents (Lachs, *Diplomatic Corps*, pp. 4–12).

[75] PRO SP 29/281A/222, Cotterell to Treasury Comissioners.

[76] De Wicquefort commented that the mission was "neither time consuming, nor thorny and ought not to require an ambassador" (*L'Ambassadeur* I 57).

[77] Godefroy, *Le Cérémonial François* II 791.

[78] "The Chair of State was placed at the focal point of the perspective so that the king's seat was the best in the house and the court arranged itself around him in a hierarchy determined by the law of optics . . ." (Stephen Orgel, "The Royal Theatre and the Role of the King," in *Patronage in the Renaissance* [n. 4] p. 266). Finet's recorded attendances of foreign

Some ambassadors were so sensitive about their country's image that they even found fault with the sequence of Finet's visits merely to offer invitations to attend. Consequently, before the performance of *Albion's Triumph* in 1632, Finet recorded, "when I asked his majesty if any ambassadors could be invited, he breefly answered: no invitations" (III 135). Instead Finet found opportunities to drop hints that a diplomat should request admission to the performance as a private person. This did not solve the problem very well. Finet recorded a variety of official excuses of illness from the Spanish diplomats, who did not in fact wish to be present alongside hostile French and Dutch ambassadors, although some of their staff did not always feel themselves to be under such restraint. The real reasons why other diplomats declined to attend could differ from a sensitivity over the higher ranks of other embassies, to the sensible fear of fighting between their liveried servants, to a dislike of the inordinate length of the performance. The same situation could prevail outside Whitehall. In 1634, when the Inns of Court prepared their famous production of the *Triumph of Peace*, no diplomats attended (IV 39ᵛ) because Finet could not give assurances that their claims to rank in the order of their seating would be accepted. It is a safe assumption from these note books that the official presence of the diplomatic leaders at court theatricals was surprisingly slight.

King Charles was well known to be deeply devoted to the Order of the Garter, "revising its statutes, increasing the splendour of its costume and ceremonies and regarding it as the most illustrious support of his kingship,"[79] yet its elaborate annual ceremony at Whitehall, or Windsor, offered new problems to Finet. This event required that diplomats arrive at the court at an early hour to be led to a closet within the king's chapel to observe the solemn religious service conducted by a prelate together with the king and the knights of the order. During it, a procession of the knights took place, for which the foreign guests were brought out of the chapel to be seated in special booths placed in a scaffolding erected at the side of the inner terrace of the palace. From this site they could look upon the king with the knights and all their attendants marching in procession in "proper liveries, colours and cognizances" (IV 138). After some time had elapsed and the procession had re-entered the chapel, the diplomats returned there as well, for the conclusion of the ceremony, under Finet's guidance. After bringing all the diplomats to

diplomats are as follows: Jan. 1631, Venice; Jan. and Feb. 1632, France and Savoy; Jan. and Feb. 1638, France and Morocco; Jan. 1640, Venice and the Dutch Republic; April 1640, Spain.

[79] Parry, *The Golden Age Restor'd*, p. 217.

a chamber to rest for a time until the knights' dinner had begun, Finet escorted them into the Banqueting House where they were led in front of the tables to greet the king and other knights present, after which they returned to their residences. Excuses to avoid attending seem to have been a fairly frequent reaction among the diplomatic corps, even if Baron Skijt of Sweden was surely unique in pleading that he had already seen the ceremony in the days of Elizabeth I. Splendor was not inevitable. Finet was relieved in 1631 that no diplomats asked to come, for it "saved the disrepect which strangers wytnessing of so poore a solemnity as that yeare brought fourth would have cast upon yt" (IV 80; III 27ᵛ). There is no doubt that Charles would have preferred the flattery of a larger diplomatic attention; however, Finet recorded five such Garter "solemnities" — 1629, 1630, 1631, and twice in 1637 — which no diplomats asked to observe.

DEPARTURE GIFTS

The public farewell of a diplomat could be as elaborate as the first audience. Finet, moreover, was charged with the presentation of a "parting gift," which was also the occasion of a last gratuity to himself and other court servants. For resident ambassadors Charles had a fixed policy to be followed. An ambassador of a monarchy was to be granted 2000 ounces of silver plate, at a fixed rate of 8 shillings an ounce, which required a warrant of £800 to the Master of the Jewels. Ambassadors from lesser states, such as Venice or The Hague, always received 1200 ounces, at a total cost of £420. Each agent was given a gold chain and medal, at a cost of £210, irrespective of the state from which he came. For temporary diplomats, there were a variety of rings, tapestries, or jewels of a high appraised cost to be awarded.

Although this gift was an English tradition, Finet recorded some unexpected responses to his presentations. Henry Oxenstierna of Sweden, smarting over the king's refusal to support him for a command in Germany, refused his gift in 1634 with the comment: "the bestowing of a present by a prince and the receyving it by an ambassador was . . . a testimony of both theyr satisfactions" (IV 52ᵛ). Juan de Necolalde of Spain refused the offered medal and chain in 1637 because he considered them suitable only for an agent, but beneath his proper rank as "resident." In 1631 a young Savoyard count begged not to be given any silver plate, with the excuse that the many pieces would be difficult, even hazardous, to transport, and in his own duchy there was "little use and regard made of our fashion of vessel." There was a higher risk, he added, that "the duke his master," Victor Amadeus, would borrow the plate and then it would "never more be restored to him" (III 107ᵛ). His present was altered to a jewel of a similar value.

The scandal associated with this practice of a gift was that each piece of plate passed through the hands of the Master of the Jewels, Henry Mildmay. His presentation of the official gift was regularly many days behind the announced date but it was far more irritating to find that it would be considerably short of the legitimate value. Finet noted several incidents. For example, when the count of Pezze, the agent of Savoy, was about to leave in 1638, he first "formalized himself" to Finet to protest that his chain, of £210 "value" officially, was in fact worth only £150, as it was short by 13 ounces. "Whether it was the basenes of the alloy or the fraud of the delyverer" (V 23ᵛ), the Master of the Jewels was responsible for this plate from the start. The case of John Zavadsky of Poland, who came to Charles's coronation in Scotland, was notorious. His official gift of plate, valued at £800, was fully paid by the city of Edinburgh, but when finally delivered to him in London it was worth only £600, or a loss of 600 ounces of silver. Even then Mildmay asked for a gratuity of £40 for his services. Finet commented: "This he (the ambassador that saw the mony, told it and founde the defalcation) stormed at but could not remedy" (IV 29ᵛ). For convenience of comparison, there is a table of the crown expenditures for the departure gifts given in the Appendix. Finet, as Master of Ceremonies, had the right of presentation of the rings, tapestries, or other gifts that were not plate.

What of the departing diplomat himself? First, it should be recalled that extraordinary ambassadors, who had enjoyed the king's "diet," were expected to be generous, on their last day of feasting, to the king's servants. Finet seemed to think that they were. George Rakowsky of Poland, who had cost the crown £300, distributed to over a score of palace porters, trumpeters, coachmen, and servants of the wardrobe a total of £250. The same sum was passed out by San Germano in 1634 after he left the court in its summer progress (III 125; IV 66). All diplomats were also liable for the customary gifts at each New Year, for which Soranzo of Venice was noted by Finet in 1630 to have distributed £90 among yeomen of the guard, palace gate porters, trumpeters, etc. (III 66ᵛ). After all these departure gifts, which were expected to be more lavish than those of New Year's, no diplomat could expect to have his household goods escape the grasp of port officials and customs farmers at Gravesend, or Dover, without a properly signed pass from the secretariate of the privy council, for which Oxenstierna, for example, left a fee of £25 in 1634 (IV 54ᵛ). In many respects, therefore, Charles's expenditures upon resident and visiting diplomats were matched by parallel costs paid out eventually by the treasuries of foreign princes to their ministers.[80] The total expenditures of the English crown in hospitality for the diplomatic corps in London are difficult to estimate in a precise amount, but it may be suggested that their annual average could not have been higher than £5500. For comparison, a recent analysis of the costs to the crown of a single session of an early Stuart parliament has concluded that it was "over all a few thousand pounds at most." A tentative estimate of the total annual receipts of the royal treasury inclines to a figure of £700,000–750,000 for 1631 to 1635, rising to a higher amount for the later years.[81] Such a large figure can be misleading. Charles's treasury was already burdened with the debts of his father's regime as well as his two earlier costly wars against Spain and France. He had numerous traditional financial obligations to his crown officials even before trying to maintain his various residences in and near London as well as separate households for the queen, the royal children, and, after 1638, his mother-in-law, Marie de Médicis. Since his ordinary revenues were hardly adequate for his annual expenses, his inability to pay for sufficient military forces to confront the Scottish challenge after 1639, without summoning a parliament, became understandable.

A final judgment, however, should not focus on the costs, but the nature of Finet's usefulness to the foreign diplomat. From his own note books it is clear that he tried to be more than a courtier speaking a welcome. To the chamberlain and the king he served as an experienced appraiser of credential and status of foreigners, a trusted escort to important interviews, the official liaison for invitations, licenses, and warrants, the link with important household officers to assure a "diet," the monitor of frictions among rival diplomats and their retinues, the astute adviser about English court customs to inquirers. Charles's sensitivity about his image as a royal diplomat was loyally protected by the judicious services of John Finet.

[80] For comparison, the Spanish resident envoy stated that he paid a total of £2243 over a period of six years in fees and gifts at the palace (AGS E 2522, Accounts of Juan de Necolalde, 1631–37).

[81] Elizabeth R. Foster, "Staging a Parliament in Early Stuart England," in *The English Commonwealth 1547–1660*, edd. Peter Clark, Alan Smith, Nicholas Tyacke (London: Athlone Press, 1979) pp. 143–46; G. Aylmer, *The King's Servants*, pp. 65–66.

NOTE ON EDITORIAL PRACTICE

EACH NOTE BOOK contains signs of later revisions by Finet in which he would cross out words, or substitute a different phrase, or add new details. He also wrote in the margins his cross-references to other pages and supplementary comments, frequently about his gratuities. Only his final text has been here transcribed, while his scattered information about his fees has been summarized in Appendix III. Other marginal notes have been included if they help to clarify his meaning. Deleted phrases or slips of the pen have not been noted. Punctuation and capitalization have not been changed except when necessary for clarity. His variations in spelling of the same word are retained except when uniformity was more desirable. In general I have tried to follow the directives of the "Report on Editing Historical Documents" in the *Bulletin of the Institute of Historical Research* 1 (1923) 6–25.

For this edition every page that records events at Whitehall palace and the London area has been included, but repetitions of information already transcribed on an earlier occasion, or lists of petty gratuities, or descriptions of typical coach journeys outside of London, and similar minor events have been omitted.

For convenient reference, the text has been divided according to the calendar year commencing on January 1st. Notes have been provided on the background of diplomatic missions, and on the identity of diplomats and persons whom Finet sometimes mentioned simply in terms of their office or country of origin. In Appendices I and II are placed lists of diplomats and court officials.

GLOSSARY OF FINET'S USAGES

cover (verb): An invitation to put on a hat, which was only given during a ceremony by the king or queen, as it was judged a privilege to wear a hat in the royal presence.

diet (noun): the free provision of food, which he sometimes called "specie," and household supplies for a limited number of days to the extraordinary ambassador's retinue on first arrival. The whole practice Finet called "entertainment," with the costs to the crown called "defrayment."

hand (noun): "To give the hand" was an invitation to walk, or be seated, at the right hand of another diplomat as the place of honor. To refuse to do so was to declare publicly the lesser status of the diplomat and the prince he represented.

formalize (verb): to protest strongly against an action.

ordinary (noun): a permanent resident diplomat, as different in status from the temporary, or extraordinary. Finet wrote, without further description, "The States ordinary" to indicate the permanent ambassador of the Dutch Republic.

plate (noun): The official parting gift of silver plate to a resident ambassador, "according to the rate" of expense to the crown of 8 shillings an ounce; the market value was lower.

punctilio (noun): a small formality of a ceremony to which a diplomat sometimes objected.

solecisme (noun): a breach of Charles's court regulation.

state (noun): a canopy with the royal coat of arms over a chair placed on a dais.

Usage for boats:

light horseman: a light-draft boat, or gig, then popular on the River Thames.

tylt: a boat with an awning, or tylt, to cover the exposed deck in bad weather.

Usage for coins:

peece: the English coin worth £1.

pistole: a Spanish gold coin in general circulation worth from 16 shillings 6 pence to 18 shillings, according to the date of issue.

THE
NOTE
BOOKS

BOOK III

October 1, 1628 to April 24, 1632

1628

[1] The fyrst of October 1628, The ambassadors extraordinary from the States (Monsieur Rantwick and Monsieur Pau[1]) were by me accompanied to an audience of his Majesty assigned them at Hampton Court, whither they, not demanding (and I forgetting to offer) the kings coache for theyr service (as they should have had, in right of extraordinaryes, according to receyved custome as well at all privat as publick audiences) they made use of theyr owne without exception. I introduced them (after some tyme of repose in the vice chamberlin viscount of Dorchesters lodgings[2]) up the back stayres and by that way to his majestyes withdrawing roome, where they had theyr audience.

At the same day the kyng of Denmarks ambassador, Monsieur Rosencrantz,[3] had an audience also of the counsell, but without my attendance, I being then imployed in service of those other ambassadors (though the inferior[4]) for an audience of his majesty.

[1ᵛ] The Venetian ambassador[5] had an audience of the king at Denmark House[6] (the queen then there), his majesty receyving him in the withdrawing room, next the privy chamber. Having surprised the court and the lord chamberlin with a sodayne unexpected coming, he, by his owne fault, lost the accustomed honor to be receyved by a noble man at the privy chamber door, and had not my attendance at the court gate at his entrance.

---

[1] Arnaut van Randwcyk and Adrian Pawe, ambassadors extraordinary (Feb. 1628 – Feb. 1629) of the Dutch Republic, who came to promote a peace settlement between England and France as well as to negotiate serious commercial disputes with the East India Company.

[2] Sir Dudley Carleton, 1st viscount Dorchester.

[3] Paulus Rosencrantz came twice to England (March–April 1627 and Aug. 1628 – May 1629) as ambassador extraordinary of Denmark, with urgent appeals for financial and military support against the Habsburg armies in North Germany.

[4] In consideration of a republic as lower in precedence to the monarchy of Denmark.

[5] Alvise Contarini, resident ambassador (Aug. 1626 – July 1629) of Venice, carried instructions to promote peace between France and England and to support the interests of the Dutch Republic and Sweden.

[6] The former name for Somerset House, in honor of King James's wife.

The 18 of October, the kyng of Denmarks ambassador having audience assigned him at Whytehall, I made offer to him of the kyngs coach for his service, but he would not accept it saying his owne coache which he had hyred that morning for visits would serve the turne, especially now that his audience was privat and that he was by thys tyme so well knowne as that he myght well dispense wyth ceremony. I introduced him by the way (not long before ordayned) through the Privy Garden up to the privy lodgings into the Wythdrawing Chamber.

[2] October the 6, A newcome commissioner sent from the Moores of Salee in Barbary to his Majestye, had together with his colleague[7] (a messenger sent hither before) access for presentation of his letters in the Stone Table chamber by the way mentioned.

The 22 of October, his majesty being the next day to go to Theobalds and the States ambassadors understanding so much, sent to me late at nyght theyr secretary with earnest request that I would procure them an audience for the next day upon important occasion, they had already sent to the lord chamberlin and the vice chamberlin, but had found one absent and the other sick. Wherupon I repayring late to the Kyng, (then with the Queene,) I with the dewe excuse of my unseasonable importunity occassioned from the ambassadors, obtayned yt and had it gyven then the next morning, when they were expecting the kyngs coache for theyr service as accustomed, I told them what use the Kyng had of yt that day (his other coache being then repayring) and [2ᵛ] how readily the kyng of Denmarcks ambassadour had not long before dispensed with that ceremony as not affecting yt in regard of the long and publicke notice there taken of hym. This example served for theyr satisfaction. About the 20th of October, A coronell and commissary of the kyng of Denmarcks (Monsieur Ferentz) came hither with letters and private negotiation from that kyng had private audience of his majesty, together with the Denmarck ambassador the 26th of October, at his dispatch, when I introduced him for his leave takeing of his Majestye, was over forwardly putt in hope by some (upon some recommendations given of his merit by my lord Conway, principal secretary) that he should be presented with a chayne of two hundred pounds but the frugality, or necessity, of the tyme, made the expectation frustrate.

---

[7] Mohammed Clavecho (June 1628 – Jan. 1629) and Ibrahim Mocaden (Oct. 1628 – Jan. 1629) represented the pirate-controlled port of Saley in Morocco, which was then in rebellion against the infamous sultan Muley Zidan. In return for arms they offered trade concessions to the Barbary Company and naval assistance against Spain and France.

[3] Towards the day of the new lord mayors show and feast,[8] I purposely repayred to him that was yet lord mayor, Sir Hugh Hammersley, to sound the intention of the city for theyr invitation of the ambassadors then here, and found that they had already invited the Venetian and States ambassadours but had omitted him of Denmarck supposing none such to be heer because of the two other ambassadours[9] fresh departure. But I removing that errour he had the next day October the 26 an invitation brought him by one of the sheriffs. This his invitation, for the regard of precedence elsewhere touched, I thought good underhand to intimate by my officer to the Venetian, imagining he would upon knowledge thereof and to prevent injuries having avoided incounter of this ambassador, spare his appearance at the feast, as he did with no other excuse than that he had bene at yt the yeare before.

There came to yt [3ᵛ] the Denmarck and the two ambassadours of the States with more followers than there was room for, especially arriving late from theyr severall stands in Cheapsyde. A cause hereof proceeding from the lords of the councell to come hastening and the lord mayors over slow motion from Westminster through Cheapsyde to his dynner wyth out convenient stay of the sayd lords for the ambassadours. Of which the two States that came soonest, came after the lordes were set at table (but were by them given theyr places on each syde at the upper end) and the Danish ambassadour at the mydst of dynner, which he himself sayd, if he had knowne in tyme enoughe at his entrance, he would have avoyded by his departure, as sensible of the litle regarde that seemed to be had of him, though excused by my lord Treasurer with the report, he sayd was brought them, that the ambassadours would not come thither at all. The Denmarck ambassadour brought with him fyve or six gentlemen, [4] his followers, besydes the agent of that kyng,[10] Mr. Wolfin, all which coming tardy to theyr room at the table were yet civilly entertayned in the Great Hall by the two sherriffs. There came with him also Colonell Ferentz, whom I would have willingly have seated at the board of Councellors, but that fayled, I lead him to the second table in that roome where were before seated the States ambassadours followers. These ill understandings I have set downe thus particularly for prevention of the lyke, upon the lyke or other occasions hereafter, when if the ambassadors will have the right of theyr intertaynment, they must leave theyr stands in Cheapsyde as soon as the lordes have passed there and immediately follow them to Guild Hall, reservyng

---

[8] Sir Cuthbert Hackett.
[9] George Brahe and Christian Tomson, ambassadors extraordinary (Aug. 1627 – Sept. 1628) of Denmark, had failed to secure Charles's help for the armies of Christian IV.
[10] J. G. Woulffen, resident agent (June 1627 – April 1632) for Denmark.

theyr better syght of the show tyll after dynner when returning to theyr standings they may have full view of all presented before dynner at the tyme that the lord mayor rydes to St. Pauls to the evensong.

[5ᵛ] In November word came to the Muscovy merchants of an ambassador[11] on his waye hither from that emperour. They gave account of it to the lords of the Councell and intimateing that he came for congratulation (though late) of the kyngs coming to the crowne, rather than about merchants busyness, would have removed the charge of his defraying from themselves to his majesty. But theyr former precedents, and the present wants of the tyme, kept it in the old way and put it upon the company, whereof the Governor, Sir John Merrick, lett me know the 18th of November that he was arrived and lodged (tyll he might have better accomodation in the city) neare where his ship lay, in a taverne at Wapping.

Whereupon I repayring to my lord chamberlin about order for his reception had yt referred to me to be ruled by former precedents, which following as neere as myne owne noates and the merchants notice could direct me, I [6ᵛ] went with the Kyngs barge (and two of his majestyes servants to accompany me) downe to Wapping, having also the attendance of a barge appointed and hyered by the city for cariage of his followers. Whyle I went towards him by water the lord viscount Monson[12] (accompanyed with only two Gentlemen of his Majestyes Privy Chamber, others excusing that service) and the Kyngs coache (followed by that lords) went by land to Tower wharfe there to receyve him at his landing, where he was mett and thence wayted on to his lodging in Threadneedle Street neer Merchant Taylors Hall, by many citizens on horseback, well cloathed with theyr chaynes of gold, and the greater part of the Aldermen, with the two sheriffs, in theyr scarlet gownes. All these takeing theyr stands on each syde of the way neer to the very doore of his lodgings, he was left there by them and us that attended him, to his full satisfaction.

[7ᵛ] About this tyme a fyre in the night takeing hold (by what meanes is unknowne) of the house of the lord viscount Wimbledon,[13] wherein Monsieur Paw, one of the extraordinarys of the States, was lodged with his wyfe and family, consumed it to the grounde and forced them almost naked to shelter

---

[11] Vasily Demetrovich, ambassador extraordinary (Nov. 1628 – April 1629) of Czar Michael Romanov. Officially, he came to greet Charles on his accession but, privately, he appealed to Charles for support against the Swedish advances in the Baltic which endangered the English trade with Russia through the Muscovy Company.

[12] William Monson, 1st viscount Monson.

[13] Edward Cecil, baron Cecil of Putney and viscount Wimbledon.

themselves in the house of the other ambassador extraordinary. I being called by the common outcry to the syght of the calamity was by the ambassador intreated my help for recovery of suche goodes as were for theyr safeguard, eyther committed or taken (during the fury of the fyre) to others protection. I hereupon instantly repayring to my lord chamberlin, and from him by his direction to the lord privy seale and lord keeper then going to sit in the Star Chamber, obteyned order (answerable to my motion and to a note delyvered by me of the substance of the busyness) for a proclamation to be drawne by the Attorney General for restitution of all goodes, chestes and papers of the am- bassadours which had bene conveyed away and were detayned by any man, upon payn of the severest punishment the lawes could inflict, which was that day published accordingly by sound of trumpet in London and Westminster, but wyth no considerable effects that I could learne for restitution.

[8] The ambassador of Russia, after a fortnights rest at the house hyred for him by the merchants, being assigned his fyrst publick audience of his majesty on Sunday the 7th of December between two and three after noone, I ac- companyed by two Gentlemen, Sir Alex Hume, gentleman of his majestyes privy chamber and Sir Harry Reeves a Gentleman Pensioner, answerable to the former stile used towards that emperor, fetched him from his lodging in the Kyngs coache, attended by my lord viscount Carletons coache with six horses, and myne owne with two, besydes 4 others with 2 horses eache ready for him at his lodging and provided by the merchants. At the Court Gate he was receyved, as his other predecessors had bene, by a baron, my lord of Castle Island,[14] and at the top of the stayres by the earl of Monmouth,[15] with eache of them three or four gentlemen, the Kyngs servants, for company [8ᵛ] thence, introduced by them through a gard up the stayers and all along to the closet chamber of the chapel, he there reposed him self tyll the Kyng being sett to receyve him, he was by the same lords conducted along the terras through a guard made all the way to the Banketting House, where at the doore the earl of Holland, Captayne of the Guard, welcomed him. Thence passing on obliquely by a syde doore (the scene formerly buylt for a maske hindring his strayght forward passadge, which I with the necessity of yt as a worke of late and future use,[16] excused to his satisfaction) he was mett at his issuing from under the scaffold by my lord chamberlin. He went towards his, his Majestye, the earles and lordes guyding him and most of his servants (not above 10 or 12), preceeding him and only 3 (whereof two were his inter-

---

14 Edward Herbert, baron Herbert of Castle Island and Cherbury.
15 Robert Carey of Lepington, 1st earl of Monmouth.
16 Performances of "unnamed and undated plays," Bentley VII 68–69.

preters) and a secretary carying his two letters following him.[17] At this fyrst reverence, after that countrys maner with his knees and head bowed to the ground, [9] he uncovered, then putt on agayne, then agayne uncovered, performing his reverence as before and so the thyrd tyme, when the Kyng only rose up put off his hatt and, imediately covering, sat downe agayne.

The ambassador proceeding to his speech, which contayned little else than the titles of his master and a message of congratulation for health, as it was by his secretary interpreted; with other words he presented his letters from the emperour, whereat his Majestye arose and putting off his hat, made a breefe answere by his interpreter, Sir John Merricke, no more covering and the ambassador having bene all the whyle uncovered. He after presented other letters from the emperours father patriarche[18] of Russia, which done he ascended the steps of the State kyssed the Kyngs hand and retyred with reverences as he entered. He had the company of the earle of Monmouth to the place where he fyrst [9ᵛ] receyved him, but not so the lord of Castle Island to the Gate (kept behynd by the crowd, forgetfulnesse, or humour) and was thence reconducted by me and the other two gentlemen to his lodging. The queene had a syght of him from a scaffold, over a boxe on the Kynges left hand, but unobserved.

It was expected he should have brought a present to his Majesty as the two severall ambassadours preceeding had done, but the reasons of that omission were alleged to be because his message was only congragulatory for the Kynges assumption of the crowne, and in that regard myght be thought to bring honour and respect enough wyth it without other present. Whereas the other two ambassadours before him were imployed, the one with thankfulnes to kyng James for his mediation[19] and composition of the difference and great war betweene that emperour and the kyng of Sweden (which might seeme to have merited more than a mere verbal acknowledgement) though [10] the Sweden ambassador sent before on the same errand[20] in his masters behalf brought no other retribution than a long oration. The other ambassador from Russia[21] brought also thanks for a good sum of money (lent by the merchants

[17] In margin: "from the emperor and patriarch."

[18] The Patriarch Filaret was the father, Fedor, of the czar.

[19] Stepan Ivanovich Volzunski and Marko Ivanovich (Nov. 1617 – March 1618) came to thank King James for mediating the completion of the treaty of Stolbova of March 1617 with Sweden.

[20] Baron John Skijt (Nov. 1617), who would also return to London in April 1635 (see IV 78ᵛ).

[21] Ivan Pogozhevo (Feb.–June 1622) reached London after the mission of John Merrick and Dudley Digges to Moscow to re-establish the privileges of the Muscovy Company.

in name of the kyng to his master) restored wyth addition of a present as an increase to the acknowledgement of the favour.

The next day the Denmarck ambassador had a private audience of the queene in her Wythdrawing Room having had the closet chamber of the chapell on her syde appoynted for his repose. He was brought to yt through the kyngs Gard Chamber and by the ordinary way to her Majestyes closet.

[13] Not long after the ambassador of Denmarck, Monsieur Rosencrantz, his arrival here, one Fosberg[22] a Douchman, sometyme imployed by that kyng as his resident with the States of the United Provinces, having exceeded or not well managed his comission and therefore bene recalled, had his letters of revocation superscribed: 'To my Resident, etc.' Of this title he planned to make use in England, when repayring hither and showing it (for confirmation of what he pretended to) to the duke of Buckingham, and therby gayning credit of access under pretence of setting on foot certayne proiects for raysing monyes to his majestyes advantage. He had oft tymes the dukes care and regard in such measure as the Denmarck ambassador [13ᵛ] understanding what colour he had sett on his negotiation, began to styrr agaynst him (especially after the dukes death) and to proceed to the kyng and councell in demand of right to be done him agaynst an imposter, that had (he sayd) assumed the name of his masters minister, and had not wyth standing refused to show otherwyse than in part, as the superscription to his pretended letters of credence which he had boasted of, to have gyven him authority in some affayres, not communicable, he sayd, to everybody even beyond the ambassador. So theyr lordships, after a debate upon his appearance before them, sent a clerk of the councell to seyze his coffers and papers and committed him prisoner to the guard of a messenger. Finally, upon answer receyved from the kyng of Denmarck to his ambassadour, who intimated to the lords Fosbergs owne offer to submitt himself to the kyng, he was by the kynges owne ansere signifyed by the lords, commanded to go to Denmarck and there to offer himself to that kynges owne pleasure, or punishment.

---

[22] Gaspar Vosberghen was accused by Rosencrantz of abusing his earlier commission, as agent of Christian IV in The Hague, by sharing in a dubious financial transaction in London, in which Buckingham had also participated (PRO SP 75/9/384, memorandum of 1628). At this time he had a different commission.

[15] The 5th of January, the ambassador of Venice having demanded an audience (*por dar il buon capo d'anno*, as he phrased it) to congragulate the kyngs happy entrance of the new year, and wyth that occasion to negotiate for the peace between us and France,[1] asked me if the other ambassadors had bene yet there on the same errand, I told him, no, but supposed they would, when he had given them an example (thoughe I had not observed that any other ambassadors but the Venetian had, here to fore, annually observed that custome). My supposition proved correct, for I had no sooner cast out a word to the Denmark ambassador of what the Venetian had done, but both he, and after him those of the States, performed the lyke office of congragulation and, wyth all of mediation for the peace, as they themselves acknowledged. The lyke office that was performed towards the kyng was not by any of them omitted with the queene, all, in several dayes, except by him of Denmark, who had audience [15ᵛ] of the kyng at one of the clock, and of the queene at three, the same day. The Venetian had demanded the lyke, perhaps to save labour, but the queene, it seemed, would be better served and appoint her owne day, whych was the next, as was that she assigned the States ambassadors. All were in her withdrawing chamber, after they had reposed themselves in the closet chappel chamber, on the queenes syde.

Neither of these extraordinarys moved me for the use of the kyngs coach, but served themselves wyth theyr owne, but I, letting fall a word to the States ambassadors of the fytness, some tymes, to keep theyr right on foot, especially now that they were to repayre to the queene, wyth whome they had bene seldome, and that synce it was so solemne a day at court as Sunday, being Twelfth day, they desyred, and had, the kyngs coach, attended by one of theyr owne for theyr service.

[16] The 17 of January, il caualiero Barozzi,[2] qualifyed secretary and privy counselor to the duke of Savoy, arrived here two or three dayes before, having had an assignation for his fyrst audience wyth the kyng, I was moved by a

---

[1] Contarini and his successor, Soranzo, continued the Venetian policy to promote peace between France and England only.

[2] Piero Lorenzo Barozzi, agent (Jan. – Sept. 1629) of Charles Emmanuel of Savoy, denounced the French plan to invade Savoy (see III 20ᵛ) in the war of the Mantuan succession and urged an English peace negotiation with Spain.

gentleman in his behalf,[3] as for his more honor, to procure hym the kyngs coache, or at least one hyred at the kyngs charge, to fetch him to court. But I answered his majestyes coache was not, by any precedent I had, or knew of, to be imployed for service of any but ambassadors, eyther extraordinarys at all theyr audiences, or ordinarys at theyr fyrst and last, and for me to hyre one for him, at the kyngs charge, would come under the same title and infringe the order established of no more defraying for ambassadors coaches. At last he that moved this in Barozzi's behalfe, descending to a request of having some lordes coach sent for him, [16ᵛ] as to be lent him out of such a lordes respect, it was allowed of, and my lord of Carlisles coache borrowed for him, which bringing him to court, I mett him at the court gate, and conducting him to the Stone Table chamber by the usuall way thither, he was called for thence to his majesty by my lord of Carlisle into the withdrawing chamber. I, in the meane tyme, repayring to the queenes syde, upon his request, for audience of her majesty with her conveniency, which was granted for an hour or two after. I, in the interim, interteyned him in the queenes Presence Chamber tyll he was by her vicechamberlin called to the person of her Majesty in her Wythdrawing Chamber, etc.

He had two privat audiences soon after of his majesty intruding himself into the privy galleryes without demand, pretending and professing to me that he entred and remayned there as in the redyest way to take the kyng in his privat passages, but I intimating his unfit forwardness therein to my lord chamberlin tooke suche course by oblique notice given him as he repayred to me wyth request of another audience the 4th of March, which he had with my introduction and reposed himself, as I appoynted him, in the Withdrawing Chamber next the Privy Chamber.

[17] The 31st of January two commissioners, Hamet Clavecho and Brahem Mocaden, sent from the Moores of Saley in Barbary who had long resided here at a charge boarne by one Captayne Harrison that solicited theyr bysyness,[4] but to be reimboursed to him by the Kyng, tooke theyr leaves presented by his Majestye with 4 cups of gylt plate wayghing 140 onces and proportioned betweene them only wyth some fyve onces odde on the part of the former as being of more merit by his longer tyme of residence and negotiation. They had away with them in theyr ship by grant from the Kyng for use of theyr

---

[3] Sir Baltazar Gerbier.

[4] John Harrison later published a narrative of the cruelties of that king of Morocco in *The Tragicall Life and Death of Muley Abdala Melek* (Delft, 1633; STC 12860).

state, fyve iron peeses of ordinance,[5] which was at fyrst opposed but after assented to by the Lord Treasurer.

[17ᵛ] When Monsieur Randwyck and Monsieur Paw had passed theyr tyme here as extraordinaryes for the States, at theyr own charges, negotiating the peace betweene us and France by the space of a year or more, they finally moved for theyr leavetaking of his Majestye which assigned for the 25th of February, my lord chamberlin wrot to the earle [18] of Stamford as signifying the Kyngs pleasure and choyce of him to accompany them to theyr last audience. His lordship obeying repayred to the Privy Chamber and theyre takeing with him some half a dozen gentlemen, his Majestyes servants, went with his Majestyes coache and half a dozen of the lordes coaches to Herr Randwycks house neer the Savoy where the other ambassadour and Herr Joachim, the ordinary of the States, receyving him but at the topp of the stayres, here was an error committed in theyr not quitting to him the precedence at the going forth of the doors in theyr owne house, though Herr Joachim made civilly many offers of it but at last also tooke yt. This observed by the gentlemen that accompanyed my lord Stamford and by his lordship not unobserved, I at our returne remedied it, by acquaynting Herr Joachim with the exception privately taken, which he conveyed to the other ambassadours notice, by his intimation for a different cariage at theyr returne, brought all strayght agayne.

[18ᵛ] There came in theyr company to the court four persons (freshly before arrived from Holland wyth H. Joachim) deputed hither for settling the disjoynted busyness of our merchants and theyrs in the East Indyes.

These I thought fytt, whyle I left my lord of Stamford to sytt with the ambassadors in the Kynges coache, to accompany in theyrs, being my lord Stewards and kept empty from charge for that purpose, with the coachman of the ambassadours opposing as an injury to his coach for a lords to precede him, I was forward to acquaint the ambassador with his coachmans punctilio for his horses sake, as if they, and not the commissioners, were to have place, so went on tyll at our returne to court I stilled the difference by placeing them in the same coach of the ambassadours and following immediately that of his Majestye. Theyr rest was in the Councell Chamber but a small tyme when his Majestye, already sett in the Presence, commanded me to introduce them. The earle of Holland, [19] as Captayne of the Guard, receyved them in the Guard

---

[5] The Barbary Company secured a royal proclamation, forbidding English ships from attacking the Saley pirates at sea, on 22 Oct. 1628 (R. Steele, *Tudor and Stuart Proclamations* I no. 1562).

Chamber and my lord Chamberlin at the Presence door. Theyr audience ended, Monsieur Joachim, the ordinary ambassador, presented the 4 deputyes mentioned, one of them served as theyr advocate makeing a speeche to his majesty.

The Sonday following according to an assignation given these ambassadours, they had theyr last publick audience of the Queene, fetched to court in two of her majestyes coaches, and two of the lords, with 2 or 3 of theyr owne, by the earl of Denbigh, with his son the lord Fielding, and three or four of the Queenes eminent servants attending. The ambassadors being come for theyr repose to the chapel closet of the queenes syde I had a command from his majesty to intertayne them there awhyle, in regard it was the pleasure of his Majestye, then at councell, that some of the principal lords should be present with the Queene as attendants at the tyme of theyr access. [19ᵛ] This was complyed by (with much honour to the ambassadours) 15 or 16 of the principal of the councell, a respect in that kynde beyond any I had seene (only once the two Denmark ambassadours M. Tomson and M. Brahe had the lyke given by the presence of fyve or six councellors). The Queenes lord chamberlin also (the earle of Dorset) came to them to the closet to fetch them beyonde custome, but as it was his pleasure, which should have brought them for theyr introduction no farther then from the Presence doore and from theyre to her Majesty. Having taken theyr leave mein Herr van Hamsted[6] would not (with all I could say for disuasion) which divers held a solecisme in manners, be disuaded from accompanying his wyfe (while my lord of Denbigh in the interim returned home with the other ambassadours) to kyss the Queenes hands for which I had formerly begd her leave at her husbands instance, which was performed in the Queenes Withdrawing Chamber, her passage [20] thither (with her husband, her daughter and 3 other gentlewomen) having bene by the conduct of the Queenes vicechamberlin, in whose lodgings she had remayned during the audience. The kyng himself being also present with the queen at the tyme of the ladyes reception, which was with a kyss fyrst from the kyng, and then from her majesty, both her and her daughter.

These two extraordinaryes (having some seavennight before receyved theyr present of gylt plate of one thousand ounces for each of them) by the handes of the Master of the Jewel House, who from theyres had no returne of acknowledgement, departed the 9th of March towards theyr imbarking at Gravesend, attended thither by myselfe with two barges and a lyght horseman. The daye before theyr departure from London Monsieur Randwyck,

---

[6] Adrian Pawe, ambassador extraordinary.

in bothe theyr names, gave me for my much paynes the not much acknowl-edgement of 50 peeces.

[20ᵛ] The 15 of March, Sonday, a publick thanksgiving for the Queen being with chyld was read in every church and gave subiect to the ambassadors here resident to demand audience for congragulation. Of these the Denmarck and the Venetian were the fyrst, and the next day after had access to the Kyng, but not without busyness (upon both theyr receypt of letters the night before) myxt with complement. The day following, the States ambassador[7] and the agent of Savoy performed the lyke, thys latter attending the kyng in his passage from dynner through the lobby to the Withdrawing Roome next the Privy Chamber, and thence taken by his Majesty into his Withdrawing Roome had his audience, which was dispatched not without serious cariage (being upon the subiect of the kyng of Frances then having passed the Alpes) as might appear by [21] his Majestyes pregnant answer, when I intimateing to him, at the departure of the agent of Savoy, that the ambassador of the States was already in the Privy Gallery attending his majesty ansered me: Well, Well intreate him to have a litle patience, I must fyrst goe in and chew an agent, before I undertake to swallow an ambassador. This sayd, entring his Bed Chamber, he soone after came forth and gave audience to the other.

According to a signification given me from my lord chamberlin and the vice chamberlin to the Queene, I expected to have the same day brought to theyr audiences of theyr majestyes the ambassadors of Denmarck, the States and the agent of Savoy, but the fayreness of that day calling the Queen abroad was occasion that it was remitted to the next, when at Two of the clock ac-companying the Denmark ambassador (as an extraordinary) from his house to the chapel closet [21ᵛ] on the Queenes syde, I sent my officer, Briscoe, to receyve the States ambassador at the Court Gate and to bring him to the place mentioned after which I went to fynd out the agent of Savoy where I had ordayned his aboad (tyll the Denmark ambassador should be dispatched) in the Privy Chamber, there leaving him in company of some ladyes under the title (that himself familiarly challenged) of a domestick. Returning to the two ambassadors, I introduced fyrst the kyng of Denmarkes, then the States and, lastly, the Savoyard agent from the Presence into the Queenes Privy Chamber, but with an errour from misadvice or mistake, synce these being no publick audiences (as are ambassadors arrivals and partings) but a privat audience of congragulation only, they should have bene receyved privately in the Withdrawing Chamber.

---

[7] This child died later at birth. Albert Joachimi returned to be the resident ambassador of the Dutch Republic.

[22] The 19 of March, newes haveing bene brought me that Sir James Spence (a Scottish gentleman long before coronel, and after general, of two or three regiments in service of the kyng of Sweden) was arrived at Gravesend, ambassador from that king, I gave account of it to my lord chamberlin and he to his majesty, who answering he had yet receyved no particular notice of his imployment, whether he was qualifyed ambassadour or agent, I, that night, intreated Sir John Waldran, a Scottish knyght who was then goeing to him to Gravesend; he sent me from thence a resolution; this being receyved the next morning, with assurance that Sir James Spence brought with him as absolute a commission,[8] as ever had bene given to any imployed from the kyng of Sweden. The earle of Kelly[9] was appoynted for his reception with the kyngs barge at Greenwiche, after I should [22ᵛ] have fetched him (as I did in two barges and a light horseman) from Gravesend. This performed, and wee all arrived at Tower wharfe, where attended us the Kyngs coache and six or seven others of noblemen, I observed that the Denmarck ambassadours coache being only there, the Venetians and the States (not wythstanding that both had promised and offered to send) were absent.

[23ᵛ] The 23 of March, I moved for the ambassador of Swedens fyrst audience both of the king and queene with intimation of his desyres of a privat audience at the same tyme, if it might stand wyth the Kyngs pleasure and convenience, which was assented to and assurance [24] given by his majesty, upon overture of the earl of Carlisle that, thoughe the ambassador were a Scottish man borne and his natural subiect, he should receyve all the honours and respects given any other ambassador, and be permitted to cover in his presence. He was the next day fetched to court by the earl of Cleavland (as the fyttest person to accompany to his fyrst audience that ambassador, for whose master he had bene a representant at his instalment of knyght of the Garter the 4th of September before at Windsor). He was accompanyed wyth the young lord Wentworth, the lord Macquay[10] the younger son of the earl of Mar, and half a dozen of the Kyngs servants, was brought to the presence of his majesty, before whome, at his approaches, giving no more humble respectes than an other ambassador would have, he was putting on his hat, after the fyrst invitation, but after that often putting it off and on agayne, as he was

---

[8] Sir James Spence, ambassador extraordinary (March–June 1629) of Gustavus Adolphus of Sweden, who sought leave to recruit four regiments in support of the coming invasion of Germany and the reappointment of Thomas Roe as ambassador to Sweden.

[9] Thomas Erskine, 1st earl of Kellie.

[10] John Erskine, lord Macquay. Earlier, Cleveland had been the proxy for the installation of Gustavus in the order of the Garter.

invited to it by his majesty. He finally went to the queene by the way of the Chappel chamber. [24ᵛ] Her majesty invited him to cover but he refused it as being (he sayd after to me) a marck of parity, which to a woman (no sovereigne) he might dispense with, wythout prejudice to the quality of the kyng that sent him, and with more praise (sayd others) to himselfe than some Danish and Dutch ambassadors had bene formerly iudged to have merited, in covering at the very instant of theyr access to her majesty without scarce staying, as if doubting to be offered, the honour of her invitation. The ambassador parting, he was mett at the Queenes Privy Chamber door and conducted thence by the Kynges vice chamberlin, the lord of Dorchester to his assigned privat audience of the Kyng in his Wythdrawing Chamber where, and after at other privat audiences, he never offered, nor was invited to cover as being then out of publick notice and therefore in duty, as he sayd after, to acknowledge and pay all dewe respectes to his naturall soverayne. These were his owne and not improper reasons. My lord of Cleaveland had, with the necessity of his pressing affayres, excused his company to his privat audience, and so did I myne at fyrst, in regard I was to introduce the Venetian ambassador to his congragulatory audience (tyll then deferred) of the Queene.[11] But this despatched, in the same roome where the other ambassador had his, I returned to the Sweden ambassador and brought him through the privy gallery, downe the back stayres of the privy lodging into the Sermon court, to the Kynges coache attending him at the court gate, and thence to his owne lodging.

One thyng was remarkable and observed by many of this ambassadours imployment, more than of any before, that having bene sent wyth ample commission from the Kyng here to the kyng of Sweden, his then master as having longed served him in his warrs as generall of the Scottish and English forces, he was trusted and returned wyth the lyke full commission by the same kyng to the kyng of England his naturall souverayne.

[26ᵛ] Three or four days before St. Georges feast to be solemnized at Whytehall, I repayred to the Russian ambassador, with intimation that his letters being now ready, he might thynke of takeing leave of his majesty, he answered he was glad to be so neer his iourney homewards, but he desyred to know whether he should not, as his predecessors had done, eate with his majesty before his departure. I said, I knowe not how the kyngs pleasure might be to honour him more than others, but I know well that his majesty had never intertayned any ambassador at his table, since his marriage, out of a resolution he had taken that since the kynges of France and Spayne gave not

---

[11] Upon the announcement of Henrietta's pregnancy.

that honour to any of his ambassadors he woud never give it to theyrs, nor to any others. To this he replyed that his predecessors had bene admitted to dyne wyth the kyng, his father, and he hoped that this kyng would not think him less worthy of that honour than the king his father thought, considering he represented [27] the same person, as they had done, and that the same peace and amity, that had held so long, did still hold betweene this state and that of Russia. I sayd, in reply, I know not his majestyes mynde, but within a daye or two I should (I thought) be able to resolve him. So three dayes after, having understood the kyngs absolute pleasure not to admit him to dyne with him, I propounded a meanes to my lord chamberlin lykely, as I thought, to admit him satisfaction, which allowed of by his majesty, I presented to the ambassadors acceptation, thus. That though his majesty had altered the course of the kyng, his father, in admitting ambassadors to his table, yet to express his disposition to do honour to the emperour of Russia in the person of his rep-resentant, he would doo more than he had yet done to any other kings am-bassadour, who usually at St. Georges feast makeing knowne theyr desyres to see it, were in the dynner tyme, without diet in court, receyved into his Majestyes presence as he sat at table, and after passage of some complement, departed wythout dyning, but if [27ᵛ] he (the ambassador of Russia) would come that day to court where the kyng was to solemnize the feast of St. George, his majesty (who neyther by the rule of his order, nor in observation of his own prescription, could admit any man at table with him) would have a dynner purposely prepared for him in the councelle chamber, where he should have two or three noblemen to accompany him and should in the midst of the feast be brought to the kyngs presence, have the health of the Emperour his master druck to him by his Majestye, and being after dinner reconducted to a place of repose, receyve his last audience and letters from the proper handes of his Majestye.

This offer makeing, he refused but modestly both in lookes and wordes, saying he humbly thanked the kyng but he myght not intertayne any invi-tation than in the kinges owne presence and at his table. He desyred his Majestye would be pleased to pardon him and giving him a gracious dis-patch from his owne hand suffer him to depart towards the emperour his master. This answere returned by me to the kyng, his dynner, already given order for, [28] was countermanded and his last publick audience assigned him for Sonday following the 26 April, when he was fetched by me alone to court in one of the Kynges best coaches, one coache of the lords and two or three others, viscount Chaworth[12] receyving hym at the Court Gate and the earle of

---

[12] Sir George Chaworth, viscount Chaworth.

Linlithgow[13] at the foot of the stone stayres. After his repose in the Council Chamber he was conducted over the terras to the Banketting House and was there met in the fyrst entrance by the earle of Holland, as Captayne of the Gard, and at the second by the lord Chamberlin and brought to the presence of his Majestye, tooke his leave, receyved his letters, was reconducted by the two fyrst lordes to theyr severall stations and by me to his lodging.

A day or two before his audience it was intimated to me by the marchants that they having already provided for him a cup of 20 or 22 £ valewe, the charge whereof, if they could produce a precedent, was by promise of my lord chamberlin to be reimbursed to them out of the Jewell House, [28ᵛ] this cup (for the reason mentioned of not dyneing in court) was yet unpresented, so they desyred my advice what was to be done in it. I told them I thought it most unfit (howsoever some would have moved it) that so poore a thing as a cupp of 22 £ should be presented or so much as spoken of at the tyme of the ambassadors audience, but that I would (with my lord chamberlins allowance which I had) present it to him at his owne house, when I should bring him back from his audience. So I did, framing my complement: that his majesty having prepared for him a dynner in court, which he, for his privat reasons thought not fyt to accept of, and having also intended to drinck to him in that cup his emperours health and after to present him with that cup, he not appearing the day of the feast in court, his majesty had now sent the cup to him and his desyre wyth it that he should drinck his health out of it, at his fyrst landing in Russia. The ambassador tooke this as a favour otherwyse then it was supposed [29] he would, and causing the cup to be immediately filled, he sayd he would disobey the kyngs pleasure of staying to drinck his health tyll his landing in Russia, and be hold to drinck it before his parting to express his thanckfulness for his majestyes favour.

Soone after he tooke occasion to let me know by his interpreter, Andrew Angler, that the secretaryes and interpreters of ambassadors, formerly imployed hither from the emperor of Russia, had receyved presents from the Kyng and that, therefore, he hoped that those two that served him in the same places should not be neglected. With this intimation of his I acquaynting the merchants, they acknowledged that some ten yeares before there had indeed byn a gift bestowed upon a secretary or interpreter then here in service of the Russian ambassador, though not of the Kyngs charge but of the Muscovy companyes, and that therefore they knew not how now to excuse the lyke, since it was by precedent obtruded and so intreated me to frame, as I did, a complement as from my lord chamberlin, which I intimated to the interpreter

---

[13] Alexander Livingstone, 2nd earl of Linlithgow.

[29ᵛ] (the day that the company made to his lord in his owne house a solemn dynner) to this purpose: that upon my report to the lord chamberlin of the ambassadours wordes to mee touching his interpreter and secretary, his lordship had let me know the kyngs pleasure to be that not wythstanding there were no precedent for any gyft, or present, to be bestowed upon the other Russian ambassadores secretary heretofore, yet that this secretary had so fayrly carryed him selfe in his charge, both now and when he was here before, and was, so the kyng understood, so ready to doo good offices for his subiects, the merchants residing in Muscovy, as he would take order that he should receyve a token of his favour. So, answerable to this civil fiction, I the next day sent my servant to him wyth a gylt cup and cover worth about 6 £ bought by the company. But to the other secretary there was none sent, nor further notice taken of him. Of this I gave account to my lord chamberlin and had for it his approbation, with caution that it might not by example redound to his majestyes charge, howsoever to the merchants, hereafter.

[30] When this Russian ambassador had, upon notice from the merchants, shipt his goods and was ready for his departure, I answerable to the stile of his predecessors treatment here, procured a baron of Scotland, the lord Macquay, to accompany him, the 2nd of May, in the Kyngs coache for his conduct from his house to his imbarking on Tower wharfe in a barge of the queenes, hyred by the merchants without notice given (which was irregular) to the Kyngs Bargemaster. Thence rowing, without the company of aldermen and merchants that had intended to have gone with him, to Gravesend but the tyde spending and busyness attending them, fayled him, they now overtook his ship (run on ground that night at Deptford) saw him there imbark and fall downe the next tyde to the other ships that then were prepared to sayll in one fleet to Greeneland, and were to bring him so far with the less (or no) scare to aryse from pyrates towards his landing at Archangel, the fyrst port in Russia. He gave me at his parting three payre of sables to serve, as he sayd, as a muff for my wyfe worth some 4 £. The merchants having given me before 20 £.

[30ᵛ] The 10th of May by agreement of both kingdomes (from interposition of the Venetian and States ambassadors here and in France) the peace between us and France was solemnly proclaimed,[14] by sound of trumpet and four heralds at Greenwiche, in the conduyt court, the Kyng and Queene in a window of the gallery there privately beholding the manner of yt. That night the Venetian

---

[14] The treaty of Suze of 24 April 1629, with a proclamation at Greenwich on 10 May (Steele, *Tudor and Stuart Proclamations* I no. 1582).

ambassador, Alviso Contarini, made in the Charterhouse yard bonefyres and fyreworkes and gave entertaynment to divers ladyes and gentlemen as a testimony of his exultation for the fruyts of his endeavours so far forth witnessed to be parte in the peace publication, but in the city were made that nyght none, there being no comand for them. The reason, as some sayd, because we not knowing theyr disposition in France to expresse theyr joye for such a worke, might not discover ours beyond theyrs, as if we had bene more fond or more in need of peace than they were.

[31] The ambassador of Denmarck, Mr. Paul Rosencrantz after monthes of negotiation, having receyved his present of two thousand ounces of gylt plate by the under officers of the Jewell House, went (and I wyth him) the 14th of May in a barge of the Kyngs for hymself and a light horseman for his goods to Gravesend and thence towards his country. The day before his parting he sent mee by one of his gentlemen in a purse three score peeces.

May the 26, late at night, whyle I was with my lord chamberlin demanding about an audience to be given the next day to the Venetian ambassador, there came to my house, in my absence, Mr. Gerbier (late servant to the duke of Buckingham and then the kyngs) together with the kings Master Bargeman to lett me know (after they had bene to seeke my lord chamberlin then absent) that a gentleman[15] from the kyng of Spayne imployed to his Majestye and lately from Brussels, by name Peter Paul Rubens, [31ᵛ] had that day had audience of the Kyng and, for that service, one of his majestyes barges to cary him to Greenwiche. This when I understood and that the barge had bene made use of irregularly for one that was not qualifyed ambassador, I made knowne to my lord chamberlin (having fyrst reproved the Master Bargeman for his so over much forwardness, without my knowledge or approbation) and had order from his lordship not to signe his byll for that service as his punishment. I also lett Mr. Gerbier know how much my lord chamberlin was displeased with that irregularity, as being both a wrong to his charge for any man to imploy one of the kynges barges in service of any inferior minister of state, without his order, or at least without my knowledge who was to impart it to his lordship, and a subiect also for ambassadores exceptions that an honour, proper only to them, should be common with a person of so inferiour quality as an envoy, though intitling himselfe Secretary of State to the Council of Flanders and otherwyse of a fayre reputation.

[15] Peter Paul Rubens, agent extraordinary (May 1629 – Jan. 1630) of both Philip IV of Spain and of the archduchess Isabella, was to urge the opening of peace negotiations, which later began in Madrid.

[32] Immediately upon publication of our peace with France my lord viscount Dorchester, principall secretary to his majesty, dispatched a gentleman thyther with order to procure knowledge how his Majestyes ambassadour designat, Sir Thomas Edmondes, should be receyved and treated that wee here myght corespond. Advyse was speedily returned hither by the sayde gentleman (the lyke advyse being brought also by one Monsieur du Moulin, who had bene secretary to Monsieur de Tillieres, when he was ambassador here, and was now imployed hither by Monsieur de Chasteauneuf, at the same tyme designed ambassador extraordinary and on the same errand as ours was to France). It was that our kyngs ambassadour should be mett at Lucherche, a towne about 18 myles on this syde of Paris, by a nobleman an officer of the crowne, should be conducted by him to his house in Paris, provided for him and furnished at theyr Kyngs charge, should be visited the fyrst night by a prince and treated in all with the lyke respectes, as had bene formerly the earles of Carlisle and of [32ᵛ] Holland, or the duke of Buckingham.

To this stipulation his majesty having consulted with the lordes signifyed his pleasure of correspondence to the sayd du Moulin, by the mouth of my lord Dorchester, in presence of the lord chamberlin and myself and the Venetian ambassadors secretary, to his purpose that in correspondence of the reception and manner of yt offered for our ambassador, the French kings ambassador should be met at Gravesend by some eminent person of the kingdom, should there have the Kyngs barges to bring him by water to London, and when coming by water he should land at Tower wharfe, the kings coache and others should be ready there to cary him to his lodging which should be provided and furnished for him at the Kynges charge, that he should have one of the Kyngs coaches dayly to attend him for his service here, for his dyett, his Majestye desyred it might be spared his ambassadour in France, as he intended it not [33] to the kyng of Frances ambassador here, and whereas further, there had bene a motion for a ship of his Majestyes for the ambassadors transport or convoy from Calais to Dover, he should have yt but not his coaches to Dover at his landing there, as had bene accustomed in the tyme of the king his father, his majesty now raygning thinking it fit to reforme that custome, being (as it was then playnly delivered) a disorder, rather than an order, crept in, and only observed in kyng Jameses tyme, wythout example of other princes.

Anserable to his resolution I having procured a warrant from the councell for du Moulin to take up horses, cartes, etc at usuall rates of payment by the ambassadour from Dover hither, du Moulin went to Dover with four hyred coaches and caryed with him, besydes his warrant from the Councell theyre severall letters (upon my proposition to that purpose and allowance of it from my lord chamberlin) wrytten by me in his Majestyes name to the mayors of Dover, Canterbury and Rochester for theyr more particular regard to the service comitted in my absence to the hand of du Moulin, a stranger.

[33ᵛ] The 22 of June, The day of Sir Thomas Edmondes, his majestyes ambassador to the French kyng, imbarking at Dover for Boulogne, Monsieur de Chasteauneuf[16] arrived at Dover from Calais, and the next day lodging at Canterbury he came the thyrd day to Rochester, where I (as was thought fit by my lord chamberlin) to prevent incumbrance or ill understanding, if he should not be in dew tyme met at Gravesend, as was ordayned, by some great lord, receyved him that night.

[34] The next day proceeding, he was met at Gads Hill by my lord Gordon, son of the Marquis Huntley, not as sent from his majestye but of himself, as captayne of 100 horse in the French kyngs service. That night lodging at Gravesend, the morning following (June 25th) the earl of Cleavland cam downe with ten barges accompanyed with his son lord Wentworth, viscount Chaworthes son,[17] and 10 gentlemen for his reception and conduct fyrst to his landing at Tower wharfe and thence in the Kyngs and 25 coaches of noblemen and others (not hyred) to his lodgings in lord Brookes house[18] taken up and firnished for him in Holborn.

The day of his arrival at Gravesend there landed also from Holland the low countryes (where he had bene ambassadour ordinary) Signor Giovanni Soranzo sent to reside here from the state of Venice.[19] To whom, with regard of the service I had then in hand for the more eminent and fyrst come ambassador, I presented only a presumptive welcome from his majesty, with offer of my service and request of the ambassadors patience, untyll I might returne from London, wyth more formall order from his majesty, for his conduction thither.

The Sonday following (two dayes after that of the French ambassadours arrival at London) being assigned for his fyrst publick audience at Greenwiche, I imployed my officer[20] for provision of coaches, whereof could not

---

[16] Charles de l'Aubespine, marquis de Chateauneuf-sur-Cher, ambassador extraordinary (Aug. 1629 – April 1630) of France, came to secure Charles's ratification of the treaty of Suze. His extended stay was devoted to obstructing a peace with Spain, and to urging military support for the Dutch, contrary to the mission of Rubens.

[17] Sir John Chaworth.

[18] Robert Greville, 2nd baron Brooke.

[19] Giovanni Soranzo, ambassador (June 1629 – May 1632) of Venice, continued Venetian objections to an English peace with Spain. He also faced the hostility of Savoy's representatives.

[20] Robert Briscoe, Marshall of Ceremonies.

be [35] procured of noblemens besydes the Kyngs above ten (the day being Sunday when all the lords made use of their coaches to come to court). So the ambassador was forced to hyre as many at his owne charge to Greenwiche; conducted by the earle of Suffolke,[21] he passed by the way of the garden (an irregularity) to the Councell Chamber, thence to the Presence where both the Kyng and Queen together receyved him. His majesty answered his fyrst complement in English by the interpretation of the viscount of Dorchester, and he was not covering for a long tyme and often invited to cover, which (tyll after his majestyes much importuneing) he excused.

After the ambassador returned to his house, the earle of Suffolk yeelded, as he ought, to precede him, though not without much contention, but at his coming forth to accompany him to his coach the earle would by no meanes, at any door, pass before him, in so far as the ambassador, overcome in the fyghte, called me for a wytnes that the fault he had committed, in takeing place of Monsieur de Suffolk in his owne house was not his, nor he gylty, but by force of that incivility as he called it.

[35ᵛ] The next day, June 29, the newly arrived Venetian ambassador, Signor Soranzo, was fetched by mee from Gravesend with three barges and being met with two others at Blackwall by his predecessor, Signor Contarini, was receyved at Tower wharfe by the lord North[22] and attended thence with fyve and twenty coaches besydes the Kyngs (whereof ten were borrowed by the old ambassador) to his lodging at Charterhouse, where was made that nyght a great supper for intertaynment of the company. The next day, June 30, the king of Swedens ambassador, Sir James Spence, went in the Kyngs barge and one other by water to Greenwych to take his leave privatly of both theyr majestyes. I offered to procure him the company of some nobleman, as was usuall and fitting at that last complement, but he refused it saying he was the Kyngs naturall subiect and would dispense with such ceremonyes. The French ambassadour had at the same tyme (but without my attendance, as I was imployed with the other ambassador) a privat audience of the Kyng in the roome over the pasage in the garden and of the Queen in her Privye Gallery.

[36] The new come Venetian ambassador, Soranzo, being at his fyrst audience to be presented to his majesty by his predecessour Contarini, this upon my intimation that his majesty would be pleased to give them theyr publick audience at Nonesuche the Sunday following, July 5th, demanded what lord was appointed to accompany them thither. I told them, as was true, that with

[21] Theophilus Howard, 2nd earl of Suffolk.
[22] Dudley North, 4th lord North.

difficulty would there be a nobleman found for so long a iorney and that also on a Sunday, when most of them would be at the court, for the kyngs, or at home, for Gods service but that my lord chamberlin conferring wyth me to that purpose had thought of only two (whereof one to be chosen) lykeliest free for that service. They were the lord Barckley an ancient baron of England,[23] and the lord Chaworth, a viscount of Ireland. At this the Signor Contarini took exceptions as at a dimunition of the respectes formerly given him fyrst at his audience and not to be given, he sayd in a less measure to his successour.

[37] The 7th of July, The French ambassador having an audience assigned him by the Councell (they were of the commission for peace) I had a sodayne warning given me by my lord of Dorchester, and after, by one of the clerckes of the Councell, yet I went in tyme to this ambassadors house and brought him to the privy lodgings, where two or three of the lordes receyving him and following him into the Councell Chamber, they after followed him out (all) to the top of the stayres descending to the garden and there left him.

[37ᵛ] The 12 of July, the Venetian ambassador, Contarini, being to take his last leave of his majesty at Nonesuch, requyred not the company of any noble man to conduct him nor the Kyngs coache to cary him, saying he was now no more ambassadour, but going thither with four coaches of his owne hyreing and one of myne, after some tyme of rest in a roome at the ryght hand of the Presence, theyr Majestyes receyved him there. After his complement the Kyng knyghted him and gave him his sword and hanger, but not the gyrdle, which he sent to him by mee. After he had given him as he requested of his Majestye a private audience in the Withdrawing Roome next the top of the garden stayres, by which he ascended to yt and by the same way descending he, after a visit or two, tooke coache and returned to London.

[42] The 27 of August, I receyved two letters, one from the Marquis Pompeio Strozzi (sent hither two yeares before ambassadour extraordinary to his Majestye from the duke of Mantua[24]) the other from the Count Francesco d'Odelingo, in whose recommendation the fyrst letter came, signyfying his arrival there from Dover, and his desyre that, being sent from the present duke[25] of Mantua to his majesty, I would direct him for his further proceeding.

---

[23] George Berkeley, 18th baron Berkeley.

[24] Strozzi had been ambassador extraordinary (Aug.–Sept. 1627) of the former duke of Mantua, Vicenzo Gonzaga II, who died on 26 Dec. 1627 without a direct heir.

[25] Odolengo, as ambassador extraordinary, sought Charles's recognition of Charles de Gonzague, duke of Rethel, who had married Maria, niece of the previous duke Vicenzo. Because of Rethel's ties to France, Spain supported a different claimant.

My answer was that understanding he was come so far privately by post and that the Kyng being far off in his progress, I would not readily have answer for his delivery from that incommodious place, [42ᵛ] wyth my personal service imployed hereby about the French ambassadour, in manner as my duty and his merit might requyre, he might be pleased to hold on his course to London by water, makeing use of such boates as the postmaster (to whome I wrot to that purpose) should provide for him and come privately to his lodging. This course observing, he arrived here the next day and that evening had my first visit wyth excuse of absence.

The next daye I sent my officer to the court then at Windsor for assignation of his audience of the kyng and queene and haveinge receyved order for it to be the 3rd of September, he then sett forth early, wyth my attendance and the service of two coaches hyred by himself came by noone to Staines and dyning there, about noone came thither to conduct him to court the earl of Abercorne²⁶ with his brother, two gentlemen, the Kyngs coach that lordes and the lord of Dorchesters. He reposed hymself [43] in the councell chamber, had audience of the kyng in his Presence and of the queene in hers, he delivered his errand in Italian to them both, by the interpretation of the lord of Dorchester to the Kyng and of myne to the Queene. He signifyed how he was sent from the Duke Charles his master, to give account of the late duke of Mantua, Vincenzo Gonzaga's death, and by it what loss theyr Majestyes had of a faythful servant, that this surviving duke, heyre to his possessions and government, would strive to show himselfe so in his zeale for service to that purpose. He was much commended for his becoming cariage of his person his approaches to the Kyng and Queene and for his modesty when invited by the Kyng to put on his hat, he with some reluctance refused it,²⁷ but when the queen moved him to yt he only covered for an instant but all the tyme after remayned uncovered. His audience passed he returned and the lord and myself with him to Staines, where leaving him that nyght with the excuse of my necessary attendance on [43ᵛ] the French ambassador then at Windsor, I returned thither.

The 13 of September, Sonday, he had his last audience of his Majesty at Theobalds, where to I accompanyed him wyth only two coaches, one lent him by my lord of Carlisle and one hyred by himself. We were mett by the earl of Tyllibarne wyth 3 gentlemen in the Kyngs coach, on the highe way a myle short of Theobalds, there shyfting coaches he came to his repose in the

²⁶ James Hamilton, 2nd earl of Abercorne.
²⁷ At this time Rethel negotiated with Charles's agents in Mantua the sale, for £18,000, of important paintings which became part of the royal collection. See Oliver Millar, *The Queen's Pictures* (London: Weidenfeld & Nicolson, 1977) pp. 40–42.

councell chamber when the kyng was at sermon, and passing the tyme a whyle in the garden and walkes he was there met and saluted by the earles of Salisbury and Holland and accompanyed by them to his dynner provided for him (not without the addition thoughe noticed of some messes of meat from the Kyngs kitchin) by my lord of Dorchester in his lodging. After dynner brought to his audience he took his leave of his Majestye, returned with my lord Tyllibarne in the Kyngs coache as far as the place where he entered yt and there agayne shifting coaches, wee came that nyght back to London. [44] The next day being appoynted his last audience of the Queene, he was fetched in her Majestyes coache from his lodging at the Italian Ordinary to Somerset house by the lord Gordon, eldest son to the Marquis Huntley, with other gentlemen and there tooke leave of her Majestye in the Presence Chamber.

The 18 of September, he parted here with one hyred coach, the Kyngs not demanded nor offered, towards Ipswych there to imbark in the fleet of the Marchant Adventurers bound for Elbing, with desyne to land at Elsinore for his negotiation (he sayd) with the kyng of Denmark. The morning of his departure I presented him wyth a diamond ring worth about four hundred. The length of his iorney to come and the small store of money he came provided with, as he spared not to profess, laying the fault and default upon the misery of wars in his country, made him present me with so poor [44ᵛ] an acknowledgement, as I told the person who from his hande gave it to myne, that but for publishing the dishonour of an ambassadour from a prince that I so much honored as the duke of Mantua, whome I had formerly knowne in France, I should give it to my servant, which he understanding, came to me later with persuasions of satisfaction for the present, confessions of his extreme danger of want in so long a iourney as he was to goe, and assurance with many oathes that he would move the duke his master at his returne (and doubted not but to have credit with him to effect itt) to send me a regalo which should be worth the accepting.

The same day the lord Spense, ambassadour of Sweden that had beene 6 monthes negotiating a levy of men for that kyngs service, and prosequiting his owne occasiones for moneyes long before dewe to him from this state, went lykewyse privatly without the Kyngs coache, which I offered, towards Ipswych there also to take shipping in the fleet mentioned, he had a good tyme before receyved his present of gylt plate consisting of two thousand onces. To me was gyven a bason and ewer and two candlesticks worth in all 43 £ 5 s.

[45] The French ambassadour being with the Kyng at Woodstock about the end of August (*in transitu* from a iourney he had privatly taken in company

of the earl of Carlisle to the earle of Barckshyres) showed his Majestye a letter he had even then receyved from the Kyng his master, expressing his intention at the tyme of the peaces ratification for 8 dayes successively to defray his majestyes ambassador Sir Thomas Edmondes. To corespond wyth this, order was given to the officers of the household and others for provisions answerable, and directions sent to me from my lord of Dorchester to lett the ambassador know his Majestyes resolution for his defraying and to refer it to his election, whether he would be served by his owne cookes and other ministerial officers (his Majestyes officers being present and takeing care for all things necessary answerable to the course taken with the duke de Chevreuse and other extraordinaryes since) or have the Kings cookes and others the Kyngs servants attendance. [45 v] The fyrst was chosen as of less incombrance and more in the way of his appetite and profit for avaoydance of rewards. Motion was lykewyse made to me by some of the court officers, to be a meanes that the ambassadour should bring with him his owne plate and table linnen. The fyrst, from example of Messers de Chevreuse, Ville-aux-clercs, and Blainville[23] was yelded to (though sought to be excused for the troublesome carriage of yt) the latter was desyred by his stewart to be supplyed out of the Kyngs store wyth only some 20 dozen of napkins and a dozen of table cloathes for ease of the trouble of often washing them in a place perhaps not so fit for yt. This assented to and theyr trayne listed at 65 persons I caused provision to be made (as I was requyred by them) of fyve hackney coaches with four horses each (payd for by themselves as were also three coaches for theyr baggage at 18 s. the cart out and home) and of his Majestyes best coache for the ambassadors owne person, to be drawn to Colebrooke with 6 hackneys hyred by me and thence with the Kyngs sent before thither for theyr more ease, to Windsor.

[46] The ambassador at the instant that he should set forth (September 1st) excused his company with the promyse, he sayd, he had made of it to my lord Carlisle that day at dynner and intreateing me to accompany his gentlemen to Windsor came thither with that earle and his ladye towards that evening. He was lodged wyth his most necessary attendants about him at the Deanes house within the castle, where he had for himself a fayre dyneing roome with a State in it, next it a bed chamber with the Kyngs richest bed and furniture sutable, within that an inner chamber, as for his cabinet, and a privat room beyond it. All the rest of that house was left to his officers and followers,

---

28 These are former ambassadors extraordinary from Louis XIII: Claude de Lorraine, duke of Chevreuse, May 1625; Jean de Varignies, sieur de Blainville, Sept. 1625 – April 1626; Henri-Auguste de Loménie, sieur de Ville-aux-Clercs, Dec. 1624 – Jan. 1625.

whereof about a dozen gentlemen sat dayly at his owne table, filled up wyth English lordes and others invited by him, or inviting themselves to him. The rest of his owne domestickes of the better sort were well lodged at the poor knights and prebends[29] houses and for his gentlemen voluntaryes and some other of his servants was taken up the Garter Inn, where the host murmuring [46ᵛ] for the hindrance of his harvest at such a tyme and the Frenche therefore not well treated by hym, the better sort of them were removed two or three nyghts after to privat houses neer the Castle. In the ambassadours house were always attendant (for the more quyet ordering and securing of it) a yeoman usher and four of the guard, one of the kyngs porters, two or three groomes of the chamber and a groome porter, a clercke of the kytchin and a clerk of the spicery for oversyght of the dyet brought in dayly in specie, three or four scalders, larders, pullers and the lyke for assistance in the kytchin, and for superintendance of all with his presence and directions which he gave with much care and diligence, Sir Harry Vane, his majestyes Cofferer.

Sunday, 6 of September, the day assigned for the ceremony being come the proceeding was thus. As soone as the sermon before his Majestye in the household chapel was ended, the earl of Carlisle accompanyed with two or three noblemens sons and 20 or 30 gentlemen of his Majestyes Privy Chamber, went with the Kyngs coache, the Queenes and three or four noblemens downe to the ambassadours lodging [47] and brought him thence on foot (the coaches being few, his owne request, the fayrnes of the way and shortnes of yt inviting them to yt) to theyr Majestyes presence in the Withdrawing Chamber. Whence marching in even ranck, the kyng in the middle, the Queene on his right hand (her trayne borne up by the duchess of Richmond) and the ambassadour on the left, all the Kyngs most eminent servants, the lordes and great officers in theyr dew places and the ladyes and maides of honour following the Queene, they went on foot to the churche of the Deanery. Then the Queen takeing her place for sight of the ceremony in the closet above and the French gentlemen bestowed by me with care and quiet for theyr sight in one corner of the chancel over agaynst the ambassadour, and the lordes over agaynst his Majestye in the other, the Kyng and the ambassador ascended the quyre towards the altar, or communion table, adorned with the Kynges richest gylt plate within some 20 foot thereof. [47ᵛ] His majesty passed to the ryght hand, and the ambassador to the left, they both of them tooke theyr chayres placed for them, within the content of a traverse for eache drawne on eyther syde so far on, as kept each from other sight, tyll at the end of an anthemn (the last of Davides psalmes sung by them of the quyre with loud

---

[29] An alms house at Windsor.

musick of organs, cornets, etc.) his majesty stepping forth, and at the same instant the ambassador, they both mett in the midway and there ioyned handes as in token of confederacy, when the Dean of Windsor, Dr. Wren,[30] the bishop of Winchester and prelat of the Garter being sick and absent, kneeling and holding a bible the kyng layd his hand and kept his hand on it, all the tyme that the lord Viscount of Dorchester principal secretary, lykewyse kneeling, read the oath in latin. Which, when his majesty had signed and redelivered to the secretary, he returned to his seat as did also the ambassador to his. There staying the singing of another anthemn they both finally left the churche, [48] took the queen with them, and wyth drums and trumpets sounding before them marched back to the courts lodgings. There resting themselves, tyll dynner was placed on the table in the great hall of the order, they there entered and sat downe to meat, the Kyng and the Queene in the mydst and at the end of yt, on theyr left, the ambassador.

Theyr majestyes were served by the great lordes, the ambassador had for cupbearer one of his owne servants, and for sewer one of his majestyes; one or other of the lordes alwayes standing at his elbow and entertayning him with discourse. The dynner for abundance and goodnes of meate orderly served in was (of all that I ever saw) incomparable. After dynner theyr majestyes retyred to theyr chambers and the ambassador wyth them tyll the evening and supper called him to his lodging. The next day the kyng and queene removing for London, the ambassador was conducted by my lord of Carlisle, and my lord Holland, to More Parke for a sight of the rare gardens and waterworks there, where having eaten his dynner at the kyngs charge, prepared and dressed by his Majestyes officers and servants he came that night in company of the lords to London.

[53ᵛ] The 19th of September, the Frenche ambassador, upon an invitation from the earl of Holland for his sight of Cambridge wherinto that lord (having bene chosen chancellor there of, in place of the duke of Buckingham deceased) had not yet made his entry, made his first dayes journey with one coache and six horses payd by the kyng to the court at Theobalds. There, after three dayes, he went accompanyed with the earle of Carlisle and Holland the fyrst night to Bishops Stortford, and the next day to Cambridge, where intertayned with orations by the vice Chancellor,[31] the university orator[32] and others in severall colleges, wyth disputations in the schooles, wyth a comedy[33]

[30] Christopher Wren, Registrar, in the absence of Richard Neile.
[31] John Bainbrigg.
[32] Robert Creighton.
[33] Stubbe's "Fraus Honesta" on Sept. 29th.

in Trinity Colledge. He was in the same colledge lodged and defrayed four meales with excessive cheer. He was made Master of Arts (together with fyve or six of his followers and Monsieur Rubens, secretary for the Spanish treaty then on foot) and was after two nights there reaccompanyed by the same lords to London.

[54] The Frenche ambassadour having receyved a solemne invitation at his house by the two sheriffs of the city to dyne with the lord mayor[34] on the day of his entrance, 29th of October, I provided a chamber for him and his gentlemen in Cheapsyde at the Fleur de Luce near Wood Street end, and because he was an extraordinary and his lodgings defrayed by his Majestye I thought it convenient (not wythstanding the course held so long to have ambassadors make theyr owne payment for stands at such shewes) to agree with the Master of the house with condition that if the ambassadour should not give him eyther by contract, or otherwyse, the full 3 £, I would; chargeing him in the meane tyme not to demand recompense but to leave it to his pleasure. The ambassador himself came not thither, but to another house, in company of my lords of Carlisle and Holland, and towards dynner tyme desyred mee to excuse to my lord mayor, or his officers, for his lordships notice, his not repayreing to his dynner in regard he could not come in tyme to it, without loss of the syght of his lordships person rydeing through the streets, which he esteemed to be more sightworthy, [54ᵛ] and would therefore make excuse rather of that then the other. So the ambassador not going to that feast, his followers were also absent.

The Venetian and the States ambassadors were present at it having bene invited as had bene the Frenche ambassadour. One of his gentleman asking me at theyr parting how they should proceed with the master of the house for theyr stand, I told him if for my lords honour he would bestow some thyng on the mistress of the house for the tyme, I would not hinder them but that for the chamber I would discharge it upon the account of his Majesty, so as the gentleman giving, in his lords name a peece to the master, I ingaged my self to him for payment of 3 £, 6 months after. The ordinary rate of standing for ambassadours and theyr followers having bene ever wont to by fyve pounds, when payd by his Majestye. But I not knowing when or how I should be reimbursed my money agreed with him at the rate mentioned.

[55] In October towards the tyme assigned for the coming hither of don Carlos Coloma, ambassadour extraordinary for the kyng of Spayne[35] for

---

[34] Sir James Campbell.
[35] Carlos Coloma, marquis of Espinar, ambassador extraordinary (Dec. 1629 – Jan. 1631)

conclusion of peace between England and Spayne, I repayred to my lord
chamberlin for preparation of a house for him at the Kyngs choyce and charge,
as had bene that for the Frenche ambassadour. The fyrst house pickt upon
(as fit for him) was that of Alderman Parkhurst[36] in the Austin fryers and this
out of a consideration taken by the lords of the councell and suggested by
other noblemen, that of late tymes noblemens houses had bene made use of for
ambassadours and not citizens, though contrary to the custome in Queene
Elizabeths, and the beginning of king Jameses tyme, when the course had bene
by both to give order to the lord mayor for discharge of that service. My lord
chamberlin therefore directed his letters to the lord mayor with intimation of
that ancient custome and wyth nomination of alderman Parkhursts house as
proper for that purpose [55ᵛ] but these letters proving of no good relish to the
city as trenching, they thought, upon theyr liberty especially for taking up of
houses of aldermen, and the alderman himself having at that tyme two daughters of his family redy to be brought to bed, the lord mayor, neyther refusing
nor excusing the service, intreated me and Sir Peter Young, Gentleman Usher
to his Majesty, to spare, if wee could, the aldermans house, which we had
alredy visited and found fit, and to make choyce of 7 or 8 which he gave me
a list of. Of these wee tooke a vew and found only one proper which was
the house of the widow lady Weld in the Old Jewry.[37] With acceptation of
this wee returned to the lord mayor and had his allowance for yt, but could
not after get the ladyes, who bearing herself upon the alliance she had in
court, made at fyrst an absolute refusall, but was at last content to make offer
of it for his Majestyes use (rather than to be sent to prison as she was threatened)
when [56] she knew before hand it would not be accepted of, if offered. There
was her pretence of some faults to be found in it, *viz.* of nearness to a church
(which might be a subiect of scandall) and of ill access of coaches, etc. These
colors were sett on itt by the ladyes friends, for shew only of her obedience,
lest others in the lyke case myght prove disobedient near her example, or
question perhaps his Majestyes prerogative power of takeing up houses upon
the lyke occasion.

So as inforced in the end to seeke further (which was the worke of the
lord mayor by his own officer and not by the Kyngs) there was found at last
a house in Aldersgate Street at that tyme leased out by the countess of Hume[38]

---

of Philip IV. He urged that Francis Cottington be sent to Madrid with full powers to negotiate, and remained in London until the ratification of the treaty of peace.

36 Sir Robert Parkhurst.

37 Mary Weld, widow of the former lord mayor, Sir Humphrey Weld.

38 Grace Fane, wife of James Home, 2nd earl of Home.

to Sir John Smyth but not possest by him and he wrytten to by the lordes about it. Their pleasure he obeying, he only requested the discharge of his security to the lady for the rent and was satisfyed with my lord chamberlins word passed for the payment of 100 £, the whole yeares rent, though the ambassadour should perhaps make but three or four monthes use of yt.

[56ᵛ] About the midst of October one of the dukes of Saxony Laumberg, by name Francis Charles,³⁹ arriving heer fell immediately sick and upon his recovery, after three weeks, sent a gentleman to me to lett me know that having letters to me from the queene of Bohemia, he was desyrous I would the next day dyne wyth him for opportunity of theyr delivery. Obeying him I found the letters to be wholy in his recommendation for my regards to him, where to applying my observance I obteyned the next day an audience for him of his majesty in the privy gallery. After he had presented the queen of Bohemias letters he receyved for answer to his complement, having continually served the king and queen of Bohemia in defense of theyr cause and his father king James under count Mansfeld, etc. that he was welcome and deserved his respects for the honour he had done to come so far to see him, and for the service he had done his sister, and his brother, in theyr wars. His Majestye sayd he had heard he had caryed [57] himself with suche brave resolution and constancy as if the rest of the princes of Germany had done lyke him, that country had not bene now in suche subiection nor in so unfavorable condition. The next day he had the lyke audience of the queene in her Withdrawing Chamber, to whome he also presented letters from the queene of Bohemia.

A day or two before the audience of this prince, a duke of Wertenberg, Julius Frederick, uncle to the now souverayne duke⁴⁰ of that title, arrived here. At the fyrst concealing himself, but after notice given of his condition he also demanded and had audience, as the former, of both theyr Majestyes, I having fetched and conducted them in theyr owne hyred coaches; neyther of them were invited to cover in presence of theyr Majestyes, though I understood after upon discourse with the duke of Saxony that a younger brother of his had bene invited to cover, and did so, in presence of bothe the kyngs of Spayne and France at his fyrst access to theyr presence.

[57ᵛ] The duke of Saxony, according to advise given him by some, made his visits (not attending theyrs fyrst) to severall lordes, to some of which he had letters to delyver from the queen of Bohemia, and speaking to them in

---

³⁹ Francis Charles, duke of Saxe-Lauenburg, sought in vain financial help for his anti-Habsburg armed forces.

⁴⁰ Louis Frederick, duke of Württemberg.

Italian gave them the title but of *Signoria* wheras the ambassadors here (as the Venetian, the Mantuan and the Savoyard) speaking Italian usually gave them *Excellenza*. I doubting the distast of some of the lordes hereupon found it in one, who gave for answere that it savored of a *douche* of eyther greatnes or ignorance, that in Italy it was a common saying: *la Signoria si da in bordello*, and that he should be sure upon his further conference with any of the lordes they would speake Frenche not to give him advantage. The duke on the other side was as much distasted that of all those he gave visits to, only the earle of Carlisle and the viscount Dorchester had yet returned theyrs, a neglect that he sayd, were he agayne to visit them he would never hazard, but eyther receyve theyr visits first or not give them any.

[58] On the birth day of the Kyng, being the 19 of November, the Queene had prepared a feast for the intertaynment of his majesty and other lordes and ladyes at Somerset house. The two dukes (of Wirtenberg and Saxony) exprest theyr desyres to be there for the sight of it. But I by oblique wayes propounding theyr invitation to theyr Majestyes not only for sight but participation also of it, if it be permitted, and the kyng expressing his consent, the Queene wythstood it, saying she should be less happy than any common country gentlewoman, if she would not make one meale in a yeer without the presence of unknowne faces. So as the dukes appeared not at it, eyther as partakers or spectators. Whereas it was offered they might, if they thought fit, be there after supper, and at the play, then prepared, they would not appear at all with this reason, that if other thought fit they should not be present as guests at supper, they themselves thought it unfit to be present at the intertaynment after supper.

[58ᵛ] The French ambassador was there, as an invited guest, together with divers lords and ladys seated at theyr majestyes table. The kyng and queene in the mydst, and on theyr left hand (with the distance of one seat) sat the ambassadour, on theyr right (wyth lyke distance) the lady marquis of Hamilton,[41] and so answerably the rest of the lordes and ladyes round about the table, except only in the opposite of theyr majestyes (where roome was left) for theyr carver, sewer, etc. At a long table in another room were bestowed the inferiour ladyes and the maydes of honour together with the French ambassadours servants. After supper was a play, with divers changes of the scene,[42] answerable to the subiect in action. The thyrd act ended there was brought in a banket of boxes of sweetmeates brought in chargers and here and there distributed among the ladyes and straungers.

[41] Mary Fielding, wife of the marquis Hamilton.
[42] Play unidentified, performance of November 19th.

[59] The duke of Wirtenberg after some fortnights stay here tooke leave of the kyng and queene severally. He was iudged both for his quality and the paynes he had taken in coming hither, without other errand than to see the kyngs Majestye and for his alliance of his children to the kyng (being his cosens germane once removed) to have deserved regards beyond those he found.[43] He was neyther invited to eate at his Majestyes charge nor at any other noblemans, nor so much as visited by them during the tyme of his stay here, in which later he was even with them. He himself never visited any of them standing upon poynt of receypt rather than returne, as being (he sayd) the right of his quality. Whereof the duke of Saxony (as appeares before) made no difficulty. He visited the French ambassadour, for respectes as he told me of the tymes and of the iourney he was to make in his returne home through France, and not that he held it a due from him, who as a prince of the Empire might, he sayd, ryghtly from the ambassadour have bene visited.

[59ᵛ] This duke of Wirtenberg, having taken his leave, was (not wythstanding) two dayes after sent to from the Kyng and Queene, as was also the duke of Saxony, to be present at the second presentation of the comedye and showes acted before (as is mentioned) at Somerset house on the Kyngs byrth day and though the former seemed to make some scruple, when my lord the earle of Holland came to him to his house, by way of visit (though some what late, which I can say had not bene at all, but by my oblique remonstrance) and with all invited him, as he had immediately before the duke of Saxony, to accept of his ordinary, as he termed it, at the court[44] and after supper, to accompany the kyng and the queene to the play. He at last assented and was conducted by the sayd earl to the kyng and queenes presence in the Wythdrawing Chamber. They were both at the comedy, seated, the duke of Wirtenberg uppermost on a bench at the left hand of theyr Majestyes, amongst the ladyes and, next beneath him, the lady Marquis of Hamilton and next her the duke of Saxony, with some reparations of former omissions, etc.

[60] This duke of Wirtenberg, not the best satisfyed, as it seemed, wyth his treatment here (his near alliance considered) parted sodaynly and wyth litle formality of leave taking, having receyved one visit only (besydes the returne of the French ambassador) of the States ambassador and repayed it. He performed lykewyse a visit to the duches of Richmond. He sent to me, the day

---

[43] His son, Julius Frederick, had married a daughter of Charles's first cousin, the duke of Holstein.

[44] Holland, as Captain of the Guard, has his own table at court.

of his departure, 24 peeces by one of his gentlemen, who, I after understood, was not of so much honesty as trust, having order from his lord to present me with thyrty.

The duke of Saxony, a fortnight or three weekes after, made a visit to that duches and one to the French ambassador, the latter whereof, if I had not prest the respects of use he might perhaps make of the French kyngs favour, he would have dispensed with.

[61ᵛ] Don Carlos de Coloma, who had bene formerly⁴⁵ imployed hither, being to come ambassadour extraordinary from the kyng of Spayne, after some tyme of our expectation, whyle Sir Francis Cottington in correspondence of this sent thither was thought to be in Spayne, arrived in the Downes from Dunkirk, in a ship of the kyngs, and passing there to Sandwyche (with conduct of Sir Harry Mervyn, vice Admiral of the Narrow Seas that brought him over) lay the second night at Sittingbourne and thence to Gravesend. There I repayring the 30th of December for his fyrst reception (which should have bene at Rochester answerable to the proceeding observed towards the Frenche ambassadour, but that his hast prevented me) I there delyvered to him his Majestyes welcome. [62ᵛ] That night, and the next day, I passed in his company, came thither, for his more honour, the earle of Newport⁴⁶ and half a score of the kyngs servants, with four barges and one light horseman, to transport him to his landing on New Years day at Tower Wharfe and there with 2 or 3 and twenty coaches to his lodging. When his landing in England was fyrst known, the French ambassador, apprehensive that his majestyes best coache appoynted for his dayly attendance should be imployed for the others entrance, cast out some wordes to me for prevention of what he supposed might be a note of his lesser respect, and playnly sayd if there should be found no way of diversion, he must formally except agaynst it, as an indignity put upon him, to have that coache that had bene continually for his service taken from him for anothers use, especially being a coache of that publicke note as to be reckoned his Majestyes best coach. [63] To prevent further inconvenience I acquaynted my lord chamberlin with his punctuality and though his lordship at first alledged that the French ambassadour could not in reason pretend to the continuall use of any one particular coache of his Majestye that being no part of the stipulation, yet after reasons alledged by me and others that the Spanish ambassadour might as well be distasted as the French to have

---

⁴⁵ As ambassador extraordinary (May 1622 – June 1624) to James I, in the absence of Gondomar in Spain for the marriage negotiations of Charles.
⁴⁶ Mountjoy Blount, 1st earl of Newport.

as it were a borrowed coache to serve him, besydes the poornes it would represent of his Majestyes want of coaches, for service of ambassadors to have but one to spare for those here, there was sent to the wharfe an other coache of the kyngs with six horses.

In the evening about six of the clock, his majesty, upon motion of my lord chamberlin from my intimation, sent Sir Robert Carr, Gentleman of his Bed Chamber, with a complement for his welcome to his lodging, to which I accompanyed him, a proceeding not formerly, or very seldome, used here towards ambassadors, yett most fitt and allwayes observed in other kyngdomes.

[64] The 6th of January don Carlos de Coloma, having assignation for his publick audience of both theyr majestyes together, extraordinary preparation was made for yt by adorning the Banketting House at Whytehal with a sute of the kings richest hangings purposely sent for from Hampton Court. The earl of Dorset[1] had bene fyrst nominated for his conduction, but upon a consideration of his being the queens lord chamberlin, it was thought improper and instead the earl of Salisbury (qualifyed as the other both a knight of the Garter and privy counceller) was made choyce of, who for his more honor (as also for the ambassadors) had himself chosen for his company (besydes the ordinary of half a dozen gentlemen of the Privy Chamber whereof there were three colonels) two barons, Compton[2] and Howard,[3] and had besides offered him by my lord chamberlin the company of his son in law the earl of Carnarvon,[4] aginst which I obiected how unfit it would be, perhaps, and without precedent (at least to my remembrance) that [64v] an earl should accompany an earl to the fetching of an ambassador to his audience, I was satisfyed by my lord chamberlins allegation that himself had often done the lyke in the company of the earl of Pembroke his brother.

After this arose another question of my propounding, that synce the kings coach was capable but of six persons and four of these must be necessarily the ambassador, the earl of Salisbury Monsieur Rubens (as a publick minister for the Archduchess) and the earl of Carnarvon, whether the other two remayning to be placed there should be don Juan Vasquez, the ambassadors son in law, and don Juan de Luna, both of eminent quality, or the two English barons Compton and Howard, whom when my lord of Salisbury stood for, as he had reason for his owne and theyr greater honor, that would honor him with theyr company (one of which was his brother in law) and that he was herein seconded by the affection of my lord chamberlin, I thought good to move that Mr. Gerbier (one of the kyngs servants and imployed in the Spanish negotiation) should [65] be sent to the ambassador for knowledge of his pleasure, as dextrously as he could carry it, and for prevention of a *malentenda*, or some

---

1 Edward Sackville, 4th earl of Dorset.
2 Lord Spencer Compton, later earl of Northampton.
3 Lord Howard of Walden, brother-in-law of Salisbury.
4 Robert Dormer, lord Dormer of Wing, 1st earl of Carnarvon.

distaste, that might perhaps grow from an over sodayne distribution of the places in question. Accordingly at his returne it should be of the ambassadors allowance, or disallowance, as it could be mannerly understood, the two lords to proceed or stay. But that gentleman not in tyme returning, we all adventured on wyth 24 coaches and at the ambassadors house found the difference alredy resolved by the two Spanish gentlemens application of themselves to the tyme (though not without some show of insatisfaction) and by theyr ready entrance with me into the second coach, one of the queens.

The place of the ambassadors repose was the Councell Chamber from whence going over the terras to the presence of theyr majestyes in the Banketting House, we found the room ordered with extraordinary care and iudgment of my lord chamberlin, a large passage made from the door up to the State, between a guard of pensioners and other gentlemen of the left hand, and [65ᵛ] of the noblest and fayrest ladyes in court or towne on the right. The ambassador presented himself to the kyng by his own interpreter fyrst in Spanish (which he told me he would do to do right to his own language and country) and after proceeded to the further discourse in French, al this tyme not so much turning his eye (except at fyrst when he made his fyrst respectes to the kyng) towards the queen, wyth whom he after passed his complement wythout an interpreter, speaking to her in French.

Before his audience the same day he, by me, propounded to his majestyes pleasure for approbation whether, since the custom of all other kingdomes was (he sayd) for kings and queens to give theyr fyrst publick audiences separat, and that in this kingdom he should fynd the custom otherwyse, which yet he held the greater honor to him, he might not have the honor of a privat audience of the queen after his publick, eyther immediatly or the next day, [66] or when her majesty should think fittest, for delyverance of letters which he had from the Archduchess to her majesty, and for communication of some particular busynes not proper, he thought, to be imparted at the fyrst sight of her majesty and in so publick an assembly. This conveyed to the knowledge of the kyng by my lord chamberlin, was assented to, and an audience soon given him by her majesty, after some small tyme spent in his retrayt in the councell chamber, in her Withdrawing chamber. There the French ambassador was present in quality, as he himself distinguisht, of her domestick, or servant. The next day I moved for him and from him for the use of one of his majestyes coaches (as of favor not of right, as he sayd himself) for some few dayes tyll one of his own then in making should be finished, which was redily granted and made use of by him, at a privat audience he had of the king the Sonday following and at other visits for the space of 8 or 10 dayes after.

[67] Monsieur Rubens, secretary to the kyng of Spayne and of the Arch-duchesses privy council of Flanders, having negotiated here the busynes of peace by the space of almost nyne monthes, took his leave of the kyng in the privy gallery and of the queen in her Wythdrawing Chamber. He having receyved an [67ᵛ] appoyntment from her majesty by the lord chamberlin to attend there her repayre thither, which might have seemed irregular but that his imployment (he being but an *envoyé*) was not of that quality to requyre the ceremony of the queens entrance there before hand, and the solemn recep-tion with the attendance of her great ladyes about her, as belonged to am-bassadors.

The 22nd of February, his majesty intending to honor him wyth a present from his own hand gave it hym in his Withdrawing Chamber, where he also knighted him.[5] (It was a diamond ring of some 200 £ valew and his majesty sent him the next day by me a diamond hat band valewed at 300 £, but both together were dewly worth 400 £.) For which some pretending fees, I re-monstrated theyr undewness by precedent, only judged it not unfit for him to give a gratuity to the pages of the Bed Chamber, which he gave of 4 £. He after gave the kings trumpets who came to his house to congragulate 3 £, but for the rest of his fees challenged, I alledged my lord chamberlins resolution declared to me, as from the kyng, that no ambassador or forayne minister of state, ought to pay them, so he saved that charge. He sent me at his parting a chayne of gold of 7 ounces weight, for which I had 22 £ 8s.

[68] The 15 February, the Spanish ambassador extraordinary having re-receyved letters from the kyng his master, and demanded audience of his majesty, made use of his own coach for his repayre to Whytehal, he neyther made show of expecting, nor I offering, the kings coach for his service, which according to custome was wont ever to be ready and to be used by extraor-dinary ambassadors at all theyr audiences, but the reason of that use might grow from the want they had of a fytting coach of theyr owne, which this ambassador had procured himself, of here bespoken and made at his own charges.

At the beginning of March the duke of Saxe Lauenberg, after almost fyve monthes stay here, took leave of theyr majestyes, presented by the king with a jewel of diamonds worth 1000 £, his expectation having carryed him to a yearly pension of that valew, and his majesty moved to that purpose, but

---

[5] Rubens presented Charles with his "Allegory of Peace and War" now in the National Gallery, London, and received the commission for the paintings in honor of James I, for the ceiling of the Banqueting House, which were completed in 1634.

refused for consequence of precedent. He gave me fyrst a chayne and his picture worth 24 £ and after a diamond ring worth 15 £.

There being to come hither, after a long expectation, an ambassador to reside here from the French king, his name Fontenay Mareuil, marquis of that place,[6] he at last landed with his lady and family in the Downs, forced in thither by wyndes and being come to Gravesend, February 23rd, the extraordinary ambassador of that king, monsieur de Chasteauneuf, was accompanyed thither by me in the kinges barge [68ᵛ] for his incounter, who that day returned and I accompanying, brought the other in four barges and two light horsemen to the Tower wharf, where he was receyved by the lord Gordon[7] and by him conducted to his lodging at the earl of Dorsets house, his lady and her attendants going thither by water. This lord that met him was thought fit for it by his majesty, as being a marquises oldest son and so equivalent with an earl. But when I acquaynted Monsieur de Chasteauneuf with the choyce, he at the fyrst excepted agaynst it, both as not being an English earl and no peer of the realm and as being a servant in the pay of the kyng his master, for his command of 100 men of armes, but I opposing the recyved course and passage here of a Scottish earl (without exception ever yet made of inequality to one of England) for intertaynment of ambassadors (affirming that if his exceptions were made by the ambassador it would beget no good [69] concept in that nation towards him) he desyred me to forebear to move for the choyce of another, when I was even then for his satisfaction going about it, though I knew the motion would have been as displeasing as it would have been unseasonable. After he had been here three or four dayes, he came, by a privat way of the water and garden, together with his lady to kiss the queens hand, the king being then at Newmarket, which had been, in his majestyes absence, a thing as improper as irregular, but that the extraordinary ambassador, monsieur de Chasteauneuf, had before hand (before the king went out of towne) asked my opinion to that purpose and had it, that if it would please him but to give a touch of it to his majesty for his allowance, before his departure to Newmarket, I presumed it would be granted. This course was taken and access yeilded to accordingly, which was given fyrst in her majestyes privy gallery, but after with more publick notice he and his lady wayted on her into her withdrawing chamber, and then returned the way of theyr privat repayre thither.

[6] François du Val, marquis de Fontenay-Mareuil, ambassador (Feb. 1630 – May 1633) of Louis XIII. Under the revised marriage treaty of Henrietta, he brought 12 Capuchins as chaplains for Somerset House. A trusted agent of Richelieu, he clashed with Henrietta later, in June 1631 (see III 110–111ᵛ).

[7] George Gordon, son of the marquis of Huntley.

[72] After a question had been propounded to me by the extraordinary and resolved by precedents, that his personal assistance to the ordinary would be requisite, my lord of Rutland[8] was made choyce of (as both an earl and a knight of the Garter) to introduce them, accordingly he fetched the new ambassador with the kings and queens coaches accompanyed with my lord viscount Savage[9] and others in 23 or 24 coaches. The ambassadors took theyr places both together in the back end of the coach and my lord Rutland at the other end with my lord Savage. At theyr setting forth I having ranged for the ordinary ambassadors fyrst coach for the third place next after the kings and queens, and then the Venetians, the coachman of his second coach would have also had the precedence of the Venetians, but this with reason would not quit it, but whether the States did ill not to stand for the like, query.

[73] Being come to the Banketting House, we found all excellently ordered by my lord chamberlin in form as it had been for the Spanish ambassador. The extraordinary, advancing fyrst towards theyr majestyes, kept the ordinary, my lord chamberlin, my lord of Rutland on his left, all theyr followers passing on before them placed themselves by my direction, on the left hand from the entrance before the file of Pensioners, to leave a full sight for the ladyes placed on the right hand. The ordinary presented to the king by the extraordinary, speaking in French, was answered by his majesty in English, with the interpretation of the principal secretary, perhaps not to vary from the course held with monsieur Chasteauneuf at his fyrst audience. He, after addressing himself to the queen (discoursed with in the interim by the other ambassador), this returned to discourse with the king, tyll all finished, the followers [73ᵛ] of both after they had kissed theyr majestyes handes, retyred out of the room, to leave the last sight of the king to the ambassadors at theyr last reverence, a defalt found in the former audience of the Spanish ambassador and repayred in this. The extraordinary, having left the ordinary at the outer doores of the Banketting House and returning (with the freedom he had given him in the kings house) to the presence of theyr majestyes, the ordinary went back to his own house accompanyed as before.

It had been at fyrst opposed by some (as a course irregular) for an ordinary ambassador to be allowed his fyrst audience in the Banketting House, a place proper only (they sayd) for audience of extraordinarys. But to this was answered that the king and queen having to be present there both together, no other place could be found near so capable of the assembly that would attend them and [74] that the Spanish ambassador having had his audience there

---

[8] George Manners, 8th earl of Rutland.
[9] Thomas Savage, 1st viscount Savage.

so freshly, the French myght think themselves less respected to have theyrs elsewhere, and that howsoever the audience then were properly given as to an ordinary, an extraordinary had his part and presence in it.

After this ambassadors wife[10] had a whyle reposed herself at her own home (without other sight of the queen then once in privat) an expectation was prepared at court for her publick access to her majesty, not without the privat indeavor of Monsieur de Chasteauneuf, that she should be allowed for her more honour a *tabouret*, or lowe stoole, to sit on in her majestyes presence, but the hour come and I wayting to be a spectator of this novelty, word was brought into the privy chamber that the queen was retyred and no lady ambassatrice lyke to appear at court that day. Hereupon I repayring for my particular information to the kings side, and find there my lord chamberlin was by him asked whether the French ambassadors lady was come, and had receyved [74ᵛ] the honor she affected of sitting in the queens presence, I answered that her majesty was retyred into her bed chamber. 'Aye, I warrant her,' replyed his lordship, 'for having that honor done her in haste, as long as all the great ladyes do and will oppose it, and protest that, if she should sit and not they, they will come no more at court.' His lordship adding further that howsoever it might perhaps be the custome of the court of France, as was objected, for some great princesses and duchesses there, and with them some time for the wife of our kings ambassador, to sit in the presence of the queen, the lyke had never been nor would be admitted here, where if any one duchess or countess should be allowed to sit, all would pretend to it, and thereby bring rather confusion and trouble than contentment and pleasure to the queen by theyr company.

The ambassatrice in the mean tyme thought fit in discretion to absent herself from court for some tyme after, as being eyther discountenanced with the deceyt of her expectation, or apprehending perhaps that none of our great ladyes would give her place, though her tytle was marquise and theyrs but countess, a tytle which here (in regard ours do wear coronets and are styled by the king cosens) is iudged more noble then that of marquis in France, where such titles were alienable with the manor or seignury that bare them.

[75] At the beginning of April 1630 the French ambassador extraordinary, Monsieur de Chasteauneuf, having receyved his revocation, presed the conclusion of a remayning busynes he had with the councell, but insisting peremptorily, amongst other things, upon the allowance of a free transport to Spayne of certayne goodes and commodoties, which tending to the strength of our

---

[10] Susanne de Monceaux-d'Auxy.

enemyes, might be liable by the custom of all nations to seysure and forfeyture, it would be no farther yeelded to then with condition of trial for some tyme what inconvenience might accrew of it, but the ambassador, not admitting of this conditional allowance, as preiudicial to his master in subiecting himself to the pleasure and courtesy of another prince, for that which he pretended right to by ancient confederation between his and this kyngdom, discovered some discontent by his altered fashion, and was thought the more to conceyve yt, when I asking him often when it would be his pleasure that I [75ᵛ] should move for his last publick audience to take leave of his majesty, his answer still was that he affected not solemnityes nor ceremonyes, but desyred he might take leave privatly and without noyse.

With this his singularity I acquaynted my lord chamberlin and his majesty and had answer (which I had charge to delyver him) that though it had seldom, or never, been seen here that an ambassador (especially an extraordinary) had taken his leave privatly, yet that his majesty was content to leave the when, where, and how to his own election. In the mean tyme some of the lords of the counsell formalized them selves at this his singularity, as proceeding (they thought) from some distast conceyved agaynst them for theyr opposition to his forementioned demand of unmolested commerce with Spayne, and that he was not therefore unwilling (as was coniectured), by such his avoydance of publick audience, to make it appear to his master at his returne that he went home unsatisfyed in his busynes (howsoever he had been honored [76] in his person) by taking his leave in privat, so as his majesty was moved by the sayd lords absolutely to refuse him such privat leave taking, if he should affect it for the reasons mentioned.

In the mean tyme when I had told him that it would not be expected (nor was it always the custom of exraordinary ambassadors) that he should take his leave with a troublesome solemnity in the Banketting House (the king and queen being both there together, as at his fyrst audience at Greenwich) and that, if he should take his leave in the kings presence chamber, where the king and some few lords would be present, it would be sufficient, he seemed to approve of yt. But when I but spake of what great lord was lyke to be appointed to conduct him and asked him how many lords and other coaches he would requyre to attend him, he would by no means hear farther of it, saying he had been too long and too often an ambassador to regard such ceremonyes. So, as the king reinformed by me of his singular humor, and unwilling (so near the tyme of his departing) to cross [76ᵛ] him sent my lord chamberlin himself to his house (whyle I was alredy accidentally there) to let him know that though he might have perhaps heard how some of the lords of the councell did not approve of his taking leave in privat (as being different from the course and style used at the parting of all ambassadors extraordinary) it proceeded not from any disaffection to his person but from theyr regard to his majestyes person, to whom was dew (and had been ever hitherto dewly given) the respect of such publick solemnity at parting, yet if he (the ambassador) were not pleased with that way, his majesty would leave him to take the liberty of his own, and to leave how, when, and where he would, since his desyre was to give him content (answerable to his merit) in all things. This message from his majesty was replyed to by the ambassador with all humble acknowledgements of so high a favor, and with demand of pardon if he had erred in his desyres to give his majesty the less trouble by his so privat [77] parting and therein to correspond, at the end of his ambassage, with the domestick treatment he had vouchsafed him from the beginning.

So, as in conclusion, after he had some 4 or 5 dayes before his departure receyved by my handes a present from his majesty of 6 peeces of rich tapestry of Arras hangings made here in England, and valewed at three thousand pounds but well worth 2000, he, on sunday the 11th of April, took his leave of both theyr majestyes at Somerset House, in as privat a manner as himself affected, the queen presenting him from her own hand with a faucet diamond ring worth about 1100, and the next morning (refusing the use of the kings barge, but that I assured him that one, which he had alredy hyred, would not be capable of half his company) he went accompanyed with the ordinary ambassador and the earl of Holland (this of a voluntary and not by appointment) together with some other gentlemen to Tower wharf to imbark with my only attendance (which he would have also excused) for Gravesend [77ᵛ] and there after dynner he went that night in two coaches which himself had hyred (his servants riding post) to Syttingborne.

[78ᵛ] My lord chamberlin having at the Spanish ambassadors entrance into his house taken for him in Aldersgate Street, at the kings charge of 100 £ (for a year or six monthes tyme as it should be possest by the ambassador) assured the ambassador himself by me that since in sommer (if his stay should be heer tyll then) he might be perhaps too much straightened, he would not fayl by that tyme to provide him of another of more receyt, this was then forecast, and in a manner bespoken, by the Spanish ambassador to be the French ambassadors house in Holborne, as soon as he should upon conclusion of his ambassage leave it, and after underhand sollicited by my lord chamberlin to the king and assent given to it. But when his majesty had recommended the cariage of it to my lord treasurer, with the least distast that might be given to the lord Brooke owner of the house, which he had been so long dispossest of by one ambassador, and was now in the lyke danger from another, [78ᵛ] the earl of Bedford,[11] his father in law, interposed for him and made offer of another house of his sons then empty in Hackney, which the Spanish ambassador taking view of and liking of, wayghing the convenience of it in a tyme, as was then of the syckness towards, did redily accept of, having his stuffe at the house in Aldersgate Street removed thither for him by the kings officers. He entered in the [blank] of April, the other house in Aldersgate Street remayning styll to his use, but unfirnished except in one room or two tyll towards winter, when (if he should stay here so long) it might be at his pleasure to return to, as after he did, but not for a continual residence but at tymes of his owne pleasure and, particularly when the peace was to be ratifyed, for the avoydance of more troublesome iourneys then to and from Hackney.

[79] The 29 of May, the Spanish ambassador, then at Hackney, having notice given him by one from me that a young prince was that day borne to his majesty, gave the messenger for his *albricias* of good news 6 peeces, and not standing upon the ceremony of demanding audience by his servant, came himself that afternoon to St. James, where the king then was, to congragulate. Upon his example I thought fit to send my officer to the other ambassadors with signification of what had passed from the Spanish to the king his visit and to leave them to theyr pleasure. This brought the Venetian and the States, after theyr demand of access, to perform the next day the lyke office to his majesty in his gallery at Whytehall, where also upon the same occasion were admitted the day following the king of Denmarcks agent, and the agent of the duke of Florence, Signor Amerigo Salvetti.

After her majesty had layn in about three weekes and that the great lordes and ladys had been admitted to her presence for theyr congragulation, [79ᵛ] the Venetian fyrst of any ambassadors wrot to me of his impatience to see the queen, knowing, he sayd, that the ambassador of France had alredy seen her. I wrot answer that the French reckoned himself as a domestick, and went and came to court at his pleasure without giving me at any tyme notice, and that for himself and the other ambassadors, I had obtayned a day of access which was set for Saturday, the 26 June, being a day or two after the queene was to be churched. In the mean tyme my lady Denbigh, as by virtue of her place of Groome of the Stoole and consequently Fyrst Lady of her majestyes bed chamber, challenged the right of introducing for that tyme the ambassadors and had it allowed for, upon my intimation to the earl of Dorset, the queens lord chamberlin (as a punctilio not worth contestation) at a tyme that might

_____
[11] Francis Russell, 4th earl of Bedford.

seem to requyre a womans service more properly than a mans. When the instant came that the Spanish ambassador, as fyrst in rank of the other two, was after repose in my lady Denbighs lodging [80] to have his access, she accompanyed him, supererogatorily from the chamber by a back stayrs, up to the queen in her withdrawing chamber, for which both her ladyship and I (supposed her director) were condemned as for a course irregular, because the queens fyrst appearing out of her bed chamber might seem to make it a publick audience, but the sudden alteration of her majestyes mind, that was once to have it in the bed chamber and then changed, was a just excuse for both of us. As soon then as the Spanish ambassador had his dismission and was accompanyed by me to his coach, I brought by the same way from the councell chamber, the Venetian ambassador, and after him the States, who had reposed themselves in the same place together, but both of them, without introduction as so much as reception, from the countess at the withdrawing chamber door, as being told perhaps (or bethinking herself) of the error committed, though neyther the lord chamberlin nor vizchamberlin were then in presence to reform or repayre it.

[80ᵛ] Sonday the 27th of June, after the king had dyned at Whytehal, his majesty and most of the great lordes and ladyes about the towne repayred to the queen, who had been some two dayes before churched at St. James. There the heralds having made theyr sumons for a general appearance of the lordes and ladys in the privy gallery, the prince was fetched and brought thither (but wyth litle attendance, which was otherwise then had been ordered) only by the countess of Denbigh appoynted that time governess, and by the nurse, mydwyfe and rockers. The march there was through the kings presence and gard chambers down the great stayrs to the chapel, all the chambers and passages for the proceeding of the ceremony being fayrly hung, and the way in the fyrst court on each syde rayled in, to keep out the crowding multitude.

The aldermen of the cyty marched foremost in theyr scarlet gownes, next them the judges, then the lord mayor,[12] after these the other lordes according [81] to theyr dignityes, next the king of France and of Bohemia (godfathers by theyr deputyes the duke of Lenox[13] and the lord marquis Hamilton[14]) and in the last place of the lordes the earl of Bedford carying a great gylded covered bason for the font. Then came the prince under a canopy (boarne up whyle he was abroad out of the house by lordes) and his highnes caryed all the way by the lady marquis of Hamilton. She was supported on the one

---

[12] Sir Robery Ducy.
[13] James Stewart, 4th duke of Lennox.
[14] James Hamilton, 3rd marquis Hamilton.

syde by the earl marshall, earl of Arundel, and on the other by the lord treasurer, the nurse following him. Next followed the duchess of Richmond, representant for the queen mother of France, lede by the earls of Exeter[15] and Bridgewater,[16] and her trayn borne up by the litle daughter of the duchess of Buckingham, the lady Mary Viliers, last of all came the great ladyes, whereof the fyrst payr were the countess of Kent[17] and the lady Strange[18] (this allowed that place as to a stranger and the duchess of Tremouilles daughter), the second payr were the countesses of Pembroke[19] and of Suffolk,[20] and in theyr proper rancks the residew, other ladys [81ᵛ] that should have preceded these had been invited, and were expected, but appeared not that day with apprehension, it was thought, that they might be called to lend a hand to the trayn of the duchess, and this held a derogation.

All these entring the chapel (at the door whereof stood the bishop of London[21] that was, in the absence of the bishop of Canterbury, to perform the ceremony, and at whose motion the quire sang) found theyr places orderly kept for the lordes on the left hand from the entrance, and for the ladys on the right. On the north side next the altar were two seates for the two kings deputyes with a traverse drawn between them, on the south syde the lyke for the queen mothers deputy and for the prince attended by the lady marquis Hamilton, the countess of Denbigh, the nurse and the mydwyf. The chapel was richly hung with cloth of gold and Arras tapestry, the gallerys or scaffolds purposely buylt on each syde for the musick, were supported by pillars covered with crimson satin flowered with gold sylk and sylver. The window of the closet above on the kings syde was possest by his majesty [82] as spectator all the tyme of the christening. This was performed on an eyght square stage erected in the mydst of the chapel, with an ascent of three or four stepps on eyther end all covered under foot with carpets and the syde barrs, or rayles, with cloath of gold. In the mydst of it was planted a large font of sylver gylt, up to which ascended (when after a tyme the service requyred it) the three deputyes from theyr several seates, the lady marquis Hamilton bearing the prince in her armes, the countess of Denbigh as governess, the bishop of London to perform the service of baptism with a rich cope upon him, the

---

15 William Cecil, 2nd earl of Exeter.

16 John Egerton, viscount Brackley, 1st earl of Bridgewater.

17 Elizabeth Talbot, wife of Henry Grey, 7th earl of Kent.

18 Charlotte de Trémouille, wife of James Stanley, lord Strange.

19 Anne Clifford, wife of Philip Herbert, 4th earl of Pembroke.

20 Elizabeth Hume, wife of Theophilus Howard, earl of Suffolk.

21 William Laud, in place of George Abbot.

bishop of Norwych,[22] as assistant, standing upon the stayre at the one end, and the nurse and the mydwyfe at the other.

The christening finished and all the actors at it returning to theyr places, an anthem was sung, after which Garter king of Armes[23] proclaimed the prince his tytles within the chapel, and without York, another herald,[24] did the lyke, to which the people having given theyr loud acclamations, seconded by the sound of drumes and [82ᵛ] trumpetts, and by the thundring of canons from the Toure and the ships on the Thames, the returne was by the same way and manner as the setting forth, tyll the prince brought to the turning on the queens syde was caryed and presented to both theyr majestyes in the queens bed chamber, there to recyve theyr blessings and thence back to the nursery. The duchess of Richmond,[25] as she had an honor done her in this solemnity to be chosen for a representant for the queen mother of France (or another godmother herself, as she then and since held herself to be) and to be fetched from her house in the queens best coach by her master of the horses (my lord Goring) her equyryes and footmen, shewed a more than ordinary bounty in her acknowledgements by presenting the prince with a diamond ring worth four or fyve thousand pounds, the queen (at her parting from her majesty) with a jewel worth a thousand, and the mydwyfe, nurse and rockers and those that had done her honor and service to the valew well neer to fyve thousand pounds more in gold plate and jewels.

[88] The 5th of September was appointed for solemnization of St. Georges feast at Windsor. According to custom, I gave notice of it to the French and Venetian ambassadors (the Spanish having at other tymes before been present at it) that if they pleased they might signify by me to his majesty theyr desyres to have a sight of it. The Venetian made no other answer in his excuse of his not coming to it then this rude one: 'bacio le mani non lo quel disegno.'[26] The French thanked me for my intimation and requested me to present to his majesty his desyre of the honor to kiss his hands and to attend him at his table the day of the festival. This come and I accordingly expecting him, he sent a lacquay to me with a letter importing his extreme sorow that, by reason that day he must take physick for an indisposition which a day or two before had seysed him, he could not have the honor he desyred to wayt on his majesty,

22 Francis White.
23 Sir William Seger.
24 Sir William le Neve.
25 Frances Howard, wife of Ludovic Stewart, 1st duke of Richmond.
26 When Finet wished a diplomatic excuse, equivalently, "I am grateful; I have no plans."

etc. So, no ambassador nor stranger of quality (excepting one French marquis) were present at it.

The 14 of September, an agent from Hamburg, Dr. Volker,[27] took his leave of the king at Theobalds, and when he had neglected (or apprehended to be refused) a present to him at his parting, I procured for him a chayn and medal of a 100 markes.

[88ᵛ] The 25th of September I receyved a letter from one of the clerks of the councell, as by direction from the lordes, the court then at Hampton, and had it seconded by another from my lord of Dorchester, principal secretary, intimating that there being occasion of conference with the Spanish ambassador (wherein no tyme was to be lost) it was the desyre of such lordes as had charge of the Spanish busynes that I should advertise him thereof, and let him know that on Sonday in the afternoon the lordes would expect him at that place, if it stood with his conveniency, that I should lodge him thereabouts, and bring him to one of the court tables which he should best lyke of to honor, *etc.* According to this direction I wrot to him about his assignation, and because some necessary occasion caryed me then imediatly to court, I intreated him to spare my personal attendance from his house at Hackney, and that I might only meet him on the way at Twickenham within two myles of court, which I did to Hampton Court whither he hastened more than needed. [89] I conducted him to his audience of the lords commissioners in the councell chamber, and after to Kingston, where according to direction I had in an inn and a house next by provided for his lodgings taken up (at my motion) by his majestyes Harbinger. The next morning he returned to London, I only conducting him as far as Twickenham.

[89ᵛ] A thyrd son of the king of Denmark, Ulrick duke of Holstein,[28] came hither and remayned concealed for a fortnight with only a gentleman, a lieutenant colonel Mr. Enhusen, a merchant for his moneys, and one servant for all his attendance. When he saw his fit tyme (doubting himself to be discovered) he went to court at Hampton in company of Mr. Burlamach[29] and Mr. [blank], and without other notice, or introduction than theyrs to my lord of Carlisle, was brought by his lordship to the king and queen in theyr withdrawing chamber, whence (after [90] some half an hour spent in complement) excusing his manner of access, and at the same tyme demanding

[27] Following the Swedish invasion of Germany in June 1630, the Hansa sought English support for a reduction of Swedish threats to their Baltic trade with England.
[28] A first cousin of Charles.
[29] The banker Philip Burlamachi.

leave for his departure out of England, he had it given him by his majesty with (as some thought) too playn a liberty, considering how neer he was in blood to his majesty. This proceeding after wayghed by Sir Thomas Roe (who had been with him upon his discovery here and had, in the tyme of his ambassade in Sweden, known and observed his valiant cariage in that kings wars) he went purposely to court and, upon intimation and discourse with my lord of Holland for his fayrer treatment, and of this lord to the king, his majesty sent his lordship after him to London, with a present of a diamond ring of above a thousand pounds valew, as a token of his welcome and with a signification of his desyre agayn to see him.

Hereupon he went the next day to court, fetched thither from London by the viscount of Doncaster,[30] son to the earl of Carlisle, and intertained at supper by his lordship and was lodged in the lord viscount of Doncasters lodgings. [90ᵛ] At his return to London the next day, I met him on the way and, descending from my coach to present him with my service and wyth a message from Sir Thomas Rowe concerning his own occasions, I had an entrance to his notice and to the attendance I two dayes after gave him, when he was formally invited by my lord of Holland, as by order from his majesty, to sup and lye that night in his lodgings at court before he should take his final leave from theyr majestyes, who would be pleased for his more honor to accompany him at supper. This performed accordingly (theyr majestyes sitting in the midst of the table, at the left hand of the queen the duke, and at the two endes four great ladyes) he was after supper taken to another room to daunce wyth theyr majestyes. The next day after breakfast in my lord of Hollands lodging he took leave, leaving behind him an extraordinary impression and applause of his fayr and well seasoned behavior. Three or four days after, making use of the kings barge (as he had done long before of a coach for his servants, by my order allowed by my lord chamberlin) he, the 30th of October, went to Gravesend and I with him for his imbarking. He gave me a chayn for which I had 10 £.

[91] The newes of the peace formally concluded in Spayne being after long expectation brought to the king on Thursday the 30th of November, by a courier express, I was sent the next day by my lord chamberlin to let the Spanish ambassador know how much his majesty was satisyed with the tydings and conditions of it, and that the publication thereof should be on Sonday, and the ratification on Thursday following. This message receyved with a corresponding alacrity by the ambassador, he repayred instantly to the lord

---

[30] James Hay, viscount Doncaster.

treasurer at his house, and after (I wyth him) to the principal secretary, the viscount of Dorchester, from whom returning, the ambassador on the way desyred me to signify (as I did immediatly) to the lord treasurer that the secretary and he being *de concierto* (as he phrased it in Spanish) agreed that he, the ambassador, should the next day dispatch letters to Dunkerk and the portes of Flanders for the stay of all farther hostility by land and sea, with intimation that from the day of the publication on Sonday no ship taken should be prisable, and that he (the treasurer) would be pleased to do the lyke[31] for [91ᵛ] admonition to the portes of his majestyes dominions. This performed, the ambassador the next day came to a privat audience which he had demanded of his majesty for congragulations, and that night returning to his house in Aldersgate Street, where he resolved thenceforth to reside (quitting his Hackney house, unless some tyme for retrayt) with his whole family, I was sent to him with signification of his majestyes pleasure for the publication to be made of the peace, the Sonday following December 5th, being the very day appoynted for it in Spayne, and the Thursday after for the ratification.

But here grew a doubt from my lord treasurer and some others whether the ambassadors own presence at the publication were requisite, which was resolved on for the affirmative, but not other wyse than for a privat audience. When I came to him, he held it showed not respect enough from him to the king, nor proper for him regarding his own quality, to receyve notice of the kings pleasure for his audience only as I had given it, but that he himself ought to demand formally an audience, and that a publick one, for that which was was to be accompanyed with the carriage of a publick busynes, [92] so consequently, as he glanced at it, some lord of quality and the kings coach to be sent to fetch him to it. I returned with this expression of his to court, but finding there neyther his majesty nor my lord chamberlin, I met with the earl marshall his secretary, who was then lykewyse in search of my lord chamberlin to deliver him from his lord the set form in wryting of the intended proceeding to the publication, which intimated that it should be after the sermon and before the diner, and the publick audience to be given the ambassador after diner, at which the ambassador was to delyver to the king (as the formal words of the note caryed it) the king of Spaynes ingagement under his hand concerning the Palatinat and the powers to treat concerning the Hollanders,[32] but this brought to the sight of my lord chamberlin, and

---

[31] In the margin Finet wrote: "yet there was otherwyse expressed after, there being, by further reason, 14 dayes allowed for notice." Spanish shipping was not protected by the cease fire until November 30th.

[32] Cottington received in Madrid a Latin protocol signed by Philip, on 17 July 1630, granting Charles "powers," jointly with the Infanta Isabella, to negotiate peace terms with

by him to his majesty, theyr concluding opinion was that my lord marshall was mistaken about the *prius* and *posterius* of the publication, and that it was improper that this should go before, but rather follow, the audience [92ᵛ] and 'the delyvering of the powers,' as they termed them, to his majesty.[33] Whereupon his majesty himself gave me a command to wryte (as I did that night) to the ambassador that if he would be pleased the next day to take a diner in court that should be provided him by his majestyes order, he should after diner have his publick audience and thence be accompanyed by his majesty to the sight and hearing of the publication.

But the next morning, upon incounter of my lord marshall and my lord chamberlin, it was cleered that his majesty and he were mistaken in regard the stipulation in Spayne between that king and our kings ambassador was that the publication on both sydes should be fyrst made, and the delivery of the king of Spaynes ingagement for the Palatinat and the powers to treat for the Hollanders were to follow it. Answerable to this resolution, the earl of Berkshire[34] (knyght of the Garter) was made choyce of for his conduct, and brought him to court accompanyed only with his brother lord Howard, two [93] gentlemen more and myself in the kings coach, his lordships own and myne following. After a small tyme of repose in my lord chamberlins lodging and the sermon ended, the king went into the councell chamber and was instantly repayred to there by the ambassador, who after some passage of complement was taken by the king to the window that hath prospect into the Preaching Court, and there (together with his majesty and divers lordes attending) heard the words of the proclamation made[35] (though not understood by the ambassador being in Englysh) by Garter king of Heraltes, the other two kings, Clarencieux[36] and Norroy,[37] and six or seven more heralts assisting, the trumpets at the end of all sounding, and the ambassador, with a very low reverence even to the kings feet, congragulating.

Thence his majesty and the ambassador parting, the heralts rode on horsebak to publish it, fyrst at St. Pauls church (where they were met and accom-

---

the Dutch Republic. On 6 May 1630, Olivares had agreed that, after the treaty was signed, Philip would also write a letter promising that he would not fail under any circumstance to seek to satisfy Charles over the Palatinate question. In effect, the Emperor was to be asked to return the occupied territory to the Count Palatine, or his heirs (PRO SP 94/36/183, memorandum of Hopton, 18 Oct. 1632; AGS E 2574, Philip to Coloma, 20 July 1630).

[33] The order of presenting the powers was written in the treaty articles.

[34] Thomas Howard, 2nd earl of Berkshire.

[35] On 5 Dec. 1630 (R. Steele, *Tudor and Stuart Proclamations* I no. 1628).

[36] Sir Richard St. George.

[37] Sir John Burroughs.

panyed by the lord mayor), and in Cheapsyde at the Exchange, and at the bridge foot next St. Magnus church. The ambassador dined in the councell chamber [93 ᵛ] accompanyed by the lords keeper, treasurer, privy seal, divers other lordes and six of his owne gentlemen. After diner he was conducted by the earl of Berkshire over the terras, through the Great Chamber to the Presence, where he had his audience, delyvered (in two letters from the king his master) the ingagement and powers mentioned, and returned.

Some question grew in the afternoon about bonfyres to be made or not that night, as the lord treasurer and lord chamberlin had propounded to his majestyes pleasure. His majesty seemed not much disposed to it, as an innovation, and more than had been done at the publication of the French peace the year before, but after I had assured that the Spanish ambassador (whom I had then come from) had alredy begun the structure of his fyres before his house, his majesty gave me a command to repayre to the lord mayor to have it done in the cyty, as it was (though not by many) with ringing of bells, with the mayors care of appoynting a city marshall (though [94] I had before done the lyke to the constables thereabouts) for setting of a gard and keeping good order before the ambassadors house among the exceeding multitude of people, flocking thither for sight of this ambassadors bonfyres, and tast of his wyne which was served forth to them plentyfully.

The Tuesday following, the 7th of December, the earl of Carlisle being made choyce of (not without regard it may seem to the parity of proceeding at the ratification of the peace with France the year before, where the same lord performed the same work of conduction) went to him to Aldersgate Street in one of the kings ordinary coaches, the best being at repayr (at least as was affirmed), accompanyed by the earl of Carnarvon, by his own son the viscount of Doncaster, Sir George Hay eldest son to the earl of Duplin, Chancellor of Scotland, myself and 9 other nominate gentlemen of the privy chamber. He had to attend him two others of the kings and queens coaches, and 15 or 16 of the lordes coaches. He came to court [94ᵛ] about half an hour after Eleven, his passage being through the great hall (then purposely hung) up the stone stayres over the terras to the councell chamber, where after he had reposed himself about half an hour, the bishop of London presented him with a paper contayning those verses of the psalmes of David in Latin, which were to be sung in Englysh by the quire before and after his majestyes oath, but the ambassador excusing theyr perusal, with saying he was no Englishman, he would not distrust what they should say or sing though in an unknown language. He was fetched to the king in his withdrawing chamber by the lord chamberlin and there accompanyed by his majesty, attended by the lordes marching before him, by the way of the privy chamber, presence and

gard chamber down to the chappel where, on one syde of it to the right hand
towards the east end, was placed a chayr for his majesty and a desk before it
with cushions imbroidered to kneel and lean on, and on the left and [95]
the lyke for the ambassador. Both of them had traverses alyke of rich cloth
of gold, which, drawn behynd and at the syde, hid them from the sight both
of one another and of all but those that stood at a convenient distance before
them, on each syde of the altar or communion table. On the one syde whereof,
in the corner before the king, were placed the great lordes, in the other, the
ambassador his gentlemen and followers, as witnesses of that dayes remarkable
action.

After all was quietly disposed and an anthemm sung by the quyre, the
bishop of London and Sir John Cook, principal secretary (in the absence of
the viscount Dorchester then lame with gout) stept forth to a square table
covered with a carpet of crimson velvet imbroidered and placed before the
communion table, the one bearing in his hand a bible in Latin, the other the
oath lykewyse in Latin fayrly written in parchment. Both kneeling the
secretary read the sayd oath[38] about the beginning whereof, at the words
'juramus in manus Illustrissimi Domini,' the [95ᵛ] king reached forth and ioyned
his hand with the ambassadors, and at the end of the oath touching the bible
and kissing it, he and the ambassador mutually saluted, and retyring to theyr
seates (the ambassador having been always accompanyed in his by the earl
of Carlisle his conductor) they, after the singing of another anthemm and
(in conclusion of all) the reading of the two usuall prayers for theyr majestyes
and the royall progeny, returned by the way they came to the privy gallerys.

Here after some litle tyme of the kings and the ambassadors stay, the queen
entred with the ladys, and as soon as word was brought that diner was set
on the table in the Bancketting House, they all three repayred thither and satt
down, his majesty in the mydst of the table, the queen on his left hand, and
beneath her at the end of the table the ambassador, who was served (as the
French had been the year before) by a servant of his own for his cup, and by
a gentleman usher quarter wayter [96] for sewer. After the service of the
second course the heralds entered and demanded largess after the accustomed
manner. After this the fyrst health was begun (to the happy continuation of
the peace) by the king, answered by the ambassador and passed to the queen,
the next health was the queens (she being then with chyld) recommended to
the king by the ambassador, the thyrd by the same to the prince of Wales, the
fourth by his majesty to the ambassador with remembrance of the queen and

[38] In margin: "which was, as for example, mutatis mutandis, as the other made to the
French ambassador."

prince of Spayne. When the last was coming from his majesty to the king of Spayne, the disturbance of the disorderly multitude scrambling for the boxes of sweet meates, thrown unseasonably and wantonly among them by the king and the great lordes, interrupted it, so as theyr majestyes rysing from table the ambassador followed them to the privy gallerys, and there took leave of them. After some small tyme of retrayt with the earl of Carlisle to his lodgings, he repayring through the gallerys and taking there a second leave of his majesty *in transitu*, returned home with his conductor and attendants *ut supra*.

[96ᵛ] The duchess of Tremouille³⁹ (mother of the lady Strange⁴⁰) who had been formerly here and was this summer (after some two or three years absence) returned hither to see her daughter, was to part a litle before Christmas, but not with that content she expected, when she undertook her second iorney to England. She, in her fyrst, receyved particular honor from the king, as the defraying all of her stay at court, lodging in the house then of the earl of Banbury,⁴¹ allowance of the *tabouret* to sit in the queens presence,⁴² etc. But now not admitted to these respectes, she discovered her sense of insatisfaction and professed by a formal message (recommended for delyvery to the earl of Carlisle) that now she found that the obligation for those honors was due to the then living duke of Buckingham, and not to his majesty, yet carying all with a countenance of acceptation and the tyme before her, she went hence, well looked on by theyr majestyes, and accompanyed out of town with many coaches filled with ladys and lords of eminent quality and others, but I could not learn that she receyved any present at her parting.

³⁹ Charlotte of Nassau, wife of Henri sieur de Trémouille, duke of Thouars.
⁴⁰ Charlotte de Trémouille.
⁴¹ William Knollys, 1st earl of Banbury.
⁴² This had been denied to the wife of the French ambassador: see III 74.

[97] When a maske[1] was to be represented by the Kyng and certain noblemen at the end of Christmas 1630 I repayred in the holydayes to bothe the French ambassador ordinary, the Marquis de Fontenay, and to the Spanish extraordinary, don Carlos de Coloma to fynd theyre dispositions to be present at it. This latter I found not any waye curious, so much as to question after it, the other profest a jelosy that the Spanish ambassador should, as he sayd, be invited and he not,[2] which playnly, he sayd, he could not but take as an absolut declaration agaynst the king his master, who, he knew, would not otherwyse resent it than if our king should send ten thousand men into France to invade yt. This formality discovered by him to me, and by me to our lord chamberlin, I was two or three dayes before the maske sent both to him and the other ambassador wyth a message to both after one form (*mutatis mutandis*) to this purpose. That his Majestye intending personally to represent a mask and apprehending that the ambassador myght perhaps expect to be invited to yt, had for theyr better satisfaction and to prevent question that myght *per adventure* grow from theyr incounter, sent me to let hym know (as I was incharged to do also to the other) that as his majesty had ever had [97ᵛ] and would have an especial care to professe good corespondence and give content to all ministers of princes his frends and allyes, so he hoped it would not be now taken in ill part, if he (the French) did not receyve an invitation no more than the other (the Spanish) should an invitation to be present at his mask, which was an intertaynment intended only for the queens particular pleasure and satisfaction. To this the French ambassador ansered that the Kyng would (he made no question) do him justice and mayntayne the right he had to precede the Spanish ambassador, which right, he sayd, would not but suffer, if the Spanish, and not he, should be invited and if neyther of them, as by my wordes, he perceyved myght be intended, he could not conceive but that it was for the satisfaction of the Spanish, and would be with some wrong to the king his master, as it myght seem a kind of questioning of his ryght. This he was bound to mayntayne but would not proceed to take further exception, till he had given an account of my mesage to the queen, his masters sister, so

[1] Jonson and Jones, *Love's Triumph through Callipolis*, on Jan. 6th.
[2] In margin: "The Frenche man came himself to my house (but in my absence) to speake wyth me to this purpose, the next day I went to his."

desyred his majesty to pardon him, if he did not by me returne then his absolute answer.

The Spanish ambassador shewed him self less tender and more observant, [98] answering merrily that he was no dancer and too old to take pleasure in those sports except as his majesty was to be an actor in them; that, in former tymes, he knew the custome was for the Spanish and French to be alternatively invited and present at such shewes and solemnityes, and yf his majesty should take such course now and hereafter, it should not be displeasing to him; that besides he had reason as he was an ambassador extraordinary to expect an invitation fyrst, before the other, an ordinary, but that he was so much a servant to the kyngs pleasure that he would obey yt in all as assuring himself that his majesty would never do any other kyngs minister an honour to the kyng his masters prejedice and with this assurance he would be present or absent as his Majesty should command him.

From the Spanish ambassador I went (as I had command) to the Venetian (this command proceeding from my intimation to his majesty how requisite it would be, in some sort, to comply with the minister of that state, regarding theyr pretence to the same treatment [98ᵛ] in poynt of ceremony as is given to *teste coronate*) and acquaynted him wyth the substance of what had passed wyth the French and Spanish as before, adding that his majesty supposed he would take the reasons of the other ambassadors absence from the maske, and why they were not invited to it, for good and apply them to himself with satisfaction. He answered that he had good reason so to do and humbly thanked his majesty for so remembering the honour of the state he represented. The next day I performed the lyke office for the ambassador of the States, going myself to him at his house in Chelsey and had from him the lyke acknowledgement as I had from the Venetian.

These ambassadors thus setled, if I may say so of the French, I had a place assigned for theyr principall followers aloft over a box at the left hand of his majestyes seat. But the Spanish, understanding that they must mingle wyth the French, excused theyr appearance wyth a modest apprehension and obiection particularly of the ambassadour himself, that some difference [99] or dispute might perhaps fall out between them about theyr placing. In the interim the count de la Porta (of Vicenza in the state of Venice) one that lived in the house wyth the Venetian ambassador, being a person titular, was assigned his place (upon my motion) to my lord chamberlin and the earl marshall on the forme of the lordes beneath our earles, when suddenly he himself came to me the same evening of the maske and demanded whether the ambassador of Venice might not have permission to be present at the mask *sconosciuto*, or unknown. I hereupon repayred to my lords chamberlin and marshall for resolution and received their allowance of it, as not inconvenient, though there was a caution and resolution taken by both theyr lordships before hand (not without the knowledge of his majesty) that the French ambassador must not come thither under the lyke disguise because it might be undersood or conceived, perhaps, by the Spanish to have bene done by designe, not wythout disadvantage to his pretensions, whereof his majesty had professed to avoyd the determination. But the Venetian (as I sayd) having allowance for it came to the [99ᵛ] maske and saw all, but seen of few, placed in a little low box (at the right hand of the kyng) capable only of fyve or six persons and wherein he might syt covered, as he was all the maske, wythout discovery or notice.

[103] Don Carlos Coloma, after a years, and some five weekes, stay here for negotiation of the peace, demanded and had his last audience the 15th of February. Conducted to it by the earle of Carlisle, from the Kyngs owne choyce, though he had previously done the lyke at the peaces ratification. He was attended only by his owne son and the lord Gorings, wyth four or fyve gentlemen the Kyngs servants, and served by his majestyes coache, two of the queenes and about a dozen other noblemens, whych was more by half than the ambassador (out of frugality or neglect of pomp) desyred, saying (upon my demand what coaches he would have to serve him) that he was too well known here to expect, or stand upon, such shewes. I demanded for him an audience by the queens lord chamberlin and had it granted him for the same day after the Kyngs. [103ᵛ] But theyr Majestyes were pleased to admit hym to their presence both together in the Kyngs Chamber of Presence, which was a reception (for a roome of so lytle capacity) of the orderlyest and syghtliest that I had before seene. All the ladyes being ranged formost, after theyr qualityes, along and on each syde of the room, the Gentlemen Pensioners wyth theyr poleaxes placed behind them and some of the ambassadors followers suffered to enter before him, but ordered to fall off at the lower end on the ryght hand, whence the sayd followers were called and came singly up to kyss theyr majestyes handes.

I entered fyrst into the roome, and wyth the ambassador syded by the lord chamberlin on the right hand and the lord of Carlisle on the left. He went strayght from theyr Majestyes presence to the lord treasurers lodging in court fayning an errant of a visit (as I had before hand disposed it) though it was intended my lord treasurer should be absent, for a sight of the rich sute of hangings valued at £3000 prepared [104] for his majestyes present to him. (It was the same story of Hero and Leander that was presented to the French, and of the same hands, but some what more large in price, and hanging in the same lodging.) This seene, he returned to his home. Two dayes after his leave takeing, I delyvered him his present mentioned from the kyng, with this formal message incharged, from the mouth of his majesty: 'Tel him I wish him as good success in his busyness at home, as he hath had here, and that all his actions may be as acceptable to the kyng, his master, as they have bene to me.'

Four presents of chaynes of gold were bestowed upon so many of his followers. One was for Cosme de Villa Viciosa,[3] of the valew of 200 £, as for a kynde of assistant (so stiled in a letter of the archduchess), a second for the ambassadors steward, a 3rd for his secretary, or gentleman of his chamber, and 4th for his ordinary negotiating secretary, each of hundred pounds valew. (These chaynes were bestowed, beyond custome, by his majesty to correspond to those bestowed in Spayne upon the gentlemen followers of Sir Francis Cottington.)

[104ᵛ] After the peace was published and ratified, he had severall feasts made him by the commissioners. The fyrst by the lord Treasurer, the next by the earl of Arundell, the 3rd by the earl of Carlisle, and after, by the earl of Montgomery, not as a commissioner but to expresse his affection to the ambassador, and last of all, the earl of Holland. The lord Conway, lord president of the counsell and a commissioner, dying in the interim of these intertaynments, and the lord viscount Dorchester being sicke of the goute, spared theyr invitations, as did also the queens lord chamberlin, as wanting tyme for it, the ambassador sodaynly departing, though having bene allways one at all these mentioned intertaynments. To all these feasts I fetched and accompanyed him from his lodging. He made a feast him self to all these lords, three or four dayes after the fyrst made by my lord Treasurer.

[105] The fourth day after he had in publick taken his leave, he desyred and had a finall access to his majesty, where he was attending for it in the Stone Table chamber, as his majesty passed that way in his retourne from ryding at St. James's. The 22 of February (having the day before left his house in Aldersgate Street, that he might with more quiet dispatch his own bysyness in the house of Monsieur Ricaut,[4] a merchant of London) he went with my attendance to Gravesend with the use of the kyngs barges, excusing the use of his majestys coache to cary him to Tower wharfe, where he imbarked. A day before his departure he had caused his goods to be shipt in a bark hired by himself that was to go along wyth the Kyngs ship appointed for his owne passage. Because the sayd bark myght perhaps run the hazzard to be examined

[3] Secretary of Languages in the London embassy under Gondomar and Coloma.
[4] Peter Ricaut, merchant.

by the Hollanders in her falling by the lands and to the Downes he requested and had the service of a seaman chosen [105ᵛ] by the Master of the Trinity House upon order for it and qualifyed as his Majestyes servant wyth allowance of a flagg to be boarne by the sayd bark for her better protection.

He had given to me at New Years tyde when he first arrived a chayne of gold of 31 £ 10 s., when I caryed him his present he gave me gilt plate for 44 £, and at his parting 70 peeces. To my officer Walther Brisco he gave 10 £.

[106] The 6 April here arrived ambassadour extraordinary (lodged at Geronimoes the Italian ordinarie, as privately as he came by post from Dover) the young count of Scarnifigi,[5] whose father had been here about fifteen years before ambassadour ordinary,[6] from the duke of Savoy. He gave no notice of his quality (with excuse of fytting himself and his servants with apparell and necessaryes) tyll a seaven night after when I returneing from a iourney I had made into the country sent my officer to him (myself being sick of an ague) and receyved his desyre of audience wherwyth my lord chamberlin acquaynting his Majestye he had it granted for the next day, not wythout some inconvenience of such haste in regard of the preparations requisite for his conduction, and preparation of coaches to serve him.

Upon my overture to my lord chamberlin of what question might perhaps grow about the person to be chosen to fetch him to his first audience, remembering the irregularity of my lord of Carlisle's discharge of that part to the Abat de la Scaglia which I had formally opposed, my lord would have made choyce of a baron and sending to me for precedents to be ground by, I sent diverse of the Venetians, the States and others that had been promiscuously conducted, sometimes by barons, sometimes by earles. So at last the earl of Stanford was made choyce of, not without regard to this ambassadours employment as [106ᵛ] the first that had ever been sent from the duke of Savoy regnant after his fathers death. That lord went with him in the Kyngs coach and 4 others to the audience of both theyre Majestyes at once in the Presence Chamber, where was observed the like order of ranging the lords, ladyes and others as at the Spanish ambassadours leave takeing.

He told me before his audience that having been at the fyrst designed by his master the deceased duke of Savoy to congragulate the Princes birth, the duke

---

[5] Antonio Ponte di Scarnifigi, count of Montanero e Castelletto, ambassador extraordinary (April–May 1631) of Victor Amadeus I, who came to congratulate Charles on the birth of the heir and to announce the succession of the new duke.

[6] Antonio Scarnifigi, resident ambassador (April 1614 – March 1617) of the former duke, Charles Emmanuel.

soon after dying he was imployed by him surviving with the account of his fathers death and [107] his assumption of that dignity. So for discharge of both parts he had purposely fashioned his apparell for his first audience, as to sute with both congragulation and condoling, of whyte and black (his doublet white satin and the rest black) and his lacquayes all clad in black and would at his next audience, which he had of both theyr majestyes severally two dayes after, appear all in black, with conformity to the part he must then act for the duke his master living and at that instant mourning for the death of the duke his father. This he performed and withall both first and last delivered such letters as he had incharged to him for both these purposes.

Eyght or ten dayes after these publick and privat audiences, upon receypt of letters from the duke and duchess[7] (syster of our queen) he demanded and had a private audience of both theyr Majestyes apart, of the one in the kyngs Withdrawing Chamber, and the other in her majestyes Privy Gallery. [107ᵛ] The 8th of May this ambassador took his leave of both theyr majestyes together in the kyngs Presence Chamber at Greenwich, conducted thither by the earl of Westmoreland,[8] corresponding to his treatment at his fyrst audience though wyth no good president for the future, when the lyke may be expected and claymed by representatives of ducal quality, etc.

Towards the tyme of his departure I put my lord chamberlin in mynde of movinge his Majestye about his present, whych was at fyrst thought fit should be a iewell as most portative for one who that was to make his way to his home in so long a iourney. But the Master of the Jewell House intimateing to my lord Treasurer and to my lord chamberlin the harme done him by presenting ambassadors wyth jewels and not plate, different from ancient custome[9] there was appoynted for him fifteen hundred onces of gylt plate, and the warrant signed for it. Wherewyth, when I had acquainted the ambassador, he semed much troubled at it and protested that [108] considering the dangers of carriage of plate by sea (he being to returne post by land) the length of tyme before it could arrive at Savoy, the litle use and regard made of our fashion of vesell in his country and (which under confidence he spared not to profess) the hazard he might undergo of having it never more restored to him if (upon some ocasion of some great feast) the duke his master or some other great person should borow it, he would thinke himself more honored to receyve from his Majestye a ring of a hundred crownes then all the benefit so much silver vesell would bring him with the

---

[7] Christine of France.
[8] Mildmay Fane, 2nd earl of Westmoreland.
[9] Henry Mildmay insisted on a gratuity for presenting the plate.

incommodity that must needs accompany it. After this expression of his mynde to me, two dayes scarce were passed when I soliciting my lord chamberlin for the despatch of the present ordayned him, his lordship told me the Kyng was pleased to alter the matter of yt from plate to a jewell as the more proper for cariage in the ambassadours so long a iourney. (I understood after that he made knowne his mynde to Mr. Francis Vercillini, a gentleman of my lord of Arundells and this dextrously to his lord, who procured the mutation of it for the reasons mentioned.) This wrought so wyth me [108ᵛ] from the conceyt I had that the Master of the Jewell House would thinke I had a double hand in it I freely made offer, not only to him, but to my lord chamberlin that conditionly it myght be no preiudice to my ryght for the future, the Master of the Jewell House should for this tyme hand the cariage of it but this was not accepted of. He had a jewell sett with diamond of 500 £ price, having under it the Kyngs and Queens pictures lyvely limmed, delyvered by me a day or two before his departure, which was private and silent, sutable to his arrival, by water to Gravesend in a barge hyred by himself, and without my attendance.

[109ᵛ] The 6 of June I moved (in the absence of my lord chamberlin) for an audience to be given to the Venetian ambassador and having it for the next day at Greenwich, the French ambassador, Monsieur de Fontenay, caused his secretary to wryte to me late that nyght, to the same purpose, for his master (who never tyll then formally demanded audience, but had it given him domestically, at fit tymes, of his ordinary repayre to court). Now a difference occuring betweene him and Monsieur du Jars,[10] a knight of Malta refuged hither, brought forth a novelty and was a cause of my jorney, next day early, to Greenwich, where propounding to his majesty the French ambassadors demand and the consideration of the concurrence, or question that myght happen, who should have the fyrst access that day, it was given to the Venetian, as the fyrst demanded, betweene whom and the French there was no competition for precedence, therefore no wrong done, if the inferior had the priority of audience, especially when it had bene already assigned him before the other [110] demanded any.

The cause of the french ambassadors demand was this. There had growne, some months before, a difference and ill correspondence between him and the same Monsieur du Jars, for supplantation indevered by him agaynst the same ambassador, and du Jars being now neere the tyme of his retourne for France,

---

[10] François du Jars, baron de Rochechuart, a personal friend of Charles and Henrietta since 1626, was watched by Fontenay because of suspected intrigues on behalf of the house of Lorraine and of the cause of Marie de Médicis.

a gentleman of the ambassadors and his steward tooke a tyme (not to be doubted but wyth the ambassadors knowledge and order, thoughe not acknowledged by him to be so) to aske for a servant of du Jars, at his lodging in Greenwich, at a tyme purposely taken, when both he and his master were absent, and wyth pretens of a debt due to him from the sayd servant, when both entring du Jars chamber and asking for a cup of beere, the mayd that went for it speedily retourning, mett them coming out of the chamber and one of them bearing a burthen under his cloake and arm. This proved (as appeared after) to be a cabinet of Monsieur du Jars, wherein were divers papers of especial consequence, the loss whereof (though the cabinet itself was soone and secretly restored and left at the door of his lodging) begot much noyse [110ᵛ] and a complaynt from him to his majesty, with demand of justice to be done him in examination and punishment of the offenders. Hereupon his majesty (by the instigation, as was thought, of some great person[11] backing du Jars) gave a charge to one of the clerckes of the counsel to repayre to the ambassador and to delyver to him a message to this purpose: 'He was informed how some of his (the ambassadors) servants had taken a cabinet out of the chamber of a gentleman of his court, wherein were papers that much concerned his service, and though the cabinet were restored, the detention of the papers was a wrong to him, and would appeare to be such by his resentment, if they were not presently brought back agayne, or the servants (that were charged with the fact) delyvered over to the hand of justice, to be examined and punished according to theyr deserving.' The ambassadors answer was, in few words, that he intended him self to speake with his majesty and doubted not but to give him satisfaction. So accordingly [111] demanding the audience mentioned, he there debated this case, for almost an hour, together wyth his majesty, and was dismissed wyth good countenance and assurance from his majesty that he should have all right done him that might be rightly challenged by an ambassador, and that, to this purpose, he would advise with such of his counsell and servants, as had bene ambassadors, and by them be better informed of the extent of the ambassadors privileges.[12]

The ambassador told me, in his coache as wee returned to London, that the kyng sayd, in his audience, that he would not believe but that his servants proceeding was with his knowledge and direction, that the message he had sent him by the clercke of his counsell was not in those premptorey termes as he (the ambassador) had repeated it, but only to this purpose, that to try

[11] Henrietta.
[12] The papers, seized by Richelieu's order, were to lead to charges against the former ambassador, Chateauneuf, and du Jars.

whether his servants were gylty of what they were accused, he wysht they myght undergo the ordinary course of justice, by the examination allowed by the lawes of the land, but with the lesst noyse that myght be, and without disparagement to theyr masters representative quality. To that purpose, in conclusion, my lord viscount Dorchester, principall secretary, was the next day sent to the ambassador from his majesty to signify his true pleasure for the freedom of his two [111ᵛ] servants (advised, but not commanded, to keep wythin his house) and after to goe abroad at theyr pleasure, without danger or feare of the hand of justice (where wyth they had bene threatened) to lay hold on them. So, for that tyme, this stirre was quieted.

About a month after, the Chevalier du Jars (having made his accomodation on the queens party) the king carrying him self with out showe of partiall regard to eyther, took his leave of both theyr majestyes, and retourned for France. But how the queen, both then and after conceyved of yt, and what regard she caryed towards him that had gotten the better hand of one she thought worthy of her favorable countenance, appeared in the ambassadors intertaynment at court during his staye heere a year and more after. In all this tyme her majesty never assented him a gracious look that myght tell shee had forgotten her interest in du Jars sufference, shee fayled not to remember the kyng her brothers honor, in bestowing those respects, which she knew dewe in publick to his ambassador, no more then the ambassador him self did, in performing all dutyfull observance to be expected of him, in his carriage towards the kyng his masters syster.

[113ᵛ] The agent being to resyde here for affayres of the kyng of Spayne (his name Juan Nicolaldi[13] of the order of St. Iago) came to London, the 20th of July, and the Monday after, 25 July, had audience of his majesty at Oatlands in his withdrawing chamber. It was indeavered, by some, that he should have the fayrest reception that could be given an agent (whome they named resident)[14] in regard his quality was pretended to be more eminent than others formerly imployed under that title by other princes, but I, not to transgress custome and to prevent the danger of precedent, observed the wonted course. Giving him signification by the Marshall of the Ceremonyes, wyth my letters, what hour the kyng would be pleased to give him audience, went overnight (to excuse my company in his coach due only to ambassadors) in myne owne

---

[13] Juan de Necolalde, "resident" (June 1631 – July 1637) of Spain, was an interim appointment until a resident ambassador would be appointed. On 8 Dec. 1634, the count of Umanes, ambassador to France, was appointed but, for personal reasons, refused to come.

[14] Necolalde insisted that his credentials were not of the agent.

coach to Oatlands. There at his lighting I receyved him together with the Archduchess Agent,[15] Mr. Taylor, who served him for interpreter, etc.

[115] The 26 of August, a gentleman of a noble house, by name Rakowsky, High Treasurer of Lithuania and ambassador,[16] from the kyng of Poland to his majesty arrived before Gravesend. He forbore to land, because of the plague then there, and let me know by the postmaster of Gravesend of it and requested my advyce for his further proceeding. I went instantly towards him by water as far as Wolwyche, where meeting him and propounding to him the conveniency of his stay at Grenwiche tyll I might receyve his majestyes pleasure for his further proceeding and reception. His majesty (then at Nonsuch) and severall of the lords were of the opinion that in regard the kyng of Poland had not long before defrayed Sir Thomas Rowe his Majestyes ambassadour thither for 14 dayes together, the lyke treatment might be given this. But my lord treasurer (as a good husband for the kyng) would have so excused it as contravening the order established for the no more defraying of ambassadors, tyll some of the lords affirming that the kyng [115ᵛ] was tyed in honour by way of retribution to do it and that the kyng of Poland being a septentrionall prynce and scarce once in a kyngs reygne sending here, his ambassador could be no precedent for other neyghbour princes of more frequent commerce wyth us, to expect the lyke from us. It was the last assented to that 20 £ per diem should be allowed for him and his followers (their number being 28 or 30) answerable to the tyme of Sir Thomas Rowes treatment in Poland and this dyet to be delyvered him dayly by peeces in specie.

[116] September 3, the earl of Clare[17] appoynted his conductor went to Greenwiche wyth 12 coaches (whereof I was forced to hyre two to supply the defects of those the lords should have sent but fayled by reason of the attendance they then gave theyr Majestyes that were that day to returne to London from the progress) and brought him to his lodging furnished wyth the Kyngs staff at Sir Abraham Williams in the palace yard of Westminster. There that night after much discourse whether the ambassadour were to

[15] Henry Taylor had been secretary of the Spanish embassy since May 1629 during the missions of Rubens and Coloma. He was now accredited as agent of the Archduchess Isabella.

[16] George Albert Rakowsky, ambassador extraordinary (Aug.–Sept. 1631) of Sigismund III, publicly expressed gratitude for the work of Sir Thomas Roe in completing the Truce of Altmark, on 16 Sept. 1629, between Poland and Sweden. Privately, he sought Charles's help for a conference of powers, concerned over the Baltic, following the success of Gustavus of Sweden in north Germany.

[17] John Holles, 1st earl of Clare.

make use of his owne plate (the Kyngs being excused as not in towne, indeed not in being [116ᵛ] whilst it was at that instant to be melted down for conversion into another fashion) his own plate, as also his own table linen, was made use of and his dyet began that night at supper. The next day he was fetched to his publick audience by the earl of Carlisle with twenty gentlemen of the court (whereof three or four were of the nobility) and brought through a lane of pikes and shott placed in the street, a reception unusuall but advised by the earl marshall in lieu of the lyke to fayle by the then absence of the great lords and ladyes. This ambassador having questioned me the day before about the formes of his approach to theyr majestyes and I, informing him of the style used here, he, when he came to his audience, varied in this. At his second reverence he called for his letters to his secretary close behynd him, who supplyed that place as of the ambassage, performed his third reverence to the kyng at the first rise of the uppermost step, without that his Majestye descended any one step down to meet him as the ambassador (answerable to his countryes custome) expected, [117] and only bowing to the Queene he proceeded to his own oration. This pronounced by him in latin was answered by the viscount Dorchester in French. After some discourse with the kyng, the ambassador speaking in Italian, his majesty in French, he addressed himself with humble respect to the Queen. He spake to her lykewyse in latin without ever putting on his hat though invited, which done, he, in manner as he came, departed.

At his arrival at Greenwich he, unseasonably, met the newes of the Queen of Polands death[18] (which changed the countenances of him and all his followers habits who had provided themselves, especially the ambassadour, to the value of at least 1000 £ of rich apparel) so, notwythstanding the reasons alleged by my self and others of his not having received a formal account of her death from the state of that kyngdome which myght [117ᵛ] perhaps have served to keep him in colours, he turned all to black, and so continued cloathed during his stay in England.

[118] Two dayes before this ambassadours remove from Greenwich to London, the abbot of Escaglia,[19] ambassadour extraordinary for the duke of Savoy, came from Spayne by sea. He had formerly bene here imployed hither

---

[18] Constance of Styria, 2nd wife of Sigismund.

[19] Alessandro-Cesare di Scaglia, abbot of Staffarda, ambassador extraordinary (Sept. 1631 – March 1632) of Savoy. This was his third mission to Charles (previously: Jan.–Feb. 1626; Oct. 1627 – Aug. 1628) in which he sought to promote peace discussions between Spain and the Dutch Republic. The French and Venetian ambassadors disliked his support of the interests of Marie de Médicis.

twyce. He sent me word of his approach as far as Canterbury and requested my opinion and direction for his further course. This I returned advising that the plague being then at Gravesend, Rochester too remote from London for dayly correspondence, Dartford not fit to harbour him because not lodgeable, he should do well to repose himself at Grenwiche, from wich the ambassadour of Poland was to remove the day following, tyll he myght by me receyve further notice of his Majestyes pleasure for his reception. This course observed, [118ᵛ] he lodged in the same house (being a tavern or inn, the Signe of the Feathers) that the ambassadour of Poland was lodged in before him. I repayred to the earle of Carlisle for his opinion and advice of my best course of proceeding and wythall acquainted his Majestye and the lord treasurer wyth what I understood of the affections and indeavours of some to have him lodged contrary to the pragmatick, though not defrayed, in a house of the Kyngs providing. I received resolution that he was to provide his own dwelling. This putting him, as it appeared, somewhat out of his way he would have entered into another of being admitted to a private audience (not wythout irregularity as not wythout endes) before his publick. But the Kyng that wanted not dutiful servants to remember him of the inconveniences accompanying such privacy and freedome of access to his presence, prevented him both by mine and the earle of Carlisles intimation [119] to that purpose. That his majesty understood of his indisposition at the end of so long a iourney and therefore desyred him to study his health, as he would his honour by letting him rest and making much of himself tyll Sunday following, when he would give him a publick audience at Theobalds as should become the dignity of his master. In conclusion all his indeavours by several wayes could not obtayne the privat audience he so much affected, both whyle the kyng remayned at Wansted and at Theobalds. There on Sunday the 11th he had a publick audience given him both by the Kyng and Queene at once, conducted to yt from Bethnel Green, where he lodged, by the earl of Carlisle. This being an incongruity for the person conducting, but as that lords affection, and professed obligation to the duke of Savoy, might excuse it and with the service of the kyngs coach, his lordships, mine and two hyred by me, and without the company of any one gentleman of the Privy Chamber, who were then most of them at court and should have bene improperly perhaps sought out in towne, the rest being caryed with disorder.

[119ᵛ] Whyle the abbot rested at Greenwiche indeavouring the privat audience mentioned, the Polish ambassador had the honour of the kyngs invitation to hunt wyth him one morning at Wansted (Sept. 8th) and after dynner to have the private audience he had by me demanded. He, the baron of Guldensterne, and his secretary of the ambassage Doctor Borastus, and two or three of his followers, were horsed by the kyngs order and intertayned at dynner by the earle of Carlisle, at his owne charge, in company with the earl of Lyndsey, Sir Thomas Edmondes, Treasurer of the household and others. He was conducted to Wansted by me in a traveling coach of the kyngs and one more that I hyred, and that night returned to London.

After nyne or 10 dayes of his stay here at the Kyngs charge I moved his majesty for his dispatch, which him self desyred, and the kyng could not dislyke, for the relation it had to his profit. So accordingly [120] I had order to assygne him the 3rd day after (Sept. 14th) for his audience at Whytehal of the lords commissioners for his busynes, which were the lord treasurer, Carlisle, Holland and Dorchester, the lord Marshall being absent. Upon this intimation he asked me whether it were the custome here for the lords of the councell to assigne or give audience to a kyngs ambassador when the errant he came on consisted of a complement, as his did, who was sent to thank the Kyng and acknowledge his favour, that in contemplation of the ancient amity betweene his majestyes father and the kyng his master and of the performance of so Christian a work as peacemaking (his Majestye had, wythout being ever sought to by his master, imployed his ambassadour Sir Thomas Rowe, for the making of a truce between him and Gustavus, as he always and no otherwise styled him). I answered that indeed I had observed that of all the ambassadours sent hither from forayne princes merely of complement as to condole, con-gragulate and the lyke, none had had accesse (no more than there was need of it) to other than his majestyes owne person, but [120ᵛ] that for his ambassage I took it yt to be more than complemental, synce he had professed in his publick oration to his majesty that he was sent hither not only wyth his masters thankes for his Majestyes most Christian indeavours in making the truce, but wyth his desyres also that the Kyng of Great Britaine would inter-pose for a peace. To this he replyed that he hoped his majesty and the lords did not so understand him, as if he were come hither wyth the kyng his masters desyres of a peace, as if he feared or apprehended the danger of a war from Gustavus, but that he was sent to observe the conditions of the truce, which had formally bound his master to give thanks to the kyng of England, by an ambassador (as he done by one sent to the kyng of France for theyr interposition) and to hearken to and imbrace any fayre overture of a peace that myght stand wyth his masters honor, but not otherwyse. He added further that it was true he had discourse with his Majestye about the fyttest place for the ambassadours of England, France and his masters [121] and of other princes to convene about it and that he had from his master propounded Konigsberg, as a place the most indifferent being neutral, and had excepted against some places propounded as Hamburg, Dansick and others which his master, with his honor and without his disadvantage, could not assent unto. He had also spoken of the tyme (as about Christmas) as most fytt for theyr convening and he had also complained of the Muscovites breaking the truce[20] before it expired, here I was bold to interupt him wyth a question whether he thought that these propositions did not exceed a complement and cary so much of a negotiation, as that it should not be fytt for his Majesty for the easing of his paynes and the more punctual debating of the busynes to referr him to his councell. The ambassador replyed that he had sayd this, as not in any sort waving or excusing his repayre to the lords, whome he knew to be most noble and most worthy representants of his majestyes person, but as one that had reason to render the honours of the kyng his master and to be cautious how he caryed his busynes in a kingdome where he knew, he sayd, there were so many Gustavians [121ᵛ] who would not stick to report that after his fyrst publick audience he had had a long private one of his Majestye and after that another of the lords of the councell and all wyth affection to that peace with Gustavus, wythout which the kyng of Poland could not subsist, whereof rather then he would give the least subiect of conceyt to his majesty or theyr lordships he would not step one foot further in his business.

In these termes, he desyred me to recommend yt to theyr lordships considerations, which he hoped would pardon him his tenderness and jelosy for his masters honour, etc. I, acquainting the lords with these formalityes, had for answer from my lord treasurer that they intended not to proceed with him, but with dew regard to his masters honour and according to the custome and course held here towards all ambassadors. With which answer satisfyed, I brought him through the garden at Whytehall to the second chamber from the stayre head adioyning to the utmost privy gallery, whither the lords coming to receyve him, [122] tooke him wyth them into the Cabinet Councell chamber (next that he had reposed in) and, after debatement of his busynes accompanying him back to the stayre head mentioned, they there left him to my reconduction.

The day following, he desyred me in his name to request of the lord of Dorchester, principal secretary, the substance of his answere in wryting, because, he sayd, he trusted not so much to his French (in which language it was given him by that lord) as that he might not err in his understanding. Whereto his lordship answered that had the ambassadour sett downe his

---

[20] The truce of Deulino (Jan. 1619) had permitted Poland to retain Smolensk, after its capture from the czar. In 1631 Gustavus of Sweden encouraged the czar to prepare for war for its recapture. Rakowsky was aware of pro-Swedish sentiment at Charles's court.

demands in wryting he should have receyved to them a wryten answere, but having verbally delyvered them, the custom here was to make theyr answere verbal. Yet that he would move his majesty and the lords (of whome he had bene but the mouth) to give him all reasonable satisfaction. So he came a day or two after to his house, as sent by his majesty to visit him, and there receyving from the ambassadors owne mouth a repetition of what he had before demanded and propounded, he repeated to him the substance of his fyrst answer, and left him to his pleasure to take notes of it if he would [122ᵛ] for his memory, but other formality of wryting there past none between them. No more then there seemed to doe in point of insatisfaction from the ambassadour.

[124] The 21 of September, he was invited to dyne the next day with the lord mayor[21] (this intended as a particular honour from the city and a meanes to indeer to him and to his kyng the Easterne Company of merchants). [124ᵛ] Accepting the invitation (contrary to the opinion of many that thought he would never do it) he came thither and was receyved by the lord mayor at his doore, gave his lordship the precedence both there and at the table, the lord mayor sitting at the boords end, and the ambassador at the bench next the wall, with his right hand uppermost and made good (what he had profest to me before) his neglect of competition for the hand with a person, he sayd, who having it given him, but as lord mayor, could not in any sort preiudice the king his master their difference of quality considered, one being so great a king, and the other but an annual magistrate.

The 26th of September after he had ordered that the greater part of his trayne (and with them the secretary of the ambassage Dr. Borastus) should go by sea to Dansick, he took poste at Lambeth (where I only saw him horsed *et non ultra* because he parted in a private manner) with the baron of Guldensterne and four more of his followers to ryde that night to Dartford, next day to Rochester, with intention to see there some of the navye, and thence to Dover [125] for inbarking to Calais, and after overland to Brussels and Polonia. He had for his present brought him by the Master of the Jewel House, 1500 ounces of gylt plate, two thousand having bene propounded, as for a kings ambassador, answerable to the rate usually alloted them. But the precedent of his predecessor, Osaliski,[22] here in king Jameses tyme, ap-

[21] Sir Robert Ducy.
[22] George Ossalinski, count of Tenczyn, ambassador extraordinary (March 1621) of Poland, had sought the support of James I in a war against the Turks. Here Finet wrote in the margin: "for this there might be good reason; he having obtayned of the kyng 10.000 li by way of loane for his master, but nought for himself."

pearing to have bene but 1500, my lord treasurers good husbandry would not suffer it to be exceeded.

[126] The ambassador of the States, receyving order from his masters to render to his majesty (at a publick audience) an account of theyr delyvery from theyr danger of theyr enemies by theyr attempt upon certayne islands betweene Holland and Zeland,[23] lett me know of yt, wyth request to moove for a publick audience, which granted for Sunday, the 9 of October, I accompanyed him in his coach, from his house at Chelsey to Hampton Court, brought him to his repose in the councell chamber, whence fetched and conducted by the lord Goring through the Gard Chamber to the king in the Presence, he there made a punctuall relation of all particulars, though a month before not unknowne to his majesty. As the kyng was ready to come forth to his audience, my lord marshall asked me if it were usual for an ambassador to demand, and have a public audience at other tymes, then at his fyrst coming, and at his parting. I answered I had knowne of none in my tyme, unless of that which don Carlos Coloma demanded for the signification that was to precede the publication of peace with Spayne,[24] that also of the Venetian, when he had protested agaynst the interruption of his letters at Dover,[25] but I thought, I sayd, that the subiect and account of the busyness tending to the kyngs honor (as contributing to his greatnes) it myght [126ᵛ] well cary it. And to this purpose, I after learned that it was an ordinary thing in France and elsewhere, upon any remarkable occurence to the good of an estate, for the ambassador of that state to demand a publick audience, and to have it given him.

[127ᵛ] The fyft of October, St. Georges feast being to be kept at Windsor, I gave knowledge of it to the ambassadours here that I myght understand theyr dispositions to be at it. The French, Monsieur de Fontenay excused it (desyring he might be so to his Majestye wyth regard of his wyfes neernes to her tyme of delivery). The Venetian Signor Soranzo exprest no affection to it, being in deed a man litle curious. The Savoyard the lyke, only he recommended to my regarde and company his nephew the Marquise de Valluse, wherewyth I served him, the States had before seene it. So none of them appearing there it saved the disrepect which strangers wytnessing of so poore a solemnity as that yeare brought forth would have cast upon yt.

---

[23] Possibly, Joachimi narrated the capture of several Spanish troopships, under the command of John of Nassau, off the Zealand coast on 12 Sept. 1631.

[24] In Nov. 1630: see III 91.

[25] The seizure, by Buckingham's order, occurred in Nov. 1627. The Venetian Republic ordered Contarini to deliver a public protest in June 1628.

[128] In the evening of November 2nd my lord chamberlin sent for me to the court at St. James's and telling me of the arrival at Gravesend of the queens natural brother,[26] the Duke of Vendosme, come from the low countryes to see his syster, and to wear out some tyme of his commanded absence from the court of France. I had order for my instant repayre in his Majestyes name to the lord mayor[27] for the provideing of a house for him (with furniture or without was left to after resolution upon taste of the dukes disposition). The lord mayor not waving or excusing the service assured me of his best endeavers wyth the advice of the aldermen his brethren, to accomplish yt and the next day assembled them but neyther his lordships nor my officer Briscoes care and paynes could in all the city procure one fitting.

In the meane tyme I, that morning went in company of the French ambassadour, Monsieur de Fontenay, to the duke at Gravesend for his fyrst reception with signification that Mr. Walter Montagu, yonger son to the earl of Manchester[28] was immediately to follow me wyth [128ᵛ] a complement from his Majestye, but he fayling (upon breach of his coache as he professed) to come in tyme to Gravesend, we set forth thence in six barges towards London (the tyde being more then halfe spent and the wynde strongly contrary) with such a storme as not able to get above Grenwiche, our barge with 12 oares for most was forced to land there at 8 of the clock at night not with out peril of drowning. The other barges ran the lyke hazard and for theyr sauvegarde landed at other places. In an houres stay that wee made at Grenwiche, I sent abroad and borrowed a coach to carry us to London where, towards midnight, the duke came to his lodgings at the French ambassadors. The next day he was visited with a welcome from the Kyng by the earle of Holland, accompanyed with the earls of Stamford, Newport and other gentlemen, wyth offer to bring him imediately to his Majestyes sight as he did in the afternoone in the privy gallery at St. James's where he presented himself wyth these words.

[129]

Sire, Je suis venu maintenant au plus hault de mon ambition qui a este de me ieter aux pieds de vostre Majesté en qualité de vostre plus humble serviteur qui vous honore come son souvereign.[29]

---

[26] César de France, duke of Vendôme, natural son of Henry IV, was allied by marriage to the house of Lorraine and was a known conspirator against Richelieu. This honor to him at Charles's court by Henrietta was an embarrassment to the French embassy. For his return to London in Feb. 1641 see V 110ᵛ.

[27] Sir George Whitmore.

[28] Henry Montagu, viscount Mandeville, 1st earl of Manchester.

[29] "Sire, I have reached the height of my ambition, which has been to place myself at the feet of your majesty as a most humble servant, who honors you as his sovereign."

The kyng returned to him, with a gracious countenance, these words:

On m'a raconté le danger que vous avez passé par l'eau. J'espere que par terre vous ne trouvierez pas que du contentement ce que je tacheray par tous moyens vous donner en qualité de vostre frere.[30]

The Kyng (during this and other passages between them) stood uncovered, as the duke did all the tyme wythout being at all invited to put on by his majesty. Theyr discourse ended, his Majestye conducted him and his son[31] (but none else of his company) to the syght of the Queene his syster wyth a French liberty, not ten hours after she had bene brought to bed of a princess.[32] Thence he was reconducted by the lords mentioned to his lodging at the ambassadoures, tyll the next day he went to another taken by his officers [129ᵛ] at Sir Abraham Williams neer Westminster Hall, for which upon agreement he was to pay 2 £ *per diem* including bedds, bedd linen, table linen and necessaryes, all else to be at his owne charge and providing.

This course of not defraying him, eyther for lodging or dyet, was profest to proceed from [130] his owne disposition and desyre, as unwilling to charge or trouble the kyng in any thyng. But our wants (too well known) were not the least cause of it, he had in his company about 15 or 16 gentlemen and of other servants, some fifty.

A day or two after his setling, I had command from his majesty himself to repayre to the lord mayor wyth intimation that he lyked well of the care and diligence imployed by him and the aldermen, about takeing up a house for the duke of Vendosme in the city, not wyth standing they had had for yt so short a warning, but that thereafter, upon the lyke occasion and upon larger tyme given them, he would expect they should not returne him such excuses as were brought him. *Viz.* Of one house to be possessed by a widow and her children whose husband was lately dead,[33] of another by a woman ready to be brought to bedd and the lyke, but that they should give him their obedience and the effects of it redily in providing some fitting house in the city (as had bene heretofore the custome) for any great person coming into this kingdome, to visit his majesty or to negotiate, and to this purpose he [130ᵛ] intended shortly to have the lord mayor sent for to appear before his counsel, for signi-

---

[30] "I have been told of the danger through which you passed at sea. I trust you will find every satisfaction on land, for I will try, in the role of your brother, to provide it for you in every way."

[31] The duke of Mercœur.

[32] Mary.

[33] The widow of Sir Thomas Middleton.

fication of his pleasure in that case, which was performed accordingly some few dayes after.

The duke having receyved the fyrst visit from the earles of Holland, Carlisle, Pembroke and Dorset within two or three dayes after returned them. But not wythout difficulty to the earl of Carlisle, who swore he would never comit that gross fault of incivility and ill manners, as to give an assignation to a prince of his quality. The duke to clear that debt, as he called it, watched a tyme immediately after dynner to surprise him at his chamber in court whyle he was sleeping. Three or four dayes after he gave me a complement for my lord treasurer and lord keeper (himself so ranking them) that knowing the multiplicity of theyr affayres he would intreat to know theyr owne best tyme of leysure for a visit, which they complementally excusing as a duty fyrst to be, [131] they sayd, performed by them, they yet at last yeelded to and had theyr discharge by the dukes repayre, fyrst to the lord treasurer and the same day and hour to the lord keeper, who fyve or six dayes after rendered him theyr visits. It had bene set downe by king Jaymes, as my lord keeper told me, that neyther the keeper nor the treasurer should returne visits to ambassadors or others, wyth regard to theyr continual imployment in affaires of state. The duke also gave the fyrst visit to the Viscount Dorchester, principal secretary with the same regard to his affayres, but none to his sycknes which at that tyme forced him for the most part to keep his chamber. From all these persons he had no other title given him then *Monsieur* and *Vous*, except that the earle of Carlisle at his fyrst visit gave him several times *Excellence*, but when my lord chamberlin gave him his visit I receyved a special *caveat* by the French ambassadours servant, whether with the dukes knowledge or not I know not, that he was not to be treated with *Excellence* here, already having had *Altesse* given him in the low countreys, which I understanding as I ought, obeying I continued to give him alwayes *vous* and *monsieur* and no other, not more did the earl of Carlisle, after I had told him what *caveat* I had receyved.

[132] The Venetian and States ambassadors demanding of the Queene congragulatory audiences for the byrth of the princess Mary had them assigned for the 1st of December, when the evening before the Venetian writing to me of his indisposition of the gout excused his coming. The States ambassadour admitted to kyss her Majestyes hand in her chyld bed chamber would have bene introduced by me, but chanceably Mr. Vice Chamberlin of the Kyng, Sir Thomas German, being at the door, performed the service. The ambassadour of Savoy had a week before discharged that complement without mentioning to me his intention for it, only making his way by some lady of the Bed Chamber, which the tyme of her Majestyes lying in and his former do-

mestick freedome of access myght perhaps allow him to make use of for his admittance.

The ambassador of Venice having (upon recovery of his gout) demanded an audience of her majesty had it, the 11 of December, at Somerset House, whereupon the ambassador of Savoy apprehending, it should seem, that his so domestick audience above mentioned, howsoever to be [132ᵛ] interpreted as an argument of his privacy at court, might not be, perhaps, of notice sufficient to the world for a publick minister, and make some think he had forgotten, omitted or neglected that ceremony, sent to me to procure a formall audience to be given, at her majestyes pleasure, and had it the next day after at Whitehall in her Privy Chamber, whence parting with a solemne leave the lord Goring, as soon as he was out of the roome, staying him, told him (whether of him self or with the queens signifyed pleasure I know not) that now that his ceremonies were past, he should do well to dismiss the Master of them and act himself. This he did, bidding me farewell and immediately returning to the Queens presence in the same chamber, where her majesty with her ladyes about her and the ambassadour passed theyr tyme a good tyme after.

[133ᵛ] The duke de Vendosme intimating to the kyng his desyre to hear the musick of the chappel at court (not withstanding his profest difference of religion) had assigned him Christmas eve to accompany his Majestye to his devotions. In his march to the closet he fell (I know not how) to go before, which was in effect behynde,[34] the lord treasurer, which I observing as a wrong to his condition and speaking of to my lord chamberlin and my lord of Holland, it was by theyr care reformed at his returne from chappel and place given him and his son next after his Majesty.

The 28 December: he having taken his leave of theyr majestyes, and rendered his final visits to all the lords that had [134] given him any, tooke his way of returne by land towards his imbarking at Dover, refusing the course usuall to Gravesend by barge in regard of the number of horses he had bought (being 44) and the conveniency of his own coach. He lodged the fyrst night at Dartford, the next at Rochester. Thither I attended him for the syght he was to have of the shipps, though this (fyrst offered by his Majesty) was after hardly yeelded to, upon the opposition of Mr. Secretary Cooke pretending the unfitness of it for a stranger, especially of France and of his eminent quality. Yet it was at last obteyned though wyth restriction by letter from the same secretary to the Masters there to suffer him to goe abord only the Prince, not to see the magazin, nor castell, nor to have any voly of shot given him, which

---

[34] To lower his rank in precedence.

was obeyed. My officious excuse for it was that, answerable to a general order (for which I sayd I had forgotten to move his Majestye for a particular dispensation), no ordinance was to be shot off from any of the kyngs ships lyeing in harber. He only passed by them all and entered only one, the Prince, as aforesayd.

[134ᵛ] Next morning, I there took leave of him to have him proceeding on his iourney with the attendance of the Marshall of the Ceremonies and returned my self to London, having bene presented by him with 200 french crownes[35] the night before his parting. He had wyth him two passes besydes that for his horses, one under the hand of fyve or six of the councell wherin they stiled him 'our very good lord', another under the hand of his majesty stiling him 'our brother.'

When this prince was upon his parting, his majesty intending him a present of a diamond ring valued at about 1500 £, some reasons of new setting it, (or rather of not in hand paying for it) kept it so long from the kyngs owne intended personal delyvery, as the duke necessarily parting (after a long intertaynment by delay) it was sent after to Rochester by my lord chamberlins secretary,[36] with strict command as from his lord as the kyngs pleasure, not to accept any offered gratification for it.

---

[35] Finet wrote in the margin that it equaled £60.
[36] Sir Edward Tavener.

[135] A maske under the title of '*Albion's Triumph*' prepared for Twelftnyght it was acted by the kyng and divers lords the Sunday after,[1] where to when I asked his majesty if any ambassadors could be invited, he breefly answered: 'No invitations.' So expecting what those ministers of princes would propound, I was only sent for by the French the day of the mask and by him demanded if I knew whether the ambassador of Savoy would be present at it. I, answering doubtfully, gave my opinion that, if he should come, I presumed he would have his place, after his wonted domesticall manner, uppermost on the ladyes syde at the left hand of the queene, which proved accordingly, he seating himself (wyth offer of taking a lower place) next above the duchess of Buckingham as the ambassadour of France did above the lords, both entering in several companyes an hour or two before the maske. The secretary of the Venetian sending to me for accomodation had a place in the seates ordeyned for the Gentlemen of the Privy Chamber.

[135ᵛ] An ambassador from Venice of the family of Gussoni[2] sent to reside here in place of Signor Giovanni Soranzo arrived at Gravesend the 12th of January. Whereof, I having receyved notice from the sayd Soranzo and preparing for his reception and my iourney thither, I was prevented by his privat repayre to London, as *sconosciuto*, with signification that wythout noyse he would returne back at Greenwiche, there to be fetched by me (for observation of dew ceremony whereon that nation so much stands) wyth the Kyngs barges, etc. For this I gave order accordingly and had my lord chamberlins allowance to the nomination of Edward lord Herbert for his reception at Tower Wharfe, the ambassador Soranzo standing in the mean tyme upon the choyce of a person of equal quality to that had bene formerly sent to receyve the French ambassadour which I found by my noates to have bene the Lord Gordon, a marquess son but intimated by me to be of the rank of one of our barons though preceeding the lord mentioned, so passed without exception. There were some dozen Gentlemen of the Privy Chamber listed for his company. When the day assigned I went in the Kyngs barge of twelve oars then newly made and fyrst imployed to Greenwiche, where were before

---

[1] Townsend's *Albion's Triumph* on Jan. 8th.

[2] Vicenzo Gussoni, ambassador (Jan. 1632 – May 1634) of Venice, continued to support friendship between England and France and promote aid to Sweden and the Dutch republic.

arrived the 2 ambassadors and theyr followers in two other barges by me appoynted for that service, there after dynner they returned to London. They landed at Tower wharfe were there receyved by the lord mentioned and came to theyr lodging at Charterhouse, where the wonted custome of preparing a supper was thriftily omitted.

[136ᵛ] From Monday the 23rd of January, the day of his coming to towne, to Sunday the 29th, the day assigned for his publick audience, there was no person of quality sent from the king, or in his name, to visit and welcome him though that complement myght have bene and perhaps was expected by him, as it had bene by some others at other tymes. He was brought to his publick audience of both the Kyng and Queen in the Presence (the Banketing House being then incumbered wyth scaffolds for the queenes mask[3] in preparation) by the earl of Warwick, wyth the attendance of some 12 Gentlemen of the Privy Chamber and others in about 20 coaches besydes the Kyngs and Queens. His predecessor Soranzo presented hym to the Kyng wyth a few wordes in French, he made a speech in Italian of length more than expected or was perhaps proper consisting of no busyness beyond complement, and after presented his letters. Then he addressed himself (with his colleague who also presented him with a fewe words in French) to the queen [137] to whom, speaking in Italian, he delyvered to her also letters from his Republick. The next day they both made visits to the Prince and Princess in theyr severall quarters at St. James.

Monsieur de Biscarat,[4] a gentleman of good quality sent to the kyng and queen, from the Queen Mother of France (then refuged to Brussels) about her repatriating wyth the kyng her son, had his despatch the 22 of January and should have been presented, as was his majestyes orders, with a diamond ring of 200 £ value but this not ready, *more nimis solito* at the instant of his parting, my opinion was followed to send Brisco, Marshall of the Ceremonyes, after him to Dover wyth my letters for excuse for that omission, and the ring delyvered and accepted with a most thankful acknowledgement and with offer of a liberal reward to the bringer but refused by him, as the Kyngs express order was it should be, in case there should be any thing offered by the gentleman. [137ᵛ] The Venetian ambassador Giovanni Soranzo was to take his leave at Whytehall on February 7 and to receyve the order of knighthood, as others of his predecessors had one before him, from the hand of his majesty. I, having before hand moved my lord chamberlin about it (as to

---

[3] Performance on Feb. 14th of Townsend's *Tempe Restored*: see III 138.

[4] The private secretary of Marie de Médicis, who sought in vain an invitation for her visit to England.

whome the carriage of a ceremony of that nature next properly belonged)
though the lord viscount of Dorchester, as principal secretary, had notice
already given him of it by the sayd ambassador, his majesty provided wyth
a sword by his syde for that purpose receyved the ambassadour in his Withdrawing Chamber. He entered in his cloak (a gowne, his usual garment at
audiences, being at that instant of his knyghting improper for him) and covered not, though invited to do it, a good tyme whyle he made his speeche to
the king, (as he that was then to receyve an honor as a dignified servant).
Tyll at last kneeling, he had the sword layd on his shoulder and imediately
given him by his Majestye together with the hangers, the gyrdle [138] having
bene before delyvered to me by Mr. Kircke, as Master of the Robes, and by
me to the ambassadour at his coming forth of the Withdrawing Chamber.
His Majestye sayd to him after he gave him his sworde:

'*Voyla que pour vous armer, je me suis desarmé,*' etc.

To a maske intitled *Tempe Restauratum* presented by the Queen and diverse
great ladyes at Shrovetyde, no ambassadour being invited, the French came
voluntarily and took his place uppermost of the lords as the Savoyard did of the
ladyes. The new Venetian ambassador Signor Gussoni, made a particular
request to my lord chamberlin (when his lordship one day rendered him a
visit at his house) for some place where he might sit and see the mask unseen,
in satisfaction whereof he had fyrst a roome assigned only for himself his
secretary and me in the box, as they call it, over the passage entry from the
privy gallery to the Banketting house [138ᵛ] but that place having bene of
custome formerly reserved for the Queens nurse and her company, his seating
there was upon better consideration thought unfitting, so a place almost under
it behind his Majestyes seat was barred and boorded up apart and reserved
for him. But the morning of the mask day, he writing to me in excuse of his
not coming by reason of some impediments as he termed them, I caused it
to be kept for the Spanish agent Señor Necolalde if he would think fitter to
accept of that place then of among the barons as had bene by me propounded.
But I two dayes before acquainting my lord chamberlin with his desires
and presuming he would continue them for a syght of that maske, had for
answer of his lordship that he might sit among the barons, if the King would
approve of it, which propounding to his Majestye (my lord chamberlin by)
I was answered that he had observed some agents of princes to have been
placed on the scaffolds, but that if I had precedents (as I said I had) for their
seating elsewhere I might use my discretion. [139] In conformity whereof
I gave that day a particular account to the agent of my proceeding and in-

timation, both to the lord chamberlin and to his majesty, for his placing among the barons, and was answered by him that having not since his arrival in England seen the queen, and being to see her wythin four or fyve days at an audience, which, he sayd, he had the day before demanded and was assigned him, he doubted whether it would be fitting for him to make his fyrst appearance in her sight at so publick an assemble. This doubt prevayled to keep him from coming at all, eyther to the seate appoynted him in publicke amongst the lords, or to the private appartment ordayned for the Venetian but not made use of, as is before mentioned.

Two dayes after, he had audience of the Kyng in the Stone Table chamber, an hour and a half together *clausis foribus et remotis arbitris,* all but my lord Cottington that served his majesty for interpreter,[5] whyle both the archduchess agent that came wyth him for that purpose and myself that introduced him, were, by his majestyes owne signified pleasure, for that tyme excluded. [139ᵛ] He had fyve or six dayes before demanded audience of the queen and had it assigned him for the Saturday following, but her majesty not pleased wyth his so long omission of that dew observance (then having passed seven monthes synce his fyrst arrival wythout any offer even made by him to performe it) it was thought fitt by her Majestye (as for a penance or correction of his er-rour) to remitt his audience if not to Newmarket (whither she was then upon removing) at least tyll Monday following. Then he was introduced by Sir Robert Ayton, secretary to her majesty, fetched by him from the Presence Chamber, to the Withdrawing Chamber and there, wyth the interpretation of the archduchess agent,[6] he presented his owne excuses of his so long for-bearance, the kyng his masters commands incharged (as he told me) in letters to him but wythout any letter formally wrytten to her Majestye.

It was discoursed of and censured by some for a solecisme in his condition of publick minister that he had not immediately upon his fyrst audience of the King eyther demanded an audience of the Queen or framed some fayne ex-cuse for default of it, that he came not imediately [140] from Spayne to Eng-land, but from Brussels, where he had receyved his charge wythout any command or direction to her majesty was no sufficient plea for him, but the hint I gave him for reparation, rather by some few sweetening wordes to acknowledge then by silence to iustify his error, salved all and brought him off with good countenance and glances of satisfaction from her Majestye.

---

[5] After Cottington's return from Spain, Necolalde was ordered to sound out Charles's in-tentions to pursue a "secret treaty" which would prepare a common attack on the Dutch.

[6] Henry Taylor.

[141ᵛ] The 7th of March, the abbot Scaglia, who had resided here about 6 months under title of ambassador extraordinary from the duke of Savoy, having before hand sent away his nephew the marquis of Valluse and part of his family (which late at night the better to avoyd notice and question went to Gravesend) left his own house wythout noyse, after he had promised so much and effected so litle in his negotiation,[7] and went wyth the agent of Spayne to his, in his coache to dyner, to bed that night to Greenwich, and thence to Margate (thence to take sea in a ship of his majestyes lying then in the Downes) for Dunkirk. This course was not intended by him, no more expected by others, tyll an emergent occasion forced him to yt thus. He had used meanes in France by some minister there of his master the duke of Savoy, who myght be thought perhaps to have given way to it for farther discovery of his doubted designes, to procure a pass from the kyng of France for his free passage through his kyngdome. [142] This pass was brought him to his house by the French ambassadors secretary, there read by him and the day of the month (when) formally sett downe wyth these limitations expressed in the sayd pass, that if after the recypt thereof he should stay above 15 dayes in England, eyght dayes in Paris and one in any other towne of the French kyngs dominions his pass should be to him *ipso facto* invalid and of no farther benefit. But it seemed that howsoever the ambassador accepted of the pass he meant not to put himself so limited upon the *casus* of makeing use of it. For eyght dayes after he took the course and way mentioned of his departure.

He left many men ill satisfyed after theyr hopes and trust given of his nobler proceeding, my self in particular who having wyth my best diligence and care performed for him the dutyes of my charge receyved not from him so much as one visit or thankes in acknowledgement.

[142ᵛ] About the same tyme came thither from the States one Monsieur Brassert, pensioner of Delft,[8] imployed wyth the opinion then of being an ambassador, but assured by herr Joachimi (the States ambassadour resident) that he was sent as a deputy for some not generall service. He had neyther reception at Gravesend nor my attendance, when in company of the States

---

7 Victor Amadeus, alarmed at French influence in Savoy and Mantua, instructed Scaglia to promote peace between Spain and the Dutch.

8 Gouvert Brassert, agent extraordinary, or Commissioner, of the Dutch Republic (March 1632 – July 1634), hoped to negotiate disputed fishing rights and conflicting claims of English trading companies.

ambassadour, he went for audience to his Majesty at Newmarket. Returned to London the kyng gave the same ambassador of the States (and wyth him the deputy mentioned) an audience in the Withdrawing Chamber at Whytehall where the deputy covered twyce in the presence of his majesty, as I was told he had done once in Newmarket, but whether out of forgetfulness or overweening (as supposing he myght performe all *pari passu* wyth the other a compleat ambassadour) I know not. Sure I am some of the lords passed theyr censure upon him, for his over forwardness and cheap carriage in the presence of his majesty, which he after reformed.

The resident of Spayne had audience the same day an hour after the States ambassador in the same room. Where it was supposed the kyng would not have given him with regard to the difference between an ambassador and an agent, this having had it wyth the same consideration some few dayes before in the Stone Table Chamber, but it was now wyth his majestyes pleasure otherwyse.

In April the agent of the king of Denmark, Mr. Wolfin, having taken leave of theyr majestyes, I moved my lord chamberlin and the Kyng about his present, which resolved by my rating according to precedent, obtayned it to be a chayne and medal of the valew of 210 £.

[143] St. Georges day approaching, I propounded to the French, Venetian and States ambassadours and to the newly come deputy of the latter, Monsieur Brassert, (of designe omitting the Spanish resident to avoyd punctilios) whether they would be present at the ceremony of the feast. Theyre answers were all doubtful with demand of some small tyme for consideration, after which sending to me theyr resolution and receyving from me an assignation for theyr repayr to court at half an hour past nyne, they then came. The French and Venetian fyrst together and after the States and the deputy, after a small tyme of repose in the Councell Chamber they were by me placed in the Kyngs chapel closet, thence conducted for syght of the procession [143ᵛ] to a scaffold purposely raysed for them at the end of the terras next the Great Chamber stayre head, and so back to the closet. The service finished I reconducted them to the Councell Chamber and about the midst of the kyngs dynner appointing my officer to observe the tyme of sending for the second course and to give me notice of yt, I brought them to the kyngs table, where after complement wyth his Majestye and that the heralds had proclaimed the kyngs title (the knights meal in the mean tyme all served in) they descended makeing theyr respectes, at theyr issuing out of the barrs placed to keep the pressing multitude, to the knyghts. They returned through the privy galeryes to theyr severall lodgings.

The Spanish resident had sent to me his servant the same morning for my advice how he myght see the ceremony wythout others notice. I propounded how it myght best be done for the syght of it in the chapel, by standing amongst the ladyes in the queens closet, the kyngs closet being to be possest by those whome I knew he would not myngle wyth, [144] but to stand un-seene and unnoted all the tyme, at his majestyes dynner I could not (I sayd) contrive any meanes. The roome being all open and in it not any corner for concealment. So, at this answer returned and left to his pleasure, his servant came agayne wythin an hour after, and told me his master was sorry he had not sent to me sooner and that, being yet scarce up and ready, he would not put me to the trouble for staying for him, etc.

BOOK IV

May 11, 1632 to November 23, 1637

[1] The 11th of May 1632, I had notice from the French ambassador ordinary, the Marquis of Fontenay, that Monsieur de St. Chaumont,[9] extraordinary from the king his master (who was then at Calais) was instantly to pass the seas hither. He arrived at Gravesend, the 17th of May, and wyth him 15 or 16 gentlemen his followers, whereof three bore the title of marquiss and one of count, the rest of his trayne being about 50. The next day, I repayred thither, with the ordinary ambassador mentioned, and the queens cheefe Almoner, to give him his welcome (they from themselves, I from his majesty) which I delyvered in these words:

> Monsieur, Le Roy mon maystre m'a faict l'honneur de me commander de vous venir le premier recevoir et donner de sa part la bienvenue en son Royaulme [1ᵛ] ou s'il a aulcune chose que vous puisse estre agreable vous en pouvre librement disposer, en particulier de mon persone qui n'attend aultre chose que l'honeur de vos commandements, aux quels ie ne manqueray pas de me porter avec toute obeissance.[10]

That night the ordinary ambassador and I returning wyth him to London, the next day the earl of Dover, chosen for this reception, went thither with the kyngs barge and four others and two light horsemen for his company with the attendance of 8 or 9 Gentlemen of the Privy Chamber to fetch him to his lodging in Westminster, but landing at Dorset House (the residence of the ordinary ambassador) he was by him receyved on the landing stayre and for that night made his guest, the rest of the company parting after supper to theyr own appointed lodgings. The morning after his arrival he sent to me to procure audience of his majesty for the day following (his occasions, he sayd pressing him) whych I obtayned and appointed [2] for his transport to

---

[9] Melchior Mitte de Miolans, marquis de Saint-Chaumont, ambassador extraordinary (May 1632), publicly presented Louis' compliments from the port of Calais, "when he is so near." Privately, he protested any English favor to Marie de Médicis and defended French hostility toward Lorraine.

[10] "Sir, The king my master has honored me with a command to come as the first to receive you and to give on his behalf the kingdom's welcome, whereby you are to command freely anything that might be to your pleasure, especially of myself who awaits nothing else but the honor of your command, to which I shall not fail to devote myself with total obedience." This typical speach is repeated with slight variations elsewhere in the note books.

Greenwich 7 barges, wherein went for his conduct the earl of Barkshire (of a somewhat preceeding condition to the former both as the ancienter earle and as knyght of the Garter) and wyth him my lord Howard, Sir William Howard, his brother, and about a dozen Gentlemen of the Privy Chamber. He landed at the ordinary stayr entred the court by the great gate, rested awhyle in the Councell Chamber and had his audience of both kyng and queen together in the Presence. Mr. Secretary Cook being there ready at hand for interpretation, if the king had been pleased to call him to it, but his Majestye spared the costome (used since the end of our warr with France) of speaking to the ambassador in his first audience in English made use of his French to answer him.

The audience passed I presented to the Queen the ambassadors desire of seeing the prince, then but newly brought thither from St. James. This permitted, the ambassador fyrst retyring a whyle to the Councell Chamber and thence passing back up the great stayres, [2ᵛ] he went through the queens Gard Chamber the Presence and Privy Chamber into the privy galleryes where he had there a second sight of theyr Majestyes and wyth them the Prince. He returned by barge, landed at Tower wharfe (the tyde not serving to shoot the bridge) found there by my order the Kyngs and Queens coaches and the Venetians and the States ambassadour with half a score other lords, for his passage through London to his lodging at Sir Abraham Williams in the pallace court at Westminster, in whose house was provided for him all fytting furniture, the Kyngs owne bed and three or four and thirty others, suting the qualityes of those of his company, besydes other beds in neyghbours houses. All these were defrayed by the Kyng but not dyet at all allowed him.

[3ᵛ] He went almost every day to Greenwich in the Kyngs coache, entered domestically wyth his colleague by the privy garden stayre leading up to the privy gallery, and passed the tyme in generall discourse wyth theyr majestyes, never offering nor invited to be covered.

When his tyme of parting (much pressed by him) was come on Tuesday the 29 of May he took his leave but wyth avoydance of publick ceremony by me offered him, beyond what Monsieur de Chasteauneuf had done before. For since he had the honour of a domestick access to theyr majestyes since the tyme of his fyrst public audience, he should [4] be ambitious to preserve it to the last and not to take leave with the ceremony of a stranger when theyr Majestyes so neer allyance to the kyng his master made him none. So as saving that ordinary trouble of imploying a lord or any of the lords coaches for his last conduction, he went wyth only the kyngs coache and the ordinary ambassadours to Greenwich, where entring the court privately as before he took leave in the queens privy gallery (diverse great ladyes and lords being there present prepared for a publick audience in case it should have been requyred) and that night returning to London, went the next morning in the kyngs barge (three others and two light horsemen for his baggage and meaner sort of followers) to Gravesend. That night he went by post horses to Rochester saw there (by permission from his Majestye with some difficulty obtayned) the ships, particularly that named the Prince, and had a voly given out of her 25 peeces of ordinance. The next morning he posted towards Dover [4ᵛ] and gave me at his parting by the hand of his not over faythful steward 60 double pistolls and fyve peeces. The pistolls being lyght and over-valued, as they went in France for 16 s. 6 d. the pistolls, this yeelded in all but 45 £.

[5ᵛ] The ambassador of the States having an audience assigned him at Greenwich the 12th of June and with him the deputy, Monsieur Brassert, I observed that the kyng at the fyrst presentation of theyr business, after he had saluted them, putting on his hat, invited the ambassador to cover, which he civilly excepted, his Majestye put on againe and intertayned them, all the tyme of theyr audience, bareheaded. This was judged done of purpose for prevention that the deputy myght not cover if the ambassadour should. The sayd deputy had over done in that poynt when he (together with the ambassador) had his fyrst access to the Kyng at Newmarket and once after in London, since being not qualifyed as joynt and full comissioner wyth the other but deputy only for some particular affayr (not relating to the generall state of the United Provinces) he ought not to cover in his majestyes presence, howsoever he had formerly once or twice done it as an act of presumption which the Kyng himselfe, as I was told by Mr. Secretary Cooke, found falt with and spake of to the Secretary, for knowledge of the ambassador and by him intimated, as it was, to the deputy.

[7] Expecting the arrival of an ambassador, or rather deputy,[11] from Hamburg sent wyth complaynt agaynst a Scottish man that having (upon pretence of wrongs receyved from that state at sea) obtayned letters of reprisal and by their virtue repayed himself in an iniust measure, news was brought me the 26th of June that he was come under title of deputy though stiled by his followers ambassador. Immediately upon his arrival he repayred to the principal secretary, Sir John Cook, with his letters of credence and, according

---

[11] Berthold Müller, agent (June 1632 – Jan. 1633) of the Hansa. He requested Charles to withdraw recent letters of reprisal granted merchants in Scotland. The Eastland Company sought closer ties with the Hansa out of resentment at the high tolls demanded by Denmark in the Baltic.

to the receyved custome of his nation, presented them to him fyrst to be after seen by his majesty, or his councell, before his fyrst audience, as others sent from that city had preposterously done before him. But Mr. Secretary, seeing theyr direction to be immediately to his majesty, returned them to this deputy saying it was not for him, but for the kyng his master to have theyr fyrst sight and opening. So he had at Greenwiche the 3rd of July in the Wythdrawing Chamber delyvering his errant in a long formall speeche in French, [7ᵛ] having bene prepared to make it in latin but upon my resolution to his demand, in which language he might properly deliver his busyness, he made use of French because he might be assured (I sayd) that so doing he should receyve his answer from his Majestyes owne mouth in the same language which in latine would be retourned to him by an interpreter.

[10ᵛ] About the beginning of October parted hence a gentleman (his name de Bonport) that had bene sent to theyr majestyes from the duke and duchess of Savoy (this the Queens sister) wyth the news of a prince[12] borne to that succession. (At the same tyme came another gentleman[13] from the Queen Mother of France, an Italian, Signor Fabroni).

I was out of towne at the tyme of his departure when a diamond ring of about 500 £ valew being sent to him as a present from his Majesty it came to the hands (from my lord chamberlins secretary) of one Mr. Woodward, a gentleman that, wyth my assent, had obtayned a grant under the privy seale for service in my place[14] (as a substitute) when I could not be present. He presenting the ring to the gentleman was gratifyed by him with a ring of 9 small diamonds worth about 10 poundes, which after some refusal (as he told me) accepting to my use (as his own condition under his hand given to me in wryting tyed him to, in case any presents should be offered him for service in my absence) he after brought it to me and in compensation of his real proceeding, answerable to his word and obligation to that purpose, I presented him wyth a payre of sylk stockings, garters and shoes.

[11] The lord maiors[15] feast drawing neer, and I knowing that, of custome, all ambassadours and agents here residing were to be invited to it, suspected that out of forgetfulness, neglect or national popular spleene, the agents of the kyng of Spayne, and the archduchess, might be perhaps omitted, so repayred to one of the sheriffs and wyth him to the other and wyth both to the lord

---

[12] Bouvier de Bonport, courier, with news of the birth of the first child, Francis Hyacinth.
[13] Luca Fabronne d'Assigny brought another appeal from Marie de Médicis for an invitation to England; he was also suspected of intrigues with the anti-Richelieu faction at court.
[14] Roland Woodward, "Officer of Assistance."
[15] Sir Nicholas Raynton.

maior and intimateing the fytness of the invitation, his lordship at fyrst made scruple of it, as an innovation, no such persons as these agents, he sayd, appearing upon his list to have been in former tymes invited, but I possessing him (among other reasons) wyth that of the exception that myght be iustly taken by the sayd agents (and perhaps by some great ones at court) for such omission, or rather exclusion, and takeing on me the prevention of all disturbance (feared by his lordship to grow from theyr incounter wyth some other ambassadours (as the States) invited) went that evening to the two agents to let them know of the lord maiors intention, the next day to invite them and receyved from them an acknowledgement of the honour, therby, done them (but with excuse and desyre from the agent of Spayne for his absence, which [11ᵛ] was the marcke aymed at) in regard of an indisposition pretended, and from the agent of the archduchess the like pleading the unfitness of this appeareance at an affayr so publick wythout the others company. So signifying theyr answere that nyght by my letter to the sherifs they were the next morning by them both personally and formally invited, and theyr appearances, as formally excused, to all partyes satisfaction.

At this feast I mett two young princes who arriving in England about fyve weeks before and concealing (as much as they could) theyr quality went obscurely to the Kyng at Newmarket wyth no great notice taken of them as it seemed they affected. They stiled themselves in latin thus *Georgius et Ludovicus, Duces Silesiae, Ligniensis et Bregensis.*[16] They were invited to the feast but being come were litle looked on, through fault of theyr conductors, tyll I fynding them there alone (theyr Governour and followers being excluded the roome where they were to dyne), I took care of them made them knowne to some of the great lordes of the councell and got them places on the bench syde next beneath the lord keeper [12] above whome sat the ambassador of the States.

The French ambassador having bene invited, excused his coming because of the mourning habit he had a few dayes before put on for the death of his mother. The Venetian came and had his place, but having made provision for his stand in Cheapside there to see the solemnity of the lord maiors passage, I took hym after dynner to my care and brought him unknowne (with his secretary only) to a chamber, which I had bespoken for the deputy of Hambrow, whom I had acquaynted before hand wyth my intention (as I had also the Venetian ambassador wyth the deputyes) to visit him at his house, after he had made his visit (which he had tyll then deferred) to the French ambassador.

---

[16] George and Louis, dukes of Liegnitz and Brieg, in Silesia.

So, as all solecisme, or subiect of exception, prevented by my caution, they inioyed one another two or three hours together, and had conference.

[12ᵛ] About the beginning of November, John Beaucler, a French gentleman (one of the band of Pensioners to his majesty and formerly, a long tyme together, servant to king James) being accused of an attempt at rape and murther upon a young wenche, who (instigated by one or two malicious persons) had taken it upon her death (which another sicknes after brought her) that the blowes he had given her had kylled her, was to be arrayned for yt at the Kyngs Benche bar. This, because the Frenche ambassador, Monsieur de Fontenay, was according to our lawes, personally to appear *ad testificandum* that the sayd Beaucler was present in his house, at the same tyme and instant, wherein he was charged to have committed the fact, there grew a difficulty to be reconciled in poynt of ceremony: whether a kyngs representatnt could be personally present in another kyngs court of justice, though sytting there in a chayre (as was offered him) in a second place inferior to the judges, wythout preiudice to the kyng his master. This stood upon by the sayd ambassador (requested by him) I acquaynted not only the lord Cheefe Justice of the Kynges Benche,[17] but the king him self also, with his desyre and proposition, which was that his oath, or affirmation, myght be personally taken by the lord Cheef Justice *in transitu*, as he should pass through Westminster Hall to the place of iudicature, or by one of the inferior judges (sent to the ambassador in some appoynted chamber neer it). But these offers not admitted (as agaynst the course of the court) which the judges affirmed was punctually to be observed, and the testimony to be given there in hearing of the jury, it was at last ordered by the judges (upon the kyngs pleasure signified to them in favour of the ambassador) that he should, in my sight and presence sett downe in wryting under his hand (upon his honour and the true fayth of a Christian) so much as he knew of the busyness. This produced, read and sworne to by me in court that I had seene him signe yt, should be accepted for a sufficient testimony. This performed accordingly, and other testimonyes of a gentleman, a coachman, and a footman of the ambassadors family, taken wyth it, proved a principal meanes to save the lyfe of a gentleman that was lyke, otherwyse, to have lost it.

[14] His majesty having bene sick of the small pox, and passed that danger, the ambassadors here resyding sent to me severally for knowledge of the first convenient tyme, wherein they might present their congragulations for his recovery. The ambassador of the States first moved for it and had his

---

17 Sir Thomas Richardson, chief justice of the King's Bench.

assignation for Tuesday the 18th of December, but I intimateing so much to the French ambassador, he sent by me a request to my lord chamberlin that he might (with regard to his preceding ranck) be first admitted to that honour. This assented to by his majesty, I introduced him by the way of the garden, because, though he were at other tymes domestically admitted, wythout demand of audience, a more punctuall proceeding was now requisite, to his Majestye in his Withdrawing Chamber. There he covered not at all though invited to it, wyth consideration, it myght seeme, that the work he had in hand was his own wythout order from the kyng his master. This performed he went with my attendance to the queen, wyth whome I left him to returne for introduction of the States ambassador who [14ᵛ] (together with the deputy Brassert) discharged the lyke part without once offering to be covered.

The same day the Spanish resident sent to me to the same purpose as the other but I thought fitt for avoydance of over much trouble to his Majestye to move for him for the next day after, which was granted.

The day following the Venetian ambassadour had the lyke congragulatory audience of the Kyng but of a mixture wyth busyness as he himself professed to me and had therefore delayed, he sayd, the demand of yt for a day or two with respect to the reiterated trouble he might bring to his Majestye so immediatly after his recovery. I observed that he stood bare (though invited to cover) tyll he had finished his complement when entring his busyness and reinvited by his Majesty, he put on.

[15] The 27 January, Heer Joachimi, ambassador resident for the States, took his leave of both theyr majestyes in theyr several withdrawing chambers, but with intention to return, so neither had, nor gave any present at his parting from his majesty, or to me. The deputy, Heer Brassert that accompanyed him, remayned here for agent for those States after him.[1]

[15ᵛ] After the deputy of Hamburg[2] had passed here about eyght months in soliciting his busynes with the Scottish, as those that had in it the greatest interest, and for this indeavour to delay his despatch, had purposely sent a messenger into Scotland, with the kings letters and pleasure to that purpose, he took his leave (as assured of the uttmost he could expect) of his majesty in his withdrawing chamber, with my attendance thither by way of the garden, and privy gallerys and without other coaches and company than his owne and mine, and some 2 or 3 merchants trading with that city. His present was ordayned after the proportion of his predecessors, a chayn of gold and a medal of 210 £. He gave to the officer that brought it 8 £, and to the servant, 1 £. Visiting me at my house for my last farewell, he presented me in a fayr wrought purse with 55 poundes, and gave to my officer Brisco, 15 peeces.

[16ᵛ] The king of Poland, Ladislaus,[3] being, after Sigismund his fathers death, elected to that crown, which Christopher Radzivil, duke of Birze (opposing the Jesuited party that would have preferred the younger brother) was a chief meanes to sett on his head, the sayd dukes son Janush Radzivil, a youth of about 20 yeares of age, (by commission sent out of Poland to him then studying at Leyden in Holland, designed ambassador fyrst to the States of the United Provinces, next to the Archduchess at Brussells and finally hither to England) whither this young prince (so stiled as being by descent prince of the Empire) sent a gentlemen wyth letters to my lord chamberlin from Brussels where he then was, wyth signification of his employment. Some few dayes after he arrived at Gravesend where I receyved him there the 3rd of February and brought him the next day wyth 3 barges and one greater

---

[1] Gouvert Brassert was agent in the absence of Joachimi until Dec. 1633.

[2] Berthold Müller for the Hansa: see IV 7.

[3] After the death of Sigismund in April 1632, his son Vladislav IV was elected in Nov. 1632 by the Diet with various factions, including the Pope and the Habsburg court, in support. His brother, John Casimir II, succeeded in Jan. 1649.

boate for his baggage and inferior followers to Greenwiche. There met with the Kyngs barge and one other by the earl of Warwick,[4] together wyth his son the lord Riche,[5] the earl Binney[6] of Scotland, the lord Paget,[7] and half a score Gentlemen [17] of his majestyes Privy Chamber, he there upon the water entered the kyngs barge and landing at Westminster bridge was (wyth two coaches that accompanyed him and some others) taken into the Kings coache, the queens and half a dozen more, that purposely there attended him, to bring him to his prepared lodging at Sir Abraham Williams in the palace yard. He there that evening began to be intertayned at the kyngs charge for his diet, ordayned and so signified by me for 8 dayes, at the allowance of about 25 £ *per diem* the provisions to be served in dayly by peeces in specie by the Kyngs clerk of the kitchin.

His majesty was pleased, upon expression of the ambassadors disposition to it, to give him so speedy an audience as the next day in the Banketing House. There entering (he and all in mourning habits, as for an account of his masters death) conducted by the earl of Lindsey, lord high chamberlin of England (which office his father bore title of in Lithuania). [17ᵛ] According to the directions I had given him, and he requested, in manner and forme for his approaches, as his predecessor Rakovski here receyved before him, he presented himself and his errand with a long speech in latine, and delivered his letters of credence, had answer from his majesty, by Mr. Secretary Cook in the same language, and performed the like with the queen (her majestyes secretary being interpreter). He covered not, though invited to it by the king, at his coming extraordinary.

I had propounded to my lord chamberlin the fitnes, and wythall the ambassadors disposition, to see the dancing for that evening appointed. To this I had so prepared him before hand, by my intimation of other ambassadors cariage in the lyke occasion, for his seat, as a private person, amongst the ladyes, as he refused not to take it there betweene the duchess of Buckingham beneath, and his conductor the lord of Lindsey above him, not covering but only once, for a small tyme, as if by that he would show the right of his quality.

He was immediately after his audience brought back to the Counsell Chamber thence (with the kyngs pleasure prepared and signified to me) to the privy gallerys and thence into the queens Withdrawing chamber [18] where passed some discourse between the king and him in Frenche, so to the hall

---

4 Robert Rich, 2nd earl of Warwick.
5 Robert Rich, 5th baron Rich.
6 Thomas Hamilton, lord Binning and Byres.
7 William Paget, 6th lord Paget.

to see the dancing and thence, before supper, to his lodging. The next day, letting me know that, having letters to delyver from the queen of Bohemia to the king, and holding it improper (he sayd) to mix other occasions wyth those of the king his master, at the time of his first audience, he desired, and had, the thyrd day after, a privat access in his majestyes withdrawing chamber. His passages to court and elsewhere were with the kyngs coach assigned for his dayly use, as were also two others, by order of my lord chamberlin, to be hyred by me for his followers.

[19ᵛ] His audience of both theyr majestyes for his dismission was appointed for the 12 of February. He was brought, in place and manner as at his fyrst audience, by the earl of Holland, captayne of his majestyes gard, accompanyed with the earles of Stamford and Newport, the lord Bruce,[8] and others for his dismission. My lord of Holland reconducting him to the Counsell Chamber, retyred thence to his owne, whyle the ambassador returning a visit (as was before ordered) to my lord chamberlin, gave one after to the other lord, and was reaccompanyed to his lodging. The day that I had intimated what was incharged to me for the ceasing of his diets defraying, he acquainted me with his desire to dine one day with the lord maior, that he might there see the entertaynment which he had heard, he sayd, Rakowsky [20] had so much extolled for the manner of it, at his returne to Poland. I told him his excellency must be then pleased, as Rakowsky was, to lay a syde all punctuality of precedence, which assuring me he would as a thing he sayd was in reason not to be stood upon with a magistrat that was but annual, etc. I sent my officer for that purpose to my lord maior[9] on the Tuesday to let his lordship know the ambassadours intention to be wythe him at dinner the Thursday following. His answer was free and with assurance of welcome which he the next day confirmed by two of his officers sent to the house of the ambassadour formally to invite him. So on Thursday morning I conducted him fyrst to the Tower for sight of what was theyr workes, which was performed with the company of the lieutenant of the Tower[10] and the attendance of 3 or 4 hundred pikes and shot, from his fyrst entrance tyll his parting on Tower hill, but his close fisted steward gave ill satisfaction both to those soldyers and to the severall officers of the magazins of armes, wardrobe, etc. not bestowing on any of them one penny for drinking money. Thence going and the lieutenant with him to the lord maiors, he had there a dinner made him for [20ᵛ] meat and manner beyond any that I had seene before at that table.

[8] Thomas Bruce, 3rd lord Bruce of Kinloss.
[9] Sir Nicholas Raynton.
[10] Sir William Balfour.

The visits he gave and had during the tyme of his stay here were these. To the archbishop of Canterbury he gave the fyrst visit and one after to the Lord Treasurer, which later he a while made scruple of as derogating from his quality and against, he sayd, his countryes cutome, tyll I had assured him by the example of sundry ambassadors here and of the duke of Buckingham and the earl of Holland in France that it was here, as there, the custome (regarding the place and multiplicity of affayres of such persons) that he should be fyrst visited. He made offer also to visit fyrst the bishop of London (Dr. Laud), but, I acquainting him with the ambassadors intention, he desyred for good reason, he sayd, to be spared that honour and kept from the envys that might perhaps follow it. Other lords that visited him and had theyr visits returned were the lord chamberlin, the lord high chamberlin, the lord Marshall, the earles of Holland and Carlisle.

[21] He invited himself one night after supper to a play at the Cockpit[11] where he sat among the ladyes covered after the kyng had by the lord chamberlin sent to him and the other lords to do so.

The desyre I had and shall have ever to preserve friendly correspondence between ministers of princes moved me one day to repayre to the Spanish resident, don Nicolaldi, to sound his intention for his visit of this ambassadour, which though he fell upon some exceptions of the rude cariage (as he called it) of Rakowsky towards him, he added that all ambassadors were not of one mould and therefore told me he would not fayle a day or two after to send to him to that purpose. But the fyrst and last I heard of him was a message brought me by his servant that excused his not coming by reason of some indisposition. After he told me himself that he abstayned to visit him in regard he was of a different religion to the king his master, whether this were a reason just and proper,[12] query.

The deputy of the States visited him and had his returne of it by the ambassadours follower but not him personnally. The French and Venetian performed and were returned all visits as amongst ambassadours accustomed.

[22] The 16 of February the baron of Oxensterne, son to the deceased king of Swedens famous chancelor of that name,[13] coming from France to see England and in his company 6 or 7 gentlemen whereof one was nephew to the famous soldier Gustavus Horne, my lord Marquis Hamilton out of his thankful memory and regard to the respectes he had receyved in Germany from

[11] Play unidentified, performance unknown.

[12] This Radziwill family was Lutheran. Possibly the real reason was the different precedence to be given to him, because of his rank as agent (or resident).

[13] Henry, son of Axel Oxenstierna.

that king and chancelor, went the fyrst night of his arrival to visit him at his
lodging and the next day brought him to the presence of his Majestye. He
sent the Kings coache (but with an errour of forgetfulnesse not to make known
to him, as I sayd soone after, that it was *traict d'office* as he was Master of his
majestyes horses and not a dew of his quality) to bring him to the court.
There he had access to the Queen in her Withdrawing Chamber and after was
present at playes and dancing[14] but always bareheaded there in the presence of
theyr Majestyes, as were also all the lords for his cause and company, in regard
of his quality of being but the son of a baron would not give him that privilege.
He was entertayned whyle he was here at the tables of my lord Hamilton,
[22ᵛ] the lord chamberlin, lord Carlisle, the treasurer, the controller and others
but not from any solemn invitation thoughe with fare that myght have well
afforded it.

He one day had a barge appoynted him by the Kyngs order for the cariage
of him and his when his Majestye went to see his two new built ships that
lay at Wollege, and were then to fall downe to Chatham. At his returne he
was called into the Kyngs owne barge leaving his company in the other.

The 5th of March he was present at a mask of the Queens at Somerset
house,[15] placed by the Kyng himself amongst the great lords and his 6 gentlemen, Gustavus Horne, et al. that accompanyed him, were placed lykewyse,
by his Majestyes owne appoyntment upon a seate above, behind his Majestye.
After he had bene here about 18 dayes he made a iourney for the sight of
Cambridge and then cross the country to Oxford, returning by Windsor and
Hampton court, I not accompanying him (or offering it) because he was no
publick minister. This iourney he professed to have passed wythe muche
satisfaction to him from his reception at both the universityes with scholastick
exercises and orations, etc. especially at Cambridge [23] where he was made
Master of Arts and had the power given him of makeing others besydes those
gentlemen of his company.

After fyve or six dayes more of stay here he departed for France wythout
any present to him from his Majestye or any from him to other as on neyther
hand to be expected, he being no publick minister though his respects were
after that stile and that he had bene visited at his lodging by the duke of
Lenox, the Marquess Hamilton, the earle of Pembroke, Holland Warwicke
and others of the best quality.

Whyle he remained here, the French ambassador one day sent to me and
for me to recommend to my conduction, a French gentlemen, one Monsieur de

---

[14] Plays unidentified, performances unknown.
[15] Play unidentified.

Mouselin imployed from the kyng his master, wyth congragulation for his majestyes recovering from his sicknes.[16] The day after his arrival, the ambassador (wyth my attendance) accompanied him to the audience he had of bothe theyr Majestyes severally in theyr Wythdrawing Chambers. Three or four dayes after he was present at a maske sett forth by the Queen and her ladyes at Somerset house.[17] [23 ᵛ] Soone after hastening his despatch, and having receyved answere from his majesty to his letters, I caryed to him from the kyng for a present a diamond ring (rather under than over valewed at 400 £) which he receyved as a marck of especiall honour to him from his Majestye. He professed, wyth all, his particular obligation to me for my paynes which (not wyth standing my excuses for the ease of his paynes) he swore he would not fayll the next day to come to acknowledg and gratify at myne owne house, but neyther coming nor sending to me all, he two dayes after unthankfully (not unlyke others of his nation) departed.

The French ambassador and his family having kept theyr Lent, according to the reformed stile, and our Lent[18] that year falling out fyve weekes after theyrs, he requested me to procure him a licence from my lord maior for his owne bucher and poultrer to buy flesh for him. Herewyth acquainting my lord chamberlin I had his opinion that it would more fitly come from the lords of the councell then from the lord mayor [24] as an acte that concerned a publick minister. Answerable to this advice, I procured one from their lordships, but wyth a restriction in express words that his bucher and poultrer should not utter any flesh to any others then to the ambassador, upon penalty etc.

A gentleman,[19] one Monsieur Colb, at the same tyme arriving here (March 17) from the Duke of Simeren[20] (administrator to the young prince palatine), not qualifying himself ambassadour that he might negotiate with the less noyse, charge and notice, desyred lykewyse the liberty of eating flesche and had it, but by a more silent way (for which I moved) under the hand of Sir John Cook, principal secretary, wyth allowance to the master of the house (where he lodged) being a cook to dress it only for him and his own company. He had his audience at such times as he demanded them (all except the fyrst to which I brought him through the garden and privy galleryes) by the

---

[16] The actual mission concerned the recent arrests of both Chateauneuf and of Rochechuart (see III 110) with charges of a conspiracy with Gaston, brother of Louis XIII.

[17] The same play of March 5th.

[18] Easter for the Catholic embassies was March 27th, for the English court April 21st.

[19] Joannes Casimir Kolb, merchant. He negotiated money to support Charles's nephew, Charles Louis, after the death of his father in 1632.

[20] Louis Philip, duke of Simmern, brother of the deceased count Palatine Frederick V.

way of the Privy Chamber *a la domestique*, regarding his imployment from a prince so neer in blood to the kyng as the young prince palatine. I procured him upon my motion intimateing those respectes a present of a chayne of gold of 250 £ for which I had from him much verbal acknowledgement, not real, answerable to the misery of the tyme and his fortune.

[24ᵛ] The Marquis de Fontenay having resided ambassadour here for the French king full three years tyme of imployment here had a publick audience the fyft of May at Whytehall in the Presence Chamber. For his conduction to it the earl of Barkshyre was appointed, as corresponding with the earl of Rutland, who being a knight of the Garter, and having introduced him to his fyrst audience after his arrival here, anno 1630, a person of lyke dignity was now requisite. But my lord of Barkshyre waving the service, I three or four tymes passing between him and the lord chamberlin before I could obtayne his assent for performance of it, he at last sayd he would acquaint the Kyng with his reasons and doubted not but they would be accepted, but these not prevayling, in regard there was not then in towne any other knight of the Garter, which was not wythall a privy councelor (and to have made choyce of such a one being both myght be a precedent of future inconvenience when other kings ambassadors might expect the like hereafter) he finally took on himself to discharge the service. He fetched him from his house to court with the attendance of half a score coaches besydes the Kyngs and Queens and so many gentlemen of the Privy Chamber, [25] my lord Weston (being returned a litle before ambassadour extraordinary out of France) went to have accompanyed him also but meeting him on the way he tourned back and following him entered the court and the Presence with him. The Kyng had before signifyed to me his pleasure that the Queen should have then also bene present, that being his last and parting audience, but the ambassadour apprehending perhaps that some countenance of disgrace or after neglect (if not affront) myght be in public cast upon him by the queen, who ever since the difference[21] between him and the chevalier du Jars had afforded him but cold respects, he intreated me to intimate to the kyng, as from himself, how troublesome it would be to her majesty, for his cause, to appear fyrst in publick and after to give him a privat access for the taking of his leave (a favour that he sayd he would beg of her) after the kyng should be gone on his iourney to Scotland. This sute easily obtayned, he and his lady took theyr leaves of the Queen without noyse or notice the same nyght that her Majestye parted from the Kyng at Theobalds and lay at Somerset house to go the next day to Greenwich. He went downe to Gravesend by water (May 20)

---

[21] Henrietta demanded his release from prison.

[25ᵛ] without my attendance (offered but not accepted by him). The evening before his departure he was presented from his majesty[22] by the officers of the Jewell House with 2000 onces of fayre gylt plate.

[26] The 27 of May arrived here the prince of Chimey, and his brother the count of Beaumont, with him,[23] aged that 15, this 14 yeares. Theyr trayne consisted of 8 or 10 gentlemen and six or seven and twenty other servants. They came to theyr lodging (provided at theyr owne charge) at Sir Abraham Williams house at Westminster without other ceremony of reception then of my incounter at theyr landing at Kyngs bridge. Three dayes after they had access to the Queen at Greenwiche conducted thither [26ᵛ] by me in the Kyngs barge and two others and rested in the councell chamber there tyll the earl of Barkshyre (who made offer of his service when I moved her majesty to make choyce of a lord for that purpose) fetched them to her Majestye in the privy gallery.

[31ᵛ] August the 27th: The Prince of Chimey and his brother expecting dayly theyr revocation from theyr unckle, the duke of Arscot, and apprehending it myght sodaynly come when the King should be further absent in his progress, they went to the court at Oatlands where in the Withdrawing Chamber on the Kyngs syde, and in the Privy Chamber on the Queens, they took leave of theyr Majestyes. Having passed theyr tyme in England and Scotland they went the 31 of August. They parted to returne to Brussels (though they had obtayned a *saufconduit* from the States to pass through the low countryes) the prince of Orange was newly entered their country with a great army. I offered them the use of the Kyngs barge to cary them to Gravesend but excusing the use of it they took post in Southwark to ryde to Dover whither they had a day or two before sent theyr baggage and meaner sort of followers and where they were to imbark in one of the Kyngs shipps by the favour of his Majestye upon my motion and answerable to the Councells letters directed to the Admiral of the Narrow Seas, Captaine Pennington. They gave to my officer Brisco — 10 £, to my servants 2 £, and to my self a purse withe 50 £.

[32] Towards the end of August came hither (at the fyrst without notice given or taken) a gentleman[24] of a noble house of Denmark, of the name of Ranzau, sayd to have estate in yearly revenue of 30000 £. After a few dayes

---

[22] In the margin he added: "a gold chain, worth 100 £, was given to M. Boutard, as secretary." See also IV 37ᵛ–38ᵛ.

[23] Albert of Arenberg, 2nd prince of Chimey, and Philip, count of Beaumont, who succeeded to his brother's title later.

[24] Possibly lord of Rantzau-Hohenfeld (?).

he presented himself to the earl of Holland for introduction to the presence of theyr Majestyes (whereto I accompanyed him) and soone after, the 21 of September, he departed giving me at his parting a small diamond ring of some 16 £ valew.

[32ᵛ] The Queen being brought to bed of a son on the 14th of October on Monday about 3 quarters after eleven at nyght,[25] the ambassadour of Venice and the deputy of the States of the United Provinces sent to me the next morning for knowledge of the fittest tyme to send or bring theyr congragulations to his Majestye, for which purpose his majesty (takeing notice of theyr respectes) assigned them Sunday following when at two of the clock they performed that complement, one after the other according to theyr rancks, in the Kyngs Withdrawing Chamber of Whytehal.

The Spanish resident (whether out of cunning to precede the States deputy or, by accident, I know not) having fyrst lett me know that to avoyd the incounter of the other two ministers he would demand access a day or two after them (as if interposition of tyme would lessen the advantage of place) sent to me three dayes before that daye of assignation to let me know he had for the next day obtayned the grant of an audience of the Kyng by the mediation of Mr. Secretary Windebank, whereat was to be present by appointment (as his servant sayd) as interpreter my lord Cottington. This was accordingly performed and the congragulatory complement with it. I had about this tyme given a touch to the agent of the Archduchess concerning the pretention of the States deputy to precede the resident of Spayne in his audiences whensoever they should at or about the same tyme incounter. [33] To which returning a scornful regard, he sayd the resident and himself were so far from appearing in competition wyth the States deputy as he and the resident had order (and would punctually observe it) from Spayne not to quit the place or acknowledge the precedence as a dewe even to the Venetian, though an ambassador and he intitled but a resident, but in all concurrences where any such should happen, he must and would preceed wyth him *del pare* and would neyther give, nor returne, other title than what he should give to him, etc.

One day invited to dyne wyth the Venetian ambassador Gussoni, he let me know he was preparing to retourne and had not forgotten, he sayd, an ejaculation of myne about the tyme of his arrival how, when I told him that some of our great lords had taken exception to the course of late years observed in the succesion and imployment of three or four ambassadors from Venice hither that they had bene sent fyrst to the low countryes, then to England and hence to France, whereby they seemed to conclude and give the

[25] James, duke of York.

precedence to the French king before ours. This, he sayd, he had particularly intimated to the reipublick and had so far forth procured an expression of theyr intentions (never yet he sayd formally declared for eyther of the three kyngdoms, England, France and Spayne before other) as that they had now purposely designated theyr ambassador, Contarini, (at that instant residing in the [33ᵛ] low countryes) for a remove not hither, but to France, and himself to returne imediately home (as he affected and had made it his sute in regard of some pressing occasions that recalled him), another ambassador[26] being to come directly from Venice thither without any stay in the low countryes which he sayd would give us satisfaction.

Towards the tyme of the Lord Maiors feast[27] I sounded the dispositions of the Spanish resident and archduchesses agent to be at it and found them averse in regard of the Venetians and States ministers unquestioned appearance there, yet procured them a formal invitation which I knew would not be (beyond wordes) accepted, neyther was it. The Venetian in the meane tyme (whome I accompanied) and the States deputy not fayling to be present, but the latter with some incongruity and presumption (as I may call it) beyond his condition of a simple deputy by seating himself (upon a very small invitation to it of the lord keeper) in the fyrst place on the right hand and bench syde (the Venetian as was his dew at the tables end) above the lord keeper, whereas the year before he had his place next beneath the carver on the other side and this then also, in regard of the great lords present, beyond his dew.

[34] After the queen had layn at St. James's nyneteene or twenty days and that divers lords had bene admitted to her presence, I thought it tyme (the Venetian ambassador refering it to my choyce) to aske her majestyes pleasure for theyr access and had it assigned for the next day being Sunday. But her Majestye demanding farther of me who they were that had moved for it, I sayd the Venetian ambassador and the States deputy, but the Spanishe resident and the archduchesses agent haveing only spoken of it but not yet formally demanded it. Why then replyed her Majestye these may come, those may tarry.

[35] About the beginning of November a gentleman (his name Cassopini) was sent from the duke of Arscot to his Majesty with letters to acknowledge the grace his Majesty had done his nephews the prince of Chimey and his brother whyle they were here. He brought letters also to the same effect to severall

---

[26] Soranzo had been transferred to London from the Dutch Republic in June 1629; Angelo Correr's arrival was delayed until Nov. 1634.

[27] Sir Nicholas Freeman.

lords, as the Treasurer, earl Marshall, the lord chamberlin, the duke of Lenox, the earle of Carlisle. I introduced him to his Majestys presence in the privy gallery at his coming and parting, the kyng returned no answere by him, beyond salutations and notice of the dukes thankfulness for that which, his Majestye sayd complementally, did not deserve it, etc.

[35ᵛ] After the queen had layn in her monthe and that answere was returned from the queen of Bohemia, the prince palatin and the prince of Orange of theyr acceptance of the honour done them by his Majestye to be invited for witnesses (by theyr deputyes when they could not be personally present) at the christening of the duke of York, the day assigned for it (November 24th) being come the ceremony and proceeding to it, wyth litle or almost no difference from that of the Prince of Wales about three years and half before, was in this manner.

The heraulds having summoned the lords and ladyes to theyr appearance and attendance in the privy galleryes at St. James, thither [36] was brought the duke of York borne by the Countess of Denbigh (First Lady of the Queens Bed Chamber) accompanyed by the lady Governess of the Prince and Duke, the Countess of Dorset,[28] and wayted on by the nurse, midwyfe and rockers. Thence they passed the Privy Chamber, Presence and Guard Chamber down the common stayrs through the fyrst court, the way there on each syde rayled in to keep crowding out, in this order. Fyrst went the Aldermen of London, next the judges of the Common Law, the barons of the Exchequer and judges of the Admiralty, the 2 cheefe justices and cheefe baron, the Lord Mayor of London. These in theyr scarlet gownes, some of them with chaynes of gold and others with the collor of **SS**, as they were dignifyed. Next came knyghts of the privy councell, then barons, viscounts and earles. All these severall degrees distinguished by officers of armes intermixed. Next, the lord chamberlin to the Queen, lord great chamberlin (in the midst) and the lord chamberlin to the king (these together). The Lord Keeper, Clarencieux king of Armes, the deputy godfathers *viz.* lord treasurer and the earl Marshall. The earl of Hertford bearing the basin assisted by the Viscount Wimbledon. A gentleman usher, Garter Kyng of Armes, and a gentleman usher. Then the duke borne by the Countess of Kent [36ᵛ] supported by the lord privy seale and the duke of Lenox. The trayne of the Dukes mantle borne by the earl of Huntington, assisted by the earles of Southampton[29] and Bedford. The canopye carryed over the Duke (out of the house) by the lord Fielding, the lord

---

[28] Mary Curzon, wife of Edward Sackville, 4th earl of Dorset.
[29] Thomas Wriothesley, 4th earl of Southampton.

Willoughby[30] of Parham, the lord North, lord Seymour,[31] lord Craven[32] and lord Cottington.[33] Next these, the Countess of Dorset. Then after her Norroy Kyng of Armes,[34] the deputy godmother (for the queene of Bohemia) the lady marchioness of Hamilton supported by the earles of Kent and Rutland, her trayne borne by the lady Mary Villiers, daughter of the late duke of Buckingham. Last of all marched all the rest of the ladyes of honour and other ladyes according to theyr degrees.

These thus marching to the chappell were there receyved at the entrance of the quire by the Archbishop of Canterbury and four other bishops his assistants, all clothed in theyr imbroidered copes, and divided themselves each to their seates. The lords were on the left hand from the Kyng (who at the wyndow of the closet above was all the whyle spectator) the ladyes on the right. On the north syde next the communion table were two seates with traverses between for the godfathers and on the south syde the lyke for the godmother, the Duke and his attendants.

In the midst of the chappel was placed an eyght square stage with an assent to yt of three or four steps covered under foot with carpets and round on the sydes with cloth of gold, as were also the chappel walls, in the mydst whereof was placed the font of sylver gylt. [37] Up to this, after an anthem sung, ascended the representants with the Duke, who baptised by the archbishop and named James, his titles were proclaimed there within and abroad, seconded with acclamations of ioy and sounde of trumpets, drumms and canons from the Tower, and so ended the ceremony. After the Duke was reconducted by the way he came to his father and mother (to receyve their blessings) in their Bed Chamber. Then the lords, ladyes and all others of fitting quality had admittance, my lord mayor amongst the rest bringing with him and presenting a bowle (sayd to be of gold but proving to be sylver) fylled with fyve hundred peeces.

[39] About the end of November the archduchess Infanta dying in Brussels,[35] neyther her agent here, nor the resident of Spayne, as yet receyving any formal account of it, I went to the fyrst as the more imediate minister and from him to the latter to performe for myself the office of condolement. The agent asked me if I knew whether his Majestye would complye in mourning,

---

[30] Francis Willoughby, 5th lord Willoughby of Parham.
[31] Possibly Francis Seymour, later lord Seymour of Trowbridge.
[32] William Craven, baron Craven of Hamsted-Marshal.
[33] Francis Cottington, baron Cottington of Hanworth.
[34] Sir William le Neve.
[35] Isabella Clara Eugenia, Infanta, died 1 Dec. 1633 (New Style).

I sayd I made no question of it, if he should receyve the signification, which he might expect to be given him to that purpose.

Four or five dayes after, I intimated by a thyrd person what had bene let fall by my lord chamberlin concerning the sayd mourning, that there would be none taken up at court till an immediate account were given of the Infantas death by her minister or the kyng of Spaynes. This brought forth the next day a letter from the Spanish resident to Mr. Secretary Cook to that purpose, but my lord chamberlin not acquainted with it (whome in his charge it most properly concerned) it rested there tyll the default discovered a more particular intimation was brought to his lordship by the agent of the Archduchess which helped him to an audience of the Kyng and Queen on Sunday the 8th of December. Whereupon order was published at the court for the mourning [39ᵛ] to begin the Sunday following December the 15th and to be continued tyll Christmas.

If the agent of the Infanta had not repayred as he did to my lord chamberlin on the Saturday and that at the same tyme as the secretary of the States ambassadour from Holland (who was then newly returned) had not deferred or taken an irregular course by going to the Kyng (then at Theobalds) for demand of audience, which he should have caryed by the lord chamberlin or by myself, then had bene an incounter of the agent of Flanders and the States ambassadours audience at one instant. This would have stirred the question and difference for precedence, though the one an ambassadour and the other an agent, for the reasons alleged.[36]

---

[36] See IV 33.

[37ᵛ] One Boutard, that had formerly, in place of secretary, served here the Marquis de Fontenay, whyle he was here resident ambassador, having passed almost three months of an employment he had hither from the French king, as an *envoyé*, tooke leave of theyr majestyes about the beginning of January. The next morning early coming to my house, under pretence of a farewell before his prest departure I accompanyed him instantly to my lord chamberlin and on the way lett him know that, intending to move his lordship about his present from this King, I thought a chayne of gold of 210 £, as usually given persons of his imployment would be more suitable than a ring, or other jewel, as the gratuity which he most affected, was more usuall and *propos* for condolement and congragulation, than negotiation. This he approved of and I, accordingly, intimated it to my lord chamberlin, who repayring to the king for knowledge of his pleasure, receyved a breef and round answer from his majesty that, synce he knew him not to be sent hither as eyther ambassadour or agent, he knew lykewyse no cause why he should have a present bestowed upon him at his partyng.[1] This answer told me by my lord chamberlin, I imparted to Boutard, as that which I could not withhold, if I would not withal hold him in a vayne expectation. But I also found that he had deserved that neglect and worse [38] for some undutyfull and unmannerly cariag of his towards the Queen, havinge given her suche cause of offense, as when he took his leave, she was heard to tell him playnly he was so far from deserving respects from her, as if she should cause him to be beaten by a lacquay, she should but reward him according to his merit.[2] He being thus frustrate of his hopes of a present rested not there (though he professed to me he would no more look after it) but three or four dayes after wrot to me to procure him (as I did) an accesse to the kyng saying he had receyved fresh letters (as indeed he had) out of France that obliged him once more before his departure to see his Majesty. With this, he took the opportunity to lett the Kyng know what he had heard from me of his majestyes words touching his qualification, wherein if he were (he sayd) deficient, he should be a most unworthy and

---

[1] After Fontenay's premature departure in May 1633, Boutard returned to London (Oct. 1633 – Feb. 1634) as envoy extraordinary. Pougny, the next ambassador, did not arrive until July 1634.

[2] Henrietta considered the theft of Rochechuart's papers (see III 110) to be partly Boutard's work.

saucy intruder into his presence and so toke the occasion to show his letters of credence to his majesty (as those that myght serve to cleere him in the kyngs opinion) touching his imployment, which he tooke to be disabled (he sayd) by his majesty, in refusall of his present. He gayned so far as that his majesty denyed he had ever sayd that he was not imployed to him as an *envoyé*. But when [38ᵛ] the day after, my lord chamberlin chalenged me for reportyng what he had told me of the Kyngs answer, and that I had, for my discharge, formally repeated it to his lordship and imediately to the kyng also, as I have before set it downe, with the limitation of ambassador and agent, whereof the kyng sayd he was neyther, both his majesty and his lordship avowed my report as agreeing wyth the truth and nothing derogating from Boutards condition, which was in very deed of an *envoyé* and neyther (as the Kyng sayd rightly) ambassador nor agent, since the fyrst was above him and the latter implying a residency (which he could not pretend to) not agreeing with him, therefore eyther an *envoyé*, or nothing. Yet 2 or 3 dayes later upon his receyt of other letters from France he demanded and had another access, upon which I incountered Mr. Vice Chamberlin, in the Privy Gallery, and gave him an account of it. My lord treasurer (then by) seemed to formalize himself in Boutards behalf and in some sort to taxe me as cause of his decrying, in not understanding (he sayd) the condition of an *envoyé* that was no other than an extraordinary agent. Of this imputation indeavouring to cleer my self, and the kyng at the instant passing by, I put myself upon his majestyes iustification, with which I was most graciously honored. My lord treasurer professed to alter his misconceyved opinion of him, whome the king had already pronounced incapable and the Queen unworthy of a present,[3] without which he parted for France, the 7th of February.

[39ᵛ] The gentlemen of the four Inns of Court having prepared a maske to be presented at Whitehall before theyr majestyes, the 4th of February, I beforehand sounded the disposition of ambassadors and agents then here for their presence at it, which finding averse in regard I could not assure (as they expected particularly the ambassadors) that they should be formally invited to it, though I pointed at theyre places to be given them uppermost of the lords, as had been accustomed ever since [40] his majestyes entrance and declaration not any more to admitt any of theyr persons to seates next him. I tooke what order I could for placing of theyr secretareys, and followers of the best sort, so got ticketts for 24, which got them entrance and seates with conveniency at the Banketting House, theyr lords in the mean tyme taking up theyr standes

---

[3] Out of consideration that an official gift was also the king's free choice.

in the streets where they thought fittest for sight of the Maskers most pompous passage through Holborne, Chancery Lane to the Strand to Whytehal.

The description of the Maske[4] being printed, I may spare the entrance to it as thus. A hundred gentlemen that rode before the maskers bravely mounted on great horses richly caparosoned themselves all in chinquant sutes (the 16 maskers were drawn in four triumphant chariots with four horses drawing each chariot) were placed all together in the Banketting House on an upper gallery there purposely reserved for them, behind and over, the Kyngs seat. These (with the maskers) were, after the mask was finished, honored by the Kyng personally going wyth them from his privy galleryes to the Guard Chamber and there leaving them with the ladyes at a sumptuous banket provided for them.

The mask, and march of it through the streets to court, was so well performed and well lyked as theyr Majestyes were after pleased to invite themselves to a supper at the Lord Maiors[5] for a second syght [40ᵛ] of it there. This they should have had the Tuesday seavennight following, but the queens indisposition that day was cause of deferring all tyll the Thursday[6] following, when theyr majestyes and some 70 great lordes and ladies and other persons of quality were entertayned at a most plentyful supper in the lord maiors house and, after this, a ball and the mask at Merchant Taylors hall. Whither they had theyr way made and covered under foot with carpets, alongst a gallery purposely raysed on one syde of the street to a citizens house a hundred yards distant and thence by a private passage and a tournpike door to the hall mentioned. Hereunto the better and handsomer sort of the aldermens and citizens wives and daughters, also the citizens themselves, had theyr entrance by the other usuall way of the street at a lyke tourning door by tykett.

After the maskers had danced, the kyng, queen, lordes and ladyes fell to dancing and, after that, was served in great silver chargers a running banket. This ended, the maskers were entertayned at a supper of cold meates and a plentiful banket set ready for them at two tables in a long gallery. Theyr majestyes in the meane tyme retourned to Whytehal. They had bene receyved at theyr entrance into the lord maiors Liberty at Temple Bar by twenty captaynes of the city on horseback attended by 200 soldyers of the artillery [41] garden, those of the military garden having before garded theyr majestyes to the place of theyr first reception mentioned. At the Kyngs descent from his coach before the lord mayors doors, his lordship receyved him on his knee

4 Shirley's *Triumph of Peace* on Feb. 4th. This edition is STC 22459.
5 Sir Nicholas Freeman.
6 February 13th.

and wyth the sword borne by himself and the mace before him ushered him to his chamber. About the mydst of supper he came forth (sicke and weak as he then was) to present theyr Majestyes with a welcome and the lords with the lyke. These and the great ladyes were feasted and served at a large oval table capable of about 40 persons in another room next to that the kyng and queen supt in. Those that attended them wayting within the center or vacuum of the oval, the meat (to avoyd interruption by passing up and down stayrs) being handed up to the wayters from the kitchin to both the kyng and the lords table as it was also by another way to a long table in a gallery apart where supt the residue of persons of quality that wayted thither upon his Majestye.

For presents to theyr Majestyes the city had provided two purses in each and for each a thousand pounds, but this golden way being disliked, and an intimation being made by the lord chamberlin that a diamond affected by the Kyng of some 4000 £ value would be much more acceptable to the Kyng, though less, perhaps, to them that looked on the more charge, the fyrst present was not without some distaste and disgrace to the citizens deferred (for the acceptation) to a further discourse and resolution, and the latter 3 or 4 dayes after presented.

[41ᵛ] On Shrove Tuesday following, a maske of his Majestye and 14 lordes was performed at Whytehal,[7] where to (as before) were not formally invited any ambassadors, only an intimation was (of desyne and with direction of the lord chamberlin) cast out by me that, if they would come, they should be welcome and have theyr seats next above the lordes or ladyes at theyr choyce, as the French and other ambassadors since his majestyes entrance had formerly had before them. But none came, some fewe followers of theyrs only entering by ticket and placeing themselves in the fyrst galleryes.

[42] The baron of Oxensterne, Henry[8] son to the famous chancelor of Sweden, who had bene here before a privat man, for syght of the court a year[9] before, arrived, the 12 of March, before Gravesend and excusing to land, though invited by the postmaster, who to that purpose went aboord his ship, he only (by him) let me know he was there without sending me formal word of it by one of his, as should have done. The other was no warrant for my stirring towards him, I attended all the next day with expectation of some other messenger which not coming, I in the mean tyme gave notice of

---

7 Carew's *Coelum Britannicum* on Feb. 18th.

8 Henry Oxenstierna, ambassador extraordinary (March–May 1634) of the regency for Christina of Sweden, sought, on behalf of the Protestant league of Heilbrunn, Charles's support against the Habsburg coalition in Germany.

9 See IV 22.

his arrival to Mr. Controller of his Majestyes household and wrote to the lord chamberlin then wyth the Kyng at Newmarket, as I had done before when I heard he lay at the Brill for a wynde, for order about his defraying (or not) by his Majestye. I receyved it fyrst from court and after (upon my intimation of his Majestyes pleasure) from my lord treasurer, Mr. controler and Mr. Secretary Windebank (residing here) affirmatively to that purpose I commanded a barge for my owne transport to Gravesend and the 14 Marche gave him his welcome.

[42ᵛ] Having made his answere, he prest his instant departure in such boates as were there ready, but I urging the necessity of his stay, in regard, I sayd, the barges were not yet come downe and that a nobleman, the earl of Rutland, appoynted for his reception before Greenwiche had already his order for it, I could obtayne no farther of him than that, upon my promise, the barges should be there for his service the next morning very early, he would dispense with his longing to be at his rest at London, and so was by 9 of the clock without finding [43] the kings coache, or any of the ambassadors there residing, at the water syde to carry him thence to his lodging. Since no earle could be there by his owne prevention to receyve him the rest myght be, as making his entrance in privat, suitable. He had for his transport the Kings barge with 12 oares, two others and a light horseman his baggage having bene sent up in one the nyght before. His dyet at the Kings charge began the 15th of March at dynner proportioned to the expense of 25 £ per diem for feeding of 44 persons, whereof sat at his owne table of the better sort about 18, the others elsewhere at his stewards table in the same room.

[43ᵛ] The day of his coming to towne the earle of Rutland (upon my intimation of the fitnes of his performing that complement) repayred to him accompanyed by the lords Newbourg[10] and Sauil[11] to excuse of (not his fault) ill fortune to have bene prevented and disappointed by his so sodayne arrival, of the honour intended him for his reception at Greenwiche.

The next day he was visited by Mr. Controler of the household[12] as cheefe officer having charge of his treatment and the same day also by my lord Weston[13] which might seem an irregularity but that the regard to whome he had relation myght seem to countenance it. He himself in the interim resolved not to visit any, nor to stir out of doors tyll his first audience were past (answerable to the customary course of ambassadors) which he could not hope

---

[10] Edward Barret, lord Barret of Newburgh.
[11] Thomas Savile, viscount Savile of Castlebar.
[12] Sir Henry Vane had previously been ambassador extraordinary to Gustavus.
[13] Sir Jerome Weston, son of the lord treasurer.

for, tyll that Sonday a seaven night at the soonest, the kyng being not to returne tyll Fryday. That day, I repayred to his majesty then at St. James's, and presented to his consideration, conformable to custome at other tymes, of sending to him some person of quality [44] wyth a complement of welcome, for which the earl of Elgin[14] there then present was made choyce, and accompanyed by me to the ambassadors lodging.

The same day he consulted wyth me about his audience, which before he had recommended to my procuring as soone as could be, but discovering some trouble for the want of his liveryes, bespoken in France, and not yet come (which could, he thought, dislustre his fyrst appearance at court) I propounded to him a reason for delay, which he professed was indeed true, in that having received, as I knew he had, fresh letters from the Director, his father, with intimation that he was speedily to receyve some inlargements to his instructions and his audience might be deferred a day or two longer, if not from his own particular request, from my discovery of his affections to yt, to which purpose I repayred to my lord chamberlin and, without touching at all the true cause, obtayned by his lordships mediation to his majestye, an adiournment tyll Wednesday following, (march 26).

For his conduction that day to court, the earl of Salisbury was made choyce of (who though in rank a younger earle yet dignifyed a knight of the Garter and a Privy Councellor) was judged more corresponding. [44ᵛ] He went accompayned in the Kyngs coach (the Queens, the States and 13 others following) with the lord viscount Wimbledon, viscount Charworth, 2 barons (Herbert and Craven) General Ruthven,[15] a brave commander under the late kyng of Sweden. In the rest of the ambassadours trayne went the Count Witchestein,[16] Count Solmes,[17] the baron of Oxensterne, baron of Limbourg,[18] and baron of Tzernesky,[19] 2 gentlemen of the Privy Chamber and some 12 of these mingled in the other coaches, besydes almost as many colonels that came over with the ambassador, in hope of leave to levy soldiers.

Thus attended he came to court the 26th of March and went for his repose to the councell chamber. Then for his audience he went downe to the Great Hall, hung with rich tapestries and made use of as the place the most capable, whyle the Banketing House was not yet cleared of the scene set up for the last maske, and the Presence would have bene much too litle for so great a

---

14 Thomas Bruce, 1st earl of Elgin.
15 Sir Patrick Ruthven.
16 Ernest, count of Sayn-Wittgenstein.
17 Frederick Henry, count of Solms-Braunfels.
18 Herman Otto, count of Limburg.
19 Possibly William Freiherr von Wannitsky.

company, where the kyng and the queene with her ladyes were to be ioyntly present. In the ambassadors proceeding over the terras, downe the stone stayres, through the great court (where the guard stood in file on both sydes of his passage) I stept before [45] to prevent the crowd of suche as would enter the hall, though none of the ambassadors followers or company, when my lord chamberlin thought fit to send me back, with a request to the ambassador, and the lords with him, that they would be pleased to come foremost for the fayrer prospect at theyr entrance both to and from theyr majestyes (whose syght by the preceding press would be unavoydably hindered) but not so, if he should place those that came with him behind him.

The ambassador passed up to the kyng, with his three reverences, without once casting his regard on eyther side. On his left hand, stood the lordes before formes planted betweene them and the band of Pensioners behynd to keep the crowd, and on his right, before other formes, the ladyes. The ambassador did (answerable to the directions I gave him upon his demand of our cutomes) salute the Kyng with his knee touching the ground and, at that tyme, only bowing to the queene. After upon the Kyngs instructions he put on his hat and spake (something at length after the custome of northern ministers) in latin. That done he presented to the kyng his credence, which could not before come by (his secretary being kept back by the pressing multitude) and with letters he had told me before (for mine and others knowledge and warrant of his qualification) [45ᵛ] came from the crown and queen of Sweden and the princes of the union of Germany.[20] After addressing himself to the Queen, to whome he spoke in French, and having finished what he had to say, he presented to theyr majestyes his followers (of these, fyrst of all, General Ruthven) made his retrayt with regardes and salutations only to the ladyes on the right hand (in the interim of his three reverences to theyr Majestyes) and returned to his lodging.

That evening when I told the lord marquess Hamilton that wee should have need of the kyngs coache the next day, for the ambassadors privat audience, his lordship sayd I might remember his majestye had about 2 yeares before signifiyed his pleasure that his coache (upon the so long and unmannerly use of it by the French ambassador Chasteauneuf) should never more be imployed except at the fyrst and last publick audience of ambassadours. Yet this ambassador, he sayd, hath so much of my respects for his particular merit as I wyll move his majestye that he may have it for his dayly service, whereto, when I replyed that the ambassador might pretend to it from precedent of the

---

[20] A league between Sweden and the Imperial circles of Franconia, Swabia, and the Upper and Lower Rhine.

French ambassadour St. Chaumont and the Polonian prince Radzivil, he sayd, I was at that tyme out of England, but I shall be glad of any example [46] for the service of one I so much honor, so went strayt to his majesty and asked, and had, his allowance for it, wyth condition urged that I would affirme that, of my certayne knowledge, that Prince Radzivil had had it before him, and with promise of my care that no other should have it dayly in that manner after him.

The day after his publick audience having had one privat of his Majestye he made a visit to the Prince, Princess and duke of Yorke at St. James's, the two fyrst together in one roome to the latter apart, as he lay sleeping in his nurses lap. Then he went to the Archbishop of Canterbury having sent before a coronel (the Master of Forbos) with signification of his desyre to kyss his hands and present to him letters from his father, the Director. The archbishop met him in his hall, but entered every door before him, as thinking it perhaps the more proper so to do, as by way of guydance and conduction in his owne house, by the old rule of *introitus Domino*, etc. but I was bold to intimate to one of his gentlemen that at his parting he should do well to offer him the precedence, as he did, being but in two words admonished of it, and excusing his former omission upon the ambassadours offer of the door to hym wyth request [46ᵛ] to me in English to tell him (haveing all the time before spoken in Latine) that to lead him as he had done in his house, he took to be a signe of love, but not so out of it. The ambassador had, the day before, sent to my lord Treasurer for access, but this excused with his lordships indisposition of health, with request that if he would give him self that trouble it might be the day following, or at some tyme when he should hear further from him. Fyrst, he performed this visit mentioned (it was a great lords advice that he should fyrst performe the visit to my lord of Canterbury). My lord treasurer recyved him at his coming to him, towards the foot of his stayre, my lord Weston, his son, at the hall doore.

My lord of Carlisle and my lord of Holland dispensing with puntilios visited him severally before his fyrst audience. Other lords after, as they were pleased to take the tyme.

After his fyfteen dayes of treatment, at the Kyngs charge, grew towards expiration, his terme having bene signifyed by me to the steward at his arrival, as in correspondence of the lyke limited to Sir Harry Vane, when he was ambassadour from his majesty to the Kyng of Sweden, his provision of wine (layd in two or three dayes before) began to fayle, so did his wood and coale, and was refused to be supplyed further by the clerke of the Kytchin, tyll by the meanes I used of a great person with Mr. Controller, two hogsheads of one, and two loades of the other brought him saved the shame of suche unseaonable good husbandry. [46a] At the tyme of the ambassadors arrival here, the Kyng being at Newmarket (and the officers of the Jewel House absent) his Majestyes plate could not be had for his use, so, Sir Abraham Williams, where he lodged, was forced (according to conditions with his majestye upon a pension of 300 £ *per annum* allowed him) to supply him with pewter. But three dayes after, when meanes was found and order given by Mr. Controller for sylver vessels, the offer of it was not accepted by the ambassadors steward with excuse that his lord having been served with pewter in the low coun-tryes, where he was defrayed, and finding pewter sufficiently serviceable, desyred he might pass with the like here. The true reason was, as appeared after, that plate being offered them with condition implyed of takeing it to their own charge, and of being answerable for it should any be lost, they were to make good, which hazzard they were with reason unwilling to under-go. But had I bene made acquainted with theyr exception I had soone recon-ciled the difference, upon knowledge I had of Mr. Controllers disposition to appoint a servant of the office [46aᵛ] for dayly attendance on that charge, which omitted begot an opinion in some that the ambassador, towards the expiration of his 15 dayes defraying having sent abroad to hyre plate, affected that richnes of a tax to our poornes. But I, upon discourse finding his intention to be more noble and not to ayme at his own honor by derogating from the kyngs, made all well by acquainting the controller with the ambassadors reasons, when upon ceasing of the kyngs dyet, he made provision of his own, he was, as I have touched, served all with plate both at his own and his stewards table, the one having on it every meal 15 covers or plates, and the other, nine, all silver, and so the rest answerable. One thing was observable and perhaps censurable, that all the gentlemen of the trayne, being 17 or 18, sat at his table alwayes bareheaded, though two of them bore the tytle of countes, and three of them barons. Two colonels that did eate often at his table were not so ob-servant no more than I and other English were, and wyth reason, the sayd colonells standing in his presence alwayes bareheaded, but he so to beare them company and to prevent theyr covering.

[47] The terme of the ambassador of Venice (Vicenzo Gusoni) his residence here being expired, and his revocation come, he demanded audience for his parting, which referred by him to me for forme of carriage for the ceremony of it. I upon search of precedents found that his two predecessors, Contarini and Soranzo, had had theyrs in privat, a day, two or three after a publike audience had bene given them together with the new ambassador last ar-rived for successor to the old. But this ambassador having none such come had none to present, so no need of a publick audience, yet being put to it by

the sayd ambassadors secretary, exemplification of one or two ambassadors that had taken theyr leaves at the last sight of his majesty, when they receyved of him theyr knighthood, with the conduct of an earle, and use of the kyngs coache, which made theyr audience publick. I acquainted his majesty with the difference and receyved the signification of his pleasure for the lyke, the queene to be also present. So the earle of Bohan[21] was made choyce of for his conduct to court in the Kyngs coache (his brother Mr. Erskin and 3 gentlemen of the privy chamber assisting) he was receyved in the Presence (the ambassador entering fyrst for the conveniencey found by yt at the former audience of the Sweden) [47ᵛ] made his harang in Italian with interpretation of the Queens secretary (in absence of the Kings and while I was kept from it by the crowd behind him) delivered letters to both theyr majestyes, was knighted there and had the sword and hangers given him, and the gyrdle awhile after sent to him, whyle he was shifting his gowne in the place of his repose the chapel closet chamber. Part of his speech was to the purpose of recommending his secretary, Zonca,[22] to his majestyes acceptance for occuring busyness tyll another ambassadour, whome he named Coraro,[23] should come to reside here as ordinary.

[48] The ambassador of Sweden, owing the returne of a visit to the earle of Holland, had it assigned for between four and fyve, the earle having in the mean tyme prepared a court supper, as he called it, with intimation that the ambassador should be pleased to take it at his lodging and after to go wyth him to a comedy in the Cockpit,[24] as he did, and was seated there (as I before had propounded and provided with giving notice thereof to my lord chamberlin and taking his resolution) amongst the lords next above the duchess of Buckingham, putting on his hat fyrst, after the lords had receyved a signification of his majestyes pleasure for them to do the lyke. The ambassador having before his entrance there made scruple of his appearance in that assembly unless he should be assured (as he was by me from my lord chamberlin) that he should sit covered.

The King being upon his remove to Greenwiche, the 28 of April, I was requested by the same ambassadour to procure him that same day three words (as he hinted it) of an audience, but his majesty, not relishing his so quicke a returne of troubling him (especially at suche an instant of his remove) refused it as an importunity, yet upon my farther [48ᵛ] intimation, granted it for the

21 Sir James Erskine, husband to the countess of Buchan.
22 Francesco Zonca, agent (May–Nov. 1634) of Venice.
23 Angelo Correr, ambassador, arrived in November.
24 Play unidentified, performance on April 8th, Bentley VII 92.

next day. When the ambassador went for it, with the use of his majestyes barge and one other (both which not sufficiently capable of all his company) some that wanted place hyred oares at theyr owne charge.

The ambassador and one of his gentlemen went to hunt the stag with his Majestye neer Croyden, caryed thither in a coach hired by himself with six horses, and horsed there by my lord Goring. The Tuesday following this in Whitsun weeke, the ambassador continuing to make use of the liberty his majesty had given him to hunt with him, and to repayre domestically to court at his pleasure, went to Greenwich in the Kyngs coach and forbearing to arrive there immediately after dinner, to avoyd invitations, went with my lord of Holland from his lodging to the queenes privy gallery, there passed the tyme in discourse with her majesty and the ladyes, tyll the king entering from councell he attended theyr majestyes to the syght of the bearbaiting and re-tyrned that night to London.

[51] Towards the end of this ambassador of Swedens three months negotia-tion here for levye of men, etc., he finding in this state litle disposition, rather opposition, to it some by questioning his commission as not formally enough framed and signed, as was pretended it ought to have bene by the princes of Germany, the queen of Sweden and the Director Oxenstierne joyntly, but presumptively carying the title of the crown of Sweden and of those Princes power as sufficient for his qualification, etc., he sent an express to Franckfort, where that body was then assembled, and at three weekes end, had his revoca-tion brought him. Upon which having first demanded and had of his majesty a privat audience to receyve intimation (as he desyred it) for his last parting publick audience [51ᵛ] of both their majestyes together at Greenwich the 8th of June, being Sunday.

To this, the earle of Exeter being invited for his conduction, but excusing himself, with his indisposition of goute and age, the earle of Holland (upon my letter to him carrying my lord chamberlins request) undertook and dis-charged the service, fetching him (with the company of the earl of Newport, two barrons, and but as many gentlemen, in the Kyngs and Queens coaches and half a score other that had all theyr rendezvous at Essex house) from his lodging at Westminster to Tower wharfe and thence in fyve barges to Green-wiche, where brought to theyr majestyes presence he made a long harang to the King in latin, passed his complements to the Queen in French and after his retrayt, tyll the turne of the tyde at the earle of Hollands lodging (where his lordship wyth excuse of the Kings command for his repayre instantly to councell left him) and was by the lord Paget and lord Craven (that had wyth him conducted him thither) reconducted to his lodging at Westminster. The excuse that the earl of Holland pleaded (and indeed seriously, his lordship having acquainted me at London before he set forth for Greenwiche with what necessity he should be forced to be present at councell after the audience and [52] not reconduct the ambassador) passed not without dystaste and suspition, as done of designe by the Kings command, or with the earles neglect, and for such he expressed it to me, two or three dayes after. But when I had assured him of the earnest of it, he was better satisfyed, yet to say the truth had reason to formalize himself as he did, the earle having none, or very litle, to lett him returne to London without his reconduction, alwayes due from whatsoever person that has charge to conduct an ambassador to his publick audience.

At this audience, some wondered, and tooke notice of a certayne unaccustomed carriage of his majesty towards him, and of the ambassador towards his majesty, when the Kyng stepping forwards to the edge of the uppermost degree under the State as if he would have hindered him from ascending to an even station with him, the ambassador stepped up to the same height and took his station at the left hand on syde of him, but I tooke this, as others, of chance, and not of designe, and for such the ambassador asking after my opinion of it, professed it.

[52ᵛ] Some 10 or 12 dayes after the preparation of his majestyes present of 2000 ounces of gylt plate (proportionable to that gyven his predecessour Sir James Spence[25] and 500 more than what had bene given to two or three ambassadors of Polonia) the Master of the Jewels House, sent his under officer for knowing of his owne fittest tyme, when he should repayre to him to present it, answer was returned from the ambassador (at that instant retyred to his study) that all that day he should be busy about dispatches, the next in making visits, but if he would the day after come to him, his person would be welcome without a present. This ambiguous answer (if dewly wayghed) myght have served to discover his intention of refusall and have prevented the insuing inconvenience, when the present being brought to the ambassadors house and set on a table to shewe (which might be thought an errour of too much, as the other was of too litle, formality) the Master of the Jewel House made his preface of presenting it, and had for answer from the ambassador that the busyness he came about (that was of his Majestyes interest as well as of the crown and of the Princes that had imployed him) being not brought to that good end he hoped and had indeavoured, he had not deserved and therefore had no reason to accept a present. The bestowing of a present by a prince, and the receyving of it by an ambassador, being, as he understood it,

---

[25] In March–June 1629: see III 22.

a testimony of both theyr satisfactions, which he for his part [53] could not acknowledge to have had, or given, having not dispatched his business, adding further that Sir Henry Vane, in his imployment, had receyved none from the king of Sweden, his deceased master, and he should not then expect, or receyve, any from the Kyng of England. To which, when it was replyed that Sir Harry Vane had had no present offered to him, his conclusion was that whatsoever had bene done or not done by others, he was resolved to recyve no present, so with humble request of his majestyes pardon, and his favourable opinion of him, he returned it back and gave subject of severall discourses passed upon such a singularity. Towards his parting certayne lords (as the earle of Carlisle, the earle of Holland, the lord Goring and others) had made promises of a dozen or more of the best horses to be found, wherwyth to present him, but the King his present refused, any to be made by his subiects was iudged a solecisme. He parted for Gravesend and thence for the low countryes in a man of war of those parts on Midsummer day and the next morning with a favorable wynde set to sea.

[53ᵛ] One thing was observable in the scutcheons of armes, according to the usuall custom of ambassadors, were caused to be made by him and sett up in his inns and lodgings at his parting, he added to the tytles of his family and seignuries nothing but, etc. omiting the title of ambassador, which might be well iudged of designe, and was so resolved by one of his gentlemen, when I asking him the reason of yt, he answered only, my lord would have it so, who since he hath not done the busynes of his ambassage, why should he stile himself ambassadour?

[55ᵛ] The Marquis de Pougny, of the family of Rambouillet in Brittany, being designed by the French king for his ambassador²⁶ ordinary with his majestye, arrived at Gravesend, the 4th of July, whereof notice being brought me, I, the next day, repayred thither with his majestyes welcome and soone after, as I was upon dispatch of my officer back to London, wyth order for preparation of coaches for reception of the sayd ambassador at Tower wharfe, and for his conduct there to his lodging by the earle of Bohan, he drewe me apart and sayd, he understood, that a Scottish earl was made choyce of for his reception at his landing in London.²⁷ He thought he could not except against his quality and person, but he owed the kyng his masters honour to move a

²⁶ Jean d'Angennes, marquis de Pougny, ambassador (July 1634 until his death in Dec. 1636), was instructed to seek strong English support for the Dutch and Swedish forces and to end the English transport of Spanish troops to Flanders.
²⁷ Buchan had been the escort for the departure of Gussoni of Venice, who stated similar reservations about Scottish peers.

question to me, whether the choyce made of an earl of Scotland was not a lessening of that honour to him, which had become due to others of his quality and nation, who had bene receyved at theyr arrival at London by an earle of England.

I answered that when I fyrst moved my lord chamberlin for choyce of some notable person for that service there was present in the roome at court the earl of Denbigh, an English earle, and the earl of Bohan, a Scottish, the fyrst being by me fyrst nominated was not approved of by his lordship as [56] wanting language, the latter was thought fytting as being not only well languaged but of a family also by the mother (sister to the late Duke of Richmond) of the Kyngs blood, by the father descended from two that had been Constables of France. To this he replyed that he intended not to question the blood or other merit of the earle of Bohan, but he had it (he sayd) in his instructions that an English earle was to receive him at his arrival at London, and if choyce of another was made for it, he was to except against it, unless the Queene should be pleased to give allowance to it. To this I answered that for the difference of quality better or worse between English and Scottish earles I had observed none but this, those had the precedence of these in England as those of ours in Scotland. Herewith I was bold to advise him not to stirr or stand upon that question, lest it might bring upon him a national quarrel (as it myght, I sayd, have done upon Monsieur de Chateauneuf moving the lyke question on behalf of Monsieur de Fontenay at his arrival here, when the lord Gordon son to the Marquis Huntley was chosen to recyve him[28]) if he had not [56ᵛ] altered his mind and yeilded, as he did, to the choyce made. Not with standing all which reasons, he stood stiff in his exceptions, tyll I offering to returne presently myself (in place of myne officer then ready to part with order for the barges to come down the next day) he descended to this conclusion that if the queen, made acquainted with the choyce should give allowance of it, he would submit. So back I went to London and imparting what had passed to my lord chamberlin he, in my hearing, to the king and the king to the queen. Her majesty, after the king expressed no smal distast for suche singularity of the ambassador and declared his intention of no difference to be made between English and Scottish earles in poynt of choyce for ambassadors receptions and conductions, commanded her chief Almoner[29] (who was present with me at Gravesend, whyle the ambassadour made his exceptions, and sayd he knew no difference made here between English and Scottish earles) to wryte to the ambassador her approbation of the choyce of the earl

---

[28] In Feb. 1630: see III 68ᵛ.
[29] Jacques de Noël, bishop of Angoulême.

of Bohan. This caryed to him the next day by a servant of the sayd chief Almoner sent wyth me in the Kyngs barge, the letter was receyved by him and read, not without alteration of countenance, and wyth this profession added that what her majesty thought fitting, he must obey, [57] but if he were now agayne newly arrived at Gravesend, he would attend there fyfteen dayes a resolution from France how to govern himself in the busyness, rather than upon these termes to proceed to London, as he imediately did wyth 3 barges, and one light horseman. Landing at Tower wharfe, he was there receyued by the said earle of Bohan and with half a score gentlemen and thence in the kyngs coache (the queenes and eight others attending) conducted to his house in St. Bartholemews.

Thence I went to court with the account of his arrival and intimated to my lord chamberlin how fit it was, after the usual course, that some nobleman should be presently sent from the Kyng to give him a welcome to towne. Nominating for that purpose the earl of Denbighs son, Lord Fielding, the complement was instantly performed wyth my attendance. The queen that night sent to him the lyke welcome by one of her gentlemen ushers, Monsieur Vantelot, and the ambassador inquired of him if it would not be too much boldness for him to beg the sight of her majesty the next morning, since he understood it would be three or four dayes before he should have admittance to his first publick audience, whereto receyving a hopeful answer, [57ᵛ] the gentleman also sent him word of her majestyes assent for his accesse the next morning, the kyng being gone early on hunting, and her majesty that day removing to Theobalds.

This ambassador, upon maturer consideration of the punctuality he had stood upon to have an English earle for his fyrst reception, (especially when he understood the general distast that the Scottish nation had taken for his exception against one of theyrs) wyshed he had heard and obeyed other counsell than was by some at his first arrival given him, but this error left to tyme for reparation, the good, growing from this yll, will be that henceforth the choyce of earles for reception and conduct of ambassadors wyll be more facil, as theyr number more plentyful consisting indifferently of both nations.

His fyrst audience was assigned to be at Theobalds on Thursday, July 10, after the Saturday of his arrival at London. For his conduction to yt by an earle that might be out of all danger of exception (to be taken perhaps as for the former) I was put to no small trouble. A privy councellor being an earle, or a knight of Garter of the same rank being no privy councelor, had been according to the wonted style of ordinary ambassadors conduction most proper, but none such were then in towne. The earl of Lindsey, lord high chamberlin of England, [58] was ambitiously propounded by some of the

French here, but this my lord chamberlin would by no meanes allow of (regarding the eminency of that earles office) no more then he would of any of the great officers which were not to be imployed, he sayd, but for the conduct of extraordinaryes. In conclusion the earl of Warwick was pitched upon, who repayring to him at his house in St. Batholomews accompanyed with his owne sone, the lord Rich, with the lord of Duplin,[30] son to the earl of Kinnoule lord chancellor of Scotland and with the earl of Devonshires younger brother, he was brought to court in the kyngs coache (the queens, the earle of Warwicks and fyve others hired attending). No lords coaches were then to be found in towne and I allowed by my lord chamberlin, in case of such necessity, to dispense with the pragmatick published agaynst hyring coaches of service for ambassadours ordinary.

He had his audience in the Great Chamber of Presence (being one at Theobalds) both theyr Majestyes being present together, where after he had passed part of his complement to the Kyng and then he had begun to speake of his letters of credence, he found he had them not about him. Then smyleing with a French confidence, he sayd your Majestye may be pleased to pardon me this errore, as one [58ᵛ] better acquainted with the formes of a soldyer than of a Statesman, so he turned to his secretary took from him his letters, presented then to his majesty, and after, his other letters to the queene.

The States ambassador, and deputy Brassert, having before demanded audience of theyr majestyes (the latter to take his leave, the other to accompany him to it) had it also assigned them for that day but with my forecast (the better to housband theyre majestyes trouble and tyme so neer theyr progresse) that they should be introduced immediately after the French ambassadors retrayt, as they were (theyre majestyes not removing from under the State) without trouble to theyr Majestyes or other incounter of disorder.

[59] The ambassador of France, having receyved a complemental acceptation of an offer he had made of his service and attendance on theyr majestyes in theyr progresse, he prepared for it and (as the queene was at fyrst pleased) had his fyrst appearance at Welbeck. To this purpose, I having a iourney to make into Lincolnshyre, concluded to meet him at Newark, whither accordingly coming I found his course altered, upon theyr majestyes more mature consideration what incumbrance and incommodity both to them and him self his company would bring, in reason of strayghtnes of lodging upon removes, etc., which dexterously intimated to him by some of his nation (my lord chamberlin also having wrytten to me for my provident care in it) he stirred not at all from London. My lord chamberlins reasons written to

---

[30] Sir George Hay, viscount Dupplin.

me for diversion were, the unusualnes of the course never practiced by an ordinary ambassador (unless upon some urgent cause and that to be followed with a present returne), inconveniency of lodging, and other accomodations, interruption of his majestyes sports and privacy, the importunity of others to pretend to the same freedom by his example, and the lyke left to me to make use of as I should see occasion.

[59ᵛ] While I was at the court in progress[31] expecting there the incounter of the French ambassador Monsieur de Pougny, I receyved news of the Marquis of St. Germans approache,[32] as neer as Paris, sent ambassador extraordinary from the duke of Savoy. I not expecting his so speedy arrival and returning at my owne leisure to London, found him come thither above a seaven night before and much troubled at that, though in absence of his majesty, he was so litle looked after. Yet had I, provisionally at my departure from London, left instructions with Mr. Rowland Woodward (who had the charge of assistance under me) in case any ambassador should arrive whyle I was absent. This that gentleman discharged by his reception of the sayd ambassador at Gravesend, the 30 of July, and the conduction of him and his trayne in the kyngs barge and 2 others, to Sir Abraham Williams house, as I had before hand ordained it. In the mean tyme, my absence at that instant from London was no ill incounter for me, nor preiudice (as it fortuned) to the kings service. The sayd ambassadour having it for his chief negotiation in charge to hym to procure for the duke his master the title of king of Cyprus, which his master had assumed not long before and which the pope, the emperor, the kyngs of France and Spayne, had refused to give him, and assisting to that purpose all of the formality of a kings ambassador, I had bene put to a streight [60] in what stile to have treated him, if he should have stood upon his reception by an earle at Greenwiche as a kings ambassador, or have refused it at Tower wharfe by a baron as the ambassadour of a duke, answerable to the stile usually observed towards those 2 different qualities.

Eight or ten dayes after his arrival and in continual expectation of order from court for his treatment, I came to towne, and, at the same instant, had delivered me a letter with my lord chamberlins directions, importing that in answer of the expectation the ambassador might perhaps have to be defrayed etc. at his arrival at London it should be intimated to him, as it was by me, that in the kyngs absence that city was no more considerable than other partes of

---

[31] Pougny's request to visit the court in progress had been refused.

[32] Gianfrancesco San Martino, marquis of San Germano, ambassador extraordinary (Aug.–Sept. 1634) of Savoy. He sought English recognition of Victor Amadeus as king of Cyprus. Venice had broken relations with Savoy, for this was a denial of its own claim to Cyprus.

the kingdome, the place of his majestyes residing being alwayes to be iudged the seat of empire, and the court the place, where ambassadors might more especially expect theyr reception and treatment as well as theyr audience. All other provisional accomodations were rather done in honour of his majestyes grace and power, and not as obligations of respect and duty, and when he should come to court he should be lodged and defrayed, tyll then he was to think himself but upon the waye, and not at the end of his iourney. He should have the kings coach to serve him in London (where his lodging was provided for him), as it should be at the court, but that on the way he must be content to hyre coaches for his own accomodation.

[60ᵛ] Before I set forth with this ambassador towards Holmbie,[33] in obedience of these directions and instructions (wherewyth acquainting the ambassadour, he discovered much the better satisfaction) I repayred to the several ministers of state here, for knowledge how they stood affected to his pretences in behalf of his master. The French ambassador said litle to it, but those about him spake the language which they sayd theyr king used, when at any tyme he fell upon that purpose, negative and slyghting. The ambassador of the States, Joachimi, sayd he wondered what reason the duke of Savoy could have hopes here of favour and intercession here from the sister, when the brother had refused to give them, adding that he thought the king would regard what scandal the Venetians, and what stomack the Turk (if we would wayghe our traffick), might conceyve at his consenting to it. The Spanish resident sayd that whyle the pope and the emperor, which were, he sayd, the only king-makers, the kings of Spayne and France denyed theyr assents, the duke of Savoy, he thought, was ill advised to make his cause worse by the more strong opposition he might be sure to meet wyth from the princes, when they should see our king assume that power which they had waved to make use of. The Venetian [61] (most interested, as whose reipublick had for 90 yeares together borne the tytle of kings of Cyprus) talked of it with scorne and contempt, as not doubting, he sayd, our kings wisdome and justice, and adding that when the princes of Europe had generally for so many years avowed theyr tytle and right for that kyngdome, for any now to give it to another would be weaknes, lightnes and contradiction. Besydes, he sayd, that upon his knowledge the duke of Florences agent here[34] had order from his master that, in case our king should give it to the duke of Savoy, he should instantly give advice of it, that an ambassador myght be despatched hither to procure the like for the duke, his master.

[33] Holdenby House, Northants.
[34] Amerigo Salvetti, agent (1625–41) of Tuscany.

These reasons and obiections I was not so ill a servant to the kyng, my master, as not to convey to his knowledge, which, from the fyrst, I had found possessed wyth the inconveniencie lyke to grow from such a novelty, which his two brother kyngs (so his majesty named them) had refused to advance, he had no reason to be the fyrst to assent to it. Yet did theyr majestyes (especially the queen in favor of her deerest syster[35]) doe this ambassador all the personal honor he could expect, and more then I have seen done to any other of his ranck.

Setting out from London, the 14 of [August], we came [61ᵛ] the next day to Northampton and lodged at the *Swan Inn* (taken up wholly for him and his trayne, consisting of 26 persons, whereof 11 or 12 were gentlemen, and satt at his owne table). Sir Robert Eyton, the queens secretary, brought him a welcome from her majesty, and the Mayor and 12 Alderman of the towne soone after (appareled in theyr scarlet gownes) presented him with half a score pots of wine, and two sugar loaves, in the name of theyr corporation. That night, he had the first meale of his plentifull entertaynment, with fishe and the lyke, the next day, with oversyght and ordering of Sir Thomas Mery, Clerk of the Greencloth, the inferior officers of the pantry, celler, etc. attending. He was, on Sunday, the 17 [August], to have his fyrst publick audience at Holmby, whither fetched and conducted by the earl of Stamford[36] in the queens coach (which was appointed to attend him dayly, the kyngs coach being otherwise employed) accompanyed with only three gentlemen, the rest that were lysted failing, these and his cheefe followers bestowed in a second coach of the queens, three noblemens coaches and 3 hackneys of the ambassadors own hiring from London, he was brought to his place of resting in a large lower roome at the left hand of the court and, after a whyle, went to his dinner prepared for him at the Kyngs charge in my lord chamberlins lodging [62] where none but his lordships servants wayted on him (this was to avoyd the usual scrambling of the guard).

Thence, after dynner, descending towards the Presence and receyved before the door thereof by the Captaine of the Guard and at the door by the lord chamberlin, he was presented to theyr majestyes. The kyng thereof four tymes inviting him to cover, he then only touched his head with his hat and standing all the tyme after beare (answerable to the intimation he had given before to me of his intention of complement) but speaking to the queen (though invited to it) he covered not at all. His audience finished, and he returned to the chamber of his fyrst repose, he was by a back stayre fetched by the earle of

---

35 Christine of France, wife of Victor Amadeus.
36 Henry Grey, 1st earl of Stamford.

Carlisle to his privat audience (before designed by him and by me demanded of his majesty) in the privy galleryes and had after that accesse to theyr majestyes in the Privy Chamber *a la domestique*. Nyght come, after his supper in my lord chamberlins lodgings, he had the sight of a mask (or rather ballet being danced unmaskt[37]) casually prepared and, at that tyme, acted by the queene in person with some other ladyes lords and gentlemen mixed, and after midnight (wythout reconduction of the earle of Stamford, excused with his ingaged attendance on some ladyes to theyr remote lodgings) he returned to Northampton. The next day a sumptuous feast provided for theyr Majestyes by the Lord Spencer[38] (a mile or two from Holmby) was a means, upon the Queens invitation as makeing him her guest, to bring together the ambassador and only three of his gentlemen [62ᵛ] fetched from Northampton by the earl of Stamford. The like occasion and compay did the following day call him to Boughton to the Lord Vaux[39] and the third day to Ashby to the earl of Northamptons where he was lodged all night and with much honour, that day and the next he hunted the buck and the stag with his majesty.

It is not to be forgotten how, at the instant before his fyrst audience, he expressed his expectation to receyve in all points the lyke treatment from his majesty, as had bene usually given kings ambassadors, regarding, he sayd, the pretence that his ambassage brought to that purpose and desiring therefore that the kings guard might be accordingly ranged for his passage to his audience. To which I answered custome here made no such distinction between a kings and a dukes ambassador, as that the latter had not the like reception in that point as the former. Yet to prevent his exception (this wythout attributing or derogating to him, or from him, beyond his due) I acquaynted the captayne of the guard to bestowe themselves on the landing place of the stayres. before the Presence door, by which, and not through the hall where that company usually gave their attendance, he was to passe in his descent from the lord chamberlins lodging, which gave him good satisfaction and which never the less (regarding our custome) was not irregular.

[63] When, towards the end of the week, I was told his dispatch was ready, I let him know from my lord chamberlin, as I had order, that the Sunday following, being the tenth day of his treatment at the kyngs charge, his majesty would give him his parting publick audience and that to that purpose his dinner should be prepared that day in court with service of the guard at it (my lord chamberlins family being, at that instant, upon remove to theyr

37 Mask unidentified; performance unknown.
38 At Althorp, Robert Spencer, 1st lord Spencer.
39 Edward Vaux, 4th lord Vaux of Harrowden.

proceeding to the rest of the progress). But the ambassadour coming the day before from Northampton to court and the queen affecting, for her sisters sake, his longer stay and repayre to her to some other house of theyr majestyes, his dinner for the next day in court was countermanded and that night supping domestically at the Countess of Denbighes table, seeing after it a comedy,[40] and returning late to Northampton he on Monday returned towards London.

[64ᵛ] All pleas and pretensions could not move the French ambassador to visit first, nor remove the other (of Savoy) from the like resolution,[41] though, at another incounter, in presence of the queen at Nonsuch, they saluted at a distance and at a neerer approach spake complementally together.

The day of this their meeting, her majesty, after the departure of the French, who had the night before lodged in court (no usuall thing) from invitation of the earl of Carlisle and in his lodgings, cast her favours so farr upon the Savoyard, for the sake of her syster the Duchess, as she consented to sing (which she knew how to do most divinely well) in hearing of the ambassador and, after supper, danced with him and others, both French and English dances tyll after midnight he returned by moonlight to London.

This course of his almost dayly going to court then at Nonsuche, and in one of the Queens coaches appoynted by the lord Goring for his attendance, continued tyll the day before his departure, which was four or five dayes after he had taken his publick leave of their majestyes [65] in the Presence there, on the 7th of September, wyth the conduction from London of the earl of Newport, and the service of a iourneying coache of the kyngs, one of the queens, that lords and one I hyred (others of the lords failing). His dynner was with plenty prepared in court at the kings charge, his company the Treasurer and Controller of the household, two or three gentlemen of the court and his own better sort of followers. The inferior of them dyned after in the same room, upon the reversion snatched at (after the disordered custome of our court) though much endeavoured to be prevented, as soon as the officers backs were turned, by the Guard that served it in, but wayted not during the dynner, yet omitted not after it (nor others also of better quality to their greater shame) to demand gratuities. This I for their satisfaction, though little to myne own, moved for, but was answered with fair words and no further. His audience passed, I presented him in the presence of the earl

---

[40] Play unidentified; performance unknown.
[41] The "first visit" would indicate parity with the French monarchy and imply recognition of the pretended "royal" title.

of Holland with a fayre diamond ring from his majesty of the value (at least so costing) of 500 £, it being of the full weight of 7 carats.

[67] This ambassador having passed here some six weeks tyme, without obtayning in favour of his negotiation, *il titolo Regio* for the duke his master, which he pretended not formally to, nor gave him, in his common appellation, beyond that of *Altezza Reale*, parted thence, the 13th of September, with good satisfaction for his own personal respect by post with only three in his company. His trayne went two or three dayes before, for their imbarking at Dover for France, etc.

[67ᵛ] The 27th of September, I receyved a letter from the French ambassador demanding audience of the kyng with expedition. This demand was so new and rare to my lord chamberlin (the ministers of France, ever since the marriage of his majesty with a daughter of that kingdome, pretending to a domestique access, and takeing the opportunity of their audience, wheresoever they found his majesty at leisure to give it) as his lordship with readiness (it being a favour he merrily said that had not bene of long time done by any ambassador of that nation) asked and obtained one of his majesty for the next day at Hampton Court. There I receyving him at the first gate introduced him to his majestyes presence (by way of the Great Hall, [68] Guard Chamber, Presence and Privy Chamber) into the wythdrawing roome and thence after to the queens quarter. This course thus begun, I that day provided (by the help of a person of quality and trust) that it might be continued as not only adding a respect to the ambassador when (lyke him self) he should wyth fitting ceremony and publick notice be conducted to his audiences but contributing also to the kyngs honour when wyth regardes dew to his person he should be free from being surprised (as otherwyse he might) without the presence of his lords to assist him (if occasion should requyre) with theyr counsel.

This French ambassador ordinary, the Marquis de Pougny, being invited by the lord maior[42] to his annual feast, and not inquiring of me before hand what was to be done for sight of that dayes solemnity, was the day before unprovided of a house or stand in Cheapsyde, for which I (though late) sent my officer to provide one (at the ambassadors charge) against after diner, all houses being taken up all ready for that morning. He about 9 of the clock that day, came to Somerset house saw there the passage of my lord maior out and home by water. Thence he went (for avoydance of the throng at Cheapside) [68ᵛ] by Smythfield and Cripplegate to Gildhall, dyned there in that hall in company of the States ambassador and divers great lords invited at a table,

---

[42] Sir Richard Parkhurst.

on the right hand of the end of the hall from the entrance (commonly called the Hoystings). That at the other end being preserved for my lord maior and his being an alteration and remove (then fyrst putt in practice) from a less, and less fit, room within that house where they were wont to sit and whither, a whyle after the ambassadors entrance, I conducted him to see and salute the city ladies and their daughters there bestowed upon that alteration.

Exception was taken by some of the Lords that at their table were placed two or three of the ambassadors followers, and in particular the French ambassadors secretary and the States, but custome and their boldnesse was all the excuse and remedy I had for it. He went immediately after dynner to his stand in Cheapside and there after almost two howers patience of expectation, saw the lord maiors and the severall companyes rydeing and marching to Pauls.

The resident of Spayne and agent of Flanders had, as at other times, their severall invitations, but came not.

The ambassador of Venice,[43] who arrived here but a fortnight before, was also invited, but improperly while he yet kept himself *sconosciuto* and had reason to refuse, as they had none to make an offer, of soe unseasonable a courtesy.

[69ᵛ] The Sunday following he (Angelo Coraro) had his first publick audience of both their Majestyes together in the Presence Chamber at Whytehal fetched to it fom his house by the earle of Winchelsey[44] wyth the company of eight gentlemen of the Privy Chamber, the kyngs [70] coach only serving and nine others. His audience of both kyng and queen finished, Francisco Zonca (secretary to his predecessor and who, upon his departure, was qualifyed resident here) took his leave of theyr majestyes.

All the tyme of this ambassadors speaking to the queen, he (in observation of what I had before told him concerning some other ambassadors censured for their over much forwardnesse to cover) stood uncovered before her majesty, so did he two dayes after (though by some advised to the contrary) when he had his access to the prince, duke of York and Princess at St. James's, whither (I not accompanying him thither as being no extraordinary) I receyved him at his descent from his coache before the great stayre in the fyrst court there.

This ambassador, two or three dayes before Christmas, asking me my opinion whether, though he had no particular busynes for subiect of an audience, it would not be fit for him to demand one were it but to present his majesty

---

[43] Angelo Correr (Nov. 1634 – Oct. 1637) continued as ambassador of Venice the policy of encouraging English ties with France and the Dutch Republic.
[44] Thomas Finch, 2nd earl of Winchelsea.

with a congragulation of the new year then beginning, I answered that
howsoever other ambassadors [70ᵛ] of late time (and particularly his predecessor Gussoni) had been so punctual in performance of that complement, it
would be well done of him I thought (were it but upon his so fresh arrival
to let himself be seen in court) and could not but be well taken by his majesty.
Hereupon, the 30th of December, he passed by the way of the Privy Garden
and galleryes to the Withdrawing Chamber, where after the three reverences
of his approach, he only touching his head with his hat, upon his majestyes
invitation to his covering, he all the tyme stood bareheaded. Though he had
caused his growne to be brought wyth him, he did not put it on, as his predecessor were wont to do, when he was to come to his Majestyes presence but
kept on his cloak. Observing this and letting fall a word or two of my notice
of it, he sayd he took it not to be of the essence of his imployment to weare
his gowne at audiences, yet that at his first and publick audience he had, for
forme and customes sake, worn it and intended so to do at his last, but for the
rest, he thought the wearing, or not wearing, it was a thing indifferent.

Some few dayes before his audience (Christmas then neer) he acquainted
me, and I my lord chamberlin, with a desyre he had to be present at theyr
majestyes and the ladyes dancing in the great hall of the court. Thither, at a
tyme assigned him, he came with my attendance, [71] after he had reposed
himself in my lord chamberlins lodgings and repayred thence to the queens
Withdrawing Chamber, thence in company of theyre majestyes (the French
ambassador being also there) to the Great Hall, where he was seated at the
upper end of the retourned forme, on the right hand of the kyng, without
the barre of theyr majestyes seat. The French ambassador sat in common
judgement beneath him, because more remote and on the Kings left hand,
but in dew account not so, because he might seem to have made choyce, and no
doubt did, of that place for entertainment of the Duchess of Buckingham
seated there, and because the known distance of theyrranckes of representation
considered, ther was no question to be made of precedence[45] (such as, if taken,
or given, might redound to eithers prejudice) and was at that tyme a voluntary
act of the French ambassadour.

[71] The 23rd of December, divers in court meeting me there, asked how
it came to pass that the day before an ambassador (as they stiled him) from the
emperor of Muscovy[46] went up and downe the lodgings of state in court,
wythout my conduct, seeking his majesty and carying his letters openly wyth
ostentation before him, and followed by some of his nation in theyr country

---

[45] Venice insisted on parity with all monarchies in precedence.
[46] A merchant with letters from Czar Michael.

habit. Of this errour and disorder I (tyll then ignorant) [71ᵛ] inquirying found certaine of our Muscovy merchants guylty, who bringing him to court wythout acquainting my lord chamberlin or me that such a one (who was indeed but a messenger and no ambassador though called so) was arrived in England. So, the next day, when I heard he was to have access to his majesty by appointment, and that he was aledly for that purpose in the Withdrawing Roome next the Privy Chamber, I remonstrated to the merchants (there wyth him) their error and presumption, and was answered that they had that morning excused it to my lord chamberlin. But this being no sufficient reparation of the disrepect to his lordship, and the wrong done me in my place, I reproved them roundly for it, intimating wyth all theyr undutifull caryage towards the Kyng in surprising him, without my dew notice fyrst given, and wythout my conduction to his presence, etc.

Some few dayes after a complaynt was brought me by the same messengers interpreter of the base treatment, as he called it, afforded them both in dyet and otherwise by the merchants. Though his commission, he sayd, was as ample (his imployment being not only hither, but to France also, and after to the low countryes) as any sent of late years from those parts. With this complaint, and wyth the man that made it, I repayred to my lord chamberlin, [72] who speaking after with Mr. Secretary about yt, such satisfaction followed as no more noyse was made of it. A few dayes after he tooke his leave of the Kyng in the Privy Gallery with the attendance of my officer and the introduction of one of the Gentleman Ushers of the Privy Chamber.

[72] While the kyng was in his progress (the year past at Ashby) his majesty, the lordes and officers of the household there present, takyng into consideration the excessive charge of defraying ambassadors without limitacion of tyme, and particularly at that instant when the ambassador of Savoy, the marquis of St. Germano,[1] had been and then was defrayed from the day of his arrival at Northampton, wythout appearance of meanes or excuse how mannerly, to desist of such a chargeable encumbrance before the courts remove or his final departure, it was then and there ordered and set downe under his majestyes hand and seal, and the act of it entered in the counting house at court, that no ambassador should be thence forward defrayed longer then tyll the day of his first audience should be past. The order carying these formall wordes:

[72ᵛ]

BY THE KING

Whereas the defraying of forayn ambassadors is now growne more exorbitant for expense then it was in former times, or is in any other country, and is occasion of competing and distast to the ambassadors themselves, everyone pretending to as much favour and respect as hath bene shown to any other (though for the measure, we will not have the honour of our princely bounty to be restreyned but extended to our frends and allyes, as we shall think meet), yet for the tyme, wee now order and declare our expresse pleasure, the defraying of no ambassador whatsoever shall continue longer then tyll the day of his fyrst audience be past, after which theyr intertainment at our charge shall determine and cease. Hereof we require our lord chamberlin and the officers of our household, secretaryes, master of Ceremonyes and all other whome it may concern to take notice that hereafter no instance be made, nor office done to the contrary but that this our command be strictly observed, which we require to be entered by them severally amongst the orders of our house to be inviolably kept. Given at Ashby, the 22 August 1634.

According to this order, when about the midst of March word came to court of the approach of a French ambassador extraordinary,[2] it was intimated to me by the Treasurer and Controler of the household that his majesty [73]

---

[1] The prolonged stay had been, according to Finet, by Henrietta's invitation. See IV 63.

[2] Henri de Senneterre (Saint-Nectaire), marquis de la Ferté Nabert, ambassador extraordinary (March 1635 – July 1637) of France. Richelieu had completed a military alliance with the Dutch Republic on 8 Feb. 1635 and now hoped to include England in the same agreement against Spain, before the official French declaration of war on June 6th.

would have his pleasure touching the said order duly observed, and notice of it given by me to the said ambassador at his first arrival, to prevent the expectation that he might perhaps have of entertaynment at the kings charge beyond the tyme limited. The same day, March 13, the marquis Hamilton, Master of the Kings Horses, let me know his majestyes express pleasure was that in regard it was neyther for the profit nor service of his majesty, and without example of other princes, that ambassadors should have the dayly use of (as had been accustomed) his majestyes coaches to cary them up and downe at theyr command, that no ambassador should thenceforth have use of any of them farther or oftener than to and from theyr audiences. Wyth this significacion given me, I that day acquainted his majesty and had from his own mouth a confirmation that such was his pleasure, and that I should make it knowne and take care to have it observed with punctuality.

[73 ᵛ] Having notice given me, the 15 of March, by the ambassador of France that the marquis de Seneterre, extraordinary from the kyng his master, was come to Gravesend, I took barge for my self to cary him his welcome from the king. I gave order for three more and a tiltboat to be there the next day and for the kinges barge also, and another attending, to be at an hour appointed for his reception by the earl of Cleveland³ at Greenwich. So I went down to Gravesend and staying there tyll the time fit for his imbarking, the wind grew so strong and contrary, as when the boat wherein I had bestowed the remaynes of his baggage and all his groomes and lacquays lay ready to depart, I perswaded him to take post for his proceeding to Greenwich, whereto assenting, we there found the earl mentioned, his son, lord Wentworth, the son of viscount Wilmot,⁴ a dozen gentlemen of the privy chamber and the French ambassador also, who, having gone by water to him at Gravesend the day before, met here the second tyme for his reception and conduction to London, whither he came that night to his lodging at Sir Abraham Williams in Westminster, the kings coach and others missing of their appearance at his landing by reason of a countermand that I had sent them to repayre to Tower wharf, doubting that the tyde might not have served to shoot the bridge. [74] He came to his fyrst supper prepared at the kyngs charge on Tuesday, the 17 of March, the species of the diet having been sent in that day (as they were every day after during the time of his defraying) by the kings officers and their dressing left to his own servants.

³ Thomas Wentworth, 1st earl of Cleveland.
⁴ Charles Wilmot, viscount Wilmot of Athlone.

Within an hour of his arrival at his lodging, the lord Clifford,[5] as I had before hand propounded lest that due complement be forgotten, brought him the kings welcome to the towne, which his majesty the day before his going to Theobalds left to be delivered by that nobleman. Soon after came, on the lyke errand from the queen, Mr. Germain,[6] one of the gentlemen ushers of her Privy Chamber, who the next day also brought him a signification of her majestyes pleasure (as the ambassador himself told me) for his access to her in privat, which he went for in company only of that gentleman and one more, wythout other attendants. He had at least three hours privat conference with her majesty but, whether this were done with communicacion of her intention to the kyng before his departure out of towne, or her owne motion for satisfaction of her desire (impatient perhaps to attend the knowledge how matters stood in France tyll the uncertain tyme of his audience) appeared not to me.

[74ᵛ] The day came that was assigned for his publick audience (Sunday 22 March), he was brought to court (in the kyngs coach, the queens and 13 or 14 others following) by the earl of Salisbury, a privy counceller and knight of the Garter (the ambassador being in the same place to the king his master and of the order of *Saint Esprit*), there went also in that lords company the lord Clifford, the lord Whartons brother,[7] and half a dozen gentlemen of the Privy Chamber, besydes the ordinary ambassador of France, accompanying him from his lodging and seating himself at the fore end of the coach, left (after some contention of courtesy) the hinder seat, on the left hand of the ambassador extraordinary, to the earl. [75] Out of the coach and in the court he marched on the right hand of (the earl of Salisbury on the left) the extraordinary, who came before theyr majestyes in the Presence Chamber (the Banquetting House being at tyme incumbered with the yet standing scene of the queens mask)[8] and presented his letters to the kyng. The ordinary ambassador held discourse with the queen tyll the other interrupted him with his address to her and presentation of his letters (which he had tyll that tyme reserved not with standing the access he had before in privat). This passed, they returned to the councell chamber and rested there tyll I had gone to know and had brought back the queens pleasure for theyr demanded privat access of the extraordinary ambassador to her majesty. This granted and ended (the earl of Salisbury in the mean tyme, though making offer to accompany him, taking leave and leaving him to go to the queen alone) he returned late to his lodging.

---

[5] Henry Clifford, son of the earl of Cumberland.
[6] Sir Henry Jermyn.
[7] Philip Wharton, 4th lord Wharton, brother-in-law of Clifford.
[8] Davenant's *Temple of Love* had been presented Feb. 12th.

[75ᵛ] For his company to his private audience of the kyng, the thyrd day after his publick, he would admit of none but myself and the gentleman of his horse, saying he went now in privat about busynes of state, as an ambassador and not as a leader of troopes (he had not the company of the ordinary which was observed and by that minister murmured at) neyther would he allow his lacquays to sett theyr foot within the privy gallery, but commanded them to attend him below in the garden. This for instruction to other ambassadors, whose followers stick not to press even into the doors where the master hath his audience.

The Venetian ambassador had audience in privat, the 2nd April, wearing then his gowne, which he had before dispensed with. My lord chamberlin (I know not whether upon some distaste of his not observance) met him neither at the first door of the privy gallery (as he usually had done other) nor receyved him at the entrance of the Withdrawing Room, no more did he accompany him to the same door at his parting. The ambassador spoke to the king by interpretation of Mr. Secretary Cook, not trusting, it seemes, to the strength he had in the French language.

[76] The thyrd day after his visit, the extraordinary, together with his colleague the ordinary, had audience of the commissioners (deputed for his busynes) in the Councell Chamber. These were the archbishop of Canterbury, the earles of Arundel, Carlisle and Holland, and the 2 principal secretaryes. I introduced them by the ordinary way together from the great gate of the court, the way through the garden being proper only for his access privatly to his majesty. He was receyved at the top of the stayre by Secretary Cook and but at the door (and that within the chamber) by the lords who, at his parting, took there also theyr leave of him, leaving him to the secretaryes conduct which extended no farther then the place he first met him at. Whether this were not too scarce and should not have reached at least to the stayres foot, query, by his countenance I am sure he showed he was not well pleased with it.

[76ᵛ] An ambassador from the queen and crowne of Sweden by name Skijt[9] (who had come here imployed hither before, the latter tyme 1627) landed at Gravesend the 4th of April, having omitted the first night of his arrival to send me notice of it, he suffered his stay there a day or two longer than he needed. His house was already provided (according to the lord cham-

---

[9] Baron John Skijt, ambassador extraordinary (April–May 1635) of Sweden, sought Charles's support during the coming negotiations at Prague with the Imperial leaders and particularly for Sweden's settlement with Poland, which was to lead to a disadvantageous truce at Stuhmsdorff in May 1635.

berlins directions) in the Deanes Yard at Westminster and the earl of Elgin[10] made choyce of by his majesty for his reception at Greenwich. The 6 of April I presented him with the kings welcome, having brought with me three barges for his transport and left order for the kings and one more to serve him for his reception by the lord mentioned. As we fell before Greenwich he came forth on the water to enter the barge the ambassador came in, delyvered there his complements, took him, in the kings barge and with him two of his three sons, together with the Agent here for Sweden, Monsieur Bloom. He conducted him to his landing at Westminster bridge, whereon he was met and welcomed in the name [77] of theyr lords by the secretaryes of the extraordinary and ordinary of France, the Venetian and States ambassadors, each in theyr masters ranks and immediatly after the other, thence in the kyngs coach, those of the ambassadors and some others, he was brought to his lodging mentioned, where an hour or two after, he had a third welcome delyvered him from his majesty by the lord Herbert in Latin. The day before his arrival at London, one of his 3 sons, that had been in England before, asked my opinion whether his father were to impart his letters of credence to his majestyes Secretary of State before his coming to London for his audience, according to the custome (he sayd) of the country he came from. I answered the custome was not so here, neyther had I [77ᵛ] ever seen princes ambassadors of the westerly or southerly parts of the world present their credence to other hands then the kings, and that at theyr first access to his person. Yet would not this serve to divert the ambassador from sending his letters by his son to his majestyes Secretary Sir John Cook, the first hour of his coming to towne, with which he was pleased that night to make me acquainted saying that, not with standing my sufficient reasons given his son, he was bound to observe the custome of his own country and not of others. He said he had it formally prescribed him in his instructions, from which he must not vary, to send his letters of credence to the king as soon as he should arrive in the kingdom. This course he intended to take in delyvery of the letters he had from the queen of Sweden to the queen of England by the hand of her majestyes secretary.

[78ᵛ] After the ambassador of Sweden had passed 14 dayes at the kyngs and his own entertaynment and his majesty had consulted and concluded with the earl of Arundel (as high Marshall of England) and some other knights companions of the order, and Garter king of Heraultes[11] about the forme of proceedings to be had for reception of the Garter brought back after the

---

[10] Thomas Bruce, lord Kinloss, 1st earl of Elgin.
[11] Sir John Burroughs.

death of the king of Sweden[12] by this ambassador, who had it for one of the principal busyneses of his imployment, his majesty was pleased to send me to him the 17 of April with this message, that being desirous to render all due honour to the memory of the king of Sweden deceased, he would the next day, at Two of the clock after noon, be ready in full chapter together with the knights companions of the order, to receyve the Garter of the king of Sweden with the honour due to it by the hand of this ambassador.

At the hour assigned the ambassador being conducted by me in the kings coach to court allighting at the gate, he commanded four of the principal gentlemen of his trayne to come forth of another coach and to carry, one after the other, next before his person, upon cushions of velvet provided for that use, each of them, a part of the ornaments of the order all covered with fine cloths of needle work. The first of them carryed the surcoat of the order, being of crimson velvet, and the book [79] of the statutes of the order placed on it. The second bore the robe of the order which was of purple velvet. The third the Garter and the two Georges (a less and a greater, this set richly with diamonds). The fourth the coler of the order being of gold inameled with roses. In this manner all his other followers marching before the four gentlemen, and the Agent and myself on each hand of the ambassador, he passed on cross the fyrst court, up the great stayres and along the terras to the Councell Chamber where, after some litle tyme of rest, the antientest knights then there, the earl of Pembroke and Montgomery lord chamberlin of the kings house, and the earl of Arundel, earl marshall of England, clothed in the habits of the order (Garter king of heralds and the Usher of the order marching before them) came to salute and welcome him in the name of the sovereine, and to conduct him to the chamber of presence, where his majesty and the other knights sitting in chapter stayed to his coming.

The order of theyr march thither, as it had been appointed, was this. In the first place went the followers of the ambassador two and two, after them the heralds (being twelve in number appareled in theyr coates of armes) two and two, then followed Garter king of Armes bearing before him on a cushion of crimson velvet [79ᵛ] all the ornaments mentioned uncovered, assisted for theyr more easy carriage by the Usher of the order, both clothed in theyr habits of office, with robes of crimson satin lyned with white taffety, in the fourth place marched the ambassador, having at his right hand the antienter knight, the earl of Pembroke, at his left the earl of Arundel, and after him came the Agent and myself.

---

[12] Gustavus Adolphus, killed at Lützen, 16 Nov. 1632.

Being all arrived in this manner at the door of the Presence Chamber which (being the place wherein was held the chapter) was kept shut, the ambassadors gentlemen, the Agent and myself were permitted to enter but commanded withal to depart after we had a sight of his majesty who, standing under the state, and more below the knights on each side four, besides the two knights conductors, the prelate of the order,[13] the chancellor,[14] and the Registrer,[15] which also assisted each in his habit of office. His majesty receyved the ambassador who, after he had made his three reverences, placed himself under the State next the king and, after invitation, covering made an eloquent oration in latin, which lasted almost half an hour. This ended, the king of heralds (all the tyme kneeling and bearing the ornaments of the order before him) presented the sayd ornaments to the ambassador, the ambassador to the king and the king delivered them to the chancellor who, after he had receyved them [80] made a speech in French much extolling the merits of that great king of Sweden, the doors of the chapter were set open. The king commanded me to bring in four of the ambassadors principal gentlemen, the younger of the 3 sons, James Skijt lord of Daderoft, Gabriel Oxenstierna lord of Murbey, John Krust of Havila and Gustave Banier of Etones. He knighted them and left the two lords mentioned to reconduct the ambassador to the Councell Chamber in the same order as he arrived. The solemnity ended, which passed all other of that kind long before it, and was in honour of the king of Sweden (by his majestyes own pleasure and direction without direction of any former precedent to be found) thus regulated.

[78ᵛ] The 22nd of April the ambassador extraordinary of France sent his secretary to me for an audience of his majesty the next day (different from his domestick condition assumed, which gave him liberty of access and so of audience at his pleasure). This audience he had, with my introduction by the usuall way to the garden, with the company of his colleague the ordinary, bringing with them letters received from the king theyr master and giving account of his denouncing war to the king of Spayne, which being so extraordinary a busynes made theyr proceeding then so different from the ordinary.[16]

[80] St. Georges feast and the presence here of so many ambassadors ordinary and extraordinary happening at one instant, I inquired after their dis-

---

[13] Walter Curle, bishop of Winchester.

[14] Sir Francis Crane.

[15] Christopher Wren, dean of Windsor.

[16] This is a marginal note by Finet. These superflous ceremonies were for propaganda purposes.

positions to be at it, and found all inclinable, except the ambassador of Sweden, who, excusing him self with the satisfaction, he sayd, to have seen it in the tyme of queen Elizabeth, could not keep undiscovered his further cause of absence [80ᵛ] when I (to sound him) obiected that perhaps he would not be there to give place to the French ordinary, no (replyed he) nor to the extraordinary, but of this (he added) say nothing, I pray, to any man since I desire not to bring it to discourse or question unless upon urgent occasion. I, who made no doubt he would so much as question precedence with the French, had five or six dayes before (upon some excuse passed to that purpose between the two French ambassadors) asked the earl of Carlisles opinion, which of them ought to have the hand in case the Swedish extraordinary should at one and the same tyme incounter with the French both ordinary and extraordinary, and had for answer that an ordinary lost no place by that title, but that his masters right was still the same, for place or prerogative in his minister, being an ordinary as well as if he were an extraordinary.

The ambassadors that came that day at the feast of St. George were the two French, the Venetian and the States for whom I, having as at other tymes caused a [81] scaffold to be set up at the end of the terras next the entrance to the Gard Chamber, and another for the placing of so many gentlemen as should attend them next the Banketting House, that from thence they might see the kings and knights passage in procession. The queen was pleased to invite the two French to stand privatly with her in a window of the lord keepers lodging next the great gate, whither also the Venetian (that had otherwise been left alone to the States ambassadors company, which he could not have indured without distaste and departure, the French ambassador being known to be in court) followed her majesty. In the mean time the States ambassador came without my knowledge to the Councell Chamber, intending no other sight that day then that of his majesty, when he should be set at diner that he might give him then the *para bien* of the feast, as he had been formerly almost every year accustomed. But I telling him how the other ambassadors were bestowed and were even then come, from seeing the procession, into the privy gallery, he was much troubled till I had acquainted my lord chamberlin with his solitary case and his lordship had referred me for resolution to the king. He thought fit and ordered that all the ambassadors should enter together with the queen, so they did to all theyr satisfactions following her majesty immediatly when she went to salute the king sitting at diner, and from him the knights, and returning with her majesty to the privy gallery.

[81ᵛ] The third of May, the ambassador of Sweden had for his parting a publick audience of both theyr majestyes conducted to it in the Presence Chamber by the earl of Bedford, who had for company in the kings coach (the 4 ambassadors, that lords and three others following) his son the lord Russell,[17] the lord viscount Doncaster son to the earl of Carlisle, the lord viscount Grandison,[18] Sir Francis Vane brother to the earl of Westmoreland, Mr. Leuke eldest son to the baron of Dancourt,[19] and half a dozen gentlemen of the Privy Chamber. He first spake to the king in Latin (as at his first audience) with Mr. Secretary Cookes interpretation, and after in French, as he did also to the queen.

[84ᵛ] At the beginning of June a gallant young gentleman, don Fernando de Teshada[20] of the family of Mendoza in Spayn, arrived here imployed from the Infante Cardinal to correspond with the congragulation that his majesty had, some three monthes before, sent by Mr. Porter of his Bed Chamber[21] to that prince upon his arrival in Flanders for government of those provinces. Two or three dayes after this gentlemans arrival, the Spanish resident don Juan de Nicolaldi demanded, and had, an audience of his majesty both for some instant busynes of the king his master and for account of the envoyes coming, who had his access assigned him for the next day in the kings Withdrawing Room at Greenwich, and went there, the 9th of June, with only my company, the Agents of Flanders[22] and three or four gentlemen, his followers. It was questioned by some whether his majesty would render the lyke (supercilious) reception as had been given Mr. Porter, to whom that prince never so much stirred his hat or vouchsafed one look of courtesy when he first came into his presence, neither was the just returne of that high carriage unapprehended and feared both by the gentleman himself and the other Spanish ministers, [85] as they spared not (in their doubts) to discover to me. But his majesty habituated in courtesy and being of too good and gracious a

17 William Russell, son of the earl of Bedford.
18 William Villiers, viscount Grandison of Limerick.
19 Nicholas Leke, son of Farncis Leke, baron Deincourt.
20 Fernando de Tejada, son of the former confidant of Olivares, Francisco de Tejada. The Cardinal Archduke assumed office on 4 Nov. 1634 as governor.
21 Endymion Porter had met Ferdinand in 1623 during Charles's visit to Spain.
22 Henry Taylor (for his career see Albert Loomie, "Canon Henry Taylor, Spanish Habsburg Diplomat," *Recusant History* 17 No. 3 [May 1985] 223–37). The coldness of the Cardinal Infante Ferdinand, the new governor of the Low Countries, was due to a mistake in King Charles's official greetings: "Mr. Coke drew the letter in French . . . and gave the Cardinal no style but *Vous*, which the Spanish abhor, a kind of Thouing of one, whereas he expected *Altesse Royale*, at least *Altesse* . . ." (*The Earl of Strafford's Letters*, ed. William Knowler, 2 vols. [London, 1739] I 359).

disposition to revenge quarells of that kind (howsoever such keeping of state had been observed to be both natural and customary in the kings of Spayn and their children) put off to him his hat at the instant of his approach and afforded him all fayr respects of welcome. The day before, when Mr. Vice Chamberlin asked his majesty whether it were his pleasure that his coach should bring this gentlemen to his first audience, as Mr. Porter had had the cardinals at Brussels to bring the envoy to his audience, his majesty answered (looking on me) 'you know whether any other French or Spanish imployed as this gentleman have had it?' Whereto I not daring to returne a definite answer, or to reply further for the use of it, he was the next day brought in the Spanish residents coach (two hyred ones and mine attending) all passing without exception or murmur, and the less no doubt for the honour of the king without resentment did him in putting off his hat to him, as hath been mentioned. From his audience of the king he went straight for one to the queens side, where he had it in her privy gallery with gracious respects, but not without exception and dislike of some great men then by to see both the ambassadors of France there present,[23] not with standing the so freshly declared war between the king their master and the cardinal Infante, but it was excused as a French liberty.

[85ᵛ] A seven night after his first audience he had his last to take leave of the king, and should have then had the like of the queen, but when I had two dayes before presented to her majestys lord chamberlin his modest doubt whether the demand of his last access, so soon after his first, besides that he had brought with him no letters to her majesty, might not be held an importunity, I was answered by his lordship that by any meanes he must not fayle at taking his leave, as he himself could not fail of demanding an hour to be assigned for it, but his lordship was forgetful of what he had promised, and the queen not prepared because not expecting to receyve him, that complement remayned unperformed. At this departure from the presence of his majesty, I left him in the Presence Chamber of the king, while I went to the queens side, when ignorant of our custome, putting on his hat, a gentleman Usher scandalized at it, overpunctually in my opinion, admonished him of it by the agent of Flanders there present, which drew him thence sooner than he intended, or I would return, for his further conduction.

The 19th of June, he parted from London presented that day by me from his majesty with a diamond ring of 400 £ valew, which some would have had less, but the precedents produced of others, who of his condition and employment and of meaner birth, had had as much (the reason also alleged

[23] Both Pougny and Senneterre pleaded "domestic" entry.

181

that envoys, being extraordinary agents, his majesty was not tyed to an [86] ordinary rate for what he would bestow on them) prevailed for the valew mentioned. He sent to me, to my house after I had taken leave of him, a bason and ewer of 80 ounces, worth 21 £.

The 14 of June, Monsieur de Cise, styling himself count de Pecet,[24] imployed hither for Agent, had his first audience of the king in his Withdrawing Chamber at Greenwich having been received by me no sooner than as he descended from his coach at the garden outer gate there only; upon notice from himself of his arrival at London about a seven night before, I gave him a welcome from his majesty at his lodging, He should have had (according to the assignation he receyved) an access also to the queen at the same tyme, but her majesty that day indisposed remitted him to the following day, when he was introduced by one of the gentlemen Ushers, and not by me, though I had order for it, as not bound to that service. Especially, he pretended, as he did, to a kind of domestick condition here by the same right that the French ministers have it, of being representants for the brother king of France, as the other is to the husband of the sister duchess of Savoy.

[86ᵛ] 23 June: Dyning with the marquis de Seneterre, ambassador extraordinary from France, a complaynt was brought to him by his almoner, as he was rysing from table, that a priest having entered the court before his house,[25] for refuge agaynst an arrest laid in him by a pursuivant[26] (with a constable his associate), was by them drawn forcibly thence and caryed to prison.[27] At this the ambassador taking an allarme desyred me to repayre instantly to some of the lords of the Councell and to let them know how his house (that was, he sayd, the king his masters more than his) had been violated and a prisoner taken forceably out of it after he made it his sanctuary, that therefore he desyred their lordships to take present order that the sayd prisoner

---

[24] Benedetto di Cize, count of Pezze, agent (June 1635 – Oct. 1638) of Savoy, came to thank Charles for his efforts to reconcile the Duke with Venice and to seek supplies for protection against France. Efforts on behalf of the "royal" title of Cyprus continued to meet no success.

[25] The house of Sir Abraham Williams, according to custom.

[26] Francis Newton, pursuivant. This diplomatic incident was fully reported to Venice: CSP V, 1632–36, pp. 422, 432.

[27] John Brown, born 1568 in Moray, Scotland, joined the order of Friars (Minims) in Paris in 1595. He later had plans to establish a college for Scottish priests in Paris but encountered opposition from Henrietta (J. Durkan, "The Career of John Brown, Minim," Innes Review 21 No. 2 [Autumn 1970] 164–69). In 1641, he caused political embarrassment for Charles by an appearance before a committee of the House of Commons with disclosures about suspicious activities of Henrietta, Laud, the Pope, and some Jesuits (ibid., "Brown's Confession," 169–70; Journals of the House of Commons II 118, 119, 144).

myght be brought back and restored to the place from whence he had been taken, otherwise he must instantly acquaynt the kyng with the affront offered him, which he was loath to do, regarding the trouble it would bring his majesty and the noyse it would make in the world, adding further that if he should not have a speedy redress in that which so neerly concerned his masters honour and his own, he should be bound to protest and give an account of it to the king his master by a messenger that was the next day to go for Paris. With this message I went to seek out Mr. Secretary Windebank, but he then absent from court, I repayred to the earl of Manchester, lord privy seal, and related to him the whole proceeding as before and brought [87] back this answer. That he knew the ambassadors person and his house to be so privileged from violence, as whosoever should in the lest measure offer any (as it seemed this fellow had done) to eyther of them, he knew it would be his majestyes pleasure, and should be his own care, to have him severely punished, that he would therefore give present order for diligent inquyry to be made after him (who was indeed at that instant not to be found) and being found should be kept under restraynt till the ambassador might receyve satisfaction.

But this satisfaction by this answer not sufficiently given to the ambassador (jelous of the wrong that myght by delay redound to his person and quality) he desired me to returne once more to my lord privy seal with request that the priest (who by that tyme was by my industry in his search found out, where he was in the hands of the pursuivant) might by that night be sent to his house (as to the sanctuary, he called it, from whence he was violently taken) till he might the next day (as he sayd he intended) acquaynt the king with the proceeding and receyve his majestyes further pleasure. At this my lord privy seal made a demur and let me know (as for the knowledge of the ambassador) that the priest having been already under an arrest, when he sought his escape, and now being a prisoner, his simple power would not serve so to dispose of him, but that all which for that instant he could (and would readily) do for the [87ᵛ] ambassadors service was to comitt the pursuivant to prison and the priest to the custody of a messenger in his owne house, to be the next day forth coming and after disposed of at the ambassadors pleasure, to which he doubted not but his majesty would refer him. With which answer the ambassador seeming satisfyed, the lord privy seal, at his further request, instantly wrot a letter to Mr. Secretary relating the whole proceeding and the ambassadors desire that it might be communicated to his majesty, with which letter I and the secretary of the ambassador went the next day early to court and delyvered it to the Secretary Windebanck, he the substance of it to the king, and the king signifying his pleasure, a warrant was signed by

Mr. Secretary for immediat delyvery of the priest to the ambassador, the warrant running thus:

> 'Whereas John Browne is committed to your charge upon suspition of being a priest, it is his majestyes pleasure that immediatly upon sight hereof you delyver him to the handes of the marquis de Senneterre, ambassador extraordinary of the French king, to be by him disposed of as he shall think fitting, and this shall be your warrant in that behalf. From the court at Greenwich the 24 June 1635.
>
> FRANCIS WINDEBANK
>
> To Francis Taylor, one of the messengers of his majestyes most honorable privy councell.'

Upon sight of this warrant the priest was delyvered (though not immediatly) to the ambassador (the messenger who had him in keeping standing upon it for a whyle [88] that having been incharged to him by the lord privy seal, he ought not upon anothers warrant to discharge himself of him). That night he was rendered to the hand of the said lord and by him sent to the ambassador, from whom he had instant liberty.[28] At the tyme that I receyved from Mr. Secretary Windebancks mouth the signification of his majestyes pleasure for this priests delivery to the ambassador, the lord keeper being present and obiecting how a priest (who upon examination and confession of a woman that she had that morning seen him saying mass was under arrest) could be in that manner lawfully delyvered, his lordship was answered that such was his majestyes pleasure and command.

[88ᵛ] The eyth of July, I receyved 21 warrants for ambassadors and agents, thus desposed of by the earl of Holland and in his hand, as Cheef Justice of Eyre at July 6, 1635.[29]

For the ambassador of France, out of Woodford walk in Essex, out of Maryborne park, out of the great park of Windsor, 3.

For the Venetian ambassador, out of the litle park of Windsor, out of Epping walk in Essex, out of Hampton Court park, 3.

For the States ambassador, out of Theobalds park, out of Chinckford walk in Essex, out of Theobalds park, 3.

For the king of Spaynes agent, out of Chappel Henault walk in Essex, out of West Henault walk in Essex, 2.

For the queen of Bohemias agent, out of Lowton walk in Essex, out of Havering park in Essex, 2.

---

[28] In London the courtyard of an ambassador's house had immunity, but not the street in front of it (P. Lachs, *Diplomatic Corps under Charles II and James II*, pp. 131–32).

[29] Annual warrants for gifts of venison from the royal forests to resident diplomats only.

For the queen of Swedens agent, out of New Lodge walk in Essex, out of Layton walk in Essex, 2.

For the king of Spayns agent for Flanders, out of Theobalds park, out of Enfield great park, 2.

[89] For the duke of Savoys agent, out of Richmond park in Surrey, out of Windsor great park, 2.

For the duke of Florences agent, out of Enfield great park, out of Walthamstowe walk in Essex, 2.

Sunday, the 12 of July, the ambassador of Venice having had an audience in the privy chamber at Theobalds to take leave of the king, then beginning his progress, he told me after it (and desyred also that I should find tyme to intimate so much to his majesty) that he had ventured more that day than ever he durst before to speak altogether French at his audience, with this consideration that his majesty being at that instant (as he knew) so prest with busynes multiplying towards his departure, and he (the ambassador) having no busynes to treat of beyond complement, he doubted lest the readyness and plenty of his mother tongue might make him inlarge too much and forget perhaps the preciousness of his majestyes tyme, which want of words to express himself in French might make him the better remember, [89ᵛ] a complement that was not ill receyved, when after it was told to his majesty. I observed that being at that tyme clothed in his journeying apparell (the wearing of his gown dispensed with, which was noted by the lookers on as unusuall) he never would cover, though invited to it by his majesty, perhaps because his audience was not for busyness of his prince, but for his owne civil respect to take leave of his majesty.

[94ᵛ] The king being returned from his progress to Windsor, the 6 September, the two French ambassadors, extraordinary and ordinary being there, desyred me to acquaynt his majesty with theyr desyre of access to kiss his hands and congragulate his returne but (sayd Monsieur de Senneterre) without demanding audience repeating twyce or thryce the last words 'without demanding audience in any case.' Which words when I had punctually delyvered (as I thought my duty) to his majesty, he merrily made answere, after he asked me where they were and I sayd they are even now walking upon the terras, 'They shall not need to come hither, I myself will go thither. But if they will not have me give them audience, they must say nothing, since if they speak I shall hear them.' Not with standing these conditions they intertayned the king, and he them, almost an hour before they departed.

Theyr majestyes being returned from theyr progress to Hampton Court, I the next day going thither met there the French extraordinary, then newly allighted and censured by some for his confident entry with his coach into the first court, where no coach but the kings and queens (and but seldom the kings) his majesty usually making his descent before the outer most gate, had entrance. I being informed of that irregularity addressed myself for reformation to Sir Henry Vane, controller of his majestyes household, [95] with report of what others had observed and told me to that purpose. He instantly called to one of the porters and railed at him for his negligence and, having heard all the excuses he or his fellows could frayme (that the ambassador had entered with so swift as they could not, though they would, hinder it), he charged them, upon penalty of being thrust out of theyr places, not to suffer any coach to enter that court, excepting his majestyes coaches or some such great lords or ladyes as should immediatly follow them, his honor commanding withal the great gate to be always kept shut, and the wicket only to be kept open, as was immediatly and after (at least during theyr majestyes stay there) carefully observed.

About a seven night after, I had his majestyes command to accompany thither from London a young nobleman of Poland, wryting himself *Georgius Carolus Hlebowitz, Comes in Dambuno, Onixteniensis Radotzkoniensis Capitaneus*, etc.[30] According to his desyre he had, with 5 or 6 gentlemen his followers, a privat access, as *Incognito*, to the king and after to the queen, without speaking scarce one word to either, for which he was not uncensured. He that day returned to London for his further iourney to France, whither his course was before designed from the low countrys.

[95ᵛ] A deputy from the Hanse Townes (Lubeck, Hamburg, Bremen, Luneburg, etc.) by tytle and name Doctor Leon Daysema, came to my house the 17th of October for address about an audience. Wherewith I acquaynting my lord chamberlin (then in town and the court at Hampton) his lordship willed me to wryte to Mr. Secretary Cook about it, to whome sending with my letters my officer to court, I had assignation for the next day, when after introducing the deputy to the presence of his majesty in his Withdrawing Chamber, he there in a brief confident and audible speach made known his errand to be the more strong confirmation and setling of the Stillyard[31] to the proper use of those Hansiatick townes, it having been lately sought to be begged from them, and a verbal grant thereof passed as of a confiscation to the king, for not having been imployed to the use it had been (hundreds of

---

[30] George Charles Lebowitz, count of Dambuno, Captain in Onix and Radocko.

[31] The Steelyard, a mercantile depot in London, had been suppressed in 1598. Leuuw van Aitzema, as agent of the Hansa (Oct. 1635 – Feb. 1636), secured support of the London merchants for its full restoration.

years before) fundamentally intended and bestowed on those townes by his majestyes predecessors, the kings and queens of England.

After he had passed here about three months in negotiations for the relation that the tyme and our affayres might seem to have with those townes, he obtayned of his majesty a grant and confirmation of what he came for. He took leave the 9th of February, having about 10 dayes after receyved his present of a chayne of gold of 210 £ with the medal, he gave to the bringers 6 £, to me in an imbroidered purse 55 £ and to my officer 15 £.

[96] Charles Prince Elector Palatine,[32] having been alredy some weeks expected here, news was brought of his stay at Flushing for a wind, and I receyved command, the 26 October, to go to Gravesend for his first reception and welcome from his majesty. Come thither I instantly wrote to the lord warden of the Cinq Portes, the earl of Suffolk then resideing at Dover castle, and sent warrants to all postmasters in those parts with advice of his majestyes speciall pleasure of theyr imployment of best care and diligence in the discharge of that service. But the wind holding contrary to his highnesses passage, I went and came thryce to and from Gravesend, the thyrd tyme I had his majestyes express command not to move from Gravesend tyll his arrival, which succeding at Dover (as there the winds forced him) the 19th of November and word brought to me of it, I instantly dispatched an express to court and posted myself to Canterbury and presented him there with his welcome from his majesty and attended him to the church, his first piously affected visit, where the dean[33] and prebends met and receyved him. I reconducted him to the post house (the mayor and his brethren on the way thither before the town house congragulating him) and there taking post (his highness refusing the offered comodity of the deanes coach) he came that night thorow wett to his lodgings at Rochester.

There I made another dispatch to court for notice to the [96ᵛ] earl marshall, the earl of Arundel, appoynted by his majesty for his reception at Gravesend. But his lordship being alredy that night come thither, accompanyed with 7 or 8 lords and about 40 gentlemen his majestyes servants, the prince elector was there welcomed by the earl in the name of the king, as he was by my lord Goring from the queen the next day by diner (provided by his majestyes

---

[32] Charles Louis (born 1617), son of Charles's sister, always received this title at Whitehall, although the electoral title had been transferred to Bavaria in Feb. 1623 and the hereditary lands of the Palatinate were occupied by Spain and Bavaria. His disappointment over the failure to secure any recognition at the Peace of Prague in May had led to this lengthy visit to London.

[33] Dr. Isaac Bargrave.

officers purposely sent down for it), he after entred the kings barge, followed
by 21 others, and (agaynst tyde) came by Four of the clock to his landing at
Tower wharf, where entering his majestyes coach there attending with 2 of
the queens and 24 of the lords, the cannon of the Tower gave him theyr
salvo. Thence passing through London (not without an excessive confluence
of people thronging to see him) he descended at Whitehall gate and was met
at the foot of the great stone stayres by the duke of Lenox, the marquis
Hamilton and the earl of Pembroke, in the Great Chamber by the earl of
Holland (in quality of Captain of the Gard there orderly disposed) at the
Presence door by the prince, and at the door of the queens Withdrawing
Chamber by the king who, after his most affectionat imbrace, presenting him
to the queen, she receyved him with a gracious kiss and a most cheerful
countenance. The great ladys ranged on eyther side he saluted with a cour-
teous regard, only as that presence and tyme required. [97] He was after
conducted by the prince and the lords mentioned to his own assigned quarter
(some time the princes) whereon was also lodged the Rhinesgrave[34] that
accompanyed his highness hither, the rest of his trayne being disposed in
places of most conveniency near the court. Of these a young count Maurice
of Nassau son to count William, Colonel Ferentz[35] a gentleman of great
valour, judgement and appearance in the wars and otherwise, his two coun-
cellers Monsieurs Rusdorf and Blarer, lieutenant Hunike and Monsieur
Beringan, a French gentleman were the most in regard, the whole number
of his trayne of all conditions amounting to seventy.

[97ᵛ] The morning after his arrival being Sonday,[36] he followed the king
with the prince to chapel and set there in the closet, on the left hand of his
majesty as the prince did on his right, both covered. The like respect he had
that day dining with his majesty in the presence chamber and washing with
him (though for a while excusing it) and uncovered.

The next day towards evening the two French ambassadors (whereof the
extraordinary had that morning sent me his request to come speak with him)
coming to court, perhaps unseasonably when they had not [98] yet seen him
but had only sent theyr secretaryes to congragulate his arrival and might be
assured they could not avoyd his encounter in presence of theyr majestyes,
entered the queens withdrawing chamber and found there her majesty, the
king and the prince elector in discourse together. The king seeing them
entered (and standing as they always used to do at theyr privat accesses bare

---

34 Otto Louis, margrave of Rhein-Pfalz, who left in December.
35 Colonel Thomas Ferentz: see III 2ᵛ.
36 Nov. 27th.

headed) put on his hat and caused the prince elector to put on his, which was thought to be done by designe which, if the ambassadors should have done the like, they should eyther have transgressed the custome they had always observed, standing uncovered in the presence of theyr masters sister and of the king, at tymes of theyr domestical access, or else they might have run a hazard (as it was conceived by divers) never more after that one presumption to be allowed the advantageous liberty they had gayned of access to his majestyes presence at theyr pleasure as domesticks.

The occasion (before touched) of Monsieur de Seneterre sending to speak with me was to know when he and his colleague might most fitly present the prince palatine with theyr congragulations and what tytle they were to give him. My formal answer was that I thought *Altesse* and *Electeur Palatin* were the tytles most fitly and justly to be given him. To this he replyed: 'For *Altesse* we will make no difficulty [98ᵛ] to give as he is a prince born and of the blood, and for the latter of *Electeur* we shall have no cause to mention it, but can you tell how he will treat us for the hand?' I answered: 'when you shall please to make your visit doubt not but he will behave himself with all dew regard to your qualityes.' To this he replyed: 'For the rest we know how to proceed but for the hand we must maintain our masters rights, or make no visits.' This they after observed excusing theyr repayre to him, not because they thought the hand should not be given them which had been of custome (as was affirmed by some that had been ambassadors in Germany) given by the electors to kings ambassadors in theyr own houses, but because of the tytle of *Altesse Electeurale*, which had been taken away by the emperor from the prince palatine and given by general consent (they said) to the duke of Bavieres, it was not for them to restore it.³⁷

Of this formality of theirs and of giving subiect to the king for his nephew to stand upon that tytle, the ambassador ordinary Monsieur de Pougny spared not to affirm to me (from others assurance to him) that I had been the author, which he and those others (it seemed) had gathered from the answer I had made (as before) to the ambassador Senneterres demands what tytle was to be given him. But I imparting this challenge of Monsieur de Pougny not only to the prince elector, but to the king himself, was cleared in that which I was not worthy to be guilty of, his majestyes wysdome having been herein his best and only counceller.

[99] When his highness had passed his tyme, about ten dayes in court and in hunting with the king at Theobalds, he made a visit to the archbishop of

---

³⁷ The French embassy had to respect Bavaria's use of the electoral title, since Richelieu wished to detach Bavaria from its Habsburg alliance.

Canterbury and had for his passage to Lambeth the kinges barge and one other. His grace receyved him at his landing and after a good tyme of discourse with him in his privy chamber and gallery, showed him his library, had him with him to prayers in his chapel, and reconducting him to his barge would not (though much importuned to return) leave his highness before he had seen him in his chamber.

That evening came to my house the agent of the cardinal Infante (Mr. Taylor) and discovered the residents of Spayne and his intentions, in theyr masters name (as they would have it believed), to visit the prince palatine, as he then styled him. I having before had a hint of this theyr disposition, was prepared more to hear then to applaud or propound, and so lett him proceed without interruption to his purpose that, whatsoever the world conceyved, the king of Spayne was not in enmity with the prince palatine rather, on the contrary, desyred for the king of Englands sake, to do for him (as he had done) all friendly offices with the emperor, and that for theyr own partes they desyred in all to express theyr respectes, and now particularly in theyr visit for congragulation of his safe arrival if he would be pleased to assigne them a tyme for it.[38] To this I answered I doubted nothing of theyr welcome to his highness no more [99ᵛ] than I would of theyr conformity in giving his electoral highness such titles as should be fitting and would (I know) be expected from them. He replyed I might be assured they would not have proceeded so far to demand of access, if they thought they should by not applying to his pleasure any way disgust him, only they would be glad to know before how he would give them theyr rights of treatment answerable to theyr qualityes, in allowing them to sit if he should sit, stand if he should stand, cover if he should cover, and the lyke.

With this account of theyr intimations and provisional cautions I, the next day, repayring to his majesty and the prince elector, the king approved of them and commanded me instantly to return with this formal condition proposed, that if they would give his nephew the formal title of electoral highness, they should have theyr reception and welcome in manner as they themselves could expect, otherwyse they should do well not to come at all. This message delyvered I had for answer that the tytle should be assuredly given by them, so it was with open repetition (the resident speaking in Spanish with the interpretation of the cardinals agent in English). Coming the next day they were receyved by his highness in his privy chamber, he stepping forward to the midst of the room as they entered it and, when they parted,

---

[38] Necolalde and Taylor were using Philip IV's excuse that the title of elector had been precipitously conferred without his advice.

leaving them within a step or two of the door, having all the whyle intertained them standing and uncovered, without inviting them to put on.

[100] The morning before this audience (which was asigned for Three of
the clock after noon) the Spanish requesting it might not be at One (because
that hour, he sayd, was the kings usuall hour of audiences)[39] I went to the
French ambassador extraordinary (first acquaynting the king with my intention and receyving his allowance) and told him he might remember I had
made him a promise (as he had desyred it) to let him know when the prince
palatine would be disposed to receyve visits that he might be the first to give
one, and though between him and the Spanish resident there was, I sayd, no
proportion of competition for precedence, I yet thought it my part to let
him know that there was an assignation given by the prince elector to the
resident of Spayne and the cardinals agent for 3 of the clock, and if in the
mean tyme he would command me any thing for his service, I was and would
be ready to obey him. The ambassador (something startled at my report and
offer) made answer thus: 'In truth I am very glad of that you have told me,
as not doubting but we shall now see an end of the busynes and the king my
master have less to do in it.' I replyed: 'I wysh it may prove so for the general
good.' 'Make no question of it (answered he smyling) otherwyse it will
prove a greater scorn and mock than that of Gondomar when he sayd to
king James (formalizing himself that the king of Spayne had contrary to his
promise possest himself of certayne townes [100ᵛ] of the Palatinat) I wish the
king my master had them all in his possession that your majesty might see how
noble and iust he would be in making a general restitution.'

The day following the agent of Florence had his access for congragulation,
and gave it with the title of electoral highness (speaking English and often
repeating it) which when I some dayes after told the French ambassador ordinary, he seemed to wonder at it and (tyll I had constantly affirmed it) not to
believe it, he being, he sayd, the minister of a prince that was nephew to the
emperor and cosen germane to his daughter now marryed to the duke of
Baverie, the present confirmed elector.[40]

[101] The same day the deputy of Hamburg performed his part as the
former, so did the States ambassador at this tyme. But the Venetian staggering,
had sent with the first, his secretary, but it was but to inquire after others
proceedings and whether he were tyed by promise to the formes of the

[39] Finet wrote in the margin: "he added smyleing his was an audience electoral not regal."
[40] Ferdinand II, duke of Tuscany, was son of duke Cosmo II and Maria Magdalena, daughter of archduke Charles of Styria. His cousin, Maria Anna, daughter of emperor Ferdinand
II, married the Elector of Bavaria, Maximilian I.

French, or would not so soon tread in the steps of the Spanish, or whether (which was of most conceyved) he meant to send to his reipublick for theyr warrant (a long way about), he kept from personal conformity. So did the resident of Savoy, yet not wythout offer of a condition that if the prince would returne his master (upon mention of him) the title of *Altesse Royale*, he would give him that of *Altesse Electorale*, but this was a bargayne of too great an odds on his masters syde whyle he pretended, as is delyvered elsewhere, to the crown of Cyprus, and would be glad to have the tytle given him for a precedent, would not be harkened to, and so fayled of conclusion.

[101ᵛ] The 28th of December being Monday, the queen was brought to bed of her second daughter[41] at St. James about Nine of the clock at night. The next day the French ambassador extraordinary came to Whytehal (while the king was yet at his sermon) to congragulate his majesty, for performance of which complement because he desyred it might pass answerable to his usually affected manner *a la domestique*, and without ceremony, I conducted him to the withdrawing chamber, next to the kings privy chamber, and there leaving him went to my lord chamberlin (where he was in the chapel chamber) with notice of both the ambassadors repayre thither (the ordinary being come soon after there also) for discharge of that complement which they instantly and breefly passed with his majesty, at his passage through that room from the chapel.

[41] Elizabeth.

[101ᵛ] The 5th day after, being New Years day, the Venetian did the like in the same place, hour and manner, as did also after dynner (as the King returned from it) the States ambassador and the deputy of the Hanseatique townes.

The Spanish resident (to be singular, perhaps, from the rest and to walk his own way without imitation) deferred the discharge of this complement, as he let me know by the Cardinal Infantes agent he would, tyll upon some occasion of repayre to court for audience he might negotiate and congratulate both together, as he did, [102] when, the 10th of January, I conducted him to his Majestyes presence at Whitehall in the Withdrawing Chamber. Two dayes before, the States ambassador having an audience assigned him at St. James's, I made known it to the king that he was there attending in the Privy Chamber, whereupon his majesty coming forth of the Queens chamber (where her Majestye lay in child bed) to the next room there, he was hymbly asked by me, whether I should bring the ambassador thither? He answered no, I will go to him for this once, but in his way the ambassadour seeing him coming and stepping towards him, his majesty made a stand in the passage and there gave him audience.

The 17th of January, a duke of Wirtenberg[1] (second brother to the duke regnant, of about twenty years of age) having with regard to the present misery of his country (and his wants accompanying it) kept himself and his small number of 7 or 8 followers unknowne and lodged with little charge for a month or more in a blind corner of London, sent at last to me for his private introduction to his majesty. This he had by the Privy Garden in the Privy Gallery, where in the Stone Table room there (the king coming forth so far, for the less notice, though this could not be avoyded divers lords being there present) he was with gracious countenance and words receyved and dismissed by his majesty.

25 January, the king being gone to Newmarket to hunt there the Prince Elector, newly recovered of measles followed his majesty in layd coaches with his physician, Dr. Harvey,[2] the earl of Essex, the Lord Craven, and colonel Ferentz for company, performing the journey the same day. Nine of his gentlemen and myself set forth in hyred coaches, each with six horses and arrived there the day after.

---

[1] Ulrich (born 1617) second brother of Eberhard (born 1614), duke of Württemberg.
[2] William Harvey, the physician.

[102ᵛ] The 4th of February his highness went in company of the earl of Holland[3] and others to Cambridge for sight of that university and of the comedyes there prepared for him. He should, as it was designed, have been received at Trinity College gate by the Vice Chancellour[4] and heads of houses. But coming thither before the appointed hour at 12 at noon, he was at the first entrance to the Masters Lodgings, for that time made his highnesses, welcomed by the Master[5] himself with a latine oration, and after with another, in the first upper chamber by the Vice Chancellour, accompanyed with the Doctors, etc. Thence he went through the common High Street (the young fry of scollars ranged in it all along on the left hand) to the Schools. The younger graduates stood on each side of his passage through the Regents walk. Thence turning to Kings College chapell (while the Regents, non Regents and Doctors took their places in the Regents House after their degrees) he had there another [103] oration pronounced to him and a hymn sung in the quire. After he had a banket in the Masters Lodgings, he went thence back to the Schooles and received the degree of Master of Arts (as did also all his followers of the better sort, whereof there were a colonel, a lieutenant colonel and a captaine) together with some of our noblemen and young gentlemen of the university. He had after this a welcoming oration in name of the university by the Publick Orator and was before four of the clock seated in the hall for sight of a latine comedy[6] then ready to be acted, which had been before appointed for after supper but was by my persuasion (with intimation to the Vice Chancellour of his but newly recovered health to be lykely to be indangered by his sitting up late and watching) turned to an afternoons work.

That finished, he was entertained by the earl of Holland with a sumptuous supper, divers great lords sitting at the table with him and his highness in the midst with a respective difference left on each side of him.

The next morning after breakfast he was present at another latine comedy and by four in the afternoon was in his coach, which carryed him that night to Bishops Stortford and the next day (his Majestye passing that way dyneing there and takeing him in his coach) brought to London.

The next day (February 7th) his highnesses second brother, prince Rupert, sent for hither by his majesty, arriving the day before at Gravesend, whereof notice [103ᵛ] being brought me, I offered, but was not suffered with respect to

[3] As chancellor of the university.
[4] Dr. William Beale.
[5] Dr. Thomas Comber.
[6] Latin plays unidentified.

privacy to contribute my service for his reception and conduction.[7] He landed late at night out of an hyred tylt boat at the garden stayres at Whytehal, where the earl of Arundel receyved him. He was by his lordship brought to the king and queen at St. James, but fyrst to the prince elector in his lodgings there, and thence with his brothers company to theyr majestyes, who had resolved not to go to rest tyll they should see him. After the king had given him the accolade with expression of much joy, he stept to the queen proferred a kiss to her gowne, which her majesty receyved on her cheek. After returning with the prince his brother to Whytehal, he there took possession of the Rhinesgraves lodgings,[8] which that gentleman had left empty, when he went to France about Christmas, and if he should return was elsewhere to be provided for. There came with him (besydes his other trayne) two counts of Nassau, Henry son of [blank], and William son of count Ernest,[9] cosen germane once removed to his majesty, by a daughter of the king of Denmark that had marryed a duke of Brunswick. These two counts were lodged out of court which will serve for a bar of precedent (with reason *a fortiori*) against the Rhinesgrave, if when he should returne, he should expect to be agayne lodged in it.

[104] Towards Shrovetyde, Mr. Richard Vivian, a gentleman student of the Middle Temple of good means and family and of parts (humored by others of his society and youthful disposition) took upon him the tyle of Prince d'Amours and had his officers, councell and state ordered after the ancient manner of that Misruleing Principality. This concuring with the Prince Electors tyme of aboad here the young gentleman resolved, with his fictitious lord councillours, upon an entertaynement for his Highness at a supper and maske.[10] But, advising with me about the carriage of the busynes I dissuaded them from the supper as impossible to be made (if they would regard sweetnesse with conveniency and avoyd confusion) in one and the same room. The hall having no second room convenient for it, I persuaded them to convert the supper into a banquet to be brought in, with some pertinent device, in the midst of their mask. This they approved of, and against the tyme made preparation answerable, inviteing to it the prince elector and his brother and

---

[7] Rupert (born 1619) was to leave England for service in the anti-Habsburg campaigns in Germany. Captured in 1638, he was imprisoned until 1641. In 1642 he began his short career as a "Cavalier" general of the Royalist forces.

[8] Otto Louis.

[9] Ernest was son of Henry Julius, duke of Brunswick, and Elizabeth of Denmark, Charles's aunt.

[10] Davenant's *Triumphs of the Prince d'Amour* on Feb. 24th, Bentley VII 101–102.

leaving to his highnesses pleasure, as to the Master of the Entertainement, to invite and bring to it all such noblemen, ladyes and others as he should think fitting. The day for the maske approaching, question was made, and my opinion asked, about the manner of his highneses reception and of his and his brothers placing. Whether [104ᵛ], (as some of them would vainly have had it) above the Prince Elector or at the least above his brother, which I, by no means, allowed so much as the discourse of. I told them what his highnes had in my hearing said, when some speech fell to that purpose that he would not be a prince, in jest, as the other was. It was agreed that in marching and sitting the Prince Elector was to have the middle place, Prince Rupert on his right hand, and the Prince d'Amours on his left. Upon this concluded order they were encountered and receyved at the watergate of the Temple, which should have been (and this but for their sudden surprise had been followed) at their landing out of the barge by the Prince d'Amours and his great officers. Having passed the tourne door into the first court, they found there a guard made them on each side by above twenty gentlemen in quality of Pensioners, all richly appareled, carrying in their hands their poleaxes. Passing forward, they entered another tourne door into the hall and proceeding came to their repose in the Parliament Chamber, as they named it. The hall appointed to dance in, being in the mean tyme with much ado cleared of the pressing number of both sexes, then they were seated, as before mentioned, in chayres all of one fashion to behold the representation.

On their right hand (upon seates [105] of a scaffold on the severall degrees whereof were placed divers gentlewomen of different conditions), sat the Queen (come thither of herself without invitation) and placed promiscuously among other women. She was together with the Lady Marquess Hamilton, her mother, the Lady Denbigh, the Countess of Holland and the Countess of Denbighs unmarryed daughter, all under a disguise of citizens wives with hats on, and so conducted in by a scampster citizen as their companion, but all their faces bare, yet with pretence not to be known in that disguise, no more than that bird, which thrusting but her head into a bush, is said then to think all her body hidn. With them came in, as of their concealed company, the earl of Holland, the Lord Goring, Mr. Henry Percy, brother to the earl of Northumberland and two or three other gentlemen of the queens family, all likewise concealed under a kynd of disguise to be mistaken for what they were, but no more taken notice of then these ladyes mentioned. The maske ended, their two highneses, wayted on by the Prince d'Amours and his grandes to their barge, returned to Whitehall, where, on Shrove Tuesday following, his majesty, at the recommendation of the Prince Elector, laying his sword on the Prince d'Amours shoulder changed that tytle of jest to a more earnest one, of Sir Richard Vivian. Three or four dayes after, he presented me with a payre of sylver candlesticks (16 £) with excuse of theyr little worth, regarding, he said, my merit of paynes for his honour. It was sayd (and confirmed by himselfe to me) that he had spent of his own purse in that time of his personated greatness about 3000 £. *Vix Priamus tanti*, etc.

[105 ^{v}] Having had notice from Gravesend that an ambassador extraordinary, Mons. Beverne, was arrived from the States of the United Provinces,[11] I went thither (March 15th) for his reception. The next day I conducted him in the Kings barge (with one more besides that I went in) to his landing at Tower wharfe. There received by the Lord Herbert of Cherbury he was by him in the kings coach (the two French ambassadors, the Venetians and the States ordinary, together with six others) brought to his lodging in Leaden-hall Street, the house appertayning by lease to certain East Indian deputyes from Holland that had dwelt in it some four yeares before, and being parted hence, had at that tyme left it empty. It was now firnished by the kings officers at his majestyes charge, the charge of hyring another being thereby saved, which must have been otherwise taken up and paid for by his majesty, answerable to the proceeding with other ambassadors. The trayne consisted of 12 or 13 persons of the better sort, which sat at his own table, and of as many more of inferior respect, all defrayed by his majesty for nine meales, from theyr fyrst nights supper after theyr arrival at theyr lodging tyll the day after his audience exclusive, at 20 £ *per diem*.

He had the 20th of March his publick audience of both theyr majestyes together, conducted to it by the lord Strange,[12] accompanyed with the earl of Berkshires eldest son, and 7 or 8 of the privy chamber in [106] the kings coach and 10 other ambassadors and noblemens, and receyved in the presence chamber by both theyr majestyes. The king (as the ambassador approached) stepped forward to the uttermost edge of the raysed degrees under the State, of designe (as most were of opinion) to prevent the ambassadors assent so high, and his standing with him on even ground, he being no kings ambassador. Upon his majestyes invitation he covered, and his colleague with him, but instantly uncovered and so stood (once or twice onely touching their heads with their hats) all the tyme of their audience. Our Prince Charles being there

---

[11] Cornelius van Beverne, ambassador extraordinary (March 1636 – July 1637) of the Dutch Republic, had a mission similar to Senneterre's to persuade Charles to join a military alliance to restore his nephew to the Palatinate. He also wished concessions for fishing licenses and a mitigation of the principles over English territorial waters asserted in Selden's *Mare clausum*.

[12] James Stanley, lord Strange.

present was saluted by the extraordinary, which hindered not their next dayes visit to his highnes at his own lodging at Wallingford House. They performed the like, immediately after, to the Prince Elector Palatine, and his brother, though not in the order that was judged proper, when there had been an hour already assigned them in the afternoon for their access to the Lady Mary at St. James's. This visit was preposterously interposed by the overdoing diligence of his inexperienced secretary.

[106ᵛ] The 23rd of March they had my attendance at St. James's for their first private audience, after which they delivered a present brought by them from their masters, the States, to his Majestye consisting of seaven goodly white coach horses, with their crimson velvet covers imbroidered with gold embroidery, four rare pictures of excellent masters[13] in their country and a fifth of admirable needlework in *Landschap* done to the naturall by a gentle-woman, a standing clock for a cabinet of a most rare motion, a peece of am-bergrase wayghing twelve pounds, three cupps to drink in of the spirit of china purslan transparent as glasse, and not admitting (as they said) poyson in them without breaking, a great chest of China-work inlayd all over with oriental mother of pearl and gold, and within severall bolts or sutes of the purest and finest cambrick and Holland.

The horses were presented in the parke, before the Gard and the rest in the privy galleryes, both their majestyes being present. I there moved his Majes-tye for the favour of his gratuity to those that had the care and charge of the present in the transport of it and was answered they should be remembered at the ambassadours departure.

[108ᵛ] The 12th of Aprill Clement Radolt (styled in French letters from Brussels *Conseiller de la Chambre Aulique de sa Majeste Imperiale*) and in latine letters of credence, *Ablegatus*,[14] arrived here from the emperour and was received and lodged for two or three dayes by the Spanish Resident.[15] After takeing a house in Drury Lane he let me know of his arrival by the Agent of the Infant Cardinal, Mr. Taylor. Whereupon I went to him, as from myself having first given notice of it to my Lord Chamberlaine, and making offer

---

[13] These important early Dutch paintings are described in O. Millar, *The Queen's Pictures*, p. 49n34.

[14] The emperor's council of state, *Hofrat*, or *Consilium Aulicum*, which handled major policy within the Empire and his hereditary lands.

[15] Clement Radolt, agent extraordinary (April – Oct. 1636) of Ferdinand II, was to explain that Elizabeth of Bohemia and her children would be assured of their property to support themselves, if there was an oral or written submission to the emperor's authority by seeking pardon.

of my service for the procuring of his audience, he referred it to his Majestyes conveniency. So he had it the 28th of April at Somerset House in the Withdrawing Chamber, accompanyed to it by the Resident of the King of Spayne and the Agent [109] of the Cardinal Infant, but without forme of being presented to the King by either of them. I fetched him from his lodging in his own coach, the Residents and myne attending him, and in the same reconducted him. Though this reconduction of mine was offered to be excused both by himself and the Resident, it was by me persisted in, being a respect I held due to him, though qualifyed but as an Envoyé, commissary, or Deputy, yet an Envoyé, from an emperour, which might, perhaps, challenge a regard and observance somewhat above that of other princes.

Their Majestyes rydeing one day on Mayeing (May 3rd or 4th as they terme it) through Hyde Park to Kensington, where a collation was prepared for them by the earle of Holland, the ambassadour ordinary of France with his coach following next after their majestyes, some younger bloods seated in the duke of Lenox his coach (he not there) strived to passe before him, wherof the ambassador, discovering some dislyke, his lacquays and the dukes fell to blows. So as one or two of the French were wounded but the ambassador keeping the hand, and the others (better advised) ceasing the strife, he after formalized himself so far as that the duke sent to him to excuse the presumption of those that had, he sayd, not understood him nor themselves.

[109ᵛ] About the beginning of May the Baron of Raschejour, Great Master, as he styled himself, of the Ordinance to the duke of Lorraine,[16] being imployed as an Envoy to his majesty, had audience, without the addresse and knowledge of the Lord Chamberlin, with success answerable, Mr. Secretary Windebank only having only introduced him. But a second private audience being assigned for his takeing leave, he (with an ill understanding between him and the king for want of due conduction) fayled of it, though he came seasonably to court and at a time of his majestyes leisure and stay for him. I was absent (unacquainted with the assignation) and none of the kings servants there present would enter where his Majestye was retyred with the queen to tell him of the envoys attendance. So as returning *re infecta* and reporting his ill successe to the Secretary he was by him advised to take the right way of the Master of Ceremonies, which that night performing it by a gentleman that he sent to me, I soon rectifyed all, obtaining an hower for his audience the next day of the King and the next day of the queen to his satisfaction.[17]

16 For his earlier visit in 1631 see III 110–11.

17 After condemnation for conspiracy against Richelieu, he had been reprieved on the scaffold. His pardon was thought to be at Henrietta's insistence.

After requesting me (since he had bene thryce he sayd at the Prince Electors lodgings to kyss his hands but in his absence) that I would procure him an access, I was (upon my demand of it) asked by his highness whether [110] he would give him the title of *Altesse Electorale* which I was not able to resolve. His highness replyed, if he will not give it let him not come. No more did he, alledging for one reason amongst others that the duke his master standing for the emperour and the Prince Palatine not reconciled to his imperial majestye (this work being at that instant in agitation by the ambassage of the earl of Arundel, and the duke of Bavaria possessed of the place and title of elector) he durst not give what he had no comission for. Only to shew his respects he would, he said, take a time to make yet once more a tender of his service to the prince at his lodging but it should be, he ingeniously sayd, when he should know he should be absent.[18] Being almost ready to depart and his dispatch preparing, letters came to him for delivery to the King from the duke his master, which I, bringing him to present, obtained that day order for a ring to be given him. A chayne of gold being held an improper present for a person of his tytle and condition, nor one, nor other, had been so much as thought on, till I remonstrating the fitnesse of it in a tyme, especially, when fortune frowning on that prince, the neglect of the servant might be thought to be of the Master, he had it presented to him by my hand of the value of 350 £. He sent me after for a present a gilt Norenberg cup and cover to the value of 12 £ - 6 s. - 0 d.

[114ᵛ] An ambassador from the King of Poland, by name Zavadsky, who had been three years before with the King in Scotland[19] and made London his passage of returne homeward, landed the 30th of May at Dover. Whereof advice was speedily brought me and, with all, of the infection that had seized four or fyve houses at Gravesend, I sent order to the postmaster there for the ambassadors diversion from the danger of that towne, and for his proceeding without stay to Greenwich where, he being arrived the last of May, I, the 2nd of June, gave him there a wellcome from his majesty and he had, the next day, the like given him by the earl of Newport, who accompanyed with Sir William Howard, brother to the earl of Suffolk, and five other gentlemen

---

[18] With an attack from France imminent, the duke of Lorraine sought allies in the Empire, even the dispossessed count Palatine.

[19] John Zawadsky, ambassador extraordinary of Vladislav IV of Poland, brought assurance that his king still sought marriage with Charles's niece, Elizabeth, a sister of the young count Palatine, but the clergy of Poland opposed any union with a Protestant. The diplomatic nuances of this moment were considerable: England's support for Poland against Sweden would be assured; since the Polish king was of influence with the emperor there was a higher chance of imperial favor for the restoration of the count Palatine.

in the Kings coach, four of the ambassadors here remayning and three lords, brought [115] him by land (he not affecting the passage by water) to his house taken up and fairly furnished for him by the King in South Lambeth. That night, or the day following, there should have been (according to custome at other tymes) brought him, by some person of quality from the King, a salutation and inquiry of his health after his journey. But it was forgotten or omitted with no great errour perhaps, the remoteness of the court[20] serving to excuse the trouble of that complement.

He was to be defrayed, according to the reglement established, till his audience should be past and so was at 25 £ *per diem*. He had his dyet sent in dayly by the officers of the household in specie, his beer, wood and coales being laid in by them without further care from them of provision of table linnen, utensills of the kitchen and the like. All which, and his cook also and servants of necessary use, were left to his own hyring. Silver vessell he had none allowed him and pewter was hyred by himself in stead of it. This treatment, though of hard digestion to him that could say, and did, that our kings ambassador, Sir George Douglas, had had his at the court of Poland a month and three dayes, with regard to even the defraying of his horsemeat and of the least particular, went down with him without repining, as being answerable to the establishment settled here and observed reciprocally by his majesty and other [115ᵛ] kings and princes his neighbours, which for the consequence so intimated to his ambassadour, his majesty would by no means consent to have broken.

The 7th of June, he was conducted to his publick audience at Hampton Court by the earl of Lindsey, lord high chamberlin, and 7 or 8 gentlemen of the Privy Chamber from his house in the Kings coach, 4 of the ambassadours, myne own and three hyred, and was received by both their majestyes publickly and jointly in the Presence Chamber of the King, and after he was privately and separately (as before hand requested) in their Withdrawing Chambers, Mr. Secretary Cook discharging the part of interpreter (the ambassador speaking latin) for the one, and the queens Chief Almoner for the other.

After these audiences he had one of the Prince Elector, where the title of *Altesse Electorale* came not in question, high Dutch being made use of, and *Durchlightiste Churfurst* being the title given without scruple from the ambassador.[21]

---

[20] Since Charles was at Hampton Court.
[21] Charles insisted that foreign diplomats recognize his nephew's disputed rights as Elector in any visit.

After that his audience and nine meales at the Kings charge were passed, his defrayed dyet ceasing, he made his visits to ambassadours and to some lords beginning with the Archbishop of Canterbury at Lambeth, who received him at his entrance into his great chamber, gave him always the hand, accompanyed him back to the porch of his hall and there left him. The 12th of June having by me made demand of his [116] audience from both their Majestyes to take his leave and letting me know that having already had the honour (customarily due to ambassadours at their first reception and first publick audience) to be received and conducted by persons of eminent quality, he would dispense, he said, with further ceremony and punctuality in that kind and content himself with my conduction only to his leave taking. For this I accordingly provided him, as he desired, of the Kings barge with 12 oars and brought him from Lambeth bridge by water to Hampton Court landing at the Privy Garden stayres. Attending in the Close Walk there the pleasure of his Majestye for his admittance, he soon had it by the way of the back cloyster court, the Presence and Privy Chamber into the Withdrawing Chamber. Thence passing to the Elector for his farewell (the Queen not having yet dyned) he after took leave of her majesty and, in his returne by water, landing and tasting of a collation in my house at Chiswick, was that night at Lambeth.

Three or four days before,[22] certain English merchants of the Eastern Company had made way for an invitation for him from my Lord Mayors[23] to dyne with him, which brought him by the sword bearer, (after I had told him how two of his predecessors, Rakovsky and duke Radzivil had accepted of the like without scruple quitting precedence) he was entertained (together with his whole company) in a free and noble fashion, but the hand [116v] never once offered to be given by his lordship, nor stood upon to be taken by the ambassador.

The negotiation that his majesty had in hand for a marriage between the king of Poland and his Majestyes neece, eldest daughter to the queen of Bohemia, begot him a general welcome hither but when after his first private audience it was known what an unfitting demand he had made (in name rather of the clergy and senate of Poland than of his king) for his majesty to be himself the persuader of his neeces change of religion as the essential condition of the marriage and with what indignation his majesty had apprehended the unworthinesse of that office, no great man of our court would come to visit him agaynst which formalizing himself, he was plainly said to by some that he deserved that and worse. The Kings goodness, nevertheless, appeared in

---

[22] Before a public audience of June 12th.
[23] Sir Edward Bromfield.

his order given for this preparation of a present for him of gylded plate more than his predecessors Rakovsky or duke Radzivil had by 500 ounces. Yet after, when there had been a day and hour assigned him for the receyuing of it, it was told him (and truly after some suspicion of his double carriage) that the delivery of it should be respited tyll his returne out of France (pretended, howsoever really intended, if [117] he should have bene once possesst of the present) he was not a little troubled. Tyll the newes brought him, the day and almost the hour of his departure, that it was on the way bringing towards him, he discovered more ioy in his countenance than nobleness in his acknowledgement to those of the kyngs servants that had with paynes attended him.

He departed in a hyred coach the 18th of June to imbark at Rye for France, not having observed the admonition I had given him of taking a bill of store for some commodities he had bought here for his own use, and were packed up like merchants goods, which occasioned their arrest till the farmers of the customes warrant came to free them. [117ᵛ] The court being at Oatlands and I going to it July the 12th Sunday for introduction of a Persian Alli Babi, an officer in that kings court[24] and sayd to be of good respect, though reputed here a merchant, who had bene at Venice to negotiate a business of money for his master, and makeing England the way of his returne as the safer though the longer, [118] he brought letters to his majestye. I met there the report of the Conde de Oñates arrival in the Downes.[25] He desired, as the reporter intimated though not formally, to remayne *Incognito* and private at Greenwich, where the plague being then at Gravesend I had before hand advised the Resident of Spayne to provide him a lodging, till such tyme as an house taken up for him at south Lambeth (as before for the Polonian ambassador) might be fitted for his use. Upon this advice I applyed myself to the King, for knowledge of his pleasure how I should proceed? I had answer that till the ambassador himself should give notice to the lord chamberlin, or to me, of his coming, or certaine place of being, I should not need to look after him. Carrying this answer to him that had first told me the news and he

---

[24] This merchant's activities are described in Nov. 1636 (see IV 127ᵛ–128) and March 1637 (see IV 136–136ᵛ).

[25] Iñigo Ladrón Vélez de Guevara y Tassis, count of Oñate and Villa Mediana, ambassador extraordinary (July 1636 – May 1638) of Spain, had two delicate missions. The first was to assure Charles of the good intentions of Philip on behalf of Arundel's mission to Vienna to resolve the dispute over the Palatinate. At this time the sickly Emperor Ferdinand II wished still to assure the final election at Regensburg of his son as successor. Secondly, he was ordered to continue the planned Spanish subsidy for an English naval squadron to protect troop convoys in Spain's widening conflict against France and the Dutch Republic.

that night reporting it to his sender (the Spanish resident) I had the next day a letter from him importing that the conde was come to Greenwich, qualifyed as extraordinary ambassador, which tytle was there purposely expressed upon some question at the first made of it. He had taken a house there to rest himself in after his long journey, whence having put himselfe in equipage, sayd the letter, he might and would give more particular notice of his arrival. This advice somewhat restraygned me, yet knowing the kyng my masters mynd [118ᵛ] that I should hasten him on to his audience, which he was suspected all he could to delay (for the advantage and use he might make of tyme) I, the next day, without further expectation of notice from him, presented him with his majestyes welcome and gave account that night by post to my lord chamberlin how I found him in disposition.

After which expecting two dayes a returne from court and receyving none, supposing withal that that complement, due by custome to ambassadors, that they be immediately upon their arrival visited and welcomed from the king by some person of quality, would be forgotten, I took on me that part (going to him without any command) and officiously faygning, said his majesty had expressly sent me, in his name, to salute him and to returne him an account in what condition of health I found him after his journey. This fiction saved for that tyme the earnest of anothers sending and the complement was well (which not performed would have perhaps bene ill) taken by the ambassador.

Two or three dayes after, I, going to the court, then at Windsor, met there a rumor that the ambassador of Spayne shunned his audience to gayne tyme for his ends, which was not unbelieved of the most and best. But his majesty, the day that he began his progress, sending Mr. Porter of his Bed Chamber (this should have been an earls son, or a baron) made choyce of because of his language, though with no good relish of the ambassador as he discovered to me after by his exception, and me with him to Greenwich with a visit. The ambassadour, having heard of that rumor pleaded his innocency, and appealed to my witness for [119] confirmation of what he had answered both of his readyness to goe and hindrances that he could not soon goe to his audience. This for good manners sake not contradicting, because I saw the time past for reparation his majesty being gone on progresse, he was left to his majestyes pleasure, with concurrence of his owne, for the tyme and place of his audience. I after going to him at Greenwich once in three or four days with tender of my services and twice or thrice sounding him for his remove to his house prepared for him at South Lambeth, could draw from him no other answer than that he knew not how the style used here would permit his remove to another house, though assigned him, till he should be fetched and brought to it from the place he was at, by some person of fitting quality and be there treated with the kings dyet and with the attendance of his officers and servants, answerable to the proceeding observed here towards others of his quality. In a word, I found him much reserved in his resolution, and disposed to make a private stay in the house he had taken at Greenwich, of very small capacity for 70 persons (so many his lyst reckoned) till the kings returne rather then to solicit a speedy (which he called a troublesome) access to his majesty in progress. Though he had not spared, in the mean tyme, to affirme by some that he had made an offer to me, with request that I present it to his majesty, for his access eyther private or publick, which I was bold for [119ᵛ] my justification playnly to deny I had ever heard of. I had no reason (had such an offer bene made) to have neglected it, whyle it would have bene after the example of other ambassadors in former tymes, who immediately upon theyr arrival, had demanded, and had, private audiences, *en courier* as one of them termed it, before theyr publick, and whych would besides have turned to myne owne ease in saving much of the paynes I should be sure otherwise to take, going or sending to court for the ambassadors occasions whyle his majesty should be far off in progress.

The reason alledged for his not having prest for an audience, so soon upon his arrival, was the indisposition he yet found, he sayd, hanging on him after his journey (it being the remaynes of a feaver that had seized him in Spayne and held him tyll his imbarking) together with the want of his bagage and necessary apparel not yet come from the kyngs ship that had emptied it into another house in the Downes. But the true cause of his delay was supposed to be the gayne of time, which he hoped he might procure, and found yet improper, for some affayres in hand, which his majesty, discovering and thinking fit to leave him to his owne way, signified his pleasure to me by my lord chamberlin that if he should continue to make no other than a complemental offer (as he hitherto had done) of wayting on his majesty, when he should please to command [120] him and not formally to demand audience, I should let him know it was not the stile his majesty used to command them, nor to take notice of theyr propension only, but of theyr absolute desyre and demand of audience.

During this suspension of resolutions (his majesty in the interim proceeding on his progress) I fayled not once in three or four dayes to repayre to him to Greenwich with tender of my services, when after a whyle he fell to question me about what house, was, or should be, provided for his ordinary residence in London. I answered, as I had order, he should have all assistance possible for the procuring of one fit for him (though the tyme of contagion would I doubted make it a difficult work) which, according to the stile of ambassadors coming to reside here must be at his own charge, his majesty discharging that taken up for him at Lambeth tyll after his first audience and no longer, when his diet at the Kings charge ceasing, the house also was to cease to be at his use, unless perhaps for a week or two tyll he could provide himself of another. His reply to this was he stood not upon charge, but conveniency, and desyred his majesty would be pleased to use his power to place him in the bishop of Elyes house in Holborne, as the king his father had done [120ᵛ], he sayd, to two of his predecessors the Count of Gondomar, and don Carlos de Coloma. I answered I knew it to be resolved that that house (for the scandals sake that came of it and for the exception taken by our bishops, agaynst the use of the chappel for the masses sayd dayly in it, and the kings subjects frequent repayre to it) should never more be dwelt in by ambassadors. Quoth he, I shall beseeche his majesty to be a meanes I may hyre the Lady Elizabeth Hattons house, the earl of Exeters in Clerkenwell or the Duchess of Buckinghams at Chelsey, and when I had returned my opinion that the difficulty of getting houses out of the hands of such powerful possessors would be no less than the former, he in some passion fell comparatively to speake of the regard showed by the kyng his master to our kings ministers imployed in Spaine where theyr houses had bene and were, he sayd, at this present not only appointed but defrayed by his majesty. I replyed severall kingdoms have theyr severall customes and ours having none such as his Excellency spake of, I thought his majesty would be tender of creating precedents, or perswading any great persons to quit his house agaynst his lyking. No, quoth he, I would not have it brought to that question for my cause but kings have certayne sweet wayes to the compassing of theyr wills which no lady, lord nor bishop can refuse obedience to.

From this he fell to quarrel at my lord chamberlins [121] unproper choyce, as he called it, of a house for him at Lambeth on the other side of the river and where he had heard that no ambassadour had ever bene lodged but a Polonian[26] whome, for the ill manage of his ambassage, he was sorry and ashamed to be made a successor to. Besides added he, it is a house that was buylt and dwelt in by one that was a rebel[27] to the Kyng, my master, and yet beares his name of Caron House. To the first, I answered that the person his Excellency took exceptions at, for having been his predecessor, was the minister of a great kyng and had been receyved here and dismissed with honour from his majesty. For the situation of the house, I sayd, it had been made choyce of by my Lord Chamberlin, with especiall regard to the ambassadors conveniency, as being remote in this tyme of plague from danger of infection. For his other objection

---

[26] John Zawadsky in June.
[27] Noël Caron, ambassador of the Dutch Republic, 1598–1624.

that it had been built and dwelt in by one he called his masters rebel, I must be bold to repeat what I had heard his majesty himselfe say, that when he was prince he had dwelt in it himself, the builder of it, Sir Noel Caron, dying, it had descended to one of the king of Spaynes owne subjects and was synce sold to one of his majestyes, and was by himself made choyce of as most fit—he thought, for the ambassadors service. To all which the ambassador answered in breefe that not [121ᵛ] withstanding the disaffection he had expressed to the house for the reasons he had touched, no reason should prevayle with him so far as to make him dispute the kings pleasure for his repayre to it, but in the meantyme he desyred it might not be imputed to him as a contempt, if after the day and hour that he should part out of it to go to his audience, he should never more set foot in it.

These punctilios being passed over, and the king in his returne from the progress, come to Oxford, I posted thither for knowledge of his Majestyes further pleasure what person of honour should conduct the ambassador at his entry and to his publick audience. Whyle this rested unresolved I pro-pounded the fitness of asking some lord to pass a complement with him from the King for which I nominating the lord Digby and the lord Russell, the latter was made choyce of by his Majestye and a letter written to him with purpose from my lord chamberlaine. In obedience whereof his lordship and I with him went to Greenwich and had there his welcome and most thankful acknowledgement of that his Majestyes favour.

Three or four dayes after he made his formal request to me to present his Majestye with his most hunble desire to have his audience assigned him for the time and at the place his Majesty should think fitting. This signified by me to my lord chamberlin, I had in returne a letter from his lordship importing that the kyng had commanded him to acquaint me that the 18th of September [122] his majesty would be at Oatlands and there give him audience and, the 12th of the same, he should be treated at Lambeth with the same proportion and respect as was the French ambassadour, Monsieur de Seneterre.

This direction brought me there was brought me with it a letter from my lord chamberlin (the place for the superscription left blank that the name of an earle, who so ever might be supplyed, as I should find and iudge him proper for conduction) which for his near abode to London then two others that were nominated with him (the earles of Warwick and Dover) I directed to the earl of Carlisle. He, readly obeying, came at an hour assigned to Lambeth bridge and brought with him two coaches and wyth only my self and two gentlemen his kinsmen and two followers (all clad in black in mourning for his father not long before deceased) and entering the Kings and Queens coaches that there by appointment attended, together with myne owne and three other that I had hyred, we found standing ready before the ambassadors gate at Greenwich four coaches of his own. Whereof one was *de parade*, no body to ryde in it, and half a dozen others. After passage of complement we brought him to South Lambeth, where the earle of Carlisle parting, I remayned there to sett thyngs in order and mett with [122ᵛ] such disorder (occasioned by the absence of the Knight Harbinger whome I had long before summoned for his care of the service of his place and by the slackness of the Gentleman Usher who had scarce appeared there at all before that instant and then instantly vanished) as I never in my lyfe saw, nor suffered, the lyke. All rested upon my disposition, when for 26 horses there was not one stable provided, nor of 45 bedds required, scarce 25 were in a readyness. The defect of this latter proceeding not from the mistaking or neglect of the officer of the wardrobe, Mr. Kynnersley, but from the singularity of divers of the ambassadours followers, 15 or 16 of them pretending a custome of theyr country and a respect of theyr persons to lye alone and refusing to lye otherwise. Tyll, at last, the horses and groomes sent by me to Lambeth, and the bedds that wanted made shift for, within the house and neer abroad, all were by one of the clock after midnight quieted, howsoever contented.

The 3rd day after his entry into Caron House (as he himself would often merrily call it when he saw he could not avoyd his coming to it) the king that had received intimation from me of the driness of that complement, from custome now that the ambassadour was come upon his masters charge, sent a congragulation of his arrival there by Mr. Nevile, gentleman of his Privy Chamber and a brothers son to the baron of Bergaveny.

[123] Remaining there at the Kings treatment from Monday the 12th of September, he was the 17th fetched from thence by the earl of Salisbury (particularly made choyce of by the King himself for his conduction) accompanyed with only two gentlemen, his Majestyes servants and three of his own, the misery of that contagious time excusing that want, the Gentlemen in ordinary of the Privy Chamber being spared from that service because the lord chamberlin made excuse for them, as they were dispersed in severall remote places for safety from the sicknesse. All these in the Kings coach, four of the Spanish ambassadours own, the earles, myne and four hyred by me, came that night to Abscourt, a handsome house fairly furnished, of the baron of Dunsmores,²⁸ two miles from Oatlands, the journey being otherwise too long to go and returne to Lambeth in one day.

---

²⁸ Francis Leigh, lord Dunsmore.

He was fetched thence the next day by the same earle accompanyed by the lord Leppinton,[29] the lord Paget, Sir Hamilton,[30] one of the earle of Haddington sons, Mr. Henry Wentworth, brother of the earle of Cleveland, and 7 or 8 Gentlemen of the Privy Chamber with addition (by a default of the King and Queens coaches) of two others of the Queen and others to the number of 18 in all.

He had audience of both their majesties in the Presence Chamber and after returning to Abscourt (where the earl of Salisbury took leave of him for his returne home to Hatfield) he the next day after dynner (his last meale at the Kings charge) visited in his way (as was designed the day before) [123ᵛ] the Prince, Princesse and duke of York at Richmond. He left the Kings coach at Kew and me, by constraynt at my house in Chiswick, as he passed by boat down the ryver and was that night at his own house at Chelsey, hyred of the lord viscount Monson,[31] that he might make good the resolution he had taken and professed never once after his audience should be past to sett foot in the house appointed him by the king at Lambeth.

[127ᵛ] The 6th of November, Monsieur Bonika,[32] formerly imployed here by the Marquis of Baden and now by duke Bernard Weymar of Saxony,[33] had audience wyth my introduction at Windsor. He took leave of his Majesty and had for his present a chayne of gold of 250 £ value, more than the ordinary for an envoy, by 40 £, with expression of his majestyes more than ordinary regard towards him. He gave me, at his parting, a ring with a diamond worth about 20 £.

November 26, the Persian gentleman[34] before mentioned having transported from Venice hither (as his safest though his farthest way from home) no small quantities of royalls of eight, bestowed in severall chests with diverse other goods of value (which he affirmed were for the kyng his masters owne use) and for which he obtained, by my sollicitation, the lord Treasurers warrant to have them deposited in the custome house freed from the charge of importation, with condition never the less that the sayd goods should not in the interim be debited here, or theyr property altered, without payment of customes he was charged by the farmers of the customes to be no better than a merchant and that howsoever he pretended the sayd goods to be to the king

---

[29] Francis Carey of Leppington had visited Spain with Charles.

[30] William Hamilton, son of the earl of Haddington.

[31] William Monson, viscount Monson of Castelmaine.

[32] H. Ponikau had visited Whitehall in Oct. 1626.

[33] Bernard duke of Saxe-Weimar sought permission to hire English troops to serve in France's anti-Habsburg coalition.

[34] See IV 117ᵛ.

his masters use, the profit accruing from their exchange or sale here would be his owne. Whereupon a lock being set by them on the door of the roome where the goods lay, he by me made his complaynt [128] to the lords of the indignity thereby offered his masters person in his, and for the purgation of the aspersion cast upon him of a mere merchant desyred that his letters of credence myght be produced and translated (which with the fault of some and not wythout just resentment of the gentleman had not yet been done) that so his condition myght be made knowne, and the goods, severall parcells whereof were perishable might be kept at the former liberty of his access for theyr ayring. This obtained, he found diverse peeces of satins and stuffs of sylke and gold discoloured and much damnified, for which he stuck not to threaten that our merchants should, at his returne to Persia, make reparation. But carrying the tyme before him, noe great difference passed between him and them tyll towards his departure, when having bought diverse peeces of clothes (besides other commodoties of this kingdom pretended for the king his masters use) he treated with them for his freight and charge of transport, for which they stuck not to demand 1000 £, he provideing his own dyet, besides 100 £, for the use of the best cabin in the ship he was to go in, for either of which he could obtain little abatement, no more than he could of any due of custome.[35] The merchants, not with standing spared not their invitation (no more than he did his coming) to a feast made him at Crosby House, where he carried himself with shewes of much satisfaction but, in substance, not without resentment of their far more merchant like dealing.

[129ᵛ] In tyme of Christmas, the Spanish ambassadour having receyved advice of the king of Hungarys election[36] for king of the Romans, gave notice of it to the Kyng (then at Hampton Court) by one of his gentlemen and to give a more punctuall account of it by hymself, demanded audience of his majesty which granted and signifiyed by one of the Bed Chamber indefinitely in these words, for what day he should be pleased to come for it, but with this restriction, that he would be pleased wyth all to make the day known the night before to the Lord Chamberlin that his majesty might not be surprised, wyth out reasonable notice, of his coming. He the next day sent to me his servant with a letter signifying the liberty his majesty had given him, which

[35] Correr, the Venetian ambassador, also reported that this Persian merchant was displeased at the heavy fees demanded by the London customs officers and the East India merchants (CSP V 1636–39, pp. 177–78).

[36] At Regensburg on December 22nd (New Style), Ferdinand, eldest son of the emperor, was elected king of the Romans (to succeed on the death of his father). Ferdinand was already king of Hungary, but never recognized by Charles as king of Bohemia.

he intended, he sayd, to make use of by his repayr to court the day after, being Wednesday. This letter coming to my hands late in the evening, I the next day went early to court for preparation and prevention of disturbance to his majesty. The ambassador in the interim having a precipitated intention of coming that day, but not giving me reasonable notice of it, I obtained an assignation of his audience for Fryday after and let him know as much. But the next day (Thursday) he seeking, as appeared, to anticipate for reasons, of his own, the hour assigned for an audience of the Earl Marshall[37] then newly arrived from his ambassage to the emperor, was already set forth wythout giving me notice of it but was not so farr [130] on his way, as that I (acquainted with his course by another hand) was not sooner at court to have prevented him, had he come (as he did not, hearing on the way that his Majesty was gone on hunting). The day following (December 30th) he had access wyth my reception at the court gate and conduction to the closet councell chamber (over the chappel) whither no lord was sent to fetch him thence to the presence of his majesty (not withstanding my intimation and five or six precedents that I had alledged of public audience with all the formes customary and proper to it) to have bene at other tymes given several ambassadors upon occasion of congragulation and the lyke of publick condition, as this might seem to be. His majesty not assenting to it, gave him a private accesse in his Withdrawing Chamber, where no Secretary of State, nor scarce three lords of the privy councell, were present. He had his majestyes ear for two houres and a half together making use (as he told me after) of the ill French he had, with mixture of Italian and Spanish, for expression of his mynde, when I had before hand offered (but was excused) my interpretation.

---

[37] Thomas Howard, earl of Arundel, left England in April to meet with Ferdinand II. After failing to secure any promises to return the count Palatine's rights and lands, he returned to England on December 27th, and reached Hampton Court to report to Charles on the 29th.

[130ᵛ] The Deputy (or Ablegate as his letters styled him) from the emperor had had towards the end of the summer an audience at Windsor to take his leave,[1] (as he pretended and gave out) after he had discovered the kings insatisfaction for the emperors formal excuse, or rather refusal, to restore the Palatinate in forme and substance as his majesty required it by his ambassador, the earl Marshall. Whereupon, having received his final dismission, as was conceyved, and withal his passport (as he demanded it) from the lords, but not any present or any motion made for it, he retyred himself for three monthes, not known where, and was generally thought to be gone out of England, when, about mid January, I receyved from him a letter and a request to procure him an audience from his majesty, for the account he said he had command to give, and letters with it brought by an expresse,[2] from the emperor and king of Hungary, of the election of this latter for king of the Romans. This he performed with my introduction at Hampton Court, the 15th of January, and the 20th he took leave of the king at St. James, with his majestyes pleasure immediatly signifyed to my lord chamberlin of a chayne of 210 £ value. A favour that seemed beyond his expectations, when he had already resolved to be gone hence within two dayes, which was, 3 or 4 dayes after his [131] departure, delivered (as he had left order to one Prilitzer, a stranger his confidant) to be brought after him to Dover.

He tooke exception at a clause in his passe signed by the Lords because after his liberty therein given for transport of himself, servants and goods (without let or molestation), it did a second tyme injoyne the searchers to an especiall care not to suffer him to passe with any goods prohibited, which was, he said, a direct contradiction in the end to the freedom given him in the beginning of his passport.

Affirming with all that though he had no goods that might be called prohibited, he would not (he said) be subject to the search of his coffers and have his papers looked into by officers. This his grievance I intimated to Mr. Secretary Cook, with request from him to have an ommission or alteration of that charge to the searchers. But I was answered it could be neither omitted nor altered, the forme having been, he said, such as the passes of all am-

---

[1] Clement Radolt, in London, April–Aug. 1636: see IV 108ᵛ.

[2] As official envoy to announce the same events that Oñate and Arundel had related in December.

bassadours of late years parting out of England, particularly of the States ambassador the summer before when he went for Holland, who though he quarrelled at his passe so drawne could get no other. No more could this deputy, who when he saw no remedy accepted of it with patience. He had intreated me to move, as I did, Mr. Secretary Cook to write to the Admiral in the Downs for a ship to transport him which would not be granted till writeing from Dover to the earl of Arundell for this favour, it was procured him, this daye.

When my Lord Chamberlin told me of his majestyes pleasure for a chayne to be provided him of 210 £ value, the earl of Arundell then by, said smiling, it is more by 40 £ than I had from the emperor. It was most true, though strange, that the emperors present to that great lord sent ambassador to him his majesty, having been but a small diamond ring of 160 £, which was sought to be excused by some tender of the Austrian honour, with saying that the emperor gave it him as a regale of his love and not of his acknowledgement. It was made a question by others whether it had not been better refused then accepted.

[133] After the Marquess de Pougny, ordinary ambassador for France, had resided here about two years and a half and, in summer, had betaken him-selfe for refuge[3] from the contagion at London to an house hyred of the Countess of Nottingham[4] at Rygate in Surrey, he, towards Christmas, fell into a lethargy whereof he dyed. He left me and others that had done him service here in our places with little hope [133 ᵛ] of gratuities from him, whose heyrs were not like, after his death, to have any from his majesty. Yet the Gentleman of his Horses (Monsieur des Bordes) repayring to me and setting on foot a pretence of the son with intimation of the merit of the father (in advancing the service of our King upon all occasions) of the neerness of the time that his ambassage was to expire, spoke above all of the precedent of a present which he alledged, had been allotted in France for Sir Isaac Wake,[5] though dead, and sent to his widow by consent of the king and ministers of that state. I moved my lord chamberlin for it and produced a letter from Mr. Burlamack[6] to me, testifying that such a present had been given, but could prevaile no further with his lordship for the advancement of the businesse than his promise that if it should be moved to his majesty, he would give it his best furtherance, but for him fyrst to propose it stood not, he said, with

---

[3] The outbreak of the plague in London in June 1636.
[4] Mary Cockayne, wife of the 2nd earl of Nottingham.
[5] Sir Isaac Wake died in Paris in June 1632.
[6] Philip Burlamachi, the banker.

the condition of his place which owed a regard not only to the Kings honour but to his profit. Upon this answer I advised des Bordes to apply himself to the queens chief Almoner, the bishop of Angoulesme, to use his mediation to her majesty for them to the king. This took effect so far as that his majesty said, if it could be proved that a present had been given to his ambassadors widdow in France, the like should be given to the French ambassadors here in England. This signified by the bishop to my lord chamberlin, and the lord [134] chamberlin leaving of it to my proof by Mr. Burlamacks letter mentioned, I produced this in the presence of his majesty. I had, therupon, his pleasure signifyed for a present to be provided but with a restriction that it should be proportioned not after the value of 1200 £, as had been bestowed on Sir Isaack Wake, who having treated the accord of our differences upon conclusion of our peace with France was considered as an extraordinary, imployed to a busynes extraordinary but according to the ordinary proportion of 2000 ounces of gylded plate usually given here to an ordinary ambassador. For this, order was given to the Master of the Jewel House and (upon attestation to me of the bishop that des Bordes had good power given him to dispose of the deceased Marquises estate here) it was presented to him for the use of the Marquis living. It met with an acknowledgement suitable to others formerly made by that nation, when after that des Bordes had professed that he would deale as bountifully with the Master of the Jewel House, and especially with my self, who had the only operative hand in the business, as ever any French ambassador ordinary had done. He was no sooner possessed of the plate, than he was dispossessed of his grateful intention, and pretending pressing necessity and the many payments he said he had to make with that supply, he sold it. With out other visit or civill excuse he sent me only a gylt cup and a salt celler of 27 £ value, the Master of the Jewel House something less, and my officer three twenty shilling peeces.

[135ᵛ] The Queen being brought to bed of a third daughter[7] on Fryday, the 17th of March, between the hours of 4 and five in the morning, the Spanish ambassador sent to me two dayes after to excuse him, as I did, to his majesty for not coming to congragulate. The sicknesse had lighted in a victualling house near his, where some of his servants were dyetted and were therefore removed thence and shut upp in his stables near his house. But the Venetian and States ambassadors, having not yet made offer of performance of that complement, had notice given them by me of the Spanish ambassadors punctuality, which brought forth both their audiences successively, the 22nd of March.

___

[7] Anne.

The 24th, the Spanish, supposed by that time to be free from danger to his majestyes person by his presence, was admitted to the like audience. All his servants came clothed in mourning for the emperours death, but himself not, having on him a black velvet cloak and suite layd with open lace, which difference he perceiving that I observed, sayd to me smyleing, I see what you look at. But I am thus apparrelled of designe, as holding it improper for me, howsoever it may be otherwise for my men, to be cladd in mourning, when my businesse now at hand it to congragulate the burthe of a princesse. This I instantly made known to one of the lords then going to the King in his Withdrawing Chamber, and that lord to his Majestye, he applauded the ambassadours conceit and reason, and gave him after it a long and gracious audience.

[138ᵛ] March 28, the Spanish ambassador had audience of his majesty at St. James's for the account[8] he was to give, as he had received order, of the emperors death. He came then completely clothed himself and all his followers in mourning. After he had passed his businesse his Majestye told him how he had observed his manner at his accesse before in the difference of his habit from his followers, they mourning he not, he made answer to his Majestye as before to me.

Towards the end of that week, my lord chamberlin signified to the Gentlemen Ushers, and these to others of the kings servants, his majestyes pleasure for a general mourning in court for the emperor to begin on Palm Sunday and to continue till Easter day, which was obeyed, though by over few. The forbearers being either disaffectionate, or pretending ignorance of the Gentleman ushers denuntiation. His majesty the first day of mourning wore his royall couler of purple, which was observed he had not put on upon any occasion of mourning, since the Kyng his fathers death. The Prince Elector having been asked the day before whether he meant to mourne the emperor, civilly answered: as long as I acknowledge him to have been the head, and myselfe to be a member of the empire, I have reason to shew what sence the one ought to have of the others losse. So his highness together with his brother, prince Rupert, appeared, as did the rest of the court, during the time ordained for mourning in colour conformable.

[136] Towards the departure of the Persian, by this time commonly styled ambassador, the earle of Arundel did him an honour more than ordinary to invite him to a diner at his house, where, after it, was a play and a bankett,[9]

[8] Ferdinand II had died 15 Jan. 1637 (New Style).
[9] Unidentified plays and performances.

and to send him home for his greater honour, in his lordships own coach. The first of April, [136ᵛ] he had had, upon his demand, another leave taking and audience, of the kyng, where his majesty was pleased (answerable to the Persians particular request, as for his greater honour) with his own hand to deliver him his letter, in answer of that he brought from the king of Persia, which, though supposed by most men to be, if not counterfeit, wrested beyond the power pretended to be given him in it to treat and conclude the setting of a trade which the Persians for their silks (all other traders excused) were privileged, would for the future hardly prove available at his returne home to save his head without help of the advantage made here, by his bought commodoties and to be made there, by bribery, etc. *Sed de hoc viderit tempus.*

This trade of silk gave subject of much discourse and was debated of before his majesty and the councell with some hope of success for a while, but the ymmense value of it, beyond our ability of satisying, the distance and difficulty of corresponding with a king and a nation so far remote, and so uncertaine, as the merchants report the Persians to be in their trading, and above all the little assurance the ambassador could give (not with standing his pretensions and confidence of his *plenipotencia*) to offer, much less to ratify, a settled trade between us,¹⁰ was cause of nothing done for that tyme. He had presented to me, at New Years tyde before, a fayre looking glass, a peece of cloth of gold flowered, and eleven yards of watered silk chamlet, and sent me from Dover, when he imbarked, seaven yards of coloured satin, all worth about 25 £.

[137] The Spanish ambassador having brought with him two gennets out of Spayne, with intention, it seemed, in his own fit time, to make present of them to the king, kept them till April and then, at an audience, offered them to his majestyes acceptation. He, three or four days after, sent them by the Master of his horses, with their clothes on of crimson velvet fringed about with gold, at an instant as his majesty was running at the ring in St. James's parke. At their first appearance the King took little notice of them, till, after a while, the ambassador himself coming thither conducted by the earle of Bohan from his house at Chelsey, (the kyng so ordering it) he viewed them, accepted of them and ordained a chayne of gold of 50 £ value to the Master of the horses and 5 £ to each of his two groomes.

The king at his parting from the manage took the ambassador along with him and shewed him his statues as he passed through the Privy Garden. Being come to the Privy Chamber he left him to the company of the Duke of

---

¹⁰ The East India Company was suffering losses, during 1635–38, because of Dutch and Portuguese competition, as well as rival expeditions to the Persian Gulf that had Charles's own approval.

Lenox, the marquis Hamilton and the earle of Arundel, whom, till he came to his coach, the ambassador could not persuade to leave him.

[137ᵛ] The feast of the knights of the order appointed for the 17th of April brought forth my wonted care of sounding what disposition the ambassadors would have to be at it. That of the States extraordinary said he thought fit to dispense with the sight of it, for prevention of quarrells that might perhaps grow from some of his madder followers with the lyke of the Spanish ambassadors to the occasion perhaps of some scandall. The Spanish, when I had let him know the usuall style of our proceeding with ambassadors towards the day of the feast (*viz.* that his majesty used not to send an invitation to any, but that such ambassadors as desyred to see it, conveyed by me their desires to his majesty and I back to them, from him an assurance of their welcome) answered that he supposed he ought not, regarding his quality, to be present at so publick a solemnity as that feast was without an invitation. To which I replyed that the solemnity of that feast was not to be accounted publick, though all that would might come to see it, but private. It was a feast annually prepared and kept by the soveraygne, his majesty, for the companions of the order of the knights only. Hereupon he refuged his intended absence from this sight to that which he thought, he said, would be more worthy, the next feast to follow. This, within a year after, he heard would afford a more fayr shewe when all the knights [138] followers and servants, who were now as he was told excused the wearing of their proper liveries, colours and cognizances to avoid the danger of the sicknesse by confluence of people, should then appear in their full bravery. This was the colour he set on his absence, when the true reason of it, as a servant of his told me, was his doubt of incountering the French ambassador,[11] who he knew, if they should meet, would have too strong a party for his opposition. Yet he recommended to me his followers, whom to the number at least of 20, I disposed altogether for their better sight and less incumberance in the upper gallery of the Banqueting House, whence they might without hinderance see his majesty and the knights sitting at their dynner, as I had before placed them in the hall, standing upon the benches there, for sight of the procession.

The 29th of April, conducting the Spanish ambassadour to an audience of his majesty at St. James's, he had it, as had other tymes, in the Privy Chamber the place also of his first rest, whither his majesty, upon my notice of his being there, came forth to him. A paynes (in the judgement of some lords) that his majesty might well have spared, as being superrogatory and a descent from

---

[11] Finet wrote in the margin: "Thus I had seen it two years before, that he hovered about the court tyll diner tyme, perhaps to scare the Spanish."

his state to come forth of the room he was in (the Withdrawing Chamber) immediately to the Privy Chamber to give an audience. Three or four dayes after the Venetian had audience in his Majesties Withdrawing Chamber in Whitehall. He, as was observed, came not in his gowne, no more than he did at diverse other audiences before, but different from the custome of his predecessors, ambassadors of that gowned reipublick, for which he gave the answer given by himself before.

[139] The Baron Kaognitz of Moravia[12] making England his way home from Spaine and bringing with him letters recommendatory to my lord chamberlin, and me, from his majestyes ambassador there, Sir Walter Aston, kissed their majestyes hands, was admitted to the sight of what amongst us might be thought sight worthy and after 6 weeks or 2 months stay here parted the 8th of June presenting me with a small diamond ring about of 5 £ value.

One Monsieur de Samarez, father of myne officer Amis Andros, Marshall of the Ceremonies,[13] dying in Guernsey, where he had been by ancient descent one of the signors, as they are there styled, of that island, his son was to do his homage for his tenure there to the king as Duke of Normandy, and by my indeavor and procurement, obtained the discharge of that duty to his majesty in person, which had been done by his father before him to the Governor in the island, though wont of ancienter tymes to be done by his ancestors to the king himself, as now here in England. The manner of it was thus.

His majesty, the sixth of June, being a sermon day, as he passed to chapel, tooke his seate in his chayr under the state in the presence chamber (the sword borne before him by the earl of [blank] and the great lords and officers of state attending) when the gentleman mentioned, wayting at the Presence door, was fetched thence by and between the Earl Marshall of England [139ᵛ] and the lord chamberlin of his majestyes household, through a gard made of the band of Gentlemen Pensioners, and after three reverences, laying down his sword and cloak, all in forme (as had been before prescribed and sett downe in wryting by Garter king of Armes, Sir John Borows) he kneeled down at the foot of his majesty and with hands closed between his majestyes hands, pronounced these words in French:

Sire, Je demure vostre homme a vous porter foy et hommage contre tous.

To which the king read this answer set down also in French:

---

[12] Probably Lev Vilem Kaunitz (?).
[13] Amias Andros was marshal Aug. 1635 – July 1640.

Nous vous y acceptons, advouant tous vos legitimes droicts et possessions relevant en ceste tenure de nous sauf pareillement a nous nos droicts et regalitez.[14]

This sayd, the Signor Samarez (by which name he was henceforth to be styled and to quit his ordinary appellation of Andros) recyving the honour of a kiss of his majestyes hande, rose up and with most humble reverence, reassuming his cloak and sword, departed.

The Prince Elector Palatine, after 20 months abode here, having made preparation for his departure and return into Holland, took leave of the King and Queen at Greenwich the 25th of June, having received many most gracious expressions from their majestyes of their especiall respects and love towards him [140] and his brother Prince Robert. The former having receyved the confirmation of a pension of 12000 £ per annum and the latter one of 2400, besides the present gift to the Elector of 3000 £, and as much more to be paid him by bills of exchange in the low countryes, and to his brother 1000 £ in present. They had also each of them a fair diamond ring given them by the Queen with her own hand, that to the Elector worth 3000 £ and that to the Prince Robert 2000 £.

The whole body of the lords of the councell then at Greenwich, having concluded the state affayrs they had that after noone in hand, went altogether to his highnes lodging in the Tylt Yard or garden, there to take their leaves of him and his brother and returned thence altogether to the presence of his majesty.

That night theyr highnesses farewelled all the great ladyes in the Queens privy gallery. The next morning his majestye rising early to hunt returned betymes to give a second farewell to his nephews, who after with the conduct and company of the earl of Arundel, of the earl of Northampton (designated for his attendance to Holland) of the earle of Warwick, of the lord viscount Grandison, the lord Craven, the lord Herbert son to the earl of Pembroke, the lord viscount Somerset[15] and some other lords that wayted [140ᵛ] on him to his imbarking. They took barge at Greenwich, and going on shore at Woolwich for a sight of that rare new ship of the Kings there in buylding, they at Gravesend entered the Kings coach, sent thither before for his highnesses service (as were also by me 8 hyred coaches, which with 4 horses for carriage of his trayne all distributed before hand by billets made and given by me for theyr placeing, five known and named men in each coach to avoyd

---

[14] "Sire, I remain your man to maintain fidelity and homage in the face of all." "We accept this from you, acknowledging all your legitimate rights and possessions pertaining to this tenure from us, save our own rights and regalities equally proper to us."

[15] Thomas Somerset, viscount Somerset of Cashel.

intruders and confusion) so came that night to their lodging at Rochester. The next day they went to the Lady Wootens[16] house provided for their entertainment at Canterbury. The next morning towards noon they were at Deale castle in the Downes where a strong wind kept them from going a board till towards night. Then the earl of Arundell takeing leave left them to the conduct and convoy overseas (at least to the other side) of the earl of Northumberland, General of his Majestyes fleet then at sea. Their highnesses for their own passage went aboard the St. George (rier Admirall) commanded by Sir Henry Marvin made choyce of out of the princes special affection himself for his transport. The next morning towards noon he set sayle with the convoy mentioned of the Admirall and 12 or 14 others of the Kings ships for Holland.

[141] In the interim of my absence for attendance of the Prince Elector to his imbarking, the States ambassador, Monsieur Beverne, after he had resided here 15 months in quality and under tytle of extraordinary, and expecting no longer the returne of Monsieur Joachimi the ordinary, demanded his parting public audience assigned for Sunday the 2nd of July. When his steward in the interim fell sick of a burning feaver (with suspicion of turning to the plague) he discreetly gave notice of it to my lord [141ᵛ] chamberlin who herewith acquainted the king and the audience thereupon was suspended. The French ambassadour Marquess de Seneterre demanded one for his parting also. This was granted for the same day at Greenwich and the earl of Bedford made choyce of for his conduction to it. I was told of it no sooner than the last of June, two days before it, when I landed at Greenwich from the attendance I had given the Prince Elector Palatine to his embarking. This news brought me that nyght, against wind and tyde I made haste to London to my lord chamberlin for direction how to proceed in such a strait of tyme when I had but one day left for provision of coaches, or barges, by land and water if he should expect the Kings coach to Tower wharfe and his barge thence to Greenwich fetching him, as was his due, from his house in Hammersmith. But an accident of his invitation the day before to a dynner at my lord of Hollands lodgings in court saved me much of that trouble and cleared all difficulties. The ambassador, of his own disposition, perhaps not without regard to the charge, which he knew would be saved by that private way, and from consideration, as he professt, of the earl of Bedfords paynes, to be taken by so long a journey, as from London to Hammersmyth and thence to Greenwich, was pleased to dispense with ceremony for a shorter journey of

[16] Margaret Wharton, widow of Lord Edward Wotten.

coming privately to court in the forenoon. After dynner [142] he went publickly to the audience he had of both theyr majestyes together in the Presence Chamber, after he had for a while reposed himself in the councell chamber, to which he was brought by the earl, his conductor. He came first, upon my intimation, to the privy chamber and took thence with him, besides his son, the lord Russell, and two others of his sons, half a score gentlemen of the Privy Chamber appoynted to accompany him. The ambassador, after his audience, went strayght to the queens quarter, and in the Privy Chamber there, dismissing with thanks his conductor and the rest, he passed to her majesty in her privy gallery, where I also left him.

[142ᵛ] After my five or six dayes sollicitation for this French ambassadors present,[17] I was told that his majesty intended to alter the property and matter of it (which according to custome and to the proportion usually allowed kings ambassadors) should have consisted of 2000 ounces of gylt plate, into a sute of Arras hangings, consisting of fyve peeces, exceeding the other in valew and much less loss and honour to the recyver, if not to the king. It was the proper manufacture of this kingdome and the peeces, at that tyme in the custody of Sir James Palmer, one of the gentlemen Ushers of his majestyes Privy Chamber, who had now conferred on him that charge and survey of that mistery (as Sir Francis Crane deceased had had it before him). But with his own, rather than the kings, interest in it, he did therupon pretend to the right of their presenting, as issued, he said, out of his office. But I opposing, pleaded not only to my lord chamberlin, but to the king himself, my right (confirmed by two particular precedents of the like present of hangings carryed and delivered by me to the French ambassador, Monsieur Chateauneuf, and the Spanish, don Carlos de Coloma) and alledging withal [143] the reason of an accord sometymes made between my predecessor and the then Master of the Jewel House, who also stuck not at this time to be a pretender, but soon surceased, and the condition withal of my office, properly fit, and justly challenging that charge, the clayme was given over by that gentleman. The hangings were committed to my delivery by virtue of a warrant directed from the lord chamberlin to Mr. Kynnersley, yeoman of the Wardrobe, for their issuing out of his office to me, and for their presentation by me to the ambassador, carrying them to him by water (he being at his house in Hammersmyth) I presented them, as I complementally said, from his majesty for the furniture of a chamber in his new built house at Paris. Receiving from him a most thankful

---

[17] The negotiations for the alliance were being conducted in Paris by the earl of Leicester and viscount Scudamore, so that Senneterre felt he was being neglected by a lack of information. Charles was annoyed at his premature departure.

acknowledgement of his majestyes so royall favor, he presented me, after I was parted from him, by the hand of the superintendant of his family, a hundred peeces.

[143 ᵛ] After I had delivered him the present, I made offer of my service for his conduction to Gravesend, as was due and usuall to extraordinary ambassadors, in his majestyes barge. But he excused it with the commodity he had, he said, for his trayne of rideing by land with use of the many horses he had bought here and with his owne intention of going by land in coaches hyred to Rochester, and thence by post to Dover.

The States ambassadors steward being by this time recovered from danger of the plague (as was confirmed by me under the hands of two or three physicians) he went for, and had, his parting audience of both their majestyes together at Oatlands, the 16th of July. He was conducted thither from London by the Baron Herbert of Cherbury, who had performed for him the like office at his first audience, with no other company than mine and of his own servants in his own coach. For the ease of the horses, it was by me appointed to meet and receive him at Shepperton bridge, a mile from the court, and there after his audience to leave him, as I did, for his returne that nyght to London.

[144] When at the approach of this ambassador to theyr majestyes (standing under the State in the presence chamber) he began, after his thyrd and last reverence, to speak not making offer to ascend the steps of the more raysed floor whereon their majestyes stood, the king with a grace and respect to him more than ordinary, beckoned him up to him, an honour which the ambassadour after told me his majesty had omitted to do him at his first publick audience. The next day I accompanyed him to the sight and farewell of the Prince, duke of York and Princesse at Richmond.

Toward the time of his departure he discovered to me a disposition he had to be knighted, which when I intimated to my lord chamberlin, his lordship professed readiness to move for it. But the ambassador, after makeing a question whether it would not be rather a derogation than an addition of honour to his quality to be knighted, when two of his countrymen meaner than himselfe, he said, had been made barronets? I plainly replyed I thought it would be a hard matter to procure the latter, his majesty haveing of late years made few or no baronets, and to make him one, would be I thought an act of consequence. It was a subject serving for the ministers of Venice their exceptions, when they having been customarily knighted at their parting, might with reason expect hereafter to be made also barronets from precedent. This answer seeming then to satisfy, he (after his request of my silence) never spake further to me to that purpose.

The Spanish Resident, don Juan Nicolalde, had his last audience for his leave takeing[18] in the Kings Withdrawing Chamber at Oatlands, private and suiting with the condition of but an agent. From thence going to the Queens quarter he had the like of her Majestye, neither of these with other conduction, or incounter, then of myne, from his home and back again and with use only of his own two coaches, returning by the way of Richmond to take leave there, as he did, of his Majestyes children.

[145] The time of the Spanish residents departure approaching I moved my lord chamberlin for the purpose of his present. I represented his fair carriage here all the time of his six years residence, during which he had the tytle commonly given him of Resident, his particular dignity of the habit he wore of Santiago which might draw (I supposed and said) so much regard from his majestye as that he would be pleased to add an hundred or two of pounds [145ᵛ] to the usuall value of a chayne and medal of 210 £ commonly bestowed on agents and envoys of princes at their parting.

His lordship held my proposition reasonable and accordingly moved for it, but his Majesty absolutely refusing to make any such addition or difference, sayd he would not acknowledge any princes minister imployed here to be other, than either ambassador or agent, with this answer resting silent. I repayred soon after to Señor Necolalde himself to sound (like an honest spye for his Majestyes more honour and better service) his resolution for the tyme of his parting. But I found his haste to part not so much as his curiosity to know what, and of what kind, the present was that was intended to him by his majesty. I sayd that it was to come to him from the hand of the Master of the Jewel House, or his officer, and should I thought be a chayne of the value usually presented to Kings Agents. At this tytle of agent he rose up from his chayre in a passion, such as I had not seen him subject to. He sayd he was qualifyed by his letters of credence whereof he would needs after shew me the copy, for the king of Spayne his masters resident, and not for his agent, in this kingdome and that he was by the same letters styled *su consejero de Estado y de Guerra*. He was *cauallero del habito de Santiago* and had been *Veedor General* of his majestyes[19] armyes in [146] the Low Countries and was at that time Secretary of State with the Infante Cardinal.[20] For him to admit of such a descent as from a resident to agent would so much reflect, not only on his own, but the king his masters honour, as if any present should be brought

18 July 19th.
19 Member of the Council of State and War, knight of Santiago, Inspector General of the Army of Flanders.
20 His next appointment was Secretary of State and War.

him under that tytle and of the valew as to an agent that he must and would refuse it. I replyed that his Majestye, and we generally here in England, made no difference of quality between that of resident and agent but as of the old and new style which might differ in court but not in time and to that purpose. But I could not drive him from his construction and resolution taken to refuse the present if it should be sent him under the tytle and value specifyed. Of this thinking it the duty of my charge to give an account, I dispatched my servant instantly to court to Mr. Secretary Windebank with a letter relateing the manner of my proceeding, of Señor Necolaldes answer, and of my reply. To which Mr. Secretary returned the same day in writeing this formall answer.

> Sir, I have acquainted his Majestye with your letter who will not depart from his rule, nor from the ancient and constant custome ever held with Ambassadours and Agents, his Majestye acknowledging no third capacity here in England, [146ᵛ] nor any such quality as a resident which is meer innovacion, whatsoever Senor Nicolalde can pretend to by his letters of credence, and therefore he is to expect no other present than of usuall value and such as hath been heretofore bestowed upon agents.
>
> So, Sir, with remembrance of my love and service I rest your most affectionate and humble servant,
>
> FRANCIS WINDEBANK
>
> Oatlands, 25 July 1637

Imparting to Señor Necolalde the substance of this letter, he, not without expression of passion as before, returned the like answer. He added that his majesty might have been pleased, when at his first coming he saw his letter of credence, to have made his exceptions and that he might have made his defence and have instantly returned home and not have been put to it so much to his dishonour. After he had for six years together publickly possessed the place and tytle of resident, he was in the end dismissed with the name and present of an agent, which was, he said, but half a resident in quality and entertainment. The king his master allowed to his agents, if he had any abroad, but 25 £ a month and his residents (as himself) five tymes as much. He said that Mr. Gerbier and Mr. Hopton,²¹ his majestyes ministers in Flanders and Spayne, had the tytle given them from hence of Residents and that the latter answerable to that tytle had been presented at his parting from Spayne with the value of 500 £ sterling and [147] for his Majestye to take that tytle from him, when he gave it to his own, and in proportioning his present to equal him with an agent, was not altogether agreeing with that justice for which his majesty was abroad so much reknowned, for that as he was Resident here for

---

²¹ Baltazar Gerbier in Brussels and Arthur Hopton (in the absence of Aston) in Madrid.

the king of Spayne he held himself equall, and so I might remember, he had heretofore profest in all regard with the ambassadors of any reipublick, giving precedence to none but kings ambassadors[22] (as the king of France his ambassador), that a resident was equivalent in all to an ambassador, except in standing bare at audiences, and in not having gyven them the *Excellenza* and that, in conclusion, his humble request was that he might have no present at all sent him, that so dishonor might pass in silence, which, if sent him and then refused by him (as it must and should be) would make too great a noyse.

The substance of this second answer I (returneing the next day to court) related to his majesty and, from his owne mouth, had this final resolution, which I delyvered to Señor Nicolaldi thus formally (in Spanish[23]): 'His majesty has commanded me to say to your lordship that, as he does not presume to dictate to the king, your master, in what fashion he is to grade his ministers, so also does he expect that his majesty would not wish to consider it any less friendly to his service, if [147ᵛ] in viewing the consequence, he should seek to preserve in every way the ancient customs of his kingdom in dealing with the ministers of kings and foreign princes. Wherefore, having ordered a present for your lordship in keeping with the norm for those same ministers who have been sent here to reside at the court of his majesty, he hopes that your lordship will accept it as an appreciation of the satisfaction that his majesty has received in the person of your lordship. Further more, it is his prayer that God may grant your lordship a long life and a fair journey homewards.'

To this his answer extended litle beyond the former purpose, only, he said, he had three or four other reasons to alledge, which he had not before called to mind to strengthen his pretence, *viz.* 1st, that at the first of his arrival he had by order from the lord treasurer, with allowance of the King, a bill for twenty tunns of wine free of impost as to a Resident, whereas Agents have but for 15 tunns (being one half of the proportion alloted to ambassadors) to put a difference between Agents and Residents. 2nd, that the king his master had never qualifyed any minister of his abroad with the tytle of Agent and

---

[22] To the complaint to Olivares against Charles, Aston commented that, although Necolalde's credentials had the title of Resident, he had been so addressed in London "more to please him, for there are no other grades known ther in substance than ambassador and agent, nor can I understand what are the rights to which the resident could pretend that are not proper to an agent, nor do I know upon what custom don Juan is able to base them. . . . We must not cast aspersions on the favors of kings, but leave them to decide how they can reward each person according to his merits . . ." (AGS E 2563, Aston to Andres Rochas, 26 Sept. 1637). The Spanish council did not pursue the grievance.

[23] Editor's translation.

that, by his letters having been qualifyed Resident, it was in the King of Englands power to add honours to him, but not to take any from him that had been conferred on him by the king his master. 3rd, that about a year after his imployment hither he received letters from the emperour qualifying [148] him his commissioner for some business then here in agitation, which qualification continued for him till the death of his imperial majesty. By virtue of it he might, he said, if he would have, stood covered in the Kings presence. But in tyme quitting these and other reasons (all which he saw would be unavailable) he professed againe his resolution not to receive the present, if brought him as to an agent, and desired me therefore to be a means to keep it from delivery, which I excuseing as an act proper to another office and not for mine, the present being already ordered by the Kyng to be presented to him, I only promised to procure (if I could) the officers repayre to him that he might privatly know from himselfe the intention of his refusal and, as silently as might be, prevent the noyse like to follow it. But the Master of the Jewel House then absent, his officer repayring twice to him with that caution, he avoyded his sight with excuse of being from home, till finally the said officer advised by me to surprise him with some feigned errand to his secretary he could no longer excuse his being then at home though not seen. But he sent him word by his secretary that don Juan Finette, knowing his reasons why he could not accept of his majestyes present, he wished the gentleman that had come so often about it not to trouble himself, or him, any further. This understood for an absolute refusal was obeyed and so he parted hence without any present to him, or from him to me and without so much as bidding me farewell. About the beginning of September after, when he imbarked at Plymouth, he wrote me a letter carrying his reasons for refusal amongst others these. That in like manner as kings are used to treat and gratify other kings and princes ambassadors, so ministers are used to make their demonstrations and acknowledgements to the conductor, [148ᵛ] officers or other servants, which had given them attendance, this course being equal and reasonable. For him to exceed the King of Great Brittayne would be imputed to him for arrogancy, or presumption and, perhaps, another might have order to receive no gratuity from him if any should be offered. But, hopeing in the spring to pass by England to Flanders without the character of a publick minister he would visit me, kiss my hands and serve me with some courtesy of Spayne without noyse or notice to be taken of it, which let them trust that have not made tryall of Spanish unthankfulnesse as I have done.

The 22nd of August, while I was at my house in Chiswick, a gentleman (who had the year before been here Secretary to the ambassador of Poland,

Zavadsky) brought me news of another ambassador[24] from thence (by name Andreas Rey de Nablowitz) arrived before Harwich and desired my assistance and addresse for delivery of his letters, but I doubting of his welcome, after so ill a carriage and fruit of his predecessors negotiation (the king of Poland was even then upon consummation of a marriage with the emperors sister, which he had so seriously pursued for our Kings neece) gave him only my directions to find those he sought [149] without going, sending, or so much as writing myself to any of them. The gentleman, as he after returning, let me know and as I received by letters from my lord chamberlins secretary, arrived at Lindhurst (at an instant that the king was going on hunting) and applyed himself to the said secretary. He was by him accompanyed to Mr. Secretary Cook, from whom he had answer by a servant (without once seeing the master) that his majesty had taken such offense at the king of Polands proceeding, as he knew him to be resolved not to admit of his ambassage, that for his part he would not see him nor receive letters from him, though the ambassador himself was a person whose merit he much honoured, till he had spoken with the king and known his pleasure. His majesty (being returned from hunting) and Mr. Secretary, my lord chamberlin and the earl of Holland, conferring together and giving an account of the busynes to his majesty, he was pleased that my lord chamberlin (when the gentleman should next returne to him) should give him this answer: His majesty esteemed himself to have been so ill used by the king of Poland, and had so just cause of resentment and offense, as he could admit of no ambassage nor receyve any message from him. The gentleman replyed with reasons to move the king to hear him and would have perswaded my lord chamberlin to represent them to his majesty, but his lordship replyed his majestyes command was absolute, and would admit of no reply, and so dismissed him.

The sayd secretary repayred to me againe three or four dyes after, and a thyrd tyme after that, [149ᵛ] but I, having understood more particularly the kinges resolution, and what had been his answer to some merchants (indeavoring to make way for the ambassadors access and pleading the danger of theyr and the states loss, etc.) that his honour was more dear to him than the merchants interest, gave over all further inquiry after his course. He remayned still retyred at Greenwich, not altogether hopeless of a change, though in show preparing dayly for his returne home. At the end of about

---

[24] Andrew Rey of Naglowice, ambassador extraordinary (Aug. – Oct. 1637) of Poland, came to placate Charles after Vladislav had married the new emperor's sister, Cecilia Renata, in March. Charles believed he had been deliberately misled over the clergy's approval of a marriage of Vladislav with his niece, the sister of the Count Palatine (see IV 116).

six weeks, I intimated to his secretary that St. Georges feast was to be kept at Windsor, and cast out (of designe to sound his disposition) that if any of the Polish gentlemen, or perhaps the ambassador himself should affect the sight of that solemnity and would be content to be there as *Incognito* at it, I would (not as Master of Ceremonyes, but as a friend and servant to straungers, as became the duty of my charge) give them my best assistance.

He with four or five of his gentlemen came thither the evening of the feast and had my private visit at his inn and the use of my directions so far (though I appeared not publickly in their company) as they saw the King and knights sitt at supper, but not without discovery to this majesty of the ambassadors concealed presence there by some of the court, who having had sight of him before, knew him. This the next day he thanked me much for, but said he feared he had offended the king with that intrusion, though as of one *Incognito*, who had, he said, an ambition of the happiness, privately at least to see his majesty, when he was not to have public [150] accesse to him, where with the next day at dynner adventureing to acquaint his majesty had for answer that he was so far from takeing offense at it, as he took it rather for a respect, which not a little (when I told it to the ambassador) pleased him.

Two or three dayes after this, his secretary coming to my house to let me know that the King after a long debate was pleased that the ambassador should have audience and had signifyed so much, he said, to Mr. Secretary Cook who desired speedily to speak with me. I repayred to him to his house at Tottenham and there had his confirmation of the Kings pleasure, which the next day I went to receive at Hampton Court. But the King not yet satisfyed, and some points of acknowledgement (to what purpose I could not penetrate) being required by his majesty to be sent to him under the ambassadors hand, two or three letters passed from him to that purpose directed to the lord chamberlin but with no effectual operation, especially after that a letter from the king of Poland to his majesty (which letter being mislayd and out of sight was out of mind till now) was found to lay so weighty a charge and aspersion upon his majesty in point of honour as all being brought into a new disorder, it brought forth his majestyes final resolution not to give him any personal accesse at all[25] but only to permit, as he did, the company of merchants interested to repayre to him for their farewell. They asked him whether they might safely or not continue their traffick as before with Poland.[26] He answered that, for his part,

[25] Charles expected all foreign diplomats in London to follow his example, but Oñate publicly visited Rey, since the Habsburg courts of both Vienna and Madrid cultivated Poland, to counter France's alliance with Sweden.

[26] The Eastland Company's merchants wished to settle in Danzig but be exempt from that port's taxes. Charles's tactics with Vladislav rendered their chances more doubtful.

they had experience of his good disposition to maintaine a firm peace and commerce between his nation and ours and that, notwithstanding the so ill success of his negotiation, they might rest assured of his best indeavour at his returne home to do all good offices, though he was likely to find the king his master sensitive of his ministers treatment here, he would pour water and not oyle into this fire, *etc.* So receiving a present, which the merchants brought him (no likelyhood being left of any to come from his majesty) he without takeing leave or leaving any acknowledgement (as to say truth he had little reason to do) to any that had served him, departed home in ship he hyred for Holland about the end of October.

[150ᵛ] The Spanish ambassador being desirous to pass the winter in London (quitting for that time his house at Chelsey) sent to me one of his gentlemen with his request to move my lord chamberlin for his assistance to procure him a house, and particularly the Lord Brooks in Holborne,²⁷ at whatsoever rent should be reasonably demanded, and at such tymes of payment, before hand or otherwise, as should be required. I hereupon repayreing to the court then at Oatlands and not finding there my lord chamberlin, presented this ambassadors request to the King himself in presence of divers of ,the lords. I had answer, to be returned to the ambassador himself, from his majestye that if the Lord Brook had any disposition to let his house, he woud take it for a respect if, upon his recommendation, the ambassador of Spayne might have it, but if he meant to keep it in his own hands, as he was told he meant to do, he should be loath against his custome to force or perswade any of his nobility to quit his own conveniency, yet to do what might be done in the business his majesty gave me command to write instantly to my lord chamberlin. To this his lordship wrote answer that I might remember how, the year before, the same ambassador had made the like request, and had his majestyes answer how unpleasing it would be to him to perswade any man, much more a nobleman to part with his house against his lykeing, though he knew his Majestye to be most graciously inclineable to give the ambassador all befitting accomodation, etc. The substance of which letter as also of his majestyes own personall answer, I imparting to the ambassador, he preceeded no further with that importunity.

[151] The Venetian ambassador, Signor Coraro, having had his parting audience assigned him of both the king and queen at Hampton Court, for Sunday the 8th of October, was then brought to it in his majestyes coach, followed by the Spanish ambassadors and five others from his house near

²⁷ Possibly because Carlos Coloma had stayed there in 1630.

Twytham park, by the earl of Denbigh, accompanyed with Sir James Douglas (a younger son of the earl of Morton) Sir James Hamilton, brother to the earl of Haddington, and six or seaven gentlemen of the Privy Chamber.

[152ᵛ] The 10th of October, two or three English merchants trading with Barbary came to the court at Hampton, with news of the arrival of an ambassador from the king of Morocco, his name Indar ben Abdula, qualifyed of that kings privy councell and his lord chamberlin. There came with him imployed as his associat and a commissioner, Mr Robert Blake,[28] an English merchant honored with that imployment by the king of Morocco, who much favoured him and stiled him in his letters of credence, translated into Spanish, *su accompañado*. This known, I had order to carry him his welcome to Gravesend, where finding and leaving him sick of feaver, I returned with a lyst of a trayne consisting of 28 persons besides 16 English captives, 350 of which that king had redeemed at his charge of about 10,000 £ (defalking the rates demanded by the owners for theyr redemption from the duties they owed him of his customes) and were brought by him, as part of his present, in the ship, which set forth the spring before for Saley in Barbary to recover thence the English captyves, which they had taken and kept, and to revenge that affront done us on our coasts[29] by their piracyes. Together with these redeemed captives he brought his Majestye a present of four hawkes and 4 Barbary horses valued at 3 or 400 £ each, and two saddles with the bridles and stirrups plated over with massif gold of rare workmanship, esteemed each worth 1000 £.

To my first demand how this ambassador should be treated it was answered by my lord chamberlin and the Comptroller of his Majestyes household that it must be at the charge of the merchants. But these affirming themselves to be few in number (not passing 4 or 5), not rich, nor joyned in one formed company and that the ambassadors imployment to his majesty tending rather to matter of state, than to commerce, or merchants benefit, his majestye, with regard to the ambassadors quality, to the weight of his negotiation, and to the rare bravery of his present, was pleased he should be treated at his charge (as other ambassadors extraordinary) till the day after his audience, and noe longer, with the allowance of 25 £ *per diem* and with the provision of a house

[28] Robert Blake, agent (Oct. 1637 – March 1638) with Indar ben Abdulah, of the new sultan of Morocco. Although Charles had once assisted the Saley rebel regime (see III 17), the English fleet had recently assisted the sultan to recapture the rebel fortress city. Blake was currently agent of the Barbary Company in Marrakesh.

[29] Pirates from Saley raided the Irish coast in 1631 and the south coast of England in 1635. See Godfrey Fisher, *Barbary Legend: War, Trade, and Piracy in North Africa, 1415–1830* (London: Oxford University Press, 1957), p. 322.

to be taken up for him by my lord chamberlins order upon a letter from his lordship to the Lord Mayor,[30] the furnishing and payment of it to come from his majesty. This settled, I propounded that whereas other ambassadors from remote parts, as from Muscovy, were seldome employed to these, whereby would follow the lesse danger from precedent, had been at their entrance into London met on Tower Hill by the aldermen and citizens, this ambassador for his more honour (which was that which he most regarded) might be received in the same manner. This assented to, a letter was to that purpose directed to the Lord Mayor, so the 18th of October, I going, with three barges and a light horseman, to Gravesend, and the next day the earl of Kenoule accompanyed with Sir James Douglas (younger son of the earl of Morton) and 14 or 15 Gentlemen of the Privy Chamber, received him at Greenwich into the Kings barge, with one barge more accompanying it. I conducted him to his landing at Tower wharfe, where he entered the Kings coach, with about 20 others following him, and passed over Tower hill. He was there met by the aldermen in their scarlet gowns and citizens with their chaynes of gold to the number of above 100, all on horseback, rideing two and two before him, he was lighted with 5 or 600 torches to his lodging in the house of Alderman Lumbley in Wood Street.[31]

Mr. Porter of his Majestyes Bed Chamber had been appointed by the King to bring him that night the *para bien* [153ᵛ] of his coming to towne, but some occasion of his service holding him at court, he came not till the 3rd day after, when finding him still sick of his feaver, he changed the complement of his welcome to that of a visit from his majesty, and inquiry after his health, with offer from his majesty of liberty to command whatsoever might be useful to him. For his encounter mentioned on Tower hill, the Lord Mayor had been in discourse, and by some of his citty brethern persuaded, to be there himself on horseback. But his lordship propounding the fitness of it to my opinion I was directly for the negative and affirmed that his lordship, being the kings lieutenant in so eminent a condition, could not properly appear in so publick an occasion for the reception of any, except of but the king himself, or by his Majestyes speciall order, which assertion prevailed so with him, that when the aldermen and other citizens appointed for that service were ready to part from Guildhall (their general rendezvous) there expecting his lordships company, which for their better readiness he had promised them, he conveyed himself away and for that night appeared no more amongst them.

---

[30] Sir Edward Bromfield.
[31] Sir Martin Lumley.

About a fortnight before the Lord Mayors annual feast, the Spanish ambassadour had an invitation brought him by the two sheriffs[32] which he accepted of. The like was brought to the king of Moroccos ambassador but his feaver (besides the reason of not having yet seen his majesty) was a just excuse for his absence. The former who had not need at that time to fear the concurrency of other ambassadors (the French then expected and landed at Dover being come yet no further) [154] provided his stand at his own charge at Milk Street end. I had given him advice for the conveniency of entering his coach there and of passing thence by the back way to Guildhall without hindrance of the thronging multitude and he attended there the sight of the Lord Mayors passage so long after the lords (invited to the feast) were passed by towards their dynner as I doubted they would hardly forbear eating till the ambassadours coming. I sent my officer to let their lordships know what he had said to me, when I perswaded him to go to this dynner, that since my Lord Mayor had done him the honour to invite him to his dynner he owed him the respect to behold him in the glory of his passage to it. But theyr lordships, whereof there were present then only 4, returned answer (some what hungerly I confess) that, if he came not speedily, they must sit down. I againe sent the same messenger with caution that if they were all ready set he should say nothing but immediately returne, as he did, telling me he found them set at table and repeating to the ambassador in French, at his request how he found them. This he hearing and instantly conceiving it to be a scorne and an affront done him, fell from some passionate expressions to a final resolution that, as soon as the Lord should be passed by, he would part home directly. This he did, setting me down at my house, as hungry as he went to his, from a feast which we had tasted only in expectation.

The next day I made report hereof, as my charge required, to my lord chamberlaine absent from that dynner, and his lordship (much condemning the litle patience of the lords there present) to the King. Offended at it the King said my Lord Mayor had done less for the ambassadour than he himself would have done for him. [154ᵛ] But his majesty satisfyed by my lord chamberlin that it was not my Lord Mayors fault, the lords there present bore the condemnation though others condemned the ambassador for not applying himself to the tyme and company. In the mean time the Lord Mayor to clear himself from blame sent the next day the two sheriffs to the ambassador at Chelsey. But those lords, not acknowledging nor excusing any error committed, answered for themselves when they were told of it, that dynner was ready to be set on before the ambassador sent to them, and they had

---

[32] Sir Richard Fenn, lord mayor, and John Garrard and William Abel, sheriffs.

businesse of the Kings to despatch after dynner, and they knew the Lord
Mayors passage through Cheapside would not be till an hour or two
after, as indeed it was not. So as for the future caution and avoydance
of the lyke ill understanding another tyme, ambassadors invited and affecting
to see it, must be made acquainted before hand. If they will be present at
dynner they must lose the sight of the show before it and content themselves
with that after it, when the Lord Mayor shall ride to Pauls Church, against
which tyme his Lordship made acquainted with their course, may for their
respects order the proceeding in the evening to be as completely set forth as
in the morning.

   The king of Moroccos ambassador recovered of his sickness, and having been
18 dayes (from the 19th of October to the 5th of November inclusive) defrayed by his majesty at 25 £ *per diem* was conducted to his audience by the
earl of Shrewsbury,[33] ryding on horseback (being a course not in use) the
ambassador had made, by me, his particular request to his majesty, professing
his extream disaffection to ryding in a coach. He affirmed also that he had
an expresse order from the king his master to pass not otherwise to his publick
audience than on horseback, his proceeding to it was by me arranged in this
manner.

   [155] First rode one of the City Marshalls with 5 or 6 servants near by him
on foot to make way. 2nd, seaven trumpeters on horseback. 3rd, the present
of four horses, two of them with their rich saddles and furnitures on covered
with cloaths of damask, and other two with their cloaths only, each of
them led by a black Moor in his red livery and a groom by him. Next
these, or before, should have been carried four hawks part of the present,
but the doubt of theyr misusage from unskillful keepers, who had charge
of them, moved the king to have them presented to him four or five dayes
before. In the 4th place marched the 16 freed captives on foot cloathed
all new at the charge of the ambassador. 5th, the Marshall of the
Ceremonyes on horseback. 6th, rode 6 or 7 city captaynes richly cloathed
having great plumes on their hats. 7th, ten Gentlemen of the Kings Privy
Chamber, twelve having been lysted but two fayleing, in black velvet foot
cloaths (all in black to comply with the pleasure and demand of his majesty
at that tyme mourning for the Duke of Savoy deceased). 8th, myself, as
Master of the Ceremonyes, ryding alone before the ambassador. 9th, the
ambassador himself, with the earl of Shrewsbury on his right hand, on his
left, but somewhat retyred to express a difference, his associate Mr. Blake,

---

[33] John Talbot, 13th earl of Shrewsbury.

and close before him on foot his page, and another of his servants carrying his scymetar and the other his pantables and part of his horses golden harness at the collar, etc., and at each side of him, walked four footmen in blew liveryes, and behind him eight of his more eminent followers, Moors in their country habits on horseback. After these rode another of the city marshall and last of all came the earl of Shrewsburys two coaches, mine and others, that carryed us from court while we sent our saddle horses privatly before to the ambassadors lodging.

[155ᵛ] In this order he marched with a slow pace along the streets till without Temple Bar, the trayned bands of Westminster (400) lead by their Captain Endymion Porter of his majestyes Bed Chamber met him and marched before him to court, where making a stand and guard on both sides of the way, he passed between them, allighted at the Court Gate and went for his repose to the Lord Keepers lodging, next by a building for maskes then in hand in the first great court, hindring and excusing his passage[34] to the place where he should have reposed, the councell chamber, being entered from out of that lodging immediately into the banketting house, which the lord chamberlins best care could not keep clear from the overpressing multitude. There, gracefully making his three bowing reverences, he spake to his majestye and after, briefly, to the queen in Arabick by the interpretation of his Associate. He returned thence to the place of his first rest and was after a while sent for, as had been before ordered for avoydance of the intruding presse, to his majestye who stayed his coming to the Privy Gallery, and went along with him to the foot of the stayre leading downward to the Park, there to receive the present of horses, which led forth, one by one, before his majesty were by him severally viewed, as were, after them, the captives.

When the kyng returning, and the ambassador attending him as far as the first privy gallery, he there had with him a short private conference, the duke of Lenox interpreting, then taking leave, the night coming on brought with it confusion and hindered the ambassadors access to his horse (as it did to all appointed to attend in the Tylt Yard, with orders for our returne home, as we came, on horseback) and forced us to make use of the princes coach (then casually present) and of two others of the earl of Shrewsbury to conduct him to his lodging.

---

[34] The Masking House under construction in the inner Sermon Court of Whitehall palace.

BOOK V

October 26, 1637 to ca. May 15, 1641

[1] Towards the end of October 1637, Monsieur de Bellievre, ambassador from the French king (sent under title of extraordinary,[35] but with designe to reside here as ordinary) after a troublesome and dangerous passage in one of his majestyes shipps, which took him in before Dieppe, landed with his wife and family at Dover. He left his plate, the best of his household stuff, his jewells, apparel (and some sayd his letters of credence, which passed not without censure) aboard a small bark, forced from his ship syde by a storm suddenly risen before it, could discharge the goods it carryed, and not arriving at Dover tyll above a fortnight, or three weekes after. He, in the mean tyme, and his lady, wearyed wyth expectation, and unfurnished with necessaryes for theyr persons, conveyed themselves privately to London. He there indeavoured, but could not obtayne, a private access to the queen, though three of his predecessors (Monsieurs de Fontenay, Pougny and Senneterre) had successively receyved that honour from her majesty. His goods at length safely landed and brought to London, he began to hearken after the making of his publick entrance, as was requisite regarding his quality and the custome of ambassadors, into the city. To this purpose he sent to me a gentleman (it was improper for me, regarding my charge personally to repayre to him, or otherwise as yet to take notice of him) and I could prescribe him no other course but this. That if he would not returne for one night [1ᵛ] to Gravesend (which perhaps would appear to him an overtroublesome ceremony) and there have his first welcome given him by me from his majesty, he might be pleased to go privately to Greenwich and there he must attend the sending of the kings barge for his conduction, by the earl of Northampton (appointed for it) to the house prepared for him, as at other tymes for other extraordinary ambassadors in Westminster,[36] where, and not at his own house, affected by him, but had been otherwise resolved on by the Lord Chamberlin and Mr. Comptroller of his majestyes household to observe custome, he was to receive

---

[35] Finet advised the chamberlain that, despite a rank of extraordinary, the duties and length of stay would be similar to that of a resident ambassador. Pierre de Bellièvre, sieur de Grignon (at court, Nov. 1637 – Jan. 1640), sought permission to levy troops in Ireland and prevent English convoys from carrying Spanish troops to Flanders.

[36] At Abraham Williams' house; later he had a residence on Aldersgate Street.

the treatment intended him by his majesty till the day of his first audience should be passed, answerable to the style in practice, and be conducted to it by the earle mentioned.

This advice observed by him brought him, the 23rd of November before noon, to the Feather Taverne in Greenwich, whither I, repayring to him (to dynner, as I had my invitation) presented him with the kings welcome. My lord of Northampton soon after came with a dozen Gentlemen of the Privy Chamber and reiterated his majestyes welcome and took him with him to his barge, attended by four others, one more which I had appointed failing to come, and landing him at Tower wharfe, placed him there in the Kings coach, followed by the queens, the States ambassadours and 14 others, and brought him through London to his house. There, about an hour after, he had a third welcome given him by Mr. Comptroller, as come then to the Kings entertainment, and immediately after a fourth, by Sir John North with inquiry from his majesty how he found himself in disposition after his journey.

[2] He that night at supper began his dyet at the Kings charge, which was sent him every morning in specie (as to other ambassadors at other tymes) without attendance of other of the kings servants for it, than of such as had particular charge of it, two clerks, or officers, of the kitchin. These disposeing of it, and one under them delivering it with a rate or bill of fare to the ambassadors steward, though the two officers themselves never once appeared, it passed not without the ambassadours notice and perhaps not without disadvantage after, in the value of their acknowledgement.

His alloweance was of 40 £ *per diem* in correspondence of that of the Marques de Senneterre, whyle he was defrayed. The number of his followers remaining with him at that house (not reckoning those left with his lady at his own house) were in proportion much after the Marqueses, about sixty, and not without regard of so much and no more alloted to the earl of Leicester, his majestyes ambassador extraordinary at that time in France, that their proceeding and ours might be at parr.

Sunday following (November the 26th), the King being at that time recovered of an indisposition he had by a boil on his thigh, he had his publick audience of both their Majestyes together. He was conducted to it by the earl of Hertford (propounded purposely by me with regard that this ambassador, being no knight of the French kings order, should have been overmatched, if I may so say, with a knight of his majestyes order[37]) and not without regard also that the second conduction was properly, and of custome,

---

[37] The order of the Holy Spirit as equal to the Garter.

to be chosen of a preceding rank (for his tyme of creation). With this earl went for company the earl of Haddington of Scotland, the lord Rich, eldest son to the earl of Warwick and 12 Gentlemen of the Privy Chamber.

[3] His audience passed, he retyred to the lord keepers lodging (provided for his repose with the like reason of necessity as before for the ambassador of Morocco) and there attending a signification of the queens pleasure for his private accesse to her after his publick, as he had before hand demanded it, word was brought of her majestyes stay for him. He was conducted to her presence in her Withdrawing Chamber by the earl of Hertford, the Gentlemen of the Privy Chamber then leaving him, as did the earl, after the ambassador had entered discourse with her majesty.

On Tuesday following his lady[38] having received notice of her majestyes allowance of her accesse to her presence, I held it a part of my charge (not as a Master of Ceremonyes but as a servant of ladyes) particularly of one so neer in relation to an ambassador, to present to her at her house my attendance in her coach to court. It was as thankfully accepted as it was opportunely offered, none then with her knowing the way, I entered with her into the Queens Withdrawing Chamber, where both their majestyes standing under the State there, she gracefully made the three approaching reverences and at the last of them received the honour of a kisse from each of their majestyes.

While she remained there in conference [3ᵛ] the bishop of Angoulesme (chief almoner of the Queen) calling me a part said he had in charge from her majesty to let me know that, if the ambassador himself should come thither that evening, as it was conceived he would while the king was present, I should give him an admonition to forbear to enter into any discourse of affayrs with his majesty and that if he would have audience he should formally demand for some other day, according to the usuall style of ambassadors. This intimated to him by me brought forth the private audience that was next day given him in the kings Withdrawing Room, I introducing him by the way of the Privy Galleryes, whence I after conducted him to St. James's, according to an assignation given that morning for the accesse he had to the prince, duke and princess in theyr severall quarters. That evening, he returned to his own house in Aldersgate Street, whither he went privatly the evening before, though the last meal of seven, which he had at the kinges charge was that night provided for him by the officers at the house for ambassadors, but was left for the entertainment of the gentlemen, his followers that were lodged there.

---

[38] Marie de Bullión, wife of Bellièvre.

Two or three dayes before the ambassadors audience, came hither the marquis de Parella,[39] Master of the Horses to the late duke of Savoy. He was sent with an account of his death to theyr majestyes, whereof I had notice given me on the nyght before his audience, when my lord chamberlin gave me breefly in charge (the king being then present) to tell the agent of Savoy that the king would give him audience at One of the clock the next day, and that coming to it he might bring with him the gentleman sent from the duke of Savoy, [4] but when I hereupon repayred to the agents lodging with this signification, I found the gentleman he was to bring with him to be qualifyed (above himself) to be a marquis and to expect, the agent intimated to me, a reception and respect beyond the ordinary of an *envoyé*.[40] Though he could not style him, he sayd, an ambassador, adding for his higher valuation that he came from discharge of the like employment in France, where he had received particular honours of that king (the use of his coach to bring him to his audience and a diner provided for him in court at the kinges charge), he had receyved lykewyse many favours of the cardinal.[41] To which presumptions I made no question but the king my masters treatment of him would be answereable to persons of his quality. But I could not promise that his majestyes coach should be for his use till I had spoken with the lord chamberlin, to whom I instantly repayring for resolution and finding him not in his lodging, I went strayght to the King himself. I acquainted him with the Agents affectation and had answer from his majestyes own mouth that he never knew of any Agent or Envoy (but only ambassadors) that had had the use of his coach to their audiences and that I should take care how I created precedents, that howsoever he styled himself, or were a marquis, he knew well enough at what rate marquises went in Italy, yet that he should not fayle of all respects fit to be given him with regard to the persons from whom he came and to his own quality and that of soe much I might assure him.

[4ᵛ] This answer, so much of it as was proper to be imparted, carryed by me to the agent, gave him satisfaction without further reply than this. What shall be his majestyes pleasure will be the marquises. So they both came to court the next day (November 30th) with my conduction from their house, by the way of the Privy Garden, to the King in his Withdrawing Chamber and after to the Queen in hers. Whence passing to Madame Vantelets lodging and

---

[39] Alessio Maurizio San Martino, marquis of Parella, agent extraordinary (Nov.– Dec. 1637), came to report the death of Victor Amadeus and the assumption of the guardianship of the children and the duchy by Henrietta's sister, Christine.

[40] Presumably as a marquis above the count of Cizze, agent.

[41] Richelieu.

spending there an hour or two of time, they returned domestically to the queen in her Privy Chamber (where the King then was) and had from both their Majestyes gracious countenances and many questions concerning the estate, growth and yeares of their nephews and neeces, the Duke of Savoy, the Prince, his brother, and two sisters. The next day they had access to the prince and princess at St. James's.

The ambassador ordinary of the States (Monsieur Joachimi) having been absent upon command of his masters, with intention of returne above a twelve month, came back hither about mid November, when giving him at his house a welcome from myself, and supposing that to a minister of so fair a comportment, and in so good esteem as he was generally held here, a welcome from the king would be fitting, I propounded it to my lord chamberlins consideration and his lordship to his majesty, and his majesty graciously allowed of it. I was sent to present one to him, and recyved from him a most thankfull acknowledgement of so especiall an honour done him. Three or four dayes after, he had private audience of his majesty *more et loco solito*.

[5ᵛ] Two or three dayes before that of the new year, the marquis de Parella imployed, as hath been touched before, from the duke of Savoy, pressed for his dispatch (not without apprehension perhaps of the charge of the tyme towards New Years gifts) had his last audience and leave without my assistance, or without my carriage to him of the present of a diamond ring of 350 £ valew bestowed on him by the king. It was delyvered him by the hand of the lord chamberlin, not without loss (I will not say with wrong) to me in my place, who should have had the presenting of it, and for that default was left (for all the service I had done him) not at all considered.

[6ᵛ] There being a mask in exercise for the Twelfthnight to be presented by the king and twelve of his lords,[1] I repayred to my lord chamberlin, and with him to his majesty, for resolution how the ambassadors were to be treated at it. When, remembering his majesty of his pleasure signifyed to me the day before for an audience to be given to the Spanish, I intimated how fit it would be (for prevencion of his majestyes surprise by that ambassador, in case he should offer his presence at the mask) that before I should deliver to him the kings pleasure for his audience, I should receyve his majestyes instrucion how to govern myself, if he should discover a disposition to be at the mask, or an expectation, at least, to be formally invited to it. His majesty gave me for answer that I knew well enough it had never been his custome to invite any ambassador to those entertainments, that therefore whosoever of them should come, must take account to come but as private persons, yet should not want such regard for theyr placing, or otherwise as should befit theyr qualityes. To this I obiected that if the [7] French and Spanish should meet upon the same floor, where there was right hand and a left, they both striving for the right might rayse some disturbance, it was answered that, if the French ambassador should seat himself below among the ladyes (as it was likely he would, by example of other ambassadors of his nation), the Spanish could not refuse a place, if offered him, above in a box (as they call it) with the countess of Arundel (the first of her rank) and with some other great ladyes. To which I replyed that places were more looked after by ambassadors than persons, so it was left to time without further resolution.

The next day, that I might feel the Spaniards pulse and bring the difference to some terme of accomodation, I went to him to Chelsey and falling (after other purpose) upon that of the mask towards, asked him if he meant not to be at it. Yes, quoth he, very willingly, if I may have the invitation that becomes my quality. The king, I replyed, never invites any ambassador to masks, but such as come to them are sure to be welcome. I shall not be sure of that, answered he againe, unless the King do me the honour to invite me and then I doubt not but he will do me the right to protect me, which I can not promise myself so assuredly if I shall be there as a private person, uninvited and receiving perhaps an affront from some that will not stick to offer

---

[1] Davenant's *Britannia Triumphans* on Jan. 7th.

it, I shall too late fly to his Majesty for my defense as for a publick minister when I have made myself private by coming thither uninvited. With this his scrupulosity acquainting the King and his majesty commanding me to leave him to his own way, I was two or three dayes [7ᵛ] after assayled by his servants particularly his steward who sent me (with his lords recommendation, as he affirmed) a lyst of one and twenty persons, all except three under the tytle of dons (though none but one, a knight of Santiago could properly assume it) I, not without difficulty and some storming of the Lord Chamberlin brought them by the Turn Door into the first entry of the Mask Room.[2] There bestowing them for a while for their ascent after to a place ordained for them on the left hand of the Kings seat some what behind over it, some of the better sort forward and ignorant of their way, took to the right hand and entering a door there, over readily opened by Mr. Comptroller of his majes- tyes household, the rest following them altogether, passed up to a stand reserved for the French, where once seated I could not with civility offer to remove them. Though in discourse with myself and with expression to Mr. Comptroller of some doubt of exception to follow from the French, I wished it otherwise. For prevention of further disorder I went strait to the French ambassador then in court in company of his gentlemen attending my call for their placing for which I was bringing them a summons. The ambassador asking me how he himselfe should be placed I answered him that comeing thither as a domestick private and uninvited he might be pleased to seat himself among the ladyes. But, quoth he, how will you place my gentlemen, in a stand, I answered, provided for them a part from the Spanish ambassadors gentlemen to avoyd the [8] disturbance that may perhaps grow from their mingling. Aye, but replyed he, if myne have not the right hand and be not placed neerer the King and Queens seate than the Spaniards, nor they nor I are like to be there and so I must be bold to tell the Queen. I desired him to containe himself for a while, till I should make a review for a remedy, though the errore, I said, if any, was not of my making. Thereupon returning to the place and acquainting my Lord Chamberlin and Mr. Comptroller with the French ambassadors formality and exception, which they said was over curious, the ambassador of Spayne himself being not to be present and that of France to be there as private. I pointed to a place capable of seaven or eight of the French on the right hand of the Queens seat amongst gentlemen, which was both nearer and more in sight then that taken by the Spaniards, which approved by the French and preserved for them was soon after pos-

---

[2] Since the Banqueting House's ceiling now had the panels by Rubens that were liable to damage by theatrical presentations.

sest by them with their satisfaction and without the other exception, as either not observing or not regarding the small or no difference of their placing.

The Morocco ambassador, and his associate Mr. Blake, having received my intimation for their welcome to the same maske, if they should come voluntarily to it, were there seated with the better sort of their attendance in a compartiment capable of a dozen persons at the left hand behind his [8ᵛ] majestyes seate. The king the next day condemned me for their placing so obscurely, though it were no fault of myne but of some that over swayed my reasons and contestation for their better placing.

The States ambassador, the 14th of January, demanded and had a sudden audience for introduction to his Majestye of Monsieur Fosbergen, forced in here from sea for safeguard from the Dunkirkers that had pursued him in his returne at sea from his imployment of Deputy, or Resident, in France,[3] where he had been honoured with the respects of an ambassador though not so intitled.

Being come in presence of the king he did not cover, nor was invited to it, not withstanding that the other both was and did, yet but for an instant only as to preserve his right of custome, and immediately uncovering. At their entrance and issuing to and from the kings presence, the ordinary took the hand, but elsewhere always gave it him, as he himselfe told me. After some few dayes of stay here for his safer passage he proceeded on his interupted journey without further accesse to his Majestye or other notice taken of him.[4]

[10] A second maske of the Queens and 14 great ladyes (being in practice)[5] for Shrove Tuesday, I, (two or three dayes before apprehending a returne of some punctilio about the ambassadors followers placing, and their number) caused my officer to sound the Spaniards (as I myself intended to do the Frenches) disposition to that purpose. The former returned word that they and their lord also expected that the same number as was at the other mask should be at this. Of this, when I but let fall a word to my Lord Chamberlaine, he storming, swore their number should not pass five or six at the most because of the exceeding number of ladyes and persons of quality which he knew would be at this maske more than at the former. Yet he did at the last allow of eight from either ambassadour when I propounding the seating of the French as before among the women, he would by no means yeild to it

---

[3] Gaspar Vosberghen visited Charles in 1628: see III 13. He now reported on Richelieu's new subsidies to the Dutch.

[4] Since he had not an official mission to Charles.

[5] Davenant's *Luminalia* on Feb. 6th.

but absolutely ordered that the French should be placed in the seates aloft where the Spaniards were placed the maske before. This I knew would breed quarrells if they should mingle or exception from the Spanish if they should be removed from where they were formerly seated, yet leaving it to hazard (after the provision I had thought on of first seating the French on the right hand of the king in the Spaniards former places and after of excusing the seating of these on the left, when the others had already, intrudingly, as I meant for excuse to say, taken up the right). I went to the French ambassador acquainted him with my course and had his [10ᵛ] ready assent to the number limited him by my Lord Chamberlin of 8 persons only. Yet with his request that four more might, with his favour, be allowed entrance though not at that instant time listed as the other, this was agreed to. I again sent my servant to the Spanish ambassadors steward with a letter intimating that I had received my Lord Chamberlins finall signification of the number of 8 followers only of each ambassadour and that the French had already sent a list of his to that number. To this the steward returned answer by letter that, having imparted what I had written to his lord, his answer was that he was not to be ruled by the example of other ambassadours but knew well enough what he had to do without their government, etc. and that if all his servants should not be admitted as before, they should returne home altogether, after they should have presented themselves, as he intended they should lest they might be thought to disesteeme his Majestyes favour, and be refused entrance.

This punctilio being made known by me to my Lord Chamberlaine and his lordship resolute not to alter his order, I placed myself at the Court Gate the first hour of entrance into the Mask Room to prevent the Spaniards entrance into the court with the worlds notice. There when the steward came I acquainted him with the final order given me. He refused to make the choyce that I entreated him of 8 out of 21 (ready in their coaches without the Gate to enter or not according to his answer). The parting did rid me of the trouble I apprehended would follow with my blame perhaps, though not with my fault, if the Spaniards should have questioned and refused their remove from their former seate on the right hand to the left with prejudice to their pretension of precedence.⁶

[12ᵛ] The ambassador of Moroccos negotiation for commerce and correspondence with this state being brought to termes of conclusion and with his satisfaction, he pressed me to demand audience for his departure, which I

⁶ No Spanish diplomats attended masks (until Velada in 1640), but their staffs were not seated by precedence.

obtained for Tuesday the 20th of March. He had the earle of Denbigh for his conductor accompanyed with the heyr of the earl of Livingstone[7] and half a score Gentlemen of the Privy Chamber in the Kings and Queens coaches and six others of the lords, to both their Majestyes presence in the Banketting House, after his repose in the Lord Keepers lodgings as at other times. Having delivered his mind in Arabick with the interpretation of his associate Mr. Blake all his followers having humbled themselves, one after the other, with their bowing reverences to their majestyes and to the lady princess there present. He returned home accompanyed as before with expression of much satisfaction for the gracious words and countenances afforded him by their Majestyes. Five or six dayes after he took leave of the Prince and duke of York at St. James's the Princess being at that time indisposed and excuse sent for her not being then visited.

When after this he had imployed 14 or 15 dayes for ordering of what concerned his journey home (whither his Majesty had appointed one of his ships and a pinnace to transport him) news was brought him of a revolt at Saley and of the repossession of some part of that towne by the king his masters enemyes which occasioned his demand of another audience in private given him in his Majestyes Withdrawing Chamber the 7th of April. After which the season and his masters affaires calling on him, he called on me to hasten his departure. [13] The present ordayned for him (after the usuall rate of the ambassadors of France and Spayne) was eight hundred pounds to be issued upon a Privy Seal (directed to Sir William Russell[8] and Mr. Robert Blake) for the buying of such commodities of this kingdome as should be most to the ambassadors appetite and use. Gilt plate (the ordinary material for that service not being of use) rather forbidden, in Barbary, as was intimated by the ambassadors associate.[9]

For those of his servants (6 or 7 that had the charge of the Hawks and Horses) there were assigned forty peeces, which had been more by twenty had not a cozening fellow of our nation, whom the Moors had set on work for their help, kept much to his own use, after it had been inconsiderately delivered him by the gentleman of the Master of the Horse to be distributed amongst such of the ambassadours as had by their pains deserved it. Two hundred and ten pounds more were specified in the same Privy Seale and directed to Sir William Russell *ut supra* was appointed to be imployed in a gold chayne and

[7] Alexander Livingstone, 2nd earl of Linlithgow.
[8] A Farmer of the customs and Collector of duties on imported cloths.
[9] Robert Blake. As protection from pirates Charles ordered an English warship to bring the Moroccan embassy home.

medal for the associate, the money to be paid to the Master of the Jewel House and the chayne to be issued thence. But not so the present for the ambassador himself, which was awhile questioned by the sayd Master, but finally adjudged by the lord chamberlin to be most properly delyvered by me, as it was, the 11th of April, by virtue of his lordships letter, I receyving, from the hands of Sir William Russell and Mr Blake, all the parcells thereof: consisting of seven peeces of fine broad clothes, twenty peeces of pure fine cambrick, 18 peeces of the finest Holland, seven bayles, or packs, of Roan linen, musketts, pistols and other armes, all specifyed in a note subscribed by those two gentlemen for my discharge. I presented them all to the ambassador at his house in Wood Street.

[13ᵛ] In April, a gentleman by name Bloom,[10] by birth a Hollander, who had formerly been imployed hither in quality of an agent for Sweden, returning with a new qualification of agency from the queen and crown, repayred upon my admonition an error he had the tyme before committed when he addressed himself, instantly upon his coming, to Mr. Secretary Cook, without once giving notice of his condition to the lord chamberlin, he lost some regardes he might have otherwyse had from his lordship, but he now recovered them by making his first repayre to him the 10th of April, and by his lordships meanes imediately to his majesty, then in company with the lords in the Stone Table chamber, where, presenting his letters, he was receyved by his majesty with gracious countenance.

The duchess of Chevreuse,[11] after an escape she had made out of France into Spayne from some dangers threatening her, having given notice to theyr majestyes here of her design (with theyr leaves and favors to come for England) had one of the kings shipps sent for her transport from the Groyne,[12] where embarking the 12th of April, she the 14th arrived at Plymouth had 3 or 4 dayes royal entertainment near thereby at the house and charge of Sir William Udall, was received and welcomed there first by Mr. Walter Montague, younger son to the earl of Manchester, and the next day by the lord Goring, both sent purposely by theyr majestyes, and the 19th of April was met and receyved at Braynford by the earl of Holland, accompanyed with most of the young lords and gallants then at court, together with gentlemen of the

---

[10] Michael de Bloom, previously agent in 1635.

[11] Marie de Rohan-Montbazon, duchess of Chevreuse, was officially a guest of Henrietta (April 1638 – April 1640). As a Spanish pensioner, she tried to promote Olivares' policies by seeking recruitments for Spanish forces and favoring a possible marriage between Philip's son, Baltazar Carlos, and a Stuart princess.

[12] La Coruña, in Galicia.

Privy Chamber appointed for that service, as I also was [14] though not in quality of Master of Ceremonyes, the busines and the person being of no publick condition. The earl of Holland had following his coach four or five and twenty noblemens coaches, each with six horses. All which, when they came to the middle gate of Hyde Park entered there, and thence found attending an empty coach of the queens (into which the duchess entered) and two more filled with her majestyes women, sent purposely to do her honour, with half a score of her majestyes footmen to run by her. Thus accompanyed and followed, she proceeded with a walking pace through the park into St. Jameses, entering at the west gate and allighting at the foot of the Tylt Yard gallery stayres, was conducted thence through the privy Gallery and the kings Privy Chamber to the queens Withdrawing Chamber, where cheerfully received and welcomed with a kisse from both their Majestyes. The queen instantly made offer to her (which she readily receyved) of the *tabouret*, presented by her majestyes lord chamberlin, the earl of Dorset.

After a while rising up and their majestyes entertaining her with discourses and questions of her journy, she took leave and parted, with her conductor, to her lodgings prepared and richly furnished for her at the end of the Privy Garden next to King Street; her dyett was likewise provided and daily attendance for that purpose by a clerk of the Kitchin etc. She had yet but one mayd servant and two or three men for all her followers, the supply of such as were necessary about her person (especially of women for her dressing, etc.) being appointed by her Majestye out of her own for her dayly service, as was also a hand chayre and two litter men of her Majestyes to carry her in it to and from her lodging through the privy garden.

[14ᵛ] In this ladyes company, with the conveniency and safety of her passage by sea from the Groyne, came a cavelier of the order of Santiago, his name don Alonso de Cardenas.[13] He was imployed from the king of Spain for his ordinary minister here but with no formall or usuall tytle given him in his letters of credence than of a gentleman of his councill sent to take charge of the busyness of his ambassage tyll an ambassador ordinary already nominated come in place for successour to the Conde de Oñate who, having of the kyng demanded audience, had it the 22nd April. Then before his entrance into the presence of his Majestye, he told me of the arrival of the cavallier mentioned, who (sayd he) now that I have receyved my revocacion (of this he gave me then a copy, though he had not yet delivered the originall to his

---

[13] Alonso de Cárdenas, agent (April 1638 – July 1640), then ambassador (1640–1655), came as an interim appointment for the ambassador designate Gaspar de Bracamonte. His first instructions placed him as an assistant to Chevreuse.

Majestye) is to remain here till the coming of don Gaspar de Bracamente not in quality (sayd he) of an ambassador but *para assistir a los negocios de la embajada*, and therefore desired me to acquaint his Majestye with his coming and to learn what I could of his Majestyes intention for the manner of his treatment. I answered his treatment will be as was that of his predecessor, don Juan Nicolalde. This replyed he, is a person of good respect with the king, a cavallier and his counsellor, and I shall be glad to know that his majesty shall afford him some more honour then ordinary. With this curiosity acquainting my Lord Chamberlin and after, in his lordships presence, his Majestye, I had the answer I expected, that what had been done to others qualifyed as he, should be done to him and no otherwise.

[15] I had before this declaration intimated to his majesty what had been wrytten out of Spaine[14] from his ambassador there to Mr. Secretary Windebank, when choyce was made of this minister, that of four qualifications of persons usually imployed abrod by that king, which were not ambassador, the lowest was that of a secretary, the next above this an agent, then a resident and the last and best of the four, a *Gentilhombre* as I heard, I sayd, this was stiled. But this my intimation boare no sway with his majesty farther then that when I propounded to his pleasure (after I had first consulted the Lord Chamberlin and bothe the Secretaryes about it) that seing he pretended to be a person of somewhat more eminency than other minsters qualified as he and that he was at that instant sick of a tertian ague, it would be, I thought, an honour to him without consequence from precedent, if the king would but send one to him both to condole his indisposition and to welcome his person. His majesty was pleased I should repayre to him to Chelsey, where finding him sick in bed, I there left him, though not cured, not the sicker for that honour his Majestye had done him to send to him. When I had returned an account to his Majestye he commanded me that makeing another visit to him two dayes after, as from myselfe, I should procure, if I could, either from himself or from the ambassadour a copy of his letter[15] of credence, where of having had the sight he might the better judge of his condition and extent of his qualification. This I obeyed and obtained it from the ambassadour which

---

14 Sir Walter Aston.

15 The copy of his credentials stated: *"eum interea mittimus cui omnia legationis nostrae munera commendamus"* (AGS E 2575, 7 March 1638). After Bracamonte's post was annulled, Cárdenas was finally raised to the rank of ambassador in January 1640; for this occasion he made a new official entry, described by Finet: see V 86ᵛ. His subsequent career is related in Loomie, "Alonso de Cárdenas and the Long Parliament, 1640–48," *English Historical Review* 97 No. 383 (April 1982) 289–307.

imparted served to satisfy his majestye [15 ᵛ] that he was no other then an agent nor otherwyse to be treated then according to the limitation expressed to me from Mr. Secretary Windebank the year before upon the like occasion for treatment of Señor Necolaldi.

The 2nd or 3rd day following a messenger came from Mr. Secretary Windebank telling me he desyred to speak wyth me about business for his majestyes service. Repayring to him I had a significacion of his majestyes pleasure for my search amongst my notes and for conference with my lord chamberlin what proceeding was fittest to be held (according to precedent) with this minister who, besides other punctualityes, insisted upon this: that howsoever his majesty should be pleased otherwise to treat him, he hoped he should not be refused the honour of his coach going to his first audience. Therefore I should do well, sayd Mr. Secretary, after conference with my Lord Chamberlin, to address myself, together with his lordship, to the King for instructions how to govern myself in the business. This I obeyed and had his Majestyes command to tell don Alonso, that for the esteem he made of his brother, the king of Spain, and of such as had imployment from him he might be assured to receive here all respects fitting his quality. But for the pretence he understood he had to the use of his coach for his first audience it was without example, not any minister but ambassadors having yet ever had it [16] and for him now to grant it to one not bearing the tytle would create a precedent for other kings and princes ministers imployed, as he to challenge the like. Further he wished him to remember how punctuall these proceedings were in Spayne for observation of their customes, which they made it a religion to depart from, and which to presse him to alter would be not equall justice. With this his Majestyes message I went to don Alonso and discharged punctually my duty in delivering it and had for answer (besides other words and countenance of insatisfaction) that though he were not formally an ambassador, he knew his own quality to be other and otherwise to be esteemed than what I had exemplyfyed (as indeed I had comparatively done) in the person of don Juan de Necolalde and others, and that, if according to the intimation I had given, of his majestyes not acknowledging any other capacity in his kingdome than of ambassadors and agents, he had known at the first of his arrival he should have been treated but as an agent he would have returned home post imediately. Having thus concluded I asked him whether he would command me any thing to the purpose of his audience he answered that he had suffered so much at sea and was so newly recovered of his feaver, as he would be bold to take some time to restore himself before he would be troublesome to his Majestye, which I judged but a delay for advice, etc.

[16ᵛ] Here arrived about the midst of April a second brother of the Land-grave[16] of Hessen Darmstat, who instantly passing to Oxford, Cambridge and other places worth sight, unknown, and so he affected, without notice, whether unknown and unnoted of the state, he being of the Emperors party and, with his brother, no friend of the Prince Elector Palatine.

After his about three weeks stay here, my Lord Chamberlin was moved to procure him accesse to the king to kisse his hand and take his leave, he not imploying me about it, while for the respects mentioned I forbore to visit him, but a gentleman of his country residing here,[17] his majestyes servant. Yet, when the service came to the instant of performance I was sent for by my Lord Chamberlin and appointed to fetch him from his lodging to conduct him to his lordship and thence to his majesty in his Privy Gallery where he was introduced by his lordship with my attendance. He was the next day, which had been once assigned for the same day, but was hindered by the Princesse Elizabeths sudden indisposition, admitted to the Queens presence in her Withdrawing Chamber, whither I alone conducted him, and having reconducted him to his lodging there takeing leave of him, I receyved from him for acknowledgement of my two dayes pains a peece of plate of about 20 marks value.

The ambassador of Morocco having received his present (as before said) and preparing for his departure,[18] his Majestye was [17] put in mind by my Lord Chamberlin, and some others, how fit it would be, and how to his majestyes honour, to disingage himself of the debt he might seem to remaine in to the king of Morocco for the present he had sent him, which he might be pleased to repay by the present opportunity of that kings ambassadors and of his majestyes own Agents returne to him. This motion entertained, the sume of 2000 £ was ordered to be issued by warrant out of the exchequer for that purpose to Mr. Blake and Sir William Russell. I having first refused the offer made me to be nominated one of the receivers and disposers of it for some reasons urging with me, whereupon, this was bespoken directione given for it, by me and by Mr. Blake, for a coach to be lined with crimson velvet, the carriage richly gylded and painted with flowers and fontage upon the gylt, and four fair Denmark horses, with a fift spare, to draw it, with all else belonging to it suitable. This cost altogether above 600 £. Besides this coach and horses, there were sent other 6 or 7 horses and mares and also divers whole peeces of the finest broad clothes of the best and newest colours,

---

[16] John, brother of George II, Landgrave of Hesse-Darmstadt.
[17] In margin Finet wrote: "Mr. Bear."
[18] See V 12ᵛ–13.

many whole peeces of the purest fine Hollands and Cambricks, the king and queens pictures drawne after the Vandikes originalls, 100 lances and some other of our rarest country comodities which together with the charge of the frayght were reckoned to make up in the valew the sume mentioned of 2000 £ allowed for it by his majesty.

This present made ready by the 10th of April, the ambassadour with his remaining followers, five or six, the rest being sent about by sea to Portsmouth, [17ᵛ] set forth from his house in Wood Street in the Kings coach with my only conduction and with the company of Mr. Blake (two coaches: one with 6 horses for himself and one with four for his servants hyred by himself attending him) tyll he came to the west corner of Hyde Park. This was according as it was by me limited upon discourse with the Lord Chamberlin and the Master of his majestyes Horses for avoydance of consequence from precedent. He there descended from his majestyes coach to his own, and gave me my farewell in many civil words, which he had the day before given me by deeds as far as six score peeces, to my officer he gave 30 peeces.

The 13 of May the king of Spaynes ambassador after he had resided here extraordinary[19] by the space of 22 months, and received letters from the king his master importing the liberty demanded and granted, as his letter carryed it, for his returne took his publick leave (May the 22nd) of both their majestyes. He was conducted to their presence from his house in Chelsey by the earl of Danby[20] (a privy councellor and knight of the Garter in [18] correspondence of the earl of Salisbury, who so dignifyed had been his conductor to his first audience). The earl went accompanyed with the lord Philip Herbert, son to the Lord Chamberlaine, his brother, Sir John Danvers, and nine or ten Gentlemen of the Privy Chamber, served by his majestyes coach the Queens and nyne lords coaches, besides three of the ambassadors own coaches. There came with him to his audience (to be presented by him, different from the intimation first given that he would come to it alone) the before mentioned don Alonso de Cardenas, whom the ambassador requested me to take and sit with him in the Queens coach to difference their qualityes, of no good relish to him as appeared by his countenance. Being presented to the King by the ambassador he spake by an interpreter of his own, whom intending to imploy for the like service to the Queen, he was prevented by the voluntary and sudden offer, *a la Francaise*, of the Duchess de Chevreuse there present for performance of that office.

---

[19] Oñate wished to leave as soon as the public audience for Cárdenas and Chevreuse was given.
[20] Henry Danvers, 1st earl of Danby.

The next day he took leave of the Prince in his Privy Chamber at St. James's (his Withdrawing Chamber being supposed by the earl of Newcastle, his Governour, and others of that court improper for it) especially when his highneses house was, as then, regulated and brought to an ordinary and settled number of gentleman and officers attending dayly on his person. The attendance and service of women being discharged at the then compleat 8th year of his age. He took leave then of the Princesse and 2 sisters in their own quarters in manner as accustomed.

[18ᵛ] About this time I thought it seasonable and my duty (now that this Spanish ambassador was towards his departure) to put my Lord Chamberlin in mind, and after him my lord Marquess Hamilton, as Master of his majestyes Horses, of a present of two gennets, which he had made a year before to his majesty and whereof I supposed it requisite that his majesty, for his disingagement, should be now remembered. This intimation approved of by their lordships and afterwards by the King himself, his Majestye thought fit to make a like returne by horses, and not by a jewel, as had been first propounded. Whereupon the number of 4, to double those of the ambassador, being appointed, two amblers and two gallopers were provided and ledd to his house at Chelsey were there by me presented with this complement. That his Majestye wishing him a happy returne home and supposing that after the dispatch of his busines at court he would be disposed some times to take the ayre, and sometimes to hunt at his country house, had provided and sent him out of his own stable two ambling and two galloping naggs for these two uses. To which he answered, I most humbly kiss his majestyes hands for the double honour he hath done me, not only to send me a present but to present me also with the use of it, wherein I will not fayle to obey his Majestye.

Two dayes after, May the 25th, having altered his first resolution to imbark at Plymouth, he requested and had the use of the Kings barge and three others to carry him, a brother of his, don Gaspar de Oñate, don Fernando de Texada, don Alonso de Cardenas, the remaining Spanish minister, and other of his followers, to Gravesend, [19] where before our arrival by four or five myles, the tyde being already spent, he made a motion, and was obeyed, for his proceeding without stop to the kings ship, the *Nonsuch*, appointed as had been requested, for his transport to Spayne, and at that tyme riding for a wind, together with sevean of his majestyes fleet then setting to sea, in Tylbury hope. Whence, after we had rowed thither against wind and tyde, and been aboard for his accomodation in the ship, he returned to Gravesend, and there took coach to proceed for his imbarking at Dover, whither he had sent before the rest of his traine, and his horses to the number of 22. He left me for my gratuity in the hands of a merchant (to be taken by me in specie, or to be converted for me into plate at my choice) four score pounds, and for my officer 20 £. He left also in the same merchants hands for the Master of the Jewel House, who had, for his present from his majesty, personally brought him to his house at Chelsey 2000 ounces of gilt plate, 40 pounds.

[22] A french gentleman (Monsieur de la Varenne) expressly sent with the news of a dauphin[21] borne to the king of France, brought it *en courrier*, without demand of audience accompanyed with the French ambassadour to their Majestyes at Oatlands. The expressions of joy for it were as may be imagined for such welcome newes with a bonefire in court and with hogsheads of wine and beer exposed to the emptying of the Gard and others. Four or five days after the Queen and hers (while the King with his rode in hunting into the Forest of Windsor) [22ᵛ] went to Whitehall and thence the next afternoon to Somerset House there to assist at the singing of *Te Deum* for Thanksgiving.

The evening before the Spanish Agent sent to me to demand an audience of her majesty (and of the king if he had been there) for congragulation which was performed the day following her Majestye receiving him with a cheerful countenance, the Duchess of Chevreuse interpreting. A noble person present at this audience saying, this ceremony may be spared when the heart goeth not with it, he was answered by another, wars between princes last not. civility and enmity *inter se destruentes*. And why added he, may not this birth deserve congragulation from the Spaniard when perhaps it may prove for the good of Spayne by a Spanish Queen Mothers power[22] in France hereafter.

[23] The Count de Cize, Agent or as he styled himselfe from the time of his first arrival here, Resident of Savoy, wrote to me the [*blank*] of October to demand audience for the account of his returne home revoked, he said in his letter, *par Madame la duchesse de Savoy*, and subscribed his name Cize with this addition, *Resident de Savoy*. I knowing the king my masters declared pleasure not to allow of other tytle or quality of publick minister here than of that of Agent and of Ambassadour wrote answer with superscription: *A Monsieur le Comte de Cize, employe de la part de son Altesse de Savoie* wherein I neither hazarded his offence by styling him agent, when he had so long assumed and had given him by others the tytle of Resident. Nor had I contradicted the application he seemed to make of his imployment and revocation to the power and will of that Duchesse by his saying: *Madame la Duchesse*

---

21 Louis, born 4 Sept. 1638 (New Style).
22 Anne, mother of the dauphin, was sister of Philip IV.

m'a rapelle, when in reason and in opinion of many *Monsieur le Duc* should have had the name, though he had not the years, being then not seven[23] years old, to recall him and when under the tytle of *Son Altesse de Savoie* both powers of both sexes were comprehended though neither specified.

In conclusion having demanded his audience he had it of both their majesties in their severall Withdrawing Rooms the [*blank*] of October after I had the same day sounded his position of accepting [23ᵛ] or refusing a chayne of gold, in case it should be presented to him under tytle of Agent as had been done and was done by the Spanish Agent Necolalde, and had his answer that what so ever the King should be pleased to present him with in quantity and quality, he held himself bound and should be honored to receive it, yet when after (in my absence for the Queen Mothers reception) he was presented with a chayne and medal of 210 £ value (after the rate usuall for agents) whether it were the baseness of the alloy or the fraud of the deliverer, both of these being by him quarreled with, which made it of less weight and so of less worth by 13 ounces, he formalized himself to me for the wrong he had received by the undervaluing of his quality, and by his being qualifyed with a present of worth, he said, not above 150 £, wheras il cavaliero Barozzi[24] (some time employed here by the old duke of Savoy deceased) under no higher tytle than secretary, had a chayne given him of 300 £, yet not with standing this exception and the strong sense he expressed of his not being so treated *di secretario*, as he termed it, he forgot not before his parting, to send me a small enamelled chayne worth 10 £, which considering the extream necessity the duke his master made him live in here, for want of his assigned entertainment (scarce ever paid him), it was from him (and as such accepted by me) a rich acknowledgement.

[27] Their majestyes[25] being come near Aldgate attended there by the band of Gentlemen Pensioners on horseback, allighted from the coach they came in thither. They entered another of more state and richnesse (a rich imbroidered litter following it) and were wythin the gate receyved by the lord maior,[26] and all his brethren in theyr scarlett gownes and chaynes of gold,

---

[23] Christine, dowager duchess of Savoy, wished to be acknowledged regent on behalf of her eldest son, Francis Hyacinth (died 1638).

[24] Barozzi had visited London in 1629: see III 16.

[25] Marie de Médicis had arrived from Holland at Harwich on Oct. 18th and finally reached London in the company of Charles by coach journey from Rumford. Since she was the symbol of resistance to Richelieu's role in Paris, this elaborate public reception was not pleasing to Louis. He told the English ambassador that she would never receive his permission to return to France and he would be reconciled to her only if she retired to Florence.

[26] Sir Richard Fenn.

placed at the left hand on a stand that yeoman had raysed, arched and raysed before, and behynd (for defense of the crowd) covered wyth carpetts overhead and with other cloathes before, as were all the stands of the severall companyes, in their ranckes, theyr severall banners and streamers placed by them from the Gate to Temple bar. The select bandes of the city and the county, were distinguished by theyr severall colors and captaynes, [27ᵛ] being placed on the right *a la file*, one by one, almost touching one another, as far as St. James (the queen mothers ordayned lodging for herself and family). Before theyr majestyes front went the messengers on horseback, all in payres, next the trumpeters, then the Gentlemen Pensioners and other gentlemen, marching behind with theyr captayne, Sir Edward Capell, standard bearer, the Sergeantes at Armes with theyr masses, and immediately before the kinges coach, two equerryes. As lieutenant, the lord Goring lead severall of that company, on each syde of the coach, where went also the kinges footmen. Behynd the coach road the earl of Salisbury, captayne of the band of Pensioners, and the earl Morton, captayne of the Gard, and after came the Gard, in theyr rich coates and the coaches wyth the ladyes and others of the trayne of the queen mother and the kinges servants.[27]

[28] When the Venetian ambassador ordinary, Signor Giovanni Giustiniano,[28] had passed his time *Incognito* and his lady wyth him, above four monthes at his house in south Lambeth,[29] without other notice taken of them than that she was once seen seated in a place set apart, appointed for her, at a comedy[30] presented before their majestyes at Somerset house (there also as *Incognita*), he sent to me (I not offering all that time to visit him, as I had reason, having receyved no hint or invitation to it) his secretary Francesco Zonca (provisionally left here by the ambassador Corero tyll the coming of his successor) let me know his lord was then ready to make his entrance and after to demand his public audience. I, being then entering upon my imployment for the queen mothers reception at her landing, excused that service as not to be performed by me tyll my returne. After this, I, the first of November, presented the ambassador wyth my first visit and offer to serve him for his entrance, which, having understood from his secretary, he meant to make in as publick a manner as if he were but that week arrived. He expected not only

---

[27] This procession continued to St. James's Palace where special apartments were arranged.

[28] Ambassador (Nov. 1638 – June 1641), he had new instructions from Venice that granted him more discretion in supporting French policy, so that in the eyes of Finet he was considered pro-Spanish.

[29] Caron House, where Oñate had been lodged.

[30] Unidentified play on July 28th.

REPRESENTATION DES FEVS DE IOYE QVIFVRENT FAICTS SVR
LEAV DANS LONDRES A L'HONNEVR DE LA REYNE LA NVICT
DVIOVR DE SON ENTREE

TOWER WHARF, LONDON

Etching (7 1/2″×9″) in the *Histoire de l'entree de la Reyne Mere . . .
dans la Grande Bretagne* (London, 1639), by Jean Puget, sieur de la
Serre. As a member of Marie de Médicis' retinue, Puget wrote this
account for a French audience to counter the decline in the political
status of the queen mother during her exile. The public entries of
ambassadors normally began at this point.

ENTRÉE ROYALLE DE LA REYNE MÈRE DU ROŸTRES-CHRESTIEN DANS LA VILLE DE LONDRES:

PROCESSION OF COACHES

In this etching, also from Puget's *Histoire* (32″×12″), the court officers and escorts—described by Finet V 27—for the public entry of Marie de Médicis are on Cheapside, London's principal street. A similar file of coaches accompanied a new ambassador on public occasions.

LE CERCLE DE LEVRS MAGESTES DANS LA CHAMBRE DE
PRESENCE A S. IAMES

Presence Chamber, St. James's Palace

Etching from Puget's *Histoire* (7 1/2″ × 9 1/4″). The king, queen, and the queen mother of France are seated in a circle of courtiers. Finet mentions similar smaller gatherings in the queen's apartments to which "domestic access" was given to French and Savoyard diplomats.

CHARLES I, HENRIETTA, AND THE TWO EARLS OF PEMBROKE

This seventeenth-century painting by several artists was possibly made to commemorate the previous services at court of the two brothers. The background and figures are copies of earlier portraits by court artists, such as Mytens and Van Dyke, with an early Stuart interior, possibly one of the residences of the earl of Pembroke. On the left is the third earl, William Herbert, as lord steward (1626–30); on the far right, the fourth earl, Philip Herbert, as lord chamberlain (1626–41). He frequently

to have my conduction and a welcome given him by me from the kyng at Greenwich, and thence my company in the kings barge to Tower wharfe, but an earl also, as was the use, he said, for the treatment of crowned heads, must receive him at the Tower and accompany him thence in the kings coach to his house. I answered to that later pretence to the kings coach and the queens both, [27ᵛ] that I would undertake the first should be for his service according to custome, but for the queens I durst not promise because the use of it, except once at the ambassador Coraros entrance by a chance or a mistake, rather than by order, was without example.

For the latter, to have an earl meet and receive him at his landing at Tower wharfe, it was also I said without precedent, none but barons, or Irish Viscounts having ever been, to my knowledge and observation, imployed about that part of reception for any ambassador of the Venetian reipublick.

According to this intimation, procuring the lord viscount of Dungannon,[31] eldest son to the earle of Cork, to receive him at the Tower, I went to Greenwich with the kings barge and one other, being all he thriftyly desired. He, his wifes brother and sixteen or 18 of his followers came thither in a barge of his own hyreing. I landed him at the Tower wharfe stayres and presented him to the further conduction of the viscount mentioned in the Kings coach, the Queens coach, which I procured also for his satisfaction, the French and States ambassadours coaches and six other noblemens following, to his house at south Lambeth.

The 11th of November, Sunday, he had his publick audience of both their Majestyes together in the Presence Chamber of Whitehall conducted to it by the earle of Huntington[32] with the same [29] coaches and same number as before, but with a trouble and travaile unusuall, though all the coaches were by me sent back before, for our lesse paines over London bridge to Lambeth with order to attend there before the Lord Archbishops house. The coming of the conductor, accompanied with half a score Gentlemen of the Privy Chamber meant passing them over in two barges appointed by me to attend that service at the Privy Garden stayres. These came to the ambassadors house, after they had measured the long way about through London to Whitehall, where after the ambassador rested a while in the Chapel closet (his majesty being then at councell in the Councell Chamber which should have otherwise been his place of rest) he had his audience. After, upon discourse with his secretary and me, who had before hand given him a touch of the trouble of our returne by so long a way, it was resolved that considering the neerness of the

[31] Richard Boyle, viscount Dungannon.
[32] Henry Hastings, 5th earl of Huntington.

night and the length of the way, he might without wrong to his quality or danger of the consequence take leave of the earl his conductor, dismiss the Kings and Queens coaches and returne privately in his own. He first made a visit, as was propounded and performed, to the Duchess of Chevreuse then in court. He protested to me that his soe private returne was for the civill reasons mentioned and must not redound to the prejudice of his successor, whomsoever or whensoever, hereafter. So punctuall and jealous he was and that Reipublick generally is, of losing any of their least rights in point of ceremony. [29ᵛ] He had his private audience of his majesty two dayes after, both then and before at his publick audience making it an essential point of ceremony, contrary to the indifference of his predecessor, Corero, at his audiences, to wear his vest or gown, putting it on in a room apart before he would enter the presence of the king, and leaving his cloak and reassuming it, at his departure.

The like he did, the 13th of November, when he had access to the Queen Mother, who, at his entrance into the Withdrawing Chamber where she received him, rose up from her seate and stood all the time of his audience. So I was told she did with Mr. Conn,[33] the Popes minister here, if I may properly call him so, not publicly avowed by the King or avowing himself to be so, at his private access to her, which gave subject of exception.

This ambassadour having not long after, another audience assigned him for One of the clock, and the King being to play a game at tennis by appointment before Two had the patience of almost an houers stay for his coming. Seing him at last not to come his Majestye in parting commanded me to tell him how long he had stayed and to say that at the place he came from where he had lately been ambassadour they used to be more punctuall.[34] This message I delieverd to him but in his ear (his servants sitting by him in his coach) as I met him on my returne home on his way to court. It was to prevent the notice that might perhaps with his disgrace be taken of his descent from it and returne into it without accesse to his Majestye. He layd the blame with much resentment [30] and passion upon his coachmans drunkeness. Wheresoever it was due, I made it a subject for my remonstrance and advice to him not to put his Majesty any more to his patience of stay for him, but as he had done and another audience before, but rather to anticipate his assigned hour,

---

[33] Finet reflected the misgivings of several in the king's household. George Conn (July 1636 – Aug. 1639) together with Gregorio Panzani (Dec. 1634 – Dec. 1636) and the later count Carlo Rossetti (Sept. 1639 – July 1641) were in fact resident agents from pope Urban VIII, but received only by Henrietta. Charles and the representatives of Protestant states did not acknowledge them publicly.

[34] He had also been ambassador to Madrid.

as other ambassadors used to do, and to stay the leisure of his majesty which he confessed was reason and should be carefully observed by him thereafter.

The 18th of November, I procured audience of the king and, the next day, of the queen for Ernestus,[35] one of the marquesses of Brandenburg, only son of the brave deceased duke Yagendorf, who having taken armes for the cause of the king of Bohemia, and being therefore proscribed by the emperor, had all his estate confiscated and was left himself to live precariously by princes courtesyes. The king of Denmark gave him for a tyme intertaynment and, at this tyme, being come from the low countrys with letters recommendatory from the queen of Bohemia to the king, he solicited as modestly as his wants would suffer him, by the means of the earls of Pembroke and Holland and by Mr. Secretary Cook, for some supply by present, or yearly pension. But the latter was an ingagement that his majesty professed himself most averse from, in regard of the consequence, the former (sued for in a tyme when extraordinary expense for prevention, and provision agaynst, stirs threatened from Scotland) made money more precious, all he could be perswaded to for a present for him was two hundred peeces in specie, which served but for his remove, and for tryall of his fortune in France, after his almost a months expectancy here in England.

[30ᵛ] The baron of Tournon, imployed from the duchess dowager of Savoy with condolement of that duke her sons[36] death (almost three months before) had audience of his majesty in his withdrawing chamber, the 16 of December, and the same day of the queen. His arrival here having beene two days before. He imediatly upon it sent to me a gentleman with signification of his coming and the cause of it, which carryed me that night late to his lodging (at an ordinary near Aldgate) to visit him, but with more special end to discover how he valued himself for an ambassador or an *envoyé*, of which before I would see him (lest I might misstyle him) I got myself informed by one of his followers that he expected to be treated in all points (he sayd) qualifyed lyke the marquis de Parella. With this resolution (after my account given of him to his majesty) I fetched him to his audience in mine own coach (the kings not allowed him, no more than it had been to that marquis) with one coach, hyred by himself following, and in the same manner reconducted him to his lodging. He was two dayes after invited by the queen to the sight of a comedy,[37] and two dayes after to another, the second part of the same, made by one of the kings servants and acted at Somerset house.

---

[35] Ernestus, son of Johannes Georg von Brandenburg zu Jagendorf.
[36] Francis Hyacinth had died 4 Oct. 1638 (New Style).
[37] Unidentified plays, Dec. 20th and 22nd.

[34] The ambassador of the States, having receyved letters from the Bourg Masters of Amsterdam to be presented by him to the queen mother (together with a book describing by pictures *en taille douche*[1] the entertainment they had given her in her passage through Holland hither), asked my opinion whether, as he had in charge [34ᵛ] to present the book and letters to her majesty, he should not demand an audience for the delivery of the like books (but with no letters, none having been sent them) to the king and queen. I answered that a demand of an audience to be given him by the king was neither needful, nor proper, for so light a subiect, especially having no mixture (as he said he had none) of busynes with it nor any letter to accompany it. According to this resolution having an hour assigned to him, the 9th of February, for his access to the queen mother, I ordered it so as that the king (having had from me the same day an intimation of the ambassadors modest regard to his majestyes trouble) was presented with a book, not by the ambassador, but by the gentleman that brought over the bookes and letters, I assisting him for the presentation of one to the king, and directing him to Madame Vantelet[2] for delivery another to the queen, this in French, that in Latin.

A day or two before, the same ambassador thanking me for my care and paynes in his occasions, presented me with a purse and 35 peeces in it as an earnest, he sayd, of better acknowledgement to follow.

[35ᵛ] Towards the end of February, the lord viscount Scudamore being returned from his imployment of ambassador ordinary in France, and having kissed here the king and queens hands, which put an end to his quality and tytle of ambassador, requested me to procure him an access to the queen mother, as to the next in order for discharge of that duty. This access being assigned for the day following, I accompanyed him to St. Jameses, not in condition of the Master of Ceremonyes, but of an assisting friend and servant. Arriving there at an hour [36] when the queen came to visit her mother, he was introduced by the Captayne of her Gard instantly as theyr majestyes were set downe for discourse in the Bed Chamber. There he made his first reverence to the queen mother, his errand, being immediatly to her, and

---

[1] Copper-plate engravings. Etchings illustrating the earlier public receptions for Marie in the Republic appeared in Jean Puget's *Histoire de l'entree de la Reyne Mere dans les Provinces Unies des Pays Bas* (London, 1639; STC 20489). See illustrations.

[2] Henrietta's personal maid since 1625.

after to our queen. The queen mother rose up to him, more than she had done before to all or any of the great lordes when they came to visit her. It was not withstanding that I had intimated to her majesty before (when she asked me of his condition) that having once seen the king he was no more an ambassador, nor had reason to expect an ambassadores treatment. Our queen also rose up for company, both so standing, tyll he had finished his complement with the queen mother, and retreated.

[38] The king parting towards Yorke, the 27 of March, gave me in charge the day before to intimate to all the ambassadors and ministers of state here residing, that for theyr busynes that might occur here in his absence, they might repayre to his Councell here residing, and that, to that purpose, I should give my diligent attendance for theyr service. This command I discharged by my repayr to them severally (according to theyr ranks) the day after his majestyes departure.

[38ᵛ] The Venetian having demanded audience of the queen for congragulation of the feast of Easter, after the custome of Italye, and to present to her majesty as his duty, he said, in absence of the king, had an assignation for the next day, the 23rd of April. He appeared not then, having been that morning seized with a second fit of a tertian ague, and sending his excuse by me to her majesty, a seven night after being recovered, he redemanded and had it with my introduction.

[39] When his majesty had been three weekes at Yorke, ordering there his affayres for Scotland, I receyved a letter from my lord chamberlin signifying in these words that: whereas Mr. Controller³ had wrytten him to move the king touching the admission of some ambassadors (disposed to follow him in his army) he had answer returned him by his majesty that I should repayre to them with intimation that if any of them had, or should have, a disposition to come to him during his stay at Yorke, where befitting accomodation might be found for them, he should be glad [39ᵛ] to see them there. But now that he was upon his remove further with his army to Newcastle (a place streightened of lodging and conveniencyes for persons of their condition) he wished they would spare their paynes which a journy of that length could not but put them to, etc.

The day after I had received this letter I opportunely addressed myself to the Venetian ambassadour at an audience he had (with my conduction) to the Queen and telling him what intimation I had from his majesty for the ease,

³ In the margin Finet added that Pembroke had given Jermyn "power of ordering busynes concerning his lordships office at court during his absence."

I said, of ambassadors, he answered me, that he hoped he should have no necessity and was sure he should take no pleasure to go so long a journey.

The next day I went to the French ambassador,[4] whom this intimation more particularly aymed at, as at one that had more expressly made known to me and others his intention to wayte on his majesty in this expedition, and acquaynting him with the Kings answer to my Lord Chamberlines overture, in the same words turned French, as I had received them in those letters, he answered smyling, I know whome his majesty especially aymes at but for my part, as I never had, so I shall never have other thought than to observe his majestyes pleasure and to obey it and of this I pray assure my Lord Chamberlin from his most humble servant.

To the States ambassador I presented the like intimation and had the satisfying answer, with profession of his application in all to his majestyes pleasure, [40] that I expected. Of all which I gave account to my Lord Chamberlin, and his lordship to the king. From whom I after receyved the honour of his approbation of my service, as having, without exception or distaste, diverted the ministers of state here residing from the affectation they either had or might have of visiting the King in his army, where, as was the opinion of some of our more considering lords, it had been most unfit that persons of such liberty for inquiry and so little subject to question or controul as were ambassadors, should have their ears and eyes at so near a distance as their quality might seem to allow of, particularly the French of so domestick accesse, to hearken after and to observe his majestyes motions and actions in a businesse of such weight and consequence, a consideration and reason that had not escaped, it seemed, the great Cardinal of France when, as I was told by an ambassador of his majesty freshly returned thence, that king marching with his army towards Italy an intimation was given to all ambassadours not to follow him, but that upon all occasion of negotiation that might occur, they should be pleased to addresse themselves to the Councell of State appointed and residing at Paris for that purpose.

[40ᵛ] News being brought, the 20th of June, of an accord made at the camp near Berwick between the King and his Covenanting subjects of Scotland, the Venetian ambassador wrote to me that having understood of the submission of his Majestyes Scottish subjects, as he knew no man could exceed him in sincerity of affection to this crowne so he would be glad no man should step before him in the exterior demonstration of it. In this regard he let me know, he said, that he was most ready and desirous to present the queen with

---

[4] It was a common rumor that the French court fomented trouble between Charles and the Scots.

his due office of congragulation when her majesty should be pleased to admit him, *et quando l'ufficio non fosse prematuro*: when the discharge of that duty should not appear unseasonable or precipitate. This he desired might be delivered by me to her majesty. Her answer was: I thank him for his respectes, but you may tell him that, though I doubt not but the news which I have received are as true as they are good and welcome to me, yet, tyll I shall have received theyr more full confirmacion by some other expresse, which I every hour expect from his majesty, I desyre he would spare his coming to me, upon further assurance he may expect to hear from me.

This significacion of her majestyes pleasure carryed by me to this ambassador, I three or four dayes after had her majestyes command to bring him to court for his congragulatory audience. For which also I brought him to the Prince the next day in his Withdrawing Chamber, at other [41] tymes the Kynges, in Whitehall. Also the States ambassadour, the 29th of June, had the like accesse to her Majestye and after to the Prince and the Duke of York together.

His majestye having long exercised his wisdome and patience for reduction of the rebellious Covenanters of Scotland to quiet and obedience, and having assigned a peremptory day for theyr final resolution to be brought to him to Berwick by 13 or 14 of the most eminent and active of them, there appeared but three. These asked by his majesty why the others came not, answered they can not come, hindered by the people whom wee can not rule. Why then, replyed his majestye, if you can not rule the people, nor I rule you, I will go where I shall find better obedience. So instantly he set down his resolution and tyme for his returne, which was hastened by the Queens persuading letters and the lords of the Councells reasons to that purpose, brought him the first night to Raby Castle. There the Prince Elector Palatine, for communication of some affayrs with his majesty, met him the fourth day after his landing at Harwich.[5] The next day he came to Doncaster, the 3rd to Abthorpe and the 4th to Theobalds. The Queen being come there the day before went the next, with diverse lords and ladyes attending in half [41ᵛ] a score coaches, three or four miles further on the way for theyr incounter. At which his majestye stepping from his own coach into the Queens, they rested that night and the next at Theobalds, where was provided a lodging and dyett of 20 dishes for the Prince Elector and his not many followers. Thence proceeding towards London without order given for a publick and

---

[5] At Raby Castle at Staindrop, co. Durham. Charles met his nephew on July 29th, who sought, without success, support for an appointment as a commander of anti-Habsburg forces in Germany.

solemn entrance into a City not thought worthy of that honour, having shewed such poornes in their offered contribution of but 5000 £ towards the charge of this northern expedition. The queen mother met his majesty on the road three miles off, he and the Queen entring there in her coach. The country people had all the way spoken theyr gladness in strewed flowers, boughs and bonefires and the City multitude as he passed their suburbs left not their acclamations of joy and welcome till their majestyes arrived at St. Jameses, where leaving the Queen Mother in her lodgings and passing on foot with the Queen over the Park, they came to their rest at Whitehall. There his majestye on Sunday, the 4th of August gave the Venetian and States ambassadors their congragulatory audiences. The French had his *a la domestique*, as he in all affected, the day before at the instant almost of the kings arrival.

[42ᵛ] The French ambassadour at the same time had, I know not upon what termes of composition, been dealt with for a visit to be given by him to the Prince Elector. He cam out from his lodging as I entered into it. There passed between them many civil complements, the Prince giving the hand to the ambassador and accompanying him to the third and last door of his lodging. The ambassadour gave him the the tytle of *Altesse* but without addition of *Electorale*, which it seemed the Prince was content, upon private stipulation, should be spared for the better advancement of his affayrs in hand which the French king had power to crosse or further. This the prince acknowledged when he said to me that he had present use of the French ambassadour, but not so of the Venetian,[6] wishing withall that the titular addition of *Electorale*, so much stood upon at another time had never been spoken of. His highnes about a seaven night [43] after returned the visit to the French ambassador at his house, and had a returne of the like respects as he had been given him by the same ambassador.

[43] Duke Radzivill, a prince of Poland cousin germane to the duke of that name that had been ambassador here in *anno* 1632,[7] arriving in England from France towards the time of the kings returne from the northern expedition had kept himself for certain days *Incognito*. He was lodging in an obscure corner neer Billingsgate with an apprehension that his sight here might be distasteful to us, if not dangerous to his owne person, in memory of the wrong done his majesty by the double carriage of Zavadsky's negotiation here for a marriage between the king his master and the Princesse Elizabeth, his Majes-

---

[6] Since he also wished French support for his appointment the Count Palatine did not insist on the "Electoral" title, but later Giustiniani, when required to give the title, refused.

[7] Possibly Albrecht Radziwill (?); Janusz had been at Whitehall early in 1633: see IV 16–18ᵛ.

tyes neece. For which that kings other ambassadour since here (Andreas Rey) was refused accesse to his majesty.[8] But the Prince Elector arriving here, and he had formerly been his acquaintance in Holland, gave him assurance of his welcome to court. He procured him the honour of an accesse (his highnes himself introducing him) to the kings presence in the Privy Galleryes. After he had kissed his majestyes hand and received his gracious respects he was with an instant invitation taken by the Prince Elector to his lodgings [43ᵛ] and entertained there at his dynner, as were his half a score followers of handsome mine and fashion at the dynner of his attending gentlemen.

Having some few days passed his time here and being once taken by the Prince Elector to ride with the king on hunting, he took leave of both their majestyes together as they chanceably met in the kings Withdrawing Chamber; and having obtained the allowance of one of his majestyes ships for his transport into Holland, he went hence the 22nd of August, not without some trouble (so often forewarned by me to be prevented) by stay made of his trunks and chests which though suffered quietly to passe out of London (as containing no goods prohibited) were stopped at Gravesend till the Lord Goreing, chief of those that farmes the customes, wrote and sent down an order to release them. He presented me at his departure a peece of silver plate of 20 £ value.

[45] After the Prince Elector had passed two months here negotiating with his majesty for his favour and assistance in procuring him the command of duke Bernard Weymars army in Germany,[9] the hope whereof had brought him thither (and to which he was in a manner invited by the four directors of it) not with standing the competition of the Duke de Longueville carryed by the French king,[10] his highnes sodaynly parted hence without noise, or so much as a farewell taken of any but their majestyes, and accompanied with only four or five confidants, whereof one was the Lord Craven, the constant follower of all his fortunes, road post to Dover for his immediate passage to Calais or Bullogne and so forward through France *Incognito.* But a great fleet come then from Spayne to convey men and money to Dunkirk for the service of the Infant Cardinall, tempting him to a sight of it, he went aboard the *Admirall* of his majestye, which lay with the rest in the Downs and giving the prince too loud a welcome for his so privat passage, the Holland fleet with their ordinance seconding her, and the Spanish then

---

[8] See IV 149ᵛ.
[9] Bernard of Saxe-Weimar's death left his command in Germany to be filled.
[10] Henri II d'Orléans, duke of Longueville.

with such emulation, as it was judged that not so few as 2000 shot were spent in that salvo. From thence his highness posted to Dover, *etc.*, but whether this busynes was caryed with dew circumstance, *viderit tempus.*

[45ᵛ] The Spanish fleet before mentioned being met in the narrow seas and fought with by some of the Holland fleet with no good success on the Spanish part, these for reparation of theyr hurts and for theyr more commodious transport of theyr men and money to Dunkirk, entered the Downs,[11] where followed by the increasing number of theyr enemyes, and putting themselves upon the kings protection, as being entered his chamber, the Spanish resident, don Alonso de Cardenas, who had been quiet here almost a year together without demand of audience, upon an ill understanding that happened between the king and him,[12] came now into play and demanding access to his majesty, had it granted the [*blank*] of September. He had audience of both theyr majestyes the 24th, and the lyke access the 4th of October of theyr highnesses at Richmond,[13] whom, in all the tyme of his being here, he had not tyll then visited, the prince receyving him in his withdrawing chamber, with regard that his quality was but of an agent, or resident, and the princesses in the accustomed places of theyr intertaynments.

About the midst of October I was sent by my lord chamberlin with signification to a young duke of Wirtenberg,[14] son to Duke Julius Frederick that had been here in *anno* 1637, that his majesty would give him accesse for his leave taking as he demanded, which he accordingly had and went hence towards his imbarking for Denmark the 22nd of October.

[46] Towards the time of the Lord Mayors[15] feast, the ambassadors and ministers of state invited to it were the French, the Venetian, the States ambassador and the Spanish agent, this last *pro forma tantum* and forbearing as at other tymes to appear there with reason of incompetency.

The eve of the day, October 29th, the French ambassador late at night sent to me his secretary with demand whether Monsieur le Croigneux and Mon-

---

[11] The famous naval battle at the Downs had ended with a Dutch victory on 21 Oct. 1639 (New Style).

[12] Late in 1638 Charles learned of a publication of a letter from Cárdenas to Castañeda, the Spanish ambassador in Vienna, which Charles believed to misrepresent his policy on the Palatinate. He refused to grant any audiences to the Spaniard for over a year.

[13] It was customary for resident diplomats to make a public visit to the children in the early months of their mission.

[14] Possibly Sylvius Frederick, son of Julius Frederick, who had visited London in 1629 (see III 57), not in 1637. Another duke, Ulrich, had come in 1636: see IV 102.

[15] Sir Henry Garway.

sieur de Monsigot, councellors to the queen mother,[16] were invited to the feast and would be present at it? I answered I heard they were and thought they would be there. Then, replyed he, my lord ambassador bid me tell you, he will not be there, holding it most unfit that persons condemned as they, for traytors to the king his master should sit and eat at the same table with his ambassador. I answered, I thought him and them to be indeed incompatible at such publick meetings but for the ambassador to absent himself for their respects I held it most improper. Yet there might be, I supposed, a means found to reconcile the differences which, to effect, I said, I would, and did, go streight to the Bishop of Angoulesme, the Queens chief Almoner, a grave and judicious person, and asking his opinion and councell propounded whether it were not fit (for prevencion of question that might insue) to acquaint [46ᵛ] the Queen with the businesse? He said he thought it not worth her majestyes knowledge and trouble, but wished that I would take the paynes to go instantly to the Lord Mayor, and acquaint him with it, as whom it most concerned to compose it, either by an absolute disinvitation of the two invited, or by bestowing them in severall roomes, or in the same room at a severed table. This intimation carrying me late that night to the Lord Mayor, it was there debated *pro* and *contra*, the City Remembrancer, Mr. Wiseman assisting,[17] and thus resolved by his Lordship, that since to disinvite persons of their place and use about the Queen Mother might be interpreted an act of little civility and of disrespect perhaps, as it might be taken, to the person of her majesty, there should be appointed one to receive them at their entrance into Guildhall and thence to conduct them immediately to the table at the lower end of it (opposite to the other where the ambassadours and the lords of the councell were to dine) there to seat them on each hand of the old Lord Mayor[18] and above all the Aldermen, which placing, he said, they could not in reason except against; but if they should they might have their remedy (and no other to be offered them) by their departures.

This order signifyed by me the next morning to the ambassador brought him to the feast but some intimation given (by [47] whom I could not learn) to the other two of his exception kept them from it and from appearing there at all. The ambassador in the mean tyme being by me conducted from his house to Somerset house and there had a sight of (though some what too

---

[16] They were two leading anti-Richelieu agitators. Le Coigneux had at first been barred from entering England, but later admitted at the request of Henrietta (CSP V 1636–39, p. 449). Monsigot, Marie's secretary, had been heard to speak in support of an Anglo-Spanish invasion of France in 1639 (ibid., pp. 277–78).

[17] Sir Richard Wiseman.

[18] Sir Richard Fenn.

late) of the lord maiors passage by water to Westminster, and after passing through Cheapsyde without stay any where, came by twelve of the clock to Guildhall where in the court before it meeting with the States ambassador, they both entered and dyned together, without company of any of the lords of the councell, these forbearing to come, upon a notice given them of some displeasure conceived by his majesty against the city.[19]

[48] About the beginning of November, letters came from the Hague bringing news that Monsieur Aersens, lord of Somersdyke, was parted thence on his imployment for extraordinary ambassador,[20] some doubted whether his errand (tending to the removal of his majestyes displeasure conceyved agaynst the Hollanders for assayling of the Spanish fleet in his harbor at the Downs) would deserve or find that welcome and reception as had been given other ambassadors before him. But I acquaynted my lord chamberlin with the news I had receyved from Gravesend, of his being landed there, and intimated to his lordship what some gave out touching his reception, that it would be with neglect if not with disgrace (intended, they said, to be put upon his person, with a prejudice unbefitting perhaps the present constitution of affayres). His lordship went strait to the king and returned with answer, that his majesty would not punish the servants for the error of the masters, but that all fitting respects should be [48ᵛ] given him in the manner of his reception, defraying, etc. as had been given other ambassadours of that state. So accordingly, I the 12th of November, was sent to Gravesend for his reception there and finding the ships with his baggage not yet arrived, propounded to him, not with standing, his repayre to London the third day after, being Fryday with supposicion that he might have his audience at the latest on Tuesday following, and in the mean time provide hymself of such necessaryes for his own person and his followers, as their ships (not yet arrived) kept from them. But my Lord Chamberlin and some other lords that wished well to his busines having occasion with leave of his majesty to be all that week out of towne and the King also having assigned Tuesday for debate of a weighty cause in question between the Lord Deputy and the Lord Chancellor of Ireland[21] Sunday was appointed for his publick audience. I, being

[19] Another gesture of resentment over the "poorness" of the city's contribution: see above V 41.

[20] Francis Aerssens had been ambassador extraordinary to greet Charles at his accession in 1625. He now came to protest against the increased efforts of Spain to hire English ships for transport of troops to Flanders.

[21] Thomas Wentworth, lord deputy of Ireland, had placed charges of misconduct against Adam Loftus, the lord chancellor. After this meeting of the council Loftus was dismissed from office for abuses of power and extortion.

returned to London, was sent back the next day with significacion of his magestyes pleasure then to give it him. So, taking with me the Kings barge and one more with six oares with intention to presse a light horseman at Gravesend I conducted him and his, about eighteen persons not reckoning those of his colleague, Monsieur Joachimi, the ordinary who went down with me in the Kings barge having been wyth him once before upon the first news received of his arrival. He was landed at Tower Wharfe, was there welcomed by the Lord Pawlett (made choyce of according to precedents) accompanied with his eldest son,[22] 14 or 15 other gentlemen, [49] proceded to Westminster in the kings coach, followed by the French ambassadours, the Venetians, the States ordinary and ten other lords coaches, besides six or seven voluntaryes of the merchants, Dutch and English well wishers. Descending at Sir Abraham Williams his house in Westminster he was there lodged and defrayed. His provision sent him in by specie (as accustomed) by Sir Thomas Murry, Clerke of the Green Cloth and Mr. Paye, Clerke of the Kitchin. No gentleman was that night sent to him from the King, as had been at other tymes the custome observed towards other ambassadors (especially of kings) nor no motion made for it by me as at other tymes. It was with regard to the resentment his majesty might justly conceive against the supposed cause of his imployment, as deserving perhaps no further expressions of welcome than what for formes sake must needs be given. No more was there any cloathe of State set up in his dyneing room nor bedd of the kings in his chamber. These were the rather because upon search and inquiry made there could be no precedent found of any other ambassadour sent from that state that had them. But query whether this was not an unjust omission.[23]

[50] On Sunday, the 17th of November, (with his colleague) he was conducted to his publick audience of both their majestyes together in the Presence Chamber at Whitehall by the lord Viscount Scudamore[24] in the kings coach with the company in it of the lord viscount Killymekin,[25] second son of the earl of Cork, Mr. George Vane, third son of the earle of Westmoreland and (in the French, the Venetians and States coaches following) ten or twelve Gentlemen of the Privy Chamber.

The Earl Morton, Captain of the Guard, received him at the Great Chamber door and at the Presence door left him to the Lord Chamberlin.

---

[22] Lord Poulett of Hinton St. George and his son, Sir John Poulett.
[23] The cloth bearing the king's coat of arms symbolized that he was Charles's guest for these days.
[24] John Scudamore, 1st viscount Scudamore.
[25] Lewis Boyle, viscount Kinelmeaky.

[50] This ambassador arriving at the house appointed for him on Friday had there his first supper and next day and Sunday (the day of his publick audience) the like treatment without the atendance or service of any one officer or servant of the kings except of such as had charge of the dyet before mentioned who appearing not at all for his welcome had not nor expected for ought I could hear any gratuities at his parting from the kings house and charge to his own, which was, haveing made his provisions elsewhere, early on Monday morning the 18th of November.

The 24th of November he had together with his colleague his first private audience [51] in the Withdrawing Chamber accompanyed to it by me only, from his house in Covent Garden. He civilly covered not (no more than did the others) though invited to it by his majesty makeing a speech of some length and pronounceing it with that audible voyce (though himselfe said after it when I obiter spoke of it he conceived he had not done so) as not only the lords but all others by, might easily hear it. His set speech ended, when he fell into interlocutory discourse with his majestye, he spake in a lower tone. At another private audience four or five days after they both (at the first show of his majestyes invitation to it) covered.

The 27th of November they presented by me (and I by my letter to the earl of Newcastle and the Countess of Roxburgh) their request for accesse to the Prince and Princesse at Richmond when having directed my letters to that lord and in case of his absence to the Bishop of Chichester (the Prince's tutor) I received answer from the former thus:

> Sir: Though you may imagine the businesse of this minor court is not so great as that you with those ambassadors can at any time come unseasonably, yet I beseech you to consult with the lord of Newcastle, who is now at his house at London and who ought to be the first wheel of all our motions here, etc.

[52] Upon returne of my messenger with this answer I wrote to the earle for his assent, had it, and went the next day with them to Richmond, introduced them ther to the presence of their highnesses (of the Prince in his Withdrawing Chamber, of the Princesse in hers) and that night returned with them to London.

Monsieur d'Aersens (supposing he had not but to halfes, as he said to me, acquited himself of those respects he owed the queen) when he presented himself to her majesty in publick at his first audience, the king [52ᵛ] being then present, requested me to demand of her majesty a private audience which was accordingly given him together with his colleague in her majestyes Withdrawing Chamber. There after they had approached her majestyes presence and were invited by her to cover, they instantly did it, not after uncovering, but now and then as her majestyes gracious words of answer moved them to it, for which the ladyes and some lords there present spared not, after theyr departure, to censure and condemn them to her majesty of rusticity, but the queen graciously excused them, as those which in theyr right of representancy (especially at the fyrst tyme of theyr coming to her) might be allowed to do it, and did it with dew performance of respects at tymes befitting them. I was bold, some few days after, to tell them what censures had passed upon them, and how the queen had apologized for them, which they acknowledged as a favour from her majesty, but would not allow theyr error to be so great as that it was not excusable by theyr qualityes.

[52ᵛ] Towards New Years day, the Venetian having, according to the custom of ambassadors of his nation, demanded and had an audience of his majesty for congragulation of Christmas, I propounded to the consideration of the States ambassador extraordinary [53] the fitnes of his and his colleagues discharge of the lyke complement for the happy entrance of the new year and, with that opportunity, to recomend to his majestyes favour the dispatch of theyr busynes, whereof the propositions had, with some length of tyme, rested in the hand of Mr. Secretary Cook unanswered. The said ambassador seemed at first not to relish my advice, as given for a course not usual, he said, in France, where he had so long lived. But I, propounding it after to his colleague, and this confering with him about it, they intreated me to procure them an audience, which obtained for them the same day wherein I demanded it, being New Years day, proved of no ill effect to them, his majesty affording them his gracious countenance and a favourable answer to the few words they let fall to the purpose of theyr busynes, which theyr modest forbearance would have kept them from.

The ambassador of France, Monsieur de Bellievre, having with much temper, wisdome and general applause passed here two years and two months of his imployment, under tytle and with all the rights of an extraordinary (though in strict construction of his letters qualifying him but with these words only *nostre ambassadeur* made him but an ordinary) came [53ᵛ] to my house to visit and acquaint me with the king his masters signifyed pleasure for his speedy returne and, with that regard, requested me to move my lord chamberlin for his majestyes appointment of a day for his publick audience and leave taking.

This granted for Sunday the 12th of January, and the earl of Devonshire[1] made choyce of for his conductor, having for his assistants and attendants, the lord Rich, son to the earl of Warwick, the lord of Dungannon, son to the earl of Cork, and five or six gentlemen of the Privy Chamber (as many more having been listed but fayled) he was fetched from his house in Tothill Street (in the kinges coach, the queens and 13 or 14 others belonging to lords) to Whytehal and brought to his repose in the lord keepers lodging, the councell chamber being held improper for that use with regard to the remoteness of it,

---

[1] William Cavendish, 4th earl of Devonshire.

and thence to the presence of their majestyes in the Banketting House, which but the night before had been ordered and was but that morning taken in hand to be hung with a sute of the kinges richest hangings fetched from the Tower, directions having been two or three days before given, but after countermanded, for his audience to be given him in the Presence Chamber.

This audience finished, and his retreat for a while made to the chamber of his repose, the gentleman [54] that accompanyed him and all his attending coaches had theyr dismission, when him self (wyth only the earl his conductor and I passing thence along with him, by the way of the privy gallery, to the queens side) we there also left him to partake of the sight, at the instant offered, of the lord viscount Wentworth, made a little before lord lieutenant generall of Ireland, and then created earl of Strafford, introduced to his majesty and the queens presence in the Presence Chamber (6 or 7 heralds of Armes preceeding) by five earls clothed in the proper robes of that dignity, in order thus. By the earl of Newcastle marching foremost and carrying on his arm the new earls upper robe or garment, after him followed the earl of Cleveland bearing his sword, and after him the earl of Clare his coronet, then came the earl of Strafford him self, supported on the right hand by the earl of Northumberland, and on the left the lord marquis of Hamilton, as earl of Cambridge. These presenting him to the king, whyle the Secretary of State, Sir Francis Winde-bank read his patent, tyll rehearcing the words of it tending to that purpose, his robe was put upon him, after the sword gyrt to him, and lastly crowne set on his head, all severally by the earls that had caryed them, who then covered and so stood covered with him in the presence of his majesty till the ceremony ended, when the same earls accompanying him in ranck as before (the drums and trumpets sounding before him) he passed over the terras to the councell chamber.

[54ᵛ] The French ambassador being finally ready for his departure (his lady and most of the trayne being gone the day before) set forth in coach from Lambeth, after noon to be that night at Dartford and the thyrd day at Dover, I having offered him, but he excusing, the use of the kinges barge for his transport by water to Gravesend. The day before he parted he sent me by Mr. Fostyr,[2] an honest English gentleman his confidant, one hundred peeces, and to Mr. Andros[3] (not long before my officer who had, with my consent,

---

[2] Possibly Sir Richard Foster (?), of Henrietta's household, an occasional courier between Secretary Windebank and Richelieu (see M. Foster, "Sir Richard Foster, 1585–1661," *Recusant History* 14 No. 2 [May 1978] 163–74).

[3] See IV 137–137ᵛ.

quitted his place of Marshall of Ceremonyes to one Mr. Nicholls[4]) thirty peeces, but with full liberty left to me to dispose so much of that sume as I should think fitting to the said Nicholls, who had only seen and served the ambassador the day of his last audience, yet pretended a right to the whole, as given (said he) after Andros his dismission and during his (Nicholls) execution of the office. But I knowing the ambassadors intention to have been, and so expressed by him to me, especially to gratify Andros (this having deserved by two years and the other by but one dayes service) gave, as I had liberty and power, twenty pounds to the former and ten to the latter, wherewith they were both contented.

His present from the king should have been (by his majestyes declared disposition) a sute of hangings, but there being none found of so low a valew by much as 2000 ounces of gylt plate [55] would come to, regard was had to the consequence, and the said 2000 ounces presented to him, but not tyll after his departure (it being not tyll then for the too common defect in readynes) by the master of the Jewel House his officers, he him self receyving after, for an acknowledgement, a chayne of about 25 £ valew, but his officers nothing, with excuse of him that should have gratifyed them, as from the ambassador, that he had no order for it from his lord, before his departure. This ambassador left here a gentleman, Monsieur de Montereuil,[5] for dispatch of busynes occuring when he should be gone, who having been recommended by the ambassador him self for that service to Mr. Secretary Windebank, was three or four dayes after presented by me, as so qualifyed, to my lord chamberlin but not at all (as he ought to have been at the ambassadors last audience) to his majesty.

Both theyr majestyes having (together with ten lords and as many ladyes) practiced a mask[6] to be represented (the queen mother to be present at it) the 21 of January, and the French ambassador having designed his departure for that day, the queen was pleased he should be honoured with a sight of the practice of the dances and of the motions of the scene, three or four dayes before the maske was to be completely acted, he and his wyfe to sitt, as they did, *al incognita* in a box, as it is called, finally reserved for the earl [55ᵛ] and countess of Arundel.

[56] Mr. Bloome, who had formerly resided here Agent for the queen and crown of Sweden, and had been twice absent in the Low Countryes,

---

[4] Sir Ralph Nicholls.
[5] Jean de Montereuil, agent (Oct. 1640 – June 1641).
[6] Rehearsals for Davenant's *Salmacida Spolia*.

the last tyme by the space of a year and half, returned here in February.[7] After some questions passed from me, and satisfaction given by him, touching the continuance of his agency, I presented him to the lord chamberlin, and his lordship immediatly to the king, where he then was in the Stone Table chamber. He had no letters for his majesty then expecting, he sayd, some to be speedily sent him from Sweden.[8]

[56v] At the same time came to see the king and this country a duke of Holstein, by name [blank], third son to [blank], and by this cousin germane in the 2nd degree to his majesty.[9] He sent me, by a gentleman of his, his intreaty to repayre to him and to procure his access to both theyr majestyes, which I did, recommending first his quality to the lord chamberlin, and his lordship, I being by, to the king, to whom and to the queen I at that time presented his letters in his recommendation from the queen of Bohemia, herein obeying his particular request, and following his custom (as he said it was) of all German princes, to have [57] theyr letters preced theyr personal access. This discharged I, the next day, by the way of the Privy Garden, introduced him to the king at that time in his privy chamber, while he re-mayned there in his passage to his dinner then setting on the table. In the after noon he had access to the queen in her new Withdrawing Chamber where, upon the premonition I was bold to give him, he repayred the error he had committed at his audience of the king, when presenting himself with some few words of complement, and his majesty receiving him with the like he, through want of confidence it might seem, returned not one word of reply but, after a long silent pause abruptly making his reverence, departed. This defect he (otherwise by me modestly instructed) supplyed with a civil complement of the happyness, he said, he had to see and the ambitious desire he had to serve her majesty. Having passed a month here in hope, and with proffer, to be imployed by his majesty in his expedition then towards, but being not admitted with regard to the dangerous consequence of bringing in strangers for the kingdomes service in busynes of war, he went hence, March the 14th, with no greater supply of his great want than 100 £ from his majesty out of the privy purse, brought him by Sir Harry Vane, Treasurer of the household, the necessity of the time being made the excuse of further in-largement.

---

[7] Michael de Bloom, agent (Feb. – Sept. 1640): see V 13v.

[8] He reported on the efforts of Sweden's ambassador in Paris to secure the release of Charles's nephew, the count Palatine.

[9] Possibly his cousin Ulrich, son of Christian IV. He sought in vain to receive a military commission in Charles's expedition to Scotland.

[57ᵛ] After the ambassador extraordinary of the States had, by the space of three months and some what more, negotiated here and found that the indisposition of his health, or rather of his busynes, would call him home *re infecta*, he requested me to procure him an audience, which, when I asked him whether I should move for to be given him in publick, as to take his leave (because I had, I said, discovered in him a disposition to part hence) and that if he so intended, there must be a nobleman appointed and the kings coaches for his conduction, his answer was he affected rather substance than shows or shadows, and desired to part with silence, leaving his busynes to his majestyes favour rather to take his leave with pomp and ceremony. This, answerable to his intimation, I demanded and he had access to the king in his Withdrawing Chamber (February 24) took leave of his majesty, and immediately after of the queen, where she expected him, leave for his access being asked and granted the day before, also in her Withdrawing Chamber.¹⁰

[58] Having had, during the time of his defraying, no attendance of any of the kings servants, except of the two officers of the household, Sir Thomas Mery and Mr. Pay, for the ordering of his dyet, who regarding the short time of his treatment and the scarce allowance for it, had forborne to appear at all before him, he had no other gratuities to bestow than on to me, whom he gave sixty peeces, and to my officer fifteen. His present of plate consisting of 1000 ounces (after the accustomed rate for an extraordinary from that state) was brought him, in the absence of the Master of the Jewel House then out of town, by his two under officers, to whom he gave 15 £.

[58ᵛ] The marquis de Ville¹¹ (who had been at other tymes here) having passed the seas in company of the marquis de Velada, ambassador extraordinary from the king of Spayne, leaving him at Dover and posting to London, demanded audience the day of his arrival (March 27) and had it the next. But first I (being sent for to come to my lord chamberlin at the instant that I was ready to accompany him to court) had an intimation from his lordship of the kings pleasure to be imparted to the sayd marquis (but not as coming from the kyng) that the lord chamberlin and two or three of the lords (supposing the marquises busynes might tend to that which all the world discoursed of, *viz.* the duke of Loraynes late unlawful marriage,¹² but this not to be

¹⁰ Aerssens was to return in January as a marriage commissioner for William of Nassau; see V 93–95.

¹¹ Henri-Charles de Livron, sieur de Ville, agent extraordinary of the duke of Lorraine. He had visited Whitehall in March 1628.

¹² His principal purpose was to support the efforts of the duchess of Chevreuse to secure troops in Ireland to serve with the duke of Lorraine against France. However, Charles IV

mentioned by me in express termes) were desirous, for the respect they bore his person, whom they had before seen and been acquaynted with in this court, but more especially to prevent the distaste they knew his majesty would conceyve of it, that whatsoever his errand might be, the busynes which the world so discoursed of concerning his master might be no part of it, unless he meant to procure an ill welcome to himself, and for the duke his master an absolute refusal, of what should be by him propounded to his majesty.

To this the marquises answer was a request that I would let the lord chamberlin know [59] that he was not come to give distaste to his majesty by making any unfit proposition but only to cleer some particulars, which his majesty might be perhaps not rightly possesst of, and that for the rest his majesty should see, he would ever have a speciall regard in all to his majestyes satisfaction. This answer reported by me to my lord chamberlin, his lordship taking me along with him caused me to make repetition of it in his majestyes presence, wherewyth his majesty satisfed and protesting wyth an oath that he would never receyve any overture, or proposition, to the disadvantage of the duchess who was in blood so neer him, commanded me to introduce him to his presence in his Withdrawing Chamber, whence after his audience, I accompanyed him to the duchess of Chevreuse and there left him.

The next day he had access to the queen, but I before entering where her majesty and the king sat together in her Withdrawing Chamber, she called me to her and bade me to tell the marques she doubted not his wisdome would be such as not to propound, or impart any thing to her but what he had imparted and found agreeable to his majesty, with which caution and with report of it to the marques, I fetched him from [59ᵛ] the duchess of Chevreuses lodging to her majestyes presence whence, after his audience, passing to the Privy Chamber, and there intreating me to forbear any further trouble (as he termed it) of his company, he with the confidence of a domestick, returned to the presence of her majesty.

The marquis of Velada before mentioned, having passed the seas from Dunkirk in one of his majestyes ships, landed the 24th of March at Dover. I had prepared and sent thither before hand, by a servant of the Spanish agent, a declaration of his majestyes pleasure under the lord chamberlins hand, directed to all mayors,[13] justices of the peace, etc. for fair treatment and civil respectes to be given him and his on his way. He came to Gravesend, the

---

of Lorraine, while still married to his first cousin Nicole of Lorraine, had entered a bigamous second marriage to Beatrix de Cusance in 1637 and was now under papal censure.

[13] In the margin Finet wrote: "This from my motion to prevent insolencyes of people on the way."

30th of March, having dispensed with the rest, he owed his Easter day after the new style,[14] and borrowed the afternoon of it (dispensing with his devotions) for his remove to Sittingborne. At Gravesend I gave him the *para bien* from his majesty, that night returning, I went again thither the next day to conduct him, the thyrd, to London. When we were ready to set forth, a stiff easternly wind blowing contrary, we were told by the watermen of that town [60] that the ten barges I had appointed could not possibly arrive at Greenwich that tyde. Whereupon I propounded it to the ambassadors pleasure and had his assent for his own passage, and some chief of his company, in four coaches (he had three of his own and one of the agents) while the rest of his trayne and the baggage for his immediate service (the rest being sent in a barke from Dover) might go by water in four light horsemen then instantly made stay of by me for that use. These provisions by land and water brought him and 20 others in coach to Greenwich and the rest by boat to Tower wharfe. In his way at Greenwich, he was receyved by the earl of Devonshire with company of lord Charles Howard,[15] of the earl of Salisburys eldest and third sons, and by half a score gentlemen of the Privy Chamber. All these entering with the ambassador the kings barge, which had brought the conductor thither, the queens and two others, which had fortunately put in there when the wind had kept them from proceeding further, came seasonably to Tower wharf and thence through London (in the kings, the queens and 14 other coaches, 7 or 8 more having been appointed but fayling by reason of the rayny weather) [60ᵛ] to the ambassadors house at Westminster on Wednesday, the first of April.

There he had his first supper at the kings charge, after the allowance of 40 £ *per diem*, that sum having been proportioned for his dayly expense in dyet, when the whole number of his followers were reckoned and listed at 88, and were not allowed any increase when, by accession of more, they were after growne (as appeared by theyr list) to 120, with what reason of proportion, or with what justice, I leave to consideration. I told the ambassadors officers that after our custom, though but a late, and to say truth, a poor one, he was to provide his own plate and table lynnen (the king furnishing neither)

---

[14] April 5th in New Style. Antonio Sancho Davila y Toledo, marquis of Velada, ambassador extraordinary (March 1640 – Feb. 1641) of Spain and field marshal of the army of Flanders, came to demand that Charles break with the Dutch Republic, since the recent defeat of the Spanish fleet occurred when the ships were sheltered in English waters. This and the other missions from Spain are well summarized in J. Elliott, "The Year of the Three Ambassadors" in *History and Imagination*, edd. H. Lloyd-Jones and V. Pearl, pp. 165–81 (see Introduction, n. 43).

[15] Viscount Andover.

which seemed, as it was indeed, a hard and improper condition and was not now observed, though the ambassador had brought with him plenty of both, Sir Abraham Williams, upon his excuse or rather his refusal to bring forth his plate, serving them with lynnen and pewter, during the time they were served with the kings dyet.

[61ᵛ] The king had assigned this ambassador publick audience for Monday following,[16] but having understood, by Mr. Porter of the Bed Chamber, that as the rich liveryes and other bravery he had put to making in this towne would not be by that time ready, his majesty was pleased he should be remitted tyll Wednesday after (April 8), for which day the Banketting House being hung with the kings richest hangings and the access to the State incompassed on eyther syde (26 foot in bredth and 70 in length) with a rayle to keep off the intruding multitude (this done upon my intimation to the lord chamberlin of the especial use thereof). The earl of Holland was made choyce of by his majesty for this ambassadors conduction, with regard to that lords rank and quality of being a privy councellor, a knight of the Garter, and first Gentleman of his majestyes Bed Chamber, in correspondence of the others being a Grande of Spayne; of the order of Calatrava, etc.

The company that sat with him in the kings coach (the queens following) were the earl of Kildare,[17] the lord viscount Grandison, the lord viscount of Dungannon, his brother the lord Killineakin, the lord of Dillan,[18] the secretary of the ambassage, Mr. Taylor,[19] the ambassadors son and myself and in other 16 or 17 other coaches half a score or dozen gentlemen of the Privy Chamber. These brought him from his house to the presence of their majestyes where, not withstanding the provisionnal care taken by the lord chamberlin in ranging next within and down along the rayle of the kings right hand the Gentlemen Pensioners, and before them the younger sort of nobility, [62ᵛ] and on his majestyes left hand, in the same order, the gentlemen of the Privy Chamber ordinary and extraordinary, and before them, all the inferior sort of ladyes and gentlemen, the greater sort of lords and ladyes standing on the steps on each syde of theyr majestyes, such was the confusion grown from the excessive number of intruders of all sortes before the ambassadors coming, and of his trayne marching before him up those blynd stayre leading to the lord keepers lodging (a most unfit place) appointed for his repose tyll he should be introduced to the Banketting House, as all that could possibly be effected

---

[16] April 6th.
[17] George Fitzgerald, earl of Kildare.
[18] Robert Dillon, lord Dillon of Kilkenny West.
[19] Henry Taylor, agent for Brussels (1630–36), returned as secretary of Velada's embassy.

by the lord chamberlin, wyth the earl marshall and gentlemen Ushers, was but to make a lane of prospect and of march for the ambassador between the lord chamberlin and the lord conductor up to theyr majestyes seates, the company falling in after them so immediatly and so confusedly together with the ambassadors followers, as no sight could be had of his gentlemen, his pages, and his lacquays bravery.

He spoke to his majesty by the interpretation of the secretary of ambassage in Spanish, and the lyke to the queen. [63] As often as he spake to her taking and holding off his hat and after he had spoken, putting and holding it on, while the interpreter presented what the ambassador had said to her majesty and, while her majesty replyed, again uncovered, a civility observed and applauded by most of the beholders, but by some censured. Don Alonso, the Spanish resident, came not with him to the audience, perhaps as not being of equall condition to present him to his majesty, or for not being of commission with him.[20]

Wednesday, the 15th of April, he had his last meal of 14 at the kings charge, when he had a day or two before newes brought him that another ambassador from Spayne, the marquis Vergilio Malvezzi,[21] was arrived at Falmouth and on his way towards London [63ᵛ] for whose readier passage and prevention of molestation in his journey (the resident having made provision of a coach to meet him) he sent to me his request for the like letter under my lord chamberlins hand as I had procured for the marques de Velada, which had been, he said, of special use to him on his way from Dover. This obtayned, word soon came that he was come as far as Brentford, which brought the marques de Velada thither to meet him, and brought forth also the offer of an English gentleman for an house in Chelsey[22] to be at his use tyll he could provide himself of another (which he hourly sought after) of more capacity and fitting for him in London. This he found in Aldersgate Street, the house of the lord Petre,[23] and taking it after the rate of 400 £ yearly rent, began to furnish it. Then intreating me (the 19th of April) to procure him an audience of the queen mother, he had it the next day with my conduction (together with one

---

[20] The difficulties of Necolalde and Cárdenas over the rank of resident have been seen before, especially in V 14.

[21] Vergilio Malvezzi, marquis of Castelguelfo, second ambassador extraordinary of Spain, was a classicist and historian with little diplomatic experience. He came directly from the court of Madrid to seek thousands of recruits in Ireland, in return for Spanish military assistance for Charles's campaign in Scotland. Velada remained the senior negotiator.

[22] Velada had left Abraham Williams' house after his public audience.

[23] William Petre, 4th baron Petre.

of her equerries) in her own coach, two others of her coaches attending from Chelsey to St. James.

In the mean tyme a question was raysed by the king (upon sight of letters from his ambassador in Spayne, Sir Arthur Hopton, giving [64] account of the marquis of Malvezzis imployment into England with letters of instruction to the marquis of Veladas concerning his busynes here) whether he were not formally an ambassador. After which I, having his majestyes command to make inquiry, and Mr. Secretary Windebank for more certain assurance writing to Mr. Taylor, secretary of the ambassage, to that purpose, the marquis showed me so much of the king his masters credential letters qualifying him ambassador extraordinary, as made that doubt cease and the tyme for his own pleasure for his entry to be hearkened after.

The 21st of April being the first day of the kings proceeding to parliament, the marques de Velada privately (after his own pleasure) chose (upon a hynt I had given of the comodiousnes of it) the house of the duchess of Chevreuse for his sight of that solemnity, whither also came *Incognito* the other ambassador mentioned,[24] the better sort of the marquises train having been by me bestowed, at their own charge of 14 £, for a greater and less window capable of 20 persons, in a house at the lower end of King Street, where they beheld in front the entire proceedings. Other ambassadors here, as the Venetian and the States, had hyred stands elsewhere, the latter paying, for a chamber and the half of a pergolo, 10 £ and the other for a chamber in another house there 5 £.

[64ᵛ] There being about this time a comedy with variation of scenes[25] to be presented at court by certayne gentlemen and gentle women of the lord chamberlins family, his son (the lord Herbert) expressing a desire that some cheefe of the ambassadors gentlemen should be at it, they were seated (8 or 10 of them) in a box apart, and were so pleased wyth the sight of it, as upon report of what they had seen the ambassador himself (hearing it was again to be acted) desired to be a spectator at it *Incognito*. He was fetched from the duchess of Chevreuses lodging by the same young lord and placed where the gentlemen were before, with no other difference of preparation than of carpets hung before and about the seate, theyr majestyes at theyr entrance into the hall taking no other notice of him than once or twice looking towards him, and the ambassador returning his respects no otherwise than of an *Incognito*. The 17 of April, he demanded and the next day had, his first private audience, bringing with him five or six of his best qualifyed gentlemen and commanding his pages (no footmen at all appearing) to descend to the

---

24 The "Short" Parliament, 13 April to 5 May.
25 Habington's *Queen of Aragon or Cleodora* on April 9th and 10th.

garden when they were already entered the first chamber of the privy gallery, and might have been allowed theyr stay there (as other the lyke had at other tymes been) without exception but this pleasure (though intreated to the contrary) gave them theyr dismission.

[65] By this tyme the marquis de Ville finding his majesty not to relish his negotiation, so confined, took leave and the opportunity then offered of the company of the duchess of Chevreuse, who after her two yeares aboad here, with no great good liking of the most and best (*et pour cause*), was so scared with the news brought her of her husbands the dukes coming into England[26] to fetch her home to France, *etc.* as obtaining of his majesty the use of one of his ships for her passage to Flanders, she suddenly departed. And with her went the marquis de Ville, who was unpresented by the king, but the duchesse not so by the queene who, as I was told, bestowed on her a favour set with diamonds of 3000 £ valew.

After the marquis Malvezzi had layne *Incognito* about a fortnight in a house lent his colleague at Chelsey, with excuse of want of health and fit equipage to appear abroad in, I received word from the marquis de Velada that he was now ready to make his entry. This was first affected to be made from Greenwich and through London, according to the received custome and as the marquis de Velada had made his, [65ᵛ] but when I had given the reasons of other ambassadors receptions and of this last, their to have been there, because Greenwich lying in the way from Gravesend was a place most proper for the encounter there of a nobleman to conduct from thence in the kinges barge, for their passage under the bridge or in his coaches through London, and that the marquis Malvezzi having landed in the west country, and made his first place of rest at Chelsey, might have, I sayd, the same ceremony performed, with as full respect, by his use of the kings barge from Chelsey to the kings bridge at Westminster, as from Greenwich, and of the kings and queens coaches, which should, I said, attend him there at his landing to the house appointed for his treatment (though but a hundred paces distant). He chose the latter and with the conduction of the earl of Monmouth, accompanyed with two of his sons, a younger son of the marquis Huntleys, and 7 or 8 gentlemen of the Privy Chamber, was brought from Chelsey in the kings barge, with three other, to the kings bridge and being landed there to his lodging (all walking on foot, the coaches driving by). The 22nd April, towards evening, when he had the first meal at the charge of his majesty [76] about an hour after his arrival there, the lord viscount Cranbourne, eldest son to the earl of

---

[26] He did not appear in London at this time.

Salisbury, came to him from the king with his welcome and with inquiry of his condition of health, etc. and had the hand given him by the ambassador at his entrance and issuing. It was observed that, whereas we found the marquis de Velada ready at Chelsey with a purpose to accompany the marquis Malvezzi at his entry, while this later civilly contended with the earl of Monmouth about the hand, which he would by no means take from him, the marquis de Velada stepping before them with his hatt in his hand, said, he would be their servant to guid them to the kings barge, and proceeding entered it, when staying with the Resident and me at the barge house door and giving way to the other ambassador to enter it, I requested him to take his place but he excused it with the pleasure he said he would lose of the fresh air by sytting under a tylt.

The true reason of his not entering might seem to be not fitting to his mind when he must, in civility, give to another a precedence not yet fully resolved on, to which purpose his majesty, about [66ᵛ] a seaven night before, asked me if I knew which of them would take place of the other. I answered that, according to custome and my observation, the ambassador that hath last seen his masters face and had brought the freshest newes commission was to have the precedence. Yes, replyed his majesty, and should I now imploy you for my ambassador into France, you must and should take place of the earl of Leicester and, if at the day that I shall give publick audience to the marquis Malvezzi, the marquis de Velada shall take the hand of him, I shall think him in error. It may be, sir, I replied the tytle and quality that he beares of a Grande may overbear the point of precedence by the king of Spaynes own pleasure signifyed to the latter. If it be so, said his majesty, his masters pleasure must be obeyed though custome and reason be both agaynst it.

The day of audience, April 26, for this ambassador being come, the earl of Rutland, of the first rank of earles but neither knight of the Garter nor privy counceller, was made choice of for his conduction to court, not without regard to consequence, when other ambassadors shall [67] perhaps expect to have their conductors in all points answerably qualifyed to the earl of Holland, conductor of the marquis de Velada, when neither the Garter nor the place of the privy counceller can serve to make an earl greater than his earldom. He was brought from his house to court in the kings coach followed by the queens, the Venetians, the ambassadors own, and 7 or 8 other, assisted by the earl Rivers,[27] the lord Willoughby of Eresby,[28] the lord Willoughby of

[27] John Savage, 6th earl Rivers.
[28] Montagu Bertie, lord Willoughby of Eresby.

Parham and the gentlemen of the Privy Chamber. The two ambassadors made choyce of the boot to sit in, the last come ambassador having the right hand place next the coachman.

[67ᵛ] Theyr passage to the chamber appointed for theyr repose in the lord keepers lodging was now made much more free and easy than before by a new payr of stayres raised up to a balcone at the end of the new masking room and thence into the old one. There the two ambassadors entryng the marquis de Velada took the hand, without once offering to present the other ambassador to the king according to custome, and putting and holding on his hat (which many censured as an act ill becoming him and not privileged as by his being a Grande of Spayne), whyle he stood in front before theyr majestyes and intertained with discourse by his interpreter with the countess of Carnarvon,²⁹ all the tyme the other ambassador spoke to both theyr majestyes, and after he had ceased to speak, making to them a reverence only and so departing. That night the marquis Malvezzi made his last meale of nine at the kings charge, and the next day dyning there at his own, left that house to lodge in part of the other [68] ambassadors in Aldersgate Street. In his way thither about One of the clock after noon, he entered the court by the Privy Garden gate for his fyrst private audience that day assigned him, he harrangued to his majesty half an hour without intermission, the king attentively hearkening to him, and, after hearing agayn distinctly read by the Secretary of the ambassage all whatsoever the ambassador had spoken, translated *verbatim* by the same Secretary into English, and delivered at parting to the hands of his majesty.

[70ᵛ] A feast of Sergeants at Law (thirteen of them selected) being to be held in the Middle Temple (June 16) and all the ambassadors invited to it, I made offer to them of my attendance, but the marques de Velada having been let blood a day or two before and being to take physick the day after, made that a reason for his (and must pass of consequence for his colleagues) absence. [71] But the States ambassador sayd to me he doubted his indisposition was but feigned and that whatsoever he pretended, he intended to be there, 'Be it,' he sayd, 'but to give the world subject of discourse from our incounter, or to confirme a report, lately raysed by some that my masters the States seek to the Spaniards for a peace, which would be thought not unlikely, if I, their ambassador, should appear in publick at a feast with the Spanish, an incounter which I had alwaies here to fore carefully avoyded.' These reasons prevailed so far as neither came. The Venetian in the mean

²⁹ Anna Sophia Herbert, wife of the 1st earl of Carnarvon.

tyme, not fayling of his appearance, had the uppermost seat on the bench and the right hand. The great lords invited were seated in theyr ranks.

The 1st of July, the Spanish agent (don Alonso de Cardenas) introduced by me to a privat audience (which Mr. Taylor, secretary of the marques de Veladas ambassage, had formally entreated me to procure for him) was intertayned by his majesty with some length and earnestness of discourse. This in the mean tyme did not pass unobserved or unwondered at, that two ambassadors of the king of Spayne, both extraordinaries and at one tyme here, a third minister, and but an agent of the same king, should demand and have audience, neyther of these other taking or giving notice of it.

[71ᵛ] The 8 of July (a day appointed and kept for a general fast) the queen was brought to bed of a thyrd prince,[30] for congragulation of whose birth the two Spanish ambassadors extraordinary had access to his majesty at Whytehal the 12th following, in theyr company came *Incognito* the duke of Albuquerque,[31] a Grande of Spayne, who landing in the west country had posted to London for his passage to Flanders, and with him the Conde [*blank*] and three or four others of quality all concealed, the duke especially who during the audience placed himself behind the company, and had there a sight only of his majesty, while the others less reserved stood foremost, but without notice given or taken of any of them.

The Venetian, having receyved his assignation for the like access the same day and hour, but nearer Two (the Spanish having had theirs for half an hour past One, with my regard to the unfitness of theyr encounter, though there was between them no ill correspondence) came not till within a quarter of Three, when his majesty, weary of longer expecting an unmannerly ambassador, went to councell and leaving him to attend (as he deserved and did) his leisure, came forth three hours after and gave him audience. The States ambassador having presented his desire of the lyke access, but [72] with regard, to be by me expressed to his majesty, of not troubling him in one and the same day with a fourth ambassador after three preceeding, had it granted and given him at Oatlands the 14th, with my introduction there, but not attendance thither, he not requesting it.

[72ᵛ] Don Alonso de Cardenas having remayned here above two yeares under the charge and title of an agent, though not without pretence of more than a resident, receyved from Spayne about mid July a commission qualifying him ordinary ambassador for that king with the same allowance expressed as

[30] Henry.
[31] Francisco Fernández de la Cueva, duke of Albuquerque.

the conde de Oñate, ambassador extraordinary, had had before him. This commission come, he desyred my opinion and assistance for his carriage and proceeding in point of ceremony answerable to precedents here, in lyke case, of remove or advancement, from an inferior condition to a superior. I told him I had never known any such before, but that if he expected that the reception usually given to kings ordinary ambassadors at their first arrival should be in all points given to him, he might be pleased to go down to Gravesend, I to go after him thither to welcome him there, to conduct him thence in the kings barge to Tower wharf, he there to be receyved by an earl, and by him to be accompanyed in the kings coach with other of the lordes coaches to his own house (not to the kings nor his majestyes proper treatment) his commission (as I have said) not qualifying him beyond ambassador ordinary. To this intimation he replyed he would be advised, and though some other opinions had almost perswaded that he, being so well [73] known here after his two years residence, might spare the trouble of a publick entry and for the worlds better notice of his condition, be content only wyth a publick audience, it was resolved and ordered, according to this insuing letter written to me by the secretary[32] of the ambassage, in answer of one of myne to that purpose:

> Sir, Signor don Alonso, having referred the busynes of his publick entry to the opinion of these marquises, they have resolved that it will be more convenient that he enjoy all the ceremonyes which are usually practiced at the arrival here of ambassadors ordinary, that though he be already here yet he is now become entirely a person of a new condition, that this is to be seen in Rome every day where ambassadors, having been in towne some dayes *Incogniti*, do agayne go forth to make theyr *cavalcatas* and solemne entryes, and that it is not fit to loose any thing of those courtesys (though but *punctilios*) lest the successors may also be frustrated of them by like or other accidents. But this I do not alledge to you as if you need to be perswaded to it, for I have told them this evening that you have all in readynes already, but it was rather sayd to me, in reply to what I alledged against the entry, as from my self, etc.

[73ᵛ] So the 24 of July, I going wyth the kinges barge and three others to Greenwich (Gravesend being thought too long a journey and too affected to satisfy only a *punctilio* so indifferent) I there landed and took into the kinges barge the same ambassador ordinary and both the extraordinarys (come hither before hand in and for his company) and landing him at Tower wharf presented him there to the further reception and conduction of the earl Rivers, assisted by the earl of Castlehaven,[33] the lord Lumley,[34] the earl Rivers his

---

[32] Henry Taylor, in this instance, disagreed with Velada.
[33] James Touchet, 3rd earl of Castlehaven.
[34] Richard Lumley, viscount Lumley.

brother, and half a score gentlemen of the Privy Chamber, in the kings coach (wythout the queens) followed by the three Spanish ambassadors coaches, the Venetians and six others to his house at St. Johns.

This ambassador having requested me to procure him his publick audience to be given him within three or four dayes after his entry, I obtained an assignation for Sunday, the 26 July, and gave order for the preparations, when late in the evening of that day, I received a letter sent post from my lord Goring (Viz chamberlin) declaring that his majesty had commanded him to let me know I should instantly repayre to the Spanish ambassador that was to have audience the next day at Hampton Court and acquaint him that there being then two or three newly dead of the plague near [74] that house, I should entreat him to have patience tyll the Sunday seven night after, when it should be given him at Oatlands. So the audience being deferred for that time, I two or three dayes after repayring to court there for the more certain carriage of that busynes and for the better remembrance of the earl of Denbigh (made choyce of for that ambassadors conduction) I found the plague entered into that towne also, the kings farier being dead of it, and his majesty doubtful when and where to receyve the ambassador, tyll at last commanding me to attend his further resolution, which I should not fail to receive from him speedyly, the 29 July he sent Sir Ferdinand Cornwallis, one of the gentlemen Ushers of his Privy Chamber with this message, that his majestys coachmen groomes houses being most of them infected with the plague, one of the coachmen dead of it, the rest banished for a time from court and theyr coache also sequestered, as not without danger if they should be sodaynly made use of, he hoped the ambassador would not interpret it as a disrepect of continuing their desires to have their audience despatched, they should have some other coach than his majestyes sent with the lord appoynted [74ᵛ] for theyr conduction to serve them. This excuse and reason taken for an increase rather than a dimunition of honor to them, they and I with them, set forth for Oatlands, the 2nd of August, in eight coaches of theyr own and of other providing, and were received a little without the west end of Kingstone town by the earl of Denbigh, accompanyed with his son the lord viscount Fielding, and 4 or 5 gentlemen. There all three ambassadors quitting theyr coach and entring the duke of Lenoxes (as the kings for that time) none of his majestyes coaches for the reasons mentioned to be made use of, they after a short time of repose in the lord chamberlins lodgings presented the ambassador ordinary to his majesty in the presence chamber (the queen then indisposed and not appearing). After the audience accompanied by the conductor to Shefferton ferry, as the next and readiest way for theyr returne, they toke theyr leaves on the far side of the

ferry, the ambassadors went that night to London, I parting from them, as
they inforced me, when I came near my house at Hammersmith.

Some few dayes after they were all invited to dine with the Reader[35] of
the Middle Temple (and no other ambassadors to prevent question) and were
[75] there seated, as at other tymes other ambassadors. The marquis de Velada
uppermost on the bench, as the best place, being next the wall and next the
Reader, though on the left hand, he holding the lords end according to
custome, upon a forme the marquis Malvezzi, and on the other side next
beneath the marquis de Velada, the ordinary ambassador. Such gentlemen
of theyr trayne as were usually admitted to theyr own tables sat now also
at the Readers table, called to it by the name of *comaradas*, while other followers, or any officers termed by them for distinctions sake, *criados*, had a
table apart at one side of the hall purposely provided for them.

[75ᵛ] An ambassage from Denmarke having been long in voyce and expectation, there arrived at Gravesend, August 26, two ioynt commissioners,
one named Corfitz Wellefeldt intitling himself viceroy of that kingdom,
particularly favoured of that king and marryed to one of his natural daughters,
and Greggers Krabbe, senator and counseller of state,[36] etc. Of theyr arrival
I had notice late at night being then at my house at Hammersmith and carryed them the kings welcome, which I told them his majesty had with special
regard incharged to me at the instant of his departure for the north, and which
I further discharged with telling them of the earl of Arundels appointment
for theyr reception at Greenwich, with the kings barges and after at Tower
wharf with the queens coach, the kings being sequestered because of the infection happening among his coachmen.

They thankfully acknowledged the favour but would not make use of it,
because (sayd they) we hold it improper to make a solemn and publick entry,
in time of his majestyes so remote absence for an occasion so important and
so displeasing, and adding that they had sent some of theyrs to London for to
provide them of a house. [76] I told them provision was made of one already
appropriated to the service of ambassadors extraordinary, as they were, and
was kept furnished for them, but for the defraying of their diet, they might be
pleased, I said, not to expect any at a time, when the kings officers of his house

[35] Probably Sir Edward Bagshaw, the official reader for the Lent term of 1640, since Sir
Richard Pepys was not to lecture as reader until the Autumn term.

[36] Cornelius Ulefeld and Gregory Krabbe, ambassadors extraordinary (Aug.–Oct. 1640)
of Denmark. They presented an appeal to form a new alliance with Denmark and Spain
against Sweden and the Dutch Republic, as well as an offer of Christian IV to mediate between
the Scots and Charles.

were all imployed for his majestyes personal service in the north. They answered they had no reason to expect one or the other, in a time of such distraction, but would be boid to make use of the house offered them and come to it on Monday following, as they did, being that day fetched by me from Gravesend with the service of the kings barge, and two others of six oars each, and two light horsemen hyred at Gravesend for theyr baggage and meaner sort of servants.

When I parted from them the first night of theyr coming to theyr house, I told them that I might the next morning go to Mr. Secretary Windebank (in the lord chamberlins absence) with the account of their coming and would gladly know whether they would (in case he would offer it) admit of his visit, or of Sir Thomas Rowes,[37] whom they familiarly knew and had lately been ambassador for our king in Denmark. Monsieur Wellefelds answered for both: 'Sir, we desire that neyther the one nor the other, nor any man else should visit us, we being resolveed that, tyll we see the king or receyve from him his pleasure, not to see any person as visitor [76ᵛ] but will tomorow early dispatch an express to his majesty to know his pleasure for our stay where we are, tyll his returne, or for our immediate repayr to him.' To this purpose they immediately asked my opinion to whom theyr messenger should address himself at York for his access and dispatch. I answered I was of opinion that his address would be most properly made for what may concern theyr persons to the lord chamberlin, the earl of Pembroke, but for theyr busynes and what they had to negotiate to the principal secretary at that tyme there, Sir Harry Vane.

Wyth this advice they, the next morning, dispatched a gentleman to the court at York, but without letters to any of those persons, it being improper for them, they sayd, to wryte as well as to speak to any tyll they should hear from his majesty. Yet two or three dayes later Sir Thomas Row and Sir Robert Anstruder,[38] who had been imployed ambassadors to Denmark and were of theyr familiar acquaintance, severally visited them, as by surprise and were admitted, not wyth standing theyr professed resolution. In the interim of theyr gentlemans dispatch to the king, I made one by post, wryting to my lord chamberlin and Mr. Secretary Vane, how pressing I found them for theyr acces to his majesty and how litle regarding any pomp of attendance,

[37] Sir Thomas Roe (Row) had visited Christian prior to his mediation of the truce between Sweden and Poland in 1629, and then negotiated an Anglo-Dutch treaty in 1630. In 1637 he had again negotiated with Christian IV concerning the financial aid due the count Palatine.

[38] Sir Robert Anstruther had represented Charles's sister, Elizabeth of Bohemia, before the assembly of Protestant princes in 1634 in Germany. He had also been ambassador at the court of Christian IV during his war against the Emperor after 1626.

beyond one or two persons each of them for necessary service. To which his lordship returning a speedy answer with his majestyes allowance [77] for theyr repayre to him and with an intimation to me to invite them to a moderation of theyr trayne, because of the then fulness of the towne. They readyly yeilded to observe what I propounded and at theyr messengers returne admitted only of the secretary of the ambassage, Frederick Gunter, of two gentlemen, two grooms of theyr ambassadors chamber, two other inferior servants, and my self and one servant, for all theyr company.

[80ᵛ] In five days and a half (as we came to York) we returned to London, where [81] the respectes the ambassadors had before caryed in not admitting visits tyll they had seen the king, they observed punctually towards the queen, tyll after the 8th of October, when having demanded audience of her majesty, they had it in the Privy Chamber of the kinges syde. For theyr conduction I had inquired after an earl, as the stile of kinges ambassadors required, but these all gone to York, except two or three *primae magnitudinis* left here for manage of state affayres in the kings absence, who might seem above that use, I repayred for advice to the earl of Dorset, lord chamberlin to the queen, and the earl of Arundel, the lord marshall, and was wished by them to go in the name of her majesty and her said lord chamberlin to the lord viscount Cambden[39] (as of the next rank to an earl, and of equal appelation of cousin given by the king in his letters as to earles so to viscounts) for performance of the service, which his lordship readyly accepting of, and the ambassador, when I told them of the choyce in such a dearth of earles, not formalizing themselves agaynst it, he the next day wrote to me how unfit he was, since I last saw him, for such a service, by an extream defluxion into his cheek. So on repayring straight to the earl of Dorset with the account [81ᵛ] of the accident and of the plunge it put us to, his lordship nobly answered: 'So it might not wrong the condition of my place in court I would myself be theyr conductor.' 'Nay', quoth my lord marshall then standing by, 'your lordship shall not wrong the condition of your place in doing an honour to the kings unckles ambassadors and a service to the queen your mistress, at such a pinch of necessity.' Whereupon his lordships resolving, I sent a messenger to my lord Cambden with a discharge of his trouble and for the time of the audience prepared the queens coach, nine other, and as many gentlemen to accompany his lordship, who fetching them from theyr lodging conducted and reconducted them to and from the audience.

39 Edward Noel, 2nd viscount Campden.

[83 ᵛ] Preparing all things for their speedy departure, a question, began at York, continued at London, concerning their presents, whether they were to have each of them two thousand [84] ounces of gylt plate being both ambassadors extraordinary, and this according to precedent of the like conferred upon Monsieurs Tompson and Brahe, some tyme ioynt commissioners as were these from the same king,[40] or each but one thousand by a divided proportion between two ambassadors, though imployed on one ambassage, which division was judged a poorness ill suiting with his majestyes honour and with his relation to the king that sent them, and with persons also who were (especially Willefeldt) of special eminency in the kingdom they came from. I was at last resolved (not wyth standing the opposition and order of some for the more frugal distribution) that a present of two thousand ounces, already prepared answerable to a signification of his majestyes pleasure to the lord chamberlin, shoud be delivered to them.

Whyle they were packing their goods for the shipping at Gravesend, an apprehension grew of theyr search by the officers of the Custom House (upon an interrupcion they met wyth of some of theyr goods fyrst sent away) which to prevent they requested my care, and protested wythall that, as they had no such sordid intention to convey away [84 ᵛ] for theyr profit any merchandise or goods prohibited, or to countenance any such, if sought to be conveyed away by theyr followers, but if any search should be made, or offered to be made, of what they were to cary away, all being for their own personal use and provision, they would never once open their mouths for their release, but would leave them here behind them and after take theyr course for reparation, when they should be returned to Denmark. This threatening language making my care the more, I addressed my self to some of the cheef officers of the customes for prevention, and procured first theyr assurance by letter to me that if eyther of the ambassadors, or theyr secretaryes would but set down under theyr hands what number of truncks, chests, or fardells they, or theyr trayne, had to transport not any of them should be once touched by any of theyr officers. But this condition of setting downe under theyr handes being not to theyr lyking and refused by them, I procured another assurance by a letter likewise to me from another of the Farmers of the Customes, intimating that if they would but call at the Custome House key, as theyr goods should pass downe before it, they should have with them a servant of the office that should see all safely shipt at Gravesend, wythout any interruption or molestation, which offer approved of, and accepted, brought a quiet end to that busynes.

[40] The embassy of Tomson and Brahe: see III 3.

The kings letter (in answer of those they had brought) wrytten at York and sent thence to them from Mr. Secretary Vane, came to theyr hands two or three days before theyr departure, but some of them (in particular that to the prince of Denmark, who qualifyed with the title of *rex electus*, and that to the princess his wife) were superscribed with a mistaken and too meane a tytle of *Excellentissime et Celsissime*, when it should have been *Serenissime et Illustrissime*. The tytle of *excellentissime* is commonly given in Germany and Italy to doctors of Physick, and men of mean condition. This error was found fault with by the ambassadors but could not then be mended, the principal secretary being so far absent at York, but when I had made known to Sir Thomas Rowe, who from the experience he had in those parts and of the style usually given there to princes, best knew what ill construction and relish would be made and had of them, he instantly repayred to the ambassadors, and redemanding the letters faithfully promised to procure their correction and corrected so to send them after them, as they should be in Denmark over land before them.

[85ᵛ] The 19th of October these ambassadors went to Gravesend, and I wyth them, in a coach of theyr own hyring (I having offered them the kings barge and others for theyr service by water but they refused it), they going immediatly aboard theyr Admirall, I there took leave of them and left them to the favour of the winds which, coming the next day fayre for them, caryed them from our coast.

[86ᵛ] The 6 of September, having the day before receyved notice from the French secretary, Monsieur de Montereuil, of an *envoyé* (Monsieur de St. Ravy[41]) from the French king and queen for congragulation of prince Henrys birth he had my assistance (being requested) at Hampton Court (the queen being then there while the king was at York) he went thence about two months after, and had for his present a diamond ring (delivered him by Mr. William Everyt her majestyes servant) that cost 400 £, to me he gave not so much as a farewell.

[86] Monsieur de Vaucour, a gentleman sent from the duchess dowager of Savoy to the queen, her sister, with the news of her reestablishment in Turin, which by the assistance of the French was (after a dangerous siege) recovered from the Spanish,[42] had audience of the queen the 23 of October fetched by me

---

[41] Guillaume de Saint-Ravy, agent extraordinary (Sept. – Oct. 1640) for offering congratulation on the birth of a prince.

[42] The factional war (1639–42) in Savoy over the rights of Christine (supported by Richelieu) to be regent on behalf of her second son, Charles Emmanuel.

(in myne own coach the use of the kings being too much for an *envoyé*) from his lodging neer Aldgate to her majesty in the kings withdrawing Chamber, the queenes being at that tyme repayring. The tytle he gave that princess his mystress, as oft as he spake of her, was *Madame Royale* and of the duke, *son Altesse Royale*. The next day I accompanyed him at his request to the queen mother, then abiding at Chiswick, surprising her majesty there immediatly after her dynner, while most of her servants were not yet risen from theirs. He parted the 14th of November presented with a diamond ring of 400 £ valew and I by him, though another delivered him his present, with a diamond ring worth 12 £.

[86ᵛ] The 25 of October, don Alonso de Cardenas, having a good tyme before had his publick access to the king at Oatlands for his reception in quality of ambassador ordinary from the king of Spayne, had now the lyke publick access, as he demanded it, to the queen at Whytehal in the Privy Chamber of the kings side. He was accompanyed only by the marques Malvezzi, one of the Spanish extraordinaryes, the other, marques de Velada being at that tyme indisposed, and conducted in the queens coach with nine others by the earl of Kennoul.[43] The coach of don Alonso, though but of an ordinary ambassador, marched next after the queens coach (the work of the day being his) after that the marques Malvezzis, after which the Venetians pretending and putting for place and the marques de Veladas second coach taking it, the Venetian made offer to depart as disrespected, which observed by the marques Malvezzi and the Secretary of the ambassage as they sat in the kings coach and a stand there-upon commanded, they caused the Venetians coach to come forward and precede [87] the marques de Veladas second coach, which quieted the differ-ence. The marques Malvezzi gave that day the precedence at all doors and passages to don Alonso, but because, in passing through rooms (as the Gard Chamber, Presence and in the Privy Chamber) where they had their audience the marques took the right hand of him, it was thought by most of the be-holders that he did precede him, but it was mistaken, the middle place of three marching together in front, being among strangers the best, and in that marched don Alonso, with the marques Malvezzi on his right and the earl of Kinnoul on the left.

The three Spanish ambassadors, the Venetian and the States being all in-vited to the lord maiors[44] annual feast for the 29th of October, the marques de Velada pretended some few dayes before a defluxion in his arm, which he doubted, he sayd, would keep him at home. But the true reason of this ab-

---

[43] George Hay, earl of Kinnoule.
[44] Sir Edmund Wright.

sence (which I perceyved he intended) was the apprehension he had that if the States ambassador should be there also, there might grow perhaps some scandall from the encounter, or some foolish action from one or other of theyr followers, or of the people apt to favour the States ambassadors party. [87ᵛ] To remove this conceyt of his I went my self to the States ambassador and, sounding as dextrously as I could, drew from him no other resolution or assurance than that he could not resolve today what he would do tomorrow. This uncertayne answer reported by me to the marques, he returned to his first excuse of his defluxion and requesting me to represent it to the lord maior, with many thanks for his and his colleagues invitation, neither he nor they came to the feast, no more then did the States ambassador, who had no more reason, than he had intention, to be there while the Spaniards were not unlikely (being invited) to be there also. The Venetian came not, remembering perhaps what exceptions he had made the year before and what subject might be given for the like now.

The next day, after the kings returne from York (which was Fryday the 30 of October) all the ambassadors here having some few dayes before intimated to me theyr desyres to present theyr congragulations to his majesty with his fyrst conveniency, his majesty was moved for it (especially for that of the Spanish who had the day before particularly sent to me about it) by the lord chamberlin, when I standing by, was bold to present to his majesty the lyke desyre of the Venetian and States ambassadors [88] which, I sayd, might (if he would be so pleased) have also theyr severall accesses the same day and hour immediatly after the Spanish, and thereby spare his majesty another dayes trouble. This was approved of, with a provisional caution that the Spanish and States ambassadors (for as for the Venetians corresponding friendly wyth the Spanish the case would be needless) might not encounter *eodem tempore et loco*. The Venetian came first to court, but had not the first access (and with reason comparing his representative quality with the Spaniards) who though last come might justly expect to be first admitted as they were, and after them the Venetian. These dismissed, the States ambassador, who, tyll the Spaniards were passed forth of the privy gallerys, remayned unseen, came forth of the lord chamberlins lodging where I had bestowed him for avoidance of incounter with the Spanish and had his audience, as the other, without interruption. This ambassador (as he had done in February 1638 with 25 £) so about this time presented me with an acknowledgement of my care with 20 peeces.

That morning Monsieur de Montereuil (who had been left here Secretary for the affayres of France by Monsieur de Bellievre) and who had often pretended to the respectes and rights of an Agent, but could not obtayne my furtherance for them, I telling him always that while I saw no letters under the French kings hand [88ᵛ] qualifying him for his agent, I could not understand him to be so, shewed me the copy of a letter directed to his majesty from that king, wherein he was styled *nostre Agent*, upon sight whereof, as of a qualification in my judgement sufficient, I brought him to my lord chamberlin, acquaynted his lordship wyth his pretence, and with the king his masters allowance by his letters for his agency, and introducing him to the presence of his majesty he delivered his original letters and was accepted as he pretended.

A Chiaus,⁴⁵ or messenger, sent from the Grand Signor Ebrahim, with an account of his assumption to that dignity having made France his passage (whither he had also the same commission) arrived at London (the [*blank*] of September the king being then at York) and attending his majestyes returne had the 8 of November his publick audience in the Banketting House purposely hung for it. I had before hand inquyred of the Turkysh Company (who had all the while lodged and defrayed him and his 15 or 16 followers at the charge of above 40 £ the week) how he was qualified and might expect to be treated. To this purpose I found, by my notes, and from conference with others, that howsoever the Chiaus⁴⁶ sent hither in *anno* 1618 had had the conduction of a lord from Gravesend [89] that it must be no ruling precedent for this Chiauses lyke treatment. So it was upon debate concluded that not any person of honorable tytle, but that only Sir Peter Wyche, who had been a year or two past ambassador resident for the kyng at Constantinople,⁴⁷ should, wyth my assistance, bring him to his majestyes presence not in the kinges coach (which his majesty himself directly opposed when it was propounded and affected by the Turkysh Company) but in the lord chamberlins. This was accordingly performed the day after I had caryed him his welcome, which I had not before done wyth regard first to the kings absence and the silence he had rested in tyll then, the merchants having given me no notice of him. The lord chamberlins coach and five other brought him from the Chiauses house thither with as many more of the merchants coaches.

---

⁴⁵ The chiaus, official courier of sultan Ibrahim I, stayed until Dec. 1640, with plans to renew the commercial agreements of the Levant Company.

⁴⁶ A previous visit of a chiaus, with audience in October 1618, and an escort by the baron Rich. The entire visit had been paid by the Levant Company.

⁴⁷ Peter Wyche had been ambassador to the sultan from April 1628 to May 1639. Although recalled in 1633, he had remained for five years, since Charles's nomination of Sackville Crowe had been protested by the Levant Company.

The conductor had five or six gentlemen voluntaryly offering to accompany him, Sir James Palmer, gentleman usher of the privy chamber being one of them who excused to summon any of the gentlemen of the chamber to accompany the conductor, according to custome, as he doubted they would refuse their service because he was no nobleman. Divers merchants came with the Chiaus from his house to court, particularly Sir Henry Garraway Gouverner of the Turkysh Company, who came in the same coach wyth him. Being entred the Banketting House, he made not his first reverence till he came [90] almost to the ascent before the State, his majesty all the tyme sitting and once (at the instance only of his reverence) a litle lifting up his hatt to him. After he had at his more neer approach bowed himself lowe to his majestyes feet, he spake with the interpretation of an English gentleman, delivered three letters, one from the Sultan himself, one from the Grand Vizier, and a third from his majestyes own ambassador at Constantinople, Sir Sackville Crowe, and having presented his followers to kiss (as they did) his majestyes garment, he returned.

The day before his audience I presented to his majestyes notice what I had understood from France, from my lord ambassadors secretary there, and from the ambassador of Constantinople, *viz.* that in correspondence of the Great Turks treatment of his majestyes and other princes ambassadors at theyr audiences, he might be pleased to spare his rising up to the Chiaus when approaching he should make his reverence, and after, when his majesty should speak to him, neither first nor last to put off his hatt but only to touch it a little. For so much and no more, I sayd, had the French king done to this Chiaus when he gave audience. But his majesty, not able to dispense with courtesy so naturall to him, rose up from his chair after the Chiaus had begun to speak and make offer to present his letters to him, and being risen up, sat not down again whyle he was in his presence.

This Chiaus had, two or three dayes before his audience, sent to the States ambassador (to none else) to let him know that after his audience he would visit him. But the ambassador preventing him with a visit, had a returne of it about a seven night after and soon receyved from him a present of four or five dishes of meat dressed *a la Turkeska*, the unusuallness thereof being excused by the lyke custome usuall in that country. The like present he sent to me in requital of a *regale* of sweetmeates I had sent him before, but I would not hazard the sending of flesh to him for the doubt I was told the Turks have of being deceyved, either of malice or ignorance, when Christians in that manner present them.

[90ᵛ] The Turkish Company wearyed wyth their so long continuing charge of this Chiauses intertaynment eating up, they said, a great part of that litle gayne they in these hard tymes made of that decayed trade (having in the space of his four monthes abode here expended for him above 240 £) intreated me to procure his parting audience (which he himself also seemed desyrous of) and had it given him by the private way (which he himself particularly affected) of the garden to and in the privy gallery, some half a score lords only there present, Sir Peter Mericke was his conductor, as at the fyrst audience (but without the assistance of the Governor or others of that company) taking his leave with lyke humble reverences as at his fyrst admission, but the king more reserved in his formes of courtesy (only once lifting up his hat). His majesty delyvred to him wyth his own hand as custome required his letters of answer to the Grand Senior and the Grand Vizier, though they were yet unsealed by the default of their wryter excused by the much curiosity necessary in theyr fayr wryting and limming.

Three or four days after his audience, the lord marshall and the lord chamberlin, having understood from me and others the different and savorous manner of dressing his diet by his own servants *a la Turkeska*, bespake, and had, a diner at his house (bringing thither 7 or 8 other great lords) in so plentyful and so unusuall a mesure and manner, [91] both Turkish and English (the Chiaus himself being seated upper most at the tables end) as the merchants, at whose charge it was prepared, observing theyr content of appetite, and doubting what charge from the prayse they gave it to other lords might per adventure follow it, made haste to set him going and finally dismisst him hence, the [*blank*] of December, for his imbarking at Dover where one of his majestyes ships was, at the Companys sute, appointed to take him in for his transport to Holland. He parted hence not thoroughly satisfyed with his present made him by the merchants (the king not making him any at all) of 220 £ in specie of Spanish peeces of eyght. The lyke insatisfaction appeared from his followers who, promising themselves (answerable to the receyved custome of those eastern nations) to have bestowed on them parcells of cloath to make them vests, were all of them disappointed. The Company, a day or two before his parting, sent me a gylt cup of about 10 or 11 £ valew, with the merchants excuse of their hard time for traffick, *etc.*

[91ᵛ] The lords of Brederode, of Somersdyke and Haenufliet imployed from the States on a joint commission[48] to treat of a marriage between the

---

[48] Jan Wolfert, lord of Brederode, Francis Aerssens, lord of Sommelsdijk (see also V 57ᵛ), Jan van der Kerkhoven, lord of Heenvliet, came to negotiate a marriage between William of Nassau and a daughter of Charles.

young prince William of Nassau and a daughter of his majesty, arrived at Gravesend, the 27th of December, having landed at Dover, and that day the ambassador ordinary went to them and I, the next day, following in a barge of six oars. But finding them in expectation of their goods (wythheld at Margate by contrary wynds and thereby unfitted for their instant repair to London) both he and I returned with intention not to move from London tyll the significacion promised to be sent us by an express should be brought us, as it was the last day of December, when in the like barge as before we went down again.

[91ᵛ] The fyrst day of the year we came in company of these ambassadors with the service of the kinges barge (six others and two other lighthorsemen for transport of theyr goodes) to Tower wharf, there they were receyved by the lord Clifford[1] (assisted by the lords Fielding and Dungannon) and a dozen gentlemen of the privy chamber. They entered the kinges coach (and 14 other of the lords coaches, besides three or four voluntarys) and proceeded to the kinges entertainment at Sir Abraham Williamses in Westminster, whither that evening they had theyr welcome brought them from the king by the lord Digby, eldest son to the earl of Bristol.

Theyr dyet began that night at the kings charge in a more pletyfull and orderly manner than had been usually afforded to ambassadors, with regard to the errand they came on, they had beds firnished them out of the kings wardrobe, but no State (though disputed whether one or none) because without precedent.

[93ᵛ] The three ambassadors extraordinary, together with the ordinary, went on January 8th, in the kinges coach followed by 14 others, and conducted by the lord Mowbray[2] (a few dayes before styled Maltravers) eldest son to the earl of Arundel, and now made choyce of, as of a baron preceeding the Lord Clifford, their first conductor, he had for assistant and company his younger brother,[3] Viscount Stafford.

The ambassadors presenting themselves in the [94] Banqueting House (purposely adorned for that day with the richest hangings) they found the throng so exceeding great of the people pressing to see those who were said to be come about a marriage between the young Prince of Orange and the Kings daughter, as not withstanding the Lord Chamberlins and other officers best endeavours for place, the ambassadors exceedingly streightned at their approach, could not at their retreat get so much as a sight of their majestyes or any space at all wherein to make their parting reverences as accustomed.

At this their first audience of both their majestyes together they were observed to have been over forward in their covering especially when they applyed themselves to the Queen, but hereof after making remonstrance to

---

[1] Sir Henry Clifford, son of the 4th earl of Cumberland.
[2] Henry Frederick Howard, son of the earl of Arundel.
[3] William Howard, viscount Stafford.

Monsieur Haenvliet and he from me to the others, they after at their private audiences of the queen forbore to cover. The lord conductor at his first coming to theyr house was met by them at the Hall door and had the hand given him at every passage till they all three entering first the coach, he took then the left hand place next the lord of Brederod first of the commission. The day following they went (according to the order established) from the kings dyett to their own, as they did also from the kings house to one they had hyred in the Piazza having been entertained six whole dayes, *viz.* 12 meales at the charge of his majesty, at their parting from it I wrote down and gave to their Steward (as at other tymes to others) the names of the kings officers and servants that had attended, but satisfaction was so long deferred, as it at length quieted expectation.

[94ᵛ] They had desired to make their visitts to those great lords who they understood to be chosen of the commission for their business and to whom they had brought with them letters commendatory from the States and the Prince of Orange, but they were prevented by diverse of them as by the Earle of Arrundell, the Lord Chamberlin, the Lord Admiral, the Lord Marques Hamilton Mr. Secretary Vane, and others who, giving them the first visits, were repayed them after, though in a promiscuous order, without punctual regard who of them were of preceding quality.

After their accesse of private audience to both their majestyes they demanded the like to be given them to the prince and Duke of York by themselves, and to the two princesses by themselves which was granted. And having one day presented their respects to the Prince and his brother at Somerset House, they two days after did the like to the princesses in the same place where the Lord of Somersdyke carrying the word for the other three (with an extent of speech too long perhaps and too serious for the years of whom it was addressed to) it was by me in my interpretation (with reason I thought) contracted. He in the first place presented to her highnes the service of the Estates General and of the Prince of Orange, represented their affections and the honour they themselves had by their imployment hither about a businesse of so particular relation [95] to her royall highnes (*Son Altesse Royale*) as he alwayes styled her. He after descended to the especiall charge (he said) they had of presenting to her acceptance the most humble service of the young Prince William of Nassau, son to the prince of Orange and his ambition to become hers in a newer condition, for which, that he might make himself more acceptable and better understood of her, when he should be so happy as to perform the journey he had designed hither, he was become (he said) a diligent student of the English toung and hoped so to profitt in the study of it as to be made able to persuade and prevail with her hignes to make a journy with his attendance on her person to the low countryes, where the States and Prince of Orange, should be most happy to see and serve her, and towards which he and his colleagues should be most glad they might receive from her selve some words of encouragement, etc. An expression judged by them that heard it overforward and too particular for a speaker of his reputed wisdom to a hearer little more than nine years of age, especially the treaty having been not long before begun and indefinitely propounded for one of the two princesses and more nominatively for the younger than the elder, and the commissioners for his majesty having not yet once met about it, [95ᵛ] passing from the princesses Mary to her sister, the lady Elizabeth, he framed his words more suitable to her infancy using only a plaine and brief complement without touch of any particulars.

Two or three dayes after they had a conference in the Council Chamber to a more particular purpose with the lords Commissioners appointed to treat with them. These were the earl of Arundel, lord high Marshal the Bishop of London,[4] Lord Treasurer, the earl of Northumberland, high Admiral, Marquis Hamilton, Master of the Horse, the Earle of Holland, Groom of the Stole, and Sir Henry Vane, principall secretary. To these were after added the two Lord Chamberlins of the king and queen, the Earles of Pembroke and Dorsett.

The 19th of January I carried the Kings pleasure to these ambassadors for their repayre first to these commissioners and after to his majesty himself and the queen jointly in her Quarters. An access not usually granted (to both their majestyes at once) for a private audience, but so it was appointed with their majestyes intentions (as after appeared) at it to declare their joint assent (which the ambassadors told me was that day given them) for a more particular and immediate treaty for the elder sister thought and reported till then to be for the younger. They had their audience to this gracious purpose in the queens Withdrawing Chamber and two dayes after had a conference to the same purpose with the commissioners.

[96] Sir Edward Littleton, Lord Chiefe Justice of the Common Pleas[5] (of his majestyes Privy Councell and upon the flight of the Lord Finch, from the punishment threatened to him by Parliament, made Lord Keeper of the Great Seale) was the first day of Hillary Terme to ride in solemnity to Westminster Hall for his investiture there. He set forth between nine and ten of the clock from Exeter House in the Strand (then the dwelling of the lady Elizabeth

---

4 William Juxon, bishop of London.
5 Edward Littleton, 1st lord Lyttleton.

Hatton) accompanied by many great lords and others on horseback. The lord keeper himself rode foremost (divers gentlemen of the Inns of court, officers of the inferior courts of law and servants marching before him on foot) between the lord treasurer and lord privy seale, all the lords, promiscuously wythout regard of theyr dew ranck, following after them, the judges, knights and gentlemen, promiscuously also, mingled in a fayre equipage and number. Then the judges and chief officers of severall courts of justice and after all came above a hundred coaches. Sir John Banks (before his majestyes attorney generall) and now successor of the mentioned lord keeper in place of cheef justice, rode in the same manner, and so accompanyed, about a seven night later.

[96ᵛ] When the two ambassadors extraordinary from the king of Spayne (marquis de Velada and marquis Vergilio Malvezzi) had spent here, the one ten monthes, and the other nine, in theyr unpenetrable negotiation,[6] the former came to my house the [blank] of January, and acquainting me with the revocacion he had received from the king his master, and intimation of his pleasure for his repaire to his charge in Flanders (whither, he sayd, the marquis Malvezzi had order also to go in company) he requested me to signify so much to his majesty, and that within four dayes they intended to present their request for their parting audience. This they desired might be given them in private, though not of custome, but as esteeming it the greater favor and more approaching the condition they affected of domesticks. This imparted to the king by my lord chamberlin (I present) had his majestyes consent, and brought them together with the ordinary, don Alonso de Cardenas on Thursday, the 4th of February, by the way of the Privy Garden and Galleryes to the kings withdrawing Chamber where, after some time of all their joint conference with his majesty, the Marquis de Velada approaching nearer his person (the other two some what retyring) had his ear a whyle alone by his interpreter;[7] the like successively had the other two, and after rejoyning all as before, they all took leave and departed.

[97] They had sent to me the evening before to move for an audience of the Queen immediately after the Kings, but I knowing it improper to present to her majesty their request at so short a warning, reserved it for the next days motion to be given with more conveniency on Sunday following. In the mean time her majestyes pleasure and leisure (it seemed) towards the instant

6 Because of his own acute needs, the Cardinal Infante had retained in Flanders the funds that might have been lent to Charles.
7 Henry Taylor.

of this audience serving for a present dispatch, I received notice of it at my first entrance into the Privy Gallery from one of her majestyes Gentlemen Ushers and from him gave it to the Ambassadors that having finished their audience of the king I should immediately bring them to the presence of the queen and so did, passing with them through his majestyes Privy Chamber to the queen in her Withdrawing Chamber, where they performed that office of leave taking so much sooner then they expected.

The day after they requested me to procure them an access to the Princes at Richmond (not once speaking of the princesses *et pour cause*) who were then come to London and known by them to be so; but the day that I was determined to send thither word came to the Queen that the Prince had all the signs of the small pox towards, which to be more fully assured of, I went my self to Richmond (though I heard he was out of danger of that disease) and found him not unwilling (no more than I did those that had the chief charge of his person, the Earle of Newcastle and the Bishop of Chichester) to be freed of that not necessary visit, especially his Highnesse being for three or four dayes to keep his Chamber to take Physick, and the ambassadors also having complyed so far to the tender of their respects as to have made a demand of their accesse, which excused with the reason of his highnesses indisposition, might (and did) pass for satisfaction, as these two persons did acknowledge as fully as if they had performed it. These reasons intimated by me at my returne unto those Ambassadours passed unto them for current and diverted their intended Journey to take their leaves of his Highnesse.

[97ᵛ] The 6th of February, the States Ambassadors sent to me a gentleman with intimation that their majestyes having given them an allowance of their access that day to the princess, but not assigned them the time and place, they desired me to know their pleasures more particularly, who appointing them Somerset House at four of the clock, they came thither all four, when Monsieur Aersens carrying the word, said to her: Madam, The last time we came to your royall highness, it was from the States of the United Provinces and the Prince of Orange, as to the Princess Mary eldest daughter to the king of Great Britayne, but now, Madam, we come to your royall highness from the King your father, not only as to his eldest daughter but as to [98] the mistress of the young Prince William of Orange, for so we have leave from both their majestyes to style your royall highness. This said, I looked towards the Countess of Roxburgh (her highnesses Governess[8] who stood at her elbow) and said, Madam, these words of the ambassador will be more proper for your

[8] Lady Jean Ker, countess of Roxburgh.

Ladyships interpretation than for myne. Truly, my lord, answered the lady (looking toward Monsieur Aersens) I am surprised with the significacion you have made of their majestyes pleasure and leave, as you say, for the style you have uttered, as I know not how the princess, or I for her, can modestly answer you. Madam, replyed the ambassador you need not doubt how the Princesse can with modesty make answer, since it is accorded by both their majestyes that we should speak in the stile we have spoken. This said, the countess applyed herselfe to the princess and, prompting her with a few words, they all departed without any notice taken of the queens presence there, who stood all the tyme of these passages in a corner of the roome concealed wyth her mask on.

The 10th of February, the king went privately by water to the higher house of Parliament, and there investing himself in his robes and the lords in theirs, he made declaration of the assent he had given to a treaty of marriage between his eldest daughter and the young Prince of Orange, which he had entertained, he said, and given his assent to for three especiall [98ᵛ] reasons. The first for the cause of religion, which their being one with ours there should be no dispensation. The second, for the neighbourhood and correspondency more useful and necessary to us than that of any other nation. And the third, for the good of his sister and of her children for their reestablishment in the Palatinate which motives had brought him to proceed so far in the treaty, as all might be said in a manner concluded, after he should have given the signification he now intended of it to the Parliament, and had received their assents upon the consideration of the propositions set down between him and the ambassadors and which he there delivered to them in writing.

[99] While the two Spanish ambassadors extraordinary were preparing for their departure, I moved my Lord Chamberlin, and his lordship the king, about the presents to be bestowed on them, as of custome. The usuall ones of 2000 ounces of gilded plate to each of them were at first resolved on, and a warrant signed for them and sent to the Jewell House and the plate alredy provided by the Kings Goldsmith, when his majestyes pleasure signified to Sir James Palmer, gentleman Usher of his Privy Chamber and Superintendant of the Manufacture of Tapistry erected by his majesty, brought forth a discourse and this a change of the present designed to the Marquis of Velada from plate to hangings, whereof four peeces appointed consisting of 217 Flemish elnes and valued at 5 £ the elne⁹ would come to about 1000 £. This was done upon consideration had by his majesty of the serviceable respects

⁹ The ell measured, if Flemish, 27 inches; if English, 45.

extraordinaryly given him by the said Marquis while he was in Spayne,[10] as having therein been of more, and of more ancient merit towards him, than the other ambassador Malvezzi. Yet this was without any shew of considerable and visible difference in the distribution. The plate, after the kings rate and payment for it, amounting to 800 £ at 8 s. per ounce though not worth to be sold above 6 s. per ounce viz. 600 £, and the hangings, with regard to the domestick manufacture, estimated at little more charge to his Majestye, but not requiring as the other did present payment. So, at this change of the property concluded on, the [99ᵛ] Master of the Jewell House and I agreed, and went both together to the ambassadors house with the severall presents. He with the plate to the Marquis de Malvezzis quarter and I with the hangings, accompanyed by Mr. Kynnersly, Chief Officer of the Removing Wardrobe, from whence they were of course to be issued, to the marquis of Veladas quarter, whom I thought fit to tell him (though from no formal instruction given me) that the king was pleased to send him a regale, not of gylded plate, the matter usuall of presents bestowed on ambassadors, but of tapistry for the ornament of his chamber where he and his posterity might behold the mark of his majestyes more especiall regard to him, witnessed, I said, by his majestyes own coat of arms which he had purposely commanded to be set on them, etc. The ambassador seemed much satisfyed with the expression and was after very inquisitive how and when he might have two peeces more made suitable to these four; so few being not sufficient (which to say truth was a narrowing of the favour) to hang a room, but of an indifferent largesse.

This Marquess de Velada, the day before his parting gave me by the hand of the Steward four score peeces with a frugall example (which the Spaniards of all nations knew best how to follow) of the Conde de Oñate. To the Marshall of the Ceremonyes he gave 12 peeces, much beneath his hungry expectation, and to the Yeoman of the Wardrobe 10 £ peeces.

[100] Towards the time of these ambassadors preparation for their departure, the Marques de Velada intreated me to move his majestye, as I did, for one of his ships to transport them safely to Dunkirk, which was granted, and neerer the time of his departure, he made request to me by my Lord Admirall, that a Quarter Master (or some other of his charge in the Kings ship he should go in) might be written for (as he was) and was imployed to come up to London and pass down by the land's end in a bark hyred by the ambassador himself for the safer passage of their goods to the kings ship ryding in the Downes, which was also granted. They went hence the 15th of February; (when though offered

---

[10] Charles's visit to the court of Philip IV in 1623.

by me as of custome my attendance and the kings barges for their conduction to Gravesend) they excused the use of them saying their own coaches should serve them and so did, yet no further then to Blackwall, where they had barges and boates attending to take them in for their transport to Gravesend and coaches there to the Downes. [100ᵛ] About the midst of February the Duke de Vendosme, refuged hither from the dangers threatened him[11] upon an attempt he was charged with against the person of the Cardinal de Richelieu, by subornation of certain persons to murder him, presented himself privately to their majestyes in the queens withdrawing Chamber, without other introduction than of Mr. Henry Germain, sufficient for me then present to containe my self from all publick demonstration of Ceremonyes toward him, and only to carry me the next day (as the honour I had by my service formerly done him might exact) to his lodging in no better than a French cookes house in the Strand, wherein he at the instant of his arrivall bestowed himself *en particulier* till three or four days after that at his own charge and with his own servants, he was provided of better accomodation in a private house of the Piazza. He saluted the queen his sister at the first sight of her majesty not other wise than with a *Baise Mains*.

[101] Towards the end of February news came to court that the Prince Elector Palatine[12] was (not with standing the care taken for prevention by the despatch of an express to Holland) arrived at Gravesend and that he would be the next day at London, as he was with a private accesse to his majestye and without public appearance at the feast of St. George held at that time, and he a knight of that Order, he was six or seaven dayes lodged at Essex House after removed thence to the Duke of Lenoxes lodgings (usually called the Princes at Whitehall) where, as I was told, a Gentleman was sent to him with intimation that his Highness should have there the attendance of such officers and others of the Kings House as he should think necessary or useful for his service, but that for his dyet he might be pleased to appoint the quantity and quality of it but the charge to be his own.

St. Georges Feast being appointed for the 2nd of March and the States ambassadors having the day before expressed to me their desires to see that solemnity, especially the person of his majestye, the Prince and knights of the order sitting at Dynner, there came to me a gentleman of the Earl and countess

[11] His previous visit was Nov. 1631 – Jan. 1632: see III 128.

[12] The Count Palatine had been released from confinement at Vincennes by Richelieu's order after Secretary Windebank's embassy in March 1640. He came to London to protest the marriage with the house of Orange and was rumored to seek the princess for his own marriage (CSP V 1640–42, p. 133).

of Arundel, in both their names, with a request (by me to be presented to the States ambassadors) that whereas they might perhaps perform too hard a penance to fast till they should see the king at his dynner, as they understood they intended, or after he had dyned to return home fasting, that they would be pleased either before or after to take a little refection at the earl of Arundels lodgings in court, this offer thankfully acknowledged, they chose rather after, than before, the sight of his majestye to make use of it. So after some little time of his Majestyes sitting at table, I asking him of his pleasure for their time of entrance had his command instantly to bring them in, the second course of meat being not yet served up, nor the Heralds entered to proclaime the kings tytles as accustomed. Of these four ambassadors two, Monsieur Haenvliet and Monsieur Joachimi only, presented themselves there to his majesty, the other two being by an indisposition suddenly seizing them the day before, forced to keep home.

It was a fault found and censured by many that they did after some few words of complement with his majesty put on their hats, against example at least that had been observed by any of the like done by either French, Spanish or other ambassadors, considering they came not hither as guests invited by his majesty but as voluntaryes out of their own curiosityes and desires and not to an audience to treat their masters business, but of this query.

From his majesty I conducted them down to the Prince and knights with whom they briefly complemented in their passage and thence to their dynner with the Countess of Arundel (the Earl being necessarily absent at dynner with his Companions of the Garter) where they had three or fower lords for company and an intertaynment suitable.

[102] The ambassadors of the States after their so diverse audiences of his majesty and conferences with the lords Commissioners for debate and remove of questions about the marriage had a meeting with their lordships the 15th of March at the Councill Chamber and at the same time an access to the King in his Withdrawing Chamber, where, having given their finall account and received his Majestyes approbation for, and to all, and after returning againe to the Councell Chamber, they there in the presence of the Lords Commissioners set their hands and seales to the articles. And the next night that the world might take a more publick notice of the treatys full conclusion they made bonefires before their houses in the Piazza,[13] but amongst us none were made, either by public order or for expression of private affection, *et pour Cause.*

---

[13] In Covent Garden.

About the beginning of March, after the many confirmed reports of the revolt of Portugal, news came to court of the arrival of two ambassadors at Falmouth and of one at Portsmouth imployed from the new crowned king there, John the fourth Duke of Braganza to his majesty. The two former don Antonio de Almada and don Francesco de Andrade[14] were [102ᵛ] signified to have one joynt commission attended by a Secretary of the ambassage, don Antonio de Soaza de Macedo,[15] and another don Tristan de Moncia,[16] to be sent single to the States of the United Provinces, this latter coming first to London, as *in transitu*, and understanding that an ambassage from those States was already here treating a marriage, etc. made offer to be their first visitor, but this excused by them, they went first to him and he the next day to them, dyning with them, together with the most of his trayne, as freely as he was invited friendly, haveing in their passage here treated with diverse English commanders for their kings personal service in Portugal, but without resolution, they requested and had allowance of one of his Majestyes ships for their transport to Holland. The other two imployed to his Majestye remained in the mean tyme in the west country without further advance than Salisbury, whence sending before to his Majestye the Secretary of their ambassage for knowledge of his pleasure of their admittance to his presence in quality of a kings ambassador *viz.* from John the 4th King of Portugal, and this after severall debates assented to, they received an expression of his Majestyes pleasure that they should be in all points and formes received and have the like treatment and accomodation in all as had been given to the kings of France and Spaynes ambassadours. Whereupon, I propounding to my Lord Chamberlin that their motion hither having been from the west as that of other ambassadours had been from the east [103] and south (the most of them landing at the Downes or at Dover and proceeding to Gravesend where I of course caryed them the kynges welcome) there might be a correspondence held with these, both for incounter and reception of places and persons, if I should be sent to them with the Kynges welcome to Staines, and an earle to Braynford, for theyr imbarking there in his Majestyes barge down, as of other kinges ambassadours from Greenwich up to London.

This course approved of, I the 23rd of March went by coach to Staines, where having performed my charge and coming back that night to London

---

[14] Antão de Almeida and Francesco de Andrade, ambassadors extraordinary (April 1641–April 1642) of John IV of Portugal. They sought recognition of the new regime and a new commercial treaty as well as permission to recruit troops for the war against Spain.

[15] Antao de Souza, secretary of the embassy.

[16] Tristan de Mendoza Furtado, ambassador to the Dutch Republic, which welcomed an alliance.

I, the 25th, returned againe to Staines and there in theyr company and in theyr owne hyred coaches brought them to East Braynford, where I having before appoynted the Kinges barge and five others to lay ready for theyr transport, and my lord Chamberlin having made choyce of his sonn in law the earle of Carnarvon for theyr reception there and conduction to London, they towards evening landed at Westminster stayres, entered there the Kynges coach to the Kinges house, though scarce to hundred paces distant,[17] in correspondence with other ambassadours use of it from Tower wharfe, and with the attendance of two coaches more sent from the States ambassadors and myne owne, to theyr first supper at the charge of his Majestye.

[103 ᵛ] I could not that evening procure a person fitting to present them with the kynges third welcome, as of custome, the lord chamberlin being busied in affayres of Parliament and his majesty retyred, but the next day after dynner Mr. William Herbert, his lordships second sonn, was made choyce of and brought them that complement.

The third day of theyr entertainment at the kings charge, being Sunday and most proper for theyr public audience, his majesty gave it them in the Banketting House, the queen not present, with regard of her then indisposition, the prince only there standing by his majesty. Their introducer was the earl of Cumberland newly, by the decease of his father,[18] come to that dignity. With him went for assistants the lords Strange and the lord Herbert of Cherburys eldest son, and a younger son of the earl of Lindsey, and half a score gentlemen of the privy chamber and with use of the kinges coach (not the queens) and nine others. The two ambassadors sat in the coach on the hinder end both together, the earl and the lord Strange before, and at the sides, the son, grand child and a son in law of the ambassadors, their interpretation was by a servant of theyr owne, an Englishman following them from Portugal.

The next morning, after seven meals, parting from the kings diet, and the day following from his house, they went to one they had hired in Lincolns Inn Fields.

[105] After some time of hindrance to the young prince of Orange his passage by cross wynds, these at last coming favorable brought him in three ships (the residue of his fleet turning for the Downs) the 19th of April to Gravesend, where I then received a letter from the ambassadors jointly, who were the day before gone thither to meet his highnes as they always stiled him, myself being disabled by sicknesse to repair personally to him, giving me

[17] Sir Abraham Williams' house.
[18] Henry Clifford (see n. 1) had succeeded to the title.

notice of his landing and requesting me to acquaint my Lord Chamberlin and Sir Henry Vane with what they had written that his highnesses accomodation for [105ᵛ] coaches, lodging of his trayne, and whatever else might tend to his reception, might be taken into care and with convenient speed resolved on, the princes particular affection, after a tedious seas journy, carrying him to go by land. These letters from the ambassadors I sent to my Lord Chamberlin, my weakness then not suffering me to go my self to his Lordship, who instantly imparting them to their majestyes, the Earle of Lindsey, Lord High Chamberlin of England, designed before for the princes reception at Gravesend, was immediately sent to, to be ready the next day for the service. Towards which I forthwith imployed my officer for the taking up of 20 hackney coaches and for the sending to Gravesend of half a score barges, with supplies of light horsemen as need should require, for transport of such of his trayne by water, as should be either not fit or not disposed to go by land. The next day my indisposition should not keep me from going myself to court, to prevent ill understanding or disorder to which purpose, the Lord Marshall, the Lord Chamberlin and myself were called to confer with his majesty, where the first question propounded by my Lord Marshal was what tytle should be given him, when the king looking towards me, I interposed that haveing been before hand curious, as I had reason, to [106] informe myself of the ambassadors (for myne my own application when I should be sent to him with the Kings first welcome) I was answered that the style usually given, as due to him was highnesse and this, I added, his majesty had seen given him the letters those ambassadors had written to me and I had communicated to my Lord Chamberlin. To which the Earl Marshall offering to make objection, the king interrupting him said, the tytle that hath been, or is now given him can not be civilly denyed him. Then Sir, replyed the Earle, the French king having been the first that gave the tytle of hignes to the father, it will be given first to the son by your majestyes daughter.

From this, they fell to other purpose concerning his reception and ordered that being come on the way as far as Blackheath, he should there leaving the kings travayling coach (not thought on till by me moved) for as fit to be sent with the earle of Lindsey for his use from Gravesend to Blackheath and enter his majestyes coach of state, that should be ready there accompanyed by the Queens, the lords coaches and other voluntaryes for his own solemn entry into the city and passage through it to Whitehall, without makeing stops at [106ᵛ] Arundel House his appointed lodging, and there after his descent from his coach to be receyved by the prince on the top of the new stayre leading into the Banqueting House, where his majestye would first receive him and thense take him with him to the queens quarter.

But this course, when all was fitted for it, was sodaynly altered, and his passage appointed to be straight to the queen and in her Withdrawing Chamber towards which ascending up the great Stone Stayrs to the Gard Chamber entring the Privy Chamber he was received by the Prince (wayted on by the Earl Marshall and Lord Chamberlin) and by them conducted through the lobby, the narrow entry next it, and the queens Privy Chamber not capable of one quarter of the company that went before and followed him. The part of service that I owed of course and duty to receive and attend him at, and from Gravesend being hindered by my sicknesse, I supplyed to my power by wayteing at the Court Gate when his coach arrived there when stepping to the side of it, I requested Monsieur Brederode (the precedent ambassadour) to excuse the unseasonable ill fortune of my sicknesse, that would not permit me to measure more paces for his service, then remained from that place to the presence of their Majestyes and back again. To which, being told who I was, I had from him a most noble acknowledgement of thanks, etc.

[107ᵛ] The prince having passed four or five dayes in giving and receiving visits, the Venetian ambassador wrote to me to procure an appointment of time for a visit his Lordship meant to make him adding that his Excellency pretended that his treatment should be in no sort different from that given by his father to the ambassador of Venice in Holland. This letter communicated by me to the prince I returned his highness answer as it was given me, *viz.* that his Excellency might rest assured to receive the like treatment in all points as the Venetian ambassadors had received in Holland but that at the returne of his visit his highness did not less expect to be also treated in all points answerable to the style practiced by that ambassador.

[108] The same day I had a message brought me by the Portugal ambassadors secretary tending to the same purpose as to the Venetians, but not with so much punctuality, which imparting likewise to the prince, I had answer and returned it that their Excellencies might rest assured to be treated by the Prince of Orange in all points, as he would treat any other kings ambassadours whereupon these first (as haveing first formally demanded what the other had first propounded) came the next day to his highness, were by him received at their descent from their coach, had the hand given them both at doors, and sitting down and were after accompanyed by him to their coach.

[109] The 29th of Aprill at a private audience assigned by the king to the Portugal Ambassadors at two a clock and the Venetian at three, those came so late and this so soon as when the former was descending about the midst of the stayres, the other was ascending at the bottom, which I perceiving and apprehending some unproper encounter to follow made a sign to the Venetians

Gentleman Usher for his Lords diversion on the left hand into an unmarkt corner of the Garden whilst the Portugal ambassadours past straight on at the right hand without observation and with prevention of their encounters.

All articles being agreed on between his majestye his Commissioners and those of the States to the purpose of the marriage, it was suddenly designed for the second of May, when the day before the Portugal ambassadors sent to me their secretary with demand, whether it were to be solemnized in publick and whether if any ambassadours were invited to it, they might not expect that honor or if in private whether they might not be allowed some corner (as *Incognito*) to see the manner of it. I answered it was intended to be carryed so in private, and so far from any ambassadors invitation to it, as I knew their majestyes were resolved that unless it were some great lords and ladyes resident in court no persons of eminentest quality should be called to it much lesse any ambassadors, whereof if any one should be invited all might expect to be so, and for their Excellencyes of Portugall [109 ᵛ] to be bestowed in a corner, where they might see and not be seen would be impossible, the Kings private household chapel wherein they were to be marryed being very little and affording no such convenience. So, as without further reply the secretary returned in appearance satisfyed.

The proceeding to the maryage was in this manner. About nine in the morning I repayring to the court (weak and indisposed as I was) found there the earle of Holland, appointed for the Princes conduction from Arundel house to court, with attendance of some other young lords in the Kings, Queens, Princes, and fifteen or sixteen noblemens coaches with six horses each, for summons whereof I had not received order till towards midnight before. This lord thought it requisite, upon my intimation for avoydance of surprise, to send me before with notice of his readiness to set forth for his highnesses conduction to court, yet came not thither tyll towards Eleaven, when entering the first court with the kinges and queenes coaches (not permitted before to any but the queen mother) they descended at the foot of the great stone stayres and ascended to the Great Chamber, which passing through, and through the Presence, the lobby and the narrow passage leading from the kinges quarter to the queenes Privy Chamber and into her Withdrawing Chamber, where the prince being left among the lords and ladyes, the earle marshall and lord chamberlin returned to the queenes Privy Chamber for consultation to distinguish between such of the princes followers, as were of properest quality to accompany him in his march down to the chapel, and such as were (for prevention of intruders, not of his trayne) fit to be bestowed before hand in [110] seates there for the most commodious sight of the ceremony, wherein the lord chamberlin so bestirred himself as all at last being brought to fair order, the prince descended. Ushered fyrst by the Lord Goring, Vice chamberlin, myself following next with the princes governor, next us the heralds, the lord marshall and the lord chamberlin. The prince himself being closely sided by the four ambassadors and immediately followed by the prince Talmond,[19] Count Henry of Nassau, Count Solmes,[20] the Landsgrave, and two or three more particularly made choyce of to march with, or next him. Being entered the chapel, his highness proceeded to a place about the midst of it (more towards the Communion Table) seperate from the rest, raised a foot above the ground, with a passage free about it and environed with a banister about three foot high, covered with cloth of gold and the pavement spread with carpets. The entrance into it, being of about five foot, double enlarged within, and the issue answerable to the entry. Within this place, the prince and the ambassadors only entryng, those chief of his trayne mentioned were by me placed close without the banisters, whereon leaning they had a most convenient standing. After a while entred the princess led by her brothers the prince of Wales and the duke of York wayted on by her bridesmayds (young daughters of principall noblemen) and her Governess, the Countess of Roxburgh, who with regard to her charge had been appointed the only woman to stand within the rayle, but the young ladyes being little and promising little incumberance, were after also admitted into it, after whom, by example, followed 3 or 4 great ladyes but were intreated to pass forwards, as they did, to the right hand corner of the chappell.

[110ᵛ] This thus ordered, his majesty came attended by the Lord Marshall, Lord High Chamberlin, Lord Treasurer, Lord Chamberlin of the Household and three or four other great lords, and entering the place separated, by this time filled beyond order, the queen and queen mother entred last into her closet above and there were beholders during the ceremony. Whereat the Bishop of Ely, Dean of the chappell,[21] officiating in word and forme in all points as is in the Book of Common Prayer, the King, giving the bride to the bridegroom, he putting the ring on her finger and the bishop blessing them, a hymn (purposely framed for the work in hand) was sung, others following, prayers read, and sermon preached by the Bishop of Rochester.[22]

The princess going first out of the chappell, as now a married woman, the ambassadors siding her and the prince of Orange following attended by marryed men of his trayne and others, they marched the way they came and

---

[19] Henri Taleran, count of Chalais and Sciales.
[20] Frederick Henry, count of Solms-Braunfels.
[21] Mathew Wren, bishop of Ely.
[22] John Warner, bishop of Rochester.

presented themselves to their majestyes most cheerful reception in the queens withdrawing Chamber by the time it was past two of the clock, the ceremony of the church having taken up an hour or more. When I conducting the ambassadors, as I had order, to the quarter prepared for their repose and dinner (some time the lodging of the duchess of Chevreuse next King Street) they turned to the Privy Garden Gate called for their coaches, appointed by themselves before hand there to attend them, for their returne home. This I should have wondered at, had I not had before a hint of their intention, but faining the ignorant and telling them that was not their way to the dynner, [111] Monsieur Brederode answered they humbly thanked his majesty for the honour he intended them, but that they having business which required dispatch they would go home to take some refection and towards eight of the clock, by which time they supposed the king would have supped, returne to the same place where they requested me to meet them for their guidance to his majesty that they might be present (as necessarily they must at the last part of that happy days work) and see the marryed couple bedded together. I leaving them to their pleasure, accompanyed some of the princes gentlemen to the dinner prepared for the ambassadours, whither came Mr. Treasurer of the Household to bear them company. After dynner acquainting my Lord Chamberlin with their formality, I had from his lordship some further light and reason for it, as how that the day before, the king having signified his pleasure *viz.*, that (in regard of the speedy dispatch he intended and the ambassadors pressed of the marriage) he would have it pass with the greatest privacy that might be and would not therefore have so much as a show of a publick feast at it, but that the dynner and supper of that day should be kept in his Withdrawing Chamber, where none should sitt as guests, but the king, the queen, the queen mother, the prince, the duke of York and the marryed couple. With which restriction the ambassadors, not pleased, formalized themselves to some noblemen as a course derogating from their quality, use and trust in such a business not to be admitted that day to eat with the bride and bridgroom. To which it was answered that if they would have the solemnity and feast to be carryed in publick, as it was at the marriage of [111ᵛ] the Elector Palatine and the Lady Elizabeth,[23] the preparative must be answerable, solemne invitations made of ambassadors to it, as then, severall tables kept in court, the king and queen to be served by themselves, masks and showes in time to be prepared and set forth, which would require a months time and more and would hinder, not hasten, the dispatch of the marriage, which they the ambassadours so much pressed for, with these reasons they

[23] 14 February 1614.

seemed to rest satisfyed, but not so, as that they would either assent or refuse, to set at a table (as I have said) provided elsewhere for them. The order of setting at the brides table was thus. The king sitting in the middle, had at his right hand the queen mother, at his left his queen, beneath her at the board end, the bride, at the returne the prince and the duke of York, and towards the midst on that side the bridegroom. So, they sat also at supper, not any of the great lords and ladyes, except some few, being allowed entrance into the room they eat in. The non appearance of the Prince Elector in that company was wondered at but reasons were given for it by some of the privacy professed to be intended by his majesty, by others that the Prince Elector having underhand opposed the conjunction and the prince of Orange resenting it, there had as yet no visits passed between them, which might serve also at that tyme for the ambassadours exclusion.

At the hour that the ambassadors had requested my attendance at the Garden Gate for their conduction to his majestyes presence, after supper they came, were wayted on by me, to the withdrawing Chamber and thence about ten of the clock [112] (when word was brought that the bride and bridgroom were in bed) into the bed chamber where they were witnesses of as much of the consommation of that marriage as so young years and the formes used in that kind would afford.

The [blank] of May my Lord Chamberlin sent me word of an audience assigned to the ambassadors at two of the clock, wherewith I acquainting them, they returned me answer by their secretary, that they would not only themselves wayte on his majesty but also the young prince of Orange with them, as they did, by the private passage of the Garden and were received as formerly, only with this difference in one particular that the King not only not invited the ambassadors to cover, but himself also all the time of the audience stood uncovered, with this reason, by conjecture, that the prince being not of the commission (though having the honour of precedence given him in all places by the ambassadors) could not cover by the tytle they did, and had no reason to expect the allowance of it there, considering the disparity betwixt his majesty and his highness. The next audience they had was to obtain by their humble request and reasons the company of the princess with the Prince of Orange and them in their return now hastening, as the season of action now requireth to Holland, but their reasons proved uneffectuall.[24]

---

[24] She left England for Holland in February 1642 with Henrietta.

APPENDICES

I

FOREIGN DIPLOMATS IN LONDON
OCTOBER 1628 – MAY 1641

Representatives with dates of residence and diplomatic rank are placed first. Visitors, if noted by Finet, are placed at the end of each country, but it is unlikely that these were the only foreigners received officially at Whitehall.

BOHEMIA (court of the exiled queen at The Hague): 1626–1640, Sir Abraham Williams, Agent; March – April 1633, John Casimir Kolb, Agent Extraordinary. *Visitors*: Nov. 1635 – June 1637, Aug. – Sept. 1639, March 1641, Charles Louis (Elector Palatine); Feb. 1636 – June 1637, Rupert.

DENMARK (Kingdom of): June 1627 – April 1632, J. G. Woulffen, Agent; Aug. 1627 – Sept. 1628, George Brahe and Christian Tomson, Ambassadors Extraordinary; Aug. 1628 – May 1629, Paulus Rosencrantz, Ambassador Extraordinary; Aug. – Sept. 1640, Gregory Krabbe and Cornelius Ulefeld, Ambassadors Extraordinary. *Visitors*: Oct. 1628, Thomas Ferentz; Sept. 1630, Feb. 1640, Ulrich, duke of Holstein; Sept. 1633, the lord of Rantzau-Hohenfeld.

DUTCH REPUBLIC (The States General of the United Provinces): June 1624 – June 1641, Albert Joachimi, Ambassador; Feb. 1628 – Feb. 1629, Adriaen Pawe and Arnaut van Randwyck, Ambassadors Extraordinary; March 1632 – July 1634, Gouvert Brassert, deputy; March 1636 – July 1637, Cornelius van Beverne, Ambassador Extraordinary; Nov. 1639 – March 1640, Francis Aerssens, Ambassador Extraordinary; Jan. – May 1641, Jan van der Kerkhoven, lord of Heenvliet, and Jan de Brederode and Francis Aerssens, Ambassadors Extraordinary. *Visitor*: Jan. 1638, Gaspard Vosberghen.

THE HOLY ROMAN EMPIRE: April–Oct. 1636, Jan. 1637, Clement Radolt, Agent Extraordinary of Ferdinand II; Sept. 1630, H. Volker, Deputy of the Hansa; June 1632 – Jan. 1633, Berthold Müller, Deputy of the Hansa; Oct. 1635 – Feb. 1636, Leeuw van Aitzema, Deputy of the Hansa; Sept. 1636, H. Ponikau, Agent Extraordinary of the duchy of Saxe-Weimar. *Visitors*: Oct. 1629 – March 1630, Francis Charles, duke of Saxe-Lauenburg; Oct. 1629, Julius Frederick, duke of Württemberg; Oct. 1632, George and Louis, dukes of Liegnitz and Brieg; Nov.–Dec. 1635, Otto Louis, margrave of Rheinfels; Jan. 1636, Ulrich, duke of Württemberg; June 1637, Lev Vilem Kaunitz of Bohemia; Oct. 1638, John, duke of Hesse-Darmstadt; Oct. 1639, Sylvius Frederick, duke of Württemberg.

FLORENCE (Duchy of): 1625–41, Amerigo Salvetti, Agent.

FRANCE (Kingdom of): Aug. 1629 – April 1630, Charles de l'Aubespine, marquis of Chateauneuf-sur-Cher, Ambassador Extraordinary; Feb. 1630 – May 1633, François du Val, marquis of Fontenay-Mareuil, Ambassador; May 1632, Melchior Mitte de Miolans, marquis of Saint-Chaumont, Ambassador Extraordinary; May 1633, M. de Mouselin, Agent Extraordinary; Oct. 1633 – Jan. 1634, M. de Boutard, Agent; July 1634 – Dec. 1636, Jean d'Angennes, marquis of Pougny, Ambassador; March 1635 – July 1637, Henri de Saint-Nectaire, or Senneterre, marquis of La Ferté Nabert, Ambassador Extraordinary; July–Dec. 1637, M. de Baigneaux, Secretary; Jan. 1638 – Jan. 1640, Pierre de Bellièvre, sieur de Grignon, Ambassador Extraordinary; Aug. 1638, M. de la Varenne, Agent Extraordinary; Jan. 1640 – June 1641, Jean de Montereuil, Secretary, Agent after Oct. 1640; Sept. 1640, Guillaume de Saint-Ravy, Agent Extraordinary. *Vistors*: Nov. 1631 – Jan. 1632, Feb. 1641, Cesar de Bourbon, duke of Vendôme; Jan. 1632, M. de Biscarat; Oct. 1632, Luca de Fabronne; April 1638 – April 1640, Marie de Rohan-Montbazon, duchess of Chevreuse; Oct. 1638 – Sept. 1641, Marie de Médicis.

LORRAINE (Duchy of): April 1636, François du Jars, baron of Rochechuart, Agent Extraordinary; March 1640, Henri-Charles de Livron, sieur de Ville, Agent Extraordinary.

MANTUA (Duchy of): Sept. 1629. Count Francesco d'Odelingo, Ambassador Extraordinary.

MOROCCO (Sultanate of): June 1628 – Jan. 1629, Mohammed Clavecho and Ibrahim Mocaden, Deputies of rebel city of Saley; Oct. 1638 – March 1638, Indar ben Abdullah and Robert Blake, Ambassadors Extraordinary.

PAPAL STATES. *Visitors*: Dec. 1634 – Dec. 1636, Gregorio Panzani; July 1636 – Aug. 1639, George Conn; Sept. 1639 – July 1641, Count Carlo Rosetti.

PERSIA (Sultanate of): July 1636 – March 1637, Ali Baba, Ambassador.

POLAND (Kingdom of): Aug.–Sept. 1631, George Albert Rakowsky, Ambassador Extraordinary; Feb. 1633, Janusz Radziwill, Ambassador Extraordinary; July 1633, June 1636, John Zawadsky, Ambassador Extraordinary; Aug.–Oct. 1637, Andrew Rey Nablowitz, Ambassador Extraordinary. *Visitors*: June 1634, Alexander Przyphowsky; Oct. 1635, George Charles Lebowitz; Aug. 1639, Duke [Albrecht?] Radziwill.

PORTUGAL (Kingdom of): April 1641 – April 1642, Antão de Almeida, Francesco de Andrade, Ambassadors Extraordinary; Antão de Souza de Macedo, Secretary. *Visitor*: Tristan de Mendoza Furtado.

RUSSIA (Czardom of): Nov. 1628 – April 1629, Vasily Demetrovich, Ambassador Extraordinary. *Visitor*: Dec. 1634 – Jan. 1635, unnamed courier.

SAVOY (Duchy of): Jan.–Sept. 1629, Piero Lorenzo Barozzi, Agent; April–May 1631, Antonio Ponte di Scarnifigi, count of Montanero e Castelletto, Ambassador Extraordinary; Sept. 1631 – March 1632, Alessandro-Cesare di Scaglia, Abbot of Staffarda, Ambassador Extraordinary; Oct. 1632, Bouvier de Bonport, Agent Extraordinary; Aug.–Sept. 1634, Gianfranceso San Martino, marquis of San Germano, Ambassador Extraordinary; June 1635 – Oct. 1638, Benedetto di Cize, count of

Pezze, Agent; Nov. 1637, Alessio Maurizio San Martino, marquis of Parella, Agent Extraordinary; Dec. 1638, Baron of Tournon, Agent Extraordinary; Oct. 1640, M. de Vaucour, Agent Extraordinary.

SPAIN (Kingdom of): May 1629 – Sept. 1631, Henry Taylor, Secretary; June 1629 – Feb. 1630, Peter Paul Rubens, Agent Extraordinary; Dec. 1629 – Feb. 1631, Carlos Coloma, Ambassador Extraordinary; June 1631 – July 1637, Juan de Necolalde, Agent; July 1636 – May 1638, Iñigo Ladrón Vélez de Guevara y Tassis, count of Oñate and Villa Mediana, Ambassador Extraordinary; April 1638 – Nov. 1655, Alonso de Cárdenas Agent, Ambassador after July 1640; March 1640 – Feb. 1641, Antonio Sancho Davila y Toledo, marquis of Velada, Vergilio Malvezzi, marquis of Castelguelfo (after April 1640), Ambassadors Extraordinary, and Henry Taylor, Secretary; *Visitor*: July 1640, Francisco Fernández de la Cueva, duke of Albuquerque.

SPANISH NETHERLANDS: June 1629 – Feb. 1630, Peter Paul Rubens, Agent Extraordinary of Archduchess Isabella; Sept. 1631 – June 1636, Henry Taylor, Agent; May 1635 and May 1638, Fernando de Texada, Agent Extraordinary; *Visitors*: May 1633, Albert d'Arenberg, prince of Chimey, Phillipe d'Arenberg, count of Beaumont; Nov. 1633, M. Cassepin.

SWEDEN (Kingdom of): March–June 1629, James Spence, Ambassador Extraordinary; March–May 1634, Henry Oxenstierna, Ambassador Extraordinary; April–May 1635, Baron John Skijt, Ambassador Extraordinary; Feb.–July 1635, April–Sept. 1638, Feb.–Sept. 1640, Michael de Bloom, Agent; *Visitor*: Feb.–March 1633, Henry Oxenstierna.

TURKEY (Sultanate of): *Visitor*: Sept.–Dec. 1640, unnamed chiaus, or courier.

VENICE (Republic of): Aug. 1626 – July 1629, Alvise Contarini, Ambassador; June 1629 – May 1632, Giovanni Soranzo, Ambassador; Jan. 1632 – May 1634, Vicenzo Gussoni, Ambassador; May–Nov. 1634, Francesco Zonca, Agent; Nov. 1634 – Oct. 1637, Angelo Correr, Ambassador; Oct. 1637 – Nov. 1638, Franceso Zonca, Agent; Nov. 1638 – June 1641, Giovanni Giustiniani, Ambassador.

II

OFFICIALS OFTEN MENTIONED IN THE NOTE BOOKS
WITH DATE OF APPOINTMENT

Chamberlain: Philip Herbert, 4th earl of Pembroke, 1626.
Cofferer of the Household: Sir John Suckling, 1628.
Comptroller of the Household: Sir Henry Vane, 1629; Sir Thomas Jermyn, 1639.
First Gentleman of the Bed Chamber: James Hay, earl of Carlisle, 1626; Henry Rich, earl of Holland, 1636.
Keeper of the Privy Seal: Henry Montagu, earl of Manchester, 1628.
Knight Harbinger: Sir Thomas Mynne, date uncertain.
Earl Marshall: Thomas Howard, earl of Arundel, 1622.
Master of the Barges: Sir Robert Clarke, date unknown.
Master of the Horse: James Hamilton, marquess of Hamilton, 1629.
Master of the Jewel House: Sir Henry Mildmay, 1618.
Secretary of State: Sir John Coke, 1625; Sir Dudley Carleton, viscount Dorchester, 1628; Sir Francis Windebank, 1632; Sir Henry Vane, 1640.
Steward: William Herbert, 3rd earl of Pembroke, 1626; Thomas Howard, earl of Arundel, 1630.
Treasurer: Richard Weston, earl of Portland, 1628; William Laud, archbishop, 1635; William Juxon, bishop, 1636; Sir Edward Littleton, 1641.
Treasurer of the Household: Sir Thomas Edmondes, 1618.
Vice Chamberlain: Sir Humphrey May, 1629; Sir Thomas Jermyn, 1630.

THE HOUSEHOLD OF HENRIETTA MARIA (AFTER 1627)

Almoner: Jacques de Noël, bishop of Angoulême.
Chamberlain: Edward Sackville, earl of Dorset, 1628.
Secretary: Sir Robert Ayton, 1627; Sir John Wynter, 1638.
Vice Chamberlain: Sir Henry Jermyn, 1628.

III

FINANCIAL REVIEW OF THE NOTE BOOKS

TABLE I

ESTIMATED INCOME FROM THE MASTERSHIP, 1627–1641

Period	Stipendiary Fee Paid £–s–d	Allowances Paid £–s–d	Gratuities Recorded £–s–d	Total £–s–d
8 Mar. '27 – 26 Mar. '28	200–0–0	[a]	228–0–0[b]	428–0–0
26 Mar. '28 – 25 Mar. '29	200–0–0	309–9–8	208–0–0	717–9–6
1 Apr. '29 – 7 Apr. '30	200–0–0	334–17–0	285–5–6	820–2–6
12 Apr. '30 – 22 May '31	232–0–0[c]	260–13–0	370–15–0	863–8–0
1 Jun. '31 – 24 Jun. '32	216–0–0[c]	143–18–6	198–15–0	558–13–6
1 Jul. '32 – 2 Nov. '33	250–0–0[c]	134–0–0	267–2–0	751–2–0
6 Nov. '33 – 25 Nov. '34	216–0–0[c]	209–13–0	223–0–0	649–13–0
2 Dec. '34 – 25 Dec. '35	216–0–0[c]	307–14–0	184–0–0	707–14–0
1 Jan. '36 – 31 Dec. '36	200–0–0	— — –[a]	87–6–0	287–6–0
1 Jan. '37 – 31 Dec. '37	200–0–0	— — –[a]	402–0–0	402–0–0
1 Jan. '38 – 30 Dec. '38	184–0–0[c]	— — –[a]	273–10–0	457–10–0
9 Dec. '38 – 30 Nov. '39	100–0–0	134–10–0	45–0–0[d]	279–10–0
1 Dec. '39 – — May '41	350–0–0[e]	442–0–0	442–0–0	1152–18–0

TOTAL: £ 8075–5–18

[a] Bills of disbursements to chamberlain not available.
[b] Finet recorded an appraised monetary value for jewels, etc. in his journals.
[c] Here prorated to allow for the dates of Finet's bills.
[d] In this year Finet protested to the chamberlain the interference of others in his office's gratuities (V 31).
[e] Payments due according to his last will. It should also be kept in mind that he did not record New Year's gifts from resident diplomats at a minimum of £100 a year.

Sources: Finet's Note Books; PRO SP 16, LC 5/134, Probate 11/187/143.

TABLE II

ESTIMATED CROWN EXPENDITURES ON GIFTS

Period	Expenditures	
8 Mar. '27 – 25 Mar. '28	£ 5700–0–0[a]	
26 Mar. '28 – 25 Mar. '29	4556–0–0[b]	
1 Apr. '29 – 7 Apr. '30	4902–0–0	
12 Apr. '30 – 22 May '31	7667–10–0	
1 Jun. '31 – 30 Jun. '32	3690–0–0	
1 Jul. '32 – 30 Oct. '33	2360–0–0[c]	
6 Nov. '33 – 30 Nov. '34	2600–0–0[d]	
2 Dec. '34 – 30 Dec. '35	1410–0–0	
1 Jan. '36 – 31 Dec. '36	1400–0–0	
1 Jan. '37 – 31 Dec. '37	5820–0–0[e] or	15,820–0–0[f]
1 Jan. '38 – 30 Nov. '38	4570–0–0[g]	
9 Dec. '38 – 30 Nov. '39	500–0–0	
1 Dec. '39 – 15 May '41	5720–0–0 or	8720–0–0[h]
TOTAL:	£ 50,895–10–0	or £ 53,895–10–0

[a] Includes a supplement of £2000 to 2 ambassadors extraordinary (Denmark) in lieu of non-"defrayment."

[b] Does not include the cost of 5 ordnance pieces presented to commissioners from Saley.

[c] Does not include the gift of £800 made by city of Edinburgh to Zawadsky of Poland.

[d] Includes the gift of £800 to Oxenstierna which was refused.

[e] Includes the chain valued at £210 to Necolalde which was refused.

[f] This adjusted total includes presents valued at £10,000 to the two Palatinate princes.

[g] Includes a supplementary warrant for £2000 to the Moroccan ambassador for "a debt."

[h] This adjusted total includes jewels valued at £3000 presented by the queen to the duchess of Chevreuse.

IV

NAMES OF THE SEVENTEENTH-CENTURY ENGLISH OFFICERS FOR CEREMONIES

THE MASTER OF CEREMONIES: 21 May 1603 – 8 March 1627, Sir Lewis Lewkenor; 13 September 1619, Reversion granted to Sir John Finet; 8 March 1627 – 15 May 1641, Sir John Finet; Sept. 1639, Reversion granted to Sir Baltazar Gerbier; 15 April 1641, Sir Baltazar Gerbier;[a] Feb. 1661 – Dec. 1686, Sir Charles Cotterell;

[a] At the Restoration the patent was resumed, but during the Commonwealth and Protectorate Oliver Fleming performed the office of Master.

27 April 1675, Reversion granted to Sir Charles Ludovic Cotterell; Dec. 1686 – 1710, Sir Charles Ludovic Cotterell; 7 Jan. 1699, Reversion granted to Sir Charles Cotterell II.

THE MARSHALL OF CEREMONIES: ca. Nov. 1605 – Nov. 1623, William Marsh; Nov. 1623 – Aug. 1635, Walter Briscoe; Aug. 1635 – Jan. 1640, Sir Amias Andros de Saumarez; 7 Oct. 1639, Reversion granted to Sir Ralph Nicholls; Jan. 1640, Sir Ralph Nicholls; 26 Oct. 1660 – ca. Sept. 1671, Sir Amias Andros de Saumarez; 1671 – ca. 1674, Thomas Sanborne; 21 March 1674 – Nov. 1704, Richard Le Bas.

THE ASSISTING OFFICER (the title varies within the patents): ca. Nov. 1605 – Oct. 1612, Sir James Murray, William Button; Oct. 1612 – 8 March 1625, Sir William Button, John Finet; 8 March 1625 – 18 March 1627, Sir John Finet; 22 July 1630 – 6 April 1636, Roland Woodward; 6 April 1636 – 15 April 1641, Sir Baltazar Gerbier; 30 July 1641 – Feb. 1686, Sir Charles Cotterell;[b] Jan 1668 – May 1672, Sir Clement Cotterell; Feb. – Dec. 1686, Sir Charles Ludovic Cotterell; Dec. 1686 – Jan. 1698, Sir John Dormer.

[b] Master *and* Assistant Jan. 1661 – Jan. 1668 and Aug. 1672 – Feb. 1686.

Sources: Finet's Note Books; PRO SP 38/11 and 39/17; Rymer, *Foedera*; CSP D; *Calendars of Treasury Books.*

INDEX

Note: Diplomats and official visitors have been listed according to country of origin, rank, and dates of residence in London in Appendix I (pp. 315–17), and English officials consulted by Finet have been identified in Appendix II (p. 318) and Appendix IV (p. 321).